"What a rich devotional! Scripture—beribboned with trenchant questions, goading insights, and invitations to sit, to pray, to write. Invitations to read Zora Neale Hurston and W. H. Auden. Yes, please!"
— Lauren F. Winner, author of *Wearing God*

"Offering excerpts from the biblical text and the Connections commentary series, questions for deeper reflection, *lectio divina*, and space for personal reflection and thoughts, *Everyday Connections* provides a rich and essential resource to strengthen and support your spiritual and devotional practice."
— Song-Mi Suzie Park, Associate Professor of Old Testament, Austin Presbyterian Theological Seminary

"Given the richness of this devotional companion to the Connections commentary, I can't imagine it sitting on your shelf unused! Designed with simplicity yet filled with depth, it is a resource that will help you engage Scripture and life both more fully and more joyfully. The flexibility built into its use—individually, in small groups, and in relation to worship—gives this guide longevity well beyond a particular lectionary year."
— Marjorie Thompson, author of *Soul Feast*

"In days of great tumult and stress, the guided meditations on Scripture and the prompts to prayer collected in *Everyday Connections* are a welcome balm and generous call to heed God's voice in the everyday life of those of us who yearn to follow Jesus. In days of joy and hope, this same book invites believers to praise a God whose word shows us the way of faithfulness and whose grace is ever abounding."
— Eric D. Barreto, Frederick and Margaret L. Weyerhaeuser Associate Professor of New Testament, Princeton Theological Seminary

"*Everyday Connections* leads readers through the spiritual practice of centering our heads and hearts in faithful reflection and connection. It resources the writings of the Bible as well as the broader spiritual and intellectual resources of the Christian tradition, inviting us to link Christian wisdom, images, and teachings to the lived experiences of our communities and the communities of others. I commend this resource to pastors, chaplains, laypeople, and teachers engaged in the hermeneutical task of rendering biblical texts meaningful for our contemporary realities. If you seek to cultivate fresh engagement with the Bible, communities, the Christian lectionary calendar, and the self and to have fresh voices accompany you along the way, this resource can guide you in that endeavor."

— Shively T. J. Smith, Assistant Professor of New Testament,
Boston University

Everyday Connections

Everyday Connections

Reflections and Practices for Year A

Edited by Heidi Haverkamp

WESTMINSTER
JOHN KNOX PRESS
LOUISVILLE • KENTUCKY

© 2022 Westminster John Knox Press
Responses and prayers © 2022 Heidi Haverkamp

First edition
Published by Westminster John Knox Press
Louisville, Kentucky

22 23 24 25 26 27 28 29 30 31—10 9 8 7 6 5 4 3 2 1

Book design by Allison Taylor
Cover design by Allison Taylor

Library of Congress Cataloging-in-Publication Data

Names: Haverkamp, Heidi, editor.
Title: Everyday connections : reflections and practices for Year C / edited by Heidi Haverkamp.
Description: First edition. | Louisville, Kentucky : Westminster John Knox Press, 2021. | Series: Connections: A Lectionary Commentary for Preaching and Worship | Includes index. | Summary: "This volume provides a full fifty-two weeks of devotional prompts based on the Revised Common Lectionary for Year C, drawing from the insightful Bible commentaries in the Connections series"—Provided by publisher.
Identifiers: LCCN 2021021819 (print) | LCCN 2021021820 (ebook) | ISBN 9780664264529 | ISBN 9781646982059 (ebook) |
Subjects: LCSH: Common lectionary (1992). Year C—Prayers and devotions. | Church year—Prayers and devotions. | LCGFT: Devotional literature.
Classification: LCC BV30 .E94 2021 (print) | LCC BV30 (ebook) | DDC 263/.9—dc23
LC record available at https://lccn.loc.gov/2021021819
LC ebook record available at https://lccn.loc.gov/2021021820

Everyday Connections, Year A
ISBN: 9780664264536 (paperback)
ISBN: 9781646982615 (ebook)

PRINTED IN THE UNITED STATES OF AMERICA

⊗ The paper used in this publication meets the minimum requirements of the American National Standard for Information Sciences—Permanence of Paper for Printed Library Materials, ANSI Z39.48-1992

Most Westminster John Knox Press books are available at special quantity discounts when purchased in bulk by corporations, organizations, and special-interest groups. For more information, please e-mail SpecialSales@wjkbooks.com.

Contents

vi

A Note from the Publisher

This devotional resource is part of the series Connections: A Lectionary Commentary for Preaching and Worship. Connections embodies two complementary convictions about the study of Scripture. First, to best understand an individual passage of Scripture, we should put it in conversation with the rest of the Bible. Second, since all truth is God's truth, we should bring as many "lenses" as possible to the study of Scripture, drawn from as many sources as we can find. The essential idea of Connections is that biblical texts display their power most fully when they are allowed to interact with a number of contexts, that is, when many connections are made between a biblical text and realities outside that text. Like the two poles of a battery, when the pole of the biblical text is connected to a different pole (another aspect of Scripture or a dimension of life outside Scripture), creative sparks fly and energy surges from pole to pole.

Based on the Revised Common Lectionary (RCL), which has wide ecumenical use, Connections offers hundreds of essays on the full array of biblical passages in the three-year cycle. Two major interpretive essays, called Commentary 1 and Commentary 2, address every scriptural reading in the RCL. Commentary 1 explores connections between a lectionary reading and other texts and themes within Scripture, and Commentary 2 makes connections between the lectionary texts and themes in the larger culture outside of Scripture. These essays have been written by pastors, biblical scholars, theologians, and others.

During the seasons of the Christian year (Advent through Epiphany and Lent through Pentecost), the RCL provides three readings and a psalm or canticle for each Sunday and feast day: (1) a first reading, usually from the Old Testament; (2) a psalm or canticle, chosen to respond to the first reading; (3) a second reading, usually from one of the New Testament epistles; and (4) a Gospel reading. The first and second readings are chosen as complements to the Gospel reading for the day.

During the time between Pentecost and Advent, the RCL includes an additional first reading for every Sunday. There is the usual complementary reading, chosen in relation to the Gospel reading, but there is also a "semicontinuous" reading. These semicontinuous first readings move through the books of the Old Testament more or less continuously in narrative sequence, offering the stories of the patriarchs (Year A), the kings of Israel (Year B), and the prophets (Year C). Connections covers both the complementary and the semicontinuous readings.

Because not all lectionary days are used in a given year, depending on how the calendar falls, you may not need some of the readings here until a subsequent lectionary cycle. Check the official RCL website at http://lectionary .library.vanderbilt.edu for a list of readings for the current year.

We want to thank the many talented individuals who made Connections possible: our general editors, Joel B. Green, Thomas G. Long, Luke A. Powery, Cynthia L. Rigby, and Carolyn J. Sharp; Psalms editor Kimberly Bracken Long and sidebar editors Bo Adams and Rachel Toombs; the esteemed members of our editorial board; our superb slate of writers; and our indefatigable project manager Joan Murchison. Finally, our sincere thanks to the administration, faculty, and staff of Austin Presbyterian Theological Seminary, our institutional partner in producing Connections.

We are deeply grateful to Heidi Haverkamp for her exhaustive editorial and creative work developing Everyday Connections for the spiritual enrichment of every Christian who desires to delve deeply into Scripture. This insightful volume pairs weekly texts and reflections with prompts, prayers, and practices to spark connections between the Bible and everyday life as well as nurture one's own connection with the Divine.

Westminster John Knox Press

How to Use This Book

In this book, you will find a panoply of modes and methods for reflection on the Sunday readings of the Revised Common Lectionary, Year A. Some are serious, some are playful, some are personal, some are relational, some are pastoral, some are prophetic, some are practical, some are poetic; all are centered in Christ's radical call and love for us. Whether you want to deepen your prayer life, your grasp of Scripture, your small-group discussions, your sermon preparation, or some other aspect of your Christian life and relationship with God, I hope you will discover in these pages a wide variety of resources, information, ideas, questions, and spiritual practices to support you.

Your conversation partners for each week's reflections are excerpts from the Connections preaching and worship commentary series, also published by Westminster John Knox Press. The series is a treasure trove of background and insights, with essays on each Scripture passage written by Bible scholars, theologians, and pastors. They are easy to read but offer significant historical and linguistic information, theological reflection, connections across the biblical text, and connections from the text to social and cultural realities in our world. Choosing a single excerpt from so many of these essays was incredibly challenging. There are great riches to be found in the full commentaries, for those seeking more.

There are many ways Everyday Connections can guide and strengthen your Christian life, leadership, and community, depending on what works best for you, your group, or your congregation in any given week:

- Personal reflection: use for prayer, study, meditation, and journaling
- Sermon or worship preparation: explore ideas, get inspired, and prepare to preach or plan worship
- Small groups: see the appendix for a suggested format to use Everyday Connections as a curriculum or study text
- Teaching: study and reflect as you prepare to teach a Bible study or class of any age
- Meetings: use an excerpt as an opening meditation or discussion for staff or committee meetings

- Beyond church: use on visits to individuals or groups in a hospital, assisted living facility, prison, or other social agency, or as part of a mission trip, retreat, or conference

Here are some other suggestions to get the most from this devotional:

Use alongside a Bible. Since this book offers only short excerpts from Scripture for the sake of length, reading the full passage in your Bible will expand your perspective.

Choose what to study. Each week of reflections offers multiple options and ideas for engagement with the texts. Focus on whatever is speaking to you that day. Or, over time, you may discover certain exercises or modules work best for you. Do not feel that you need to interact with every single entry, every single week.

Choose what order. Reflections have been laid out in a certain order, but you can use them in any order you like.

Choose what frequency. You may want to use this book every day, studying one or two entries at a time, or just once or twice a week, studying several or most of a week's entries at once.

The material for each week is divided into these sections:

1. **A Scripture Overview.** On the first page of each week, a selection of verses excerpted from that week's readings gives you a sense of what to expect. (Excerpts from psalms and canticles are omitted in the season after Pentecost in order to accommodate excerpts from the two Old Testament tracks.) Then, a shortened form of **Lectio Divina**, Latin for "holy reading," is suggested, as a way to begin to reflect on the week's Scriptures: choose a phrase or a few words that speak to you, then listen in prayer or meditation for what God might be saying to you through those words. Benedictine monks have prayed in this way for centuries.
2. **Themes from This Week's Writers.** Two themes, drawn from the week's commentary essays, are suggested for study, reflection, or sermon preparation. Brief quotes from the essays that support the theme are provided. See if the commentators' words inspire you or other connections emerge for you. A **Spiritual Practice** associated with the themes or liturgical season is also suggested. The practice

can be done on your own, as a family, with a friend or prayer partner, or as a small-group activity, and on any day of the week.

3. **First Reading, Canticle, Second Reading, and Gospel.** A deeper dive into four of the week's readings (five for Palm/Passion Sunday and six for Easter Sunday) includes a verse or two of Scripture, an excerpt from a commentary essay, some reflection questions, and a brief prayer. These reflections will invite you to make connections that (usually) go in different directions from the two themes. You could read one each day, read them all at once, or pick just one or two to read, depending on the week.

4. **Weekend Reflections.** Choose a way to wrap up the week's study and Scripture connections, perhaps on the day you are sitting down to write a sermon or plan worship. First, a **Further Connection** is offered: a quote from a source outside of Scripture and the commentary essays, which may speak to you in a new way or deepen a connection you have made with a theme or reading already that week. Full sources and citations for these quotes are available in the appendix. **Making the Connections** invites you to consider one of four questions (repeated each week) to focus your reflections and connections from the readings to a conclusion, sermon, or final theme for the week. **My Connections** provides extra space to write your own notes.

5. **Sabbath Day.** These exercises are meant to be done on a day you consider the end of the week or a day off. The **Scripture of Assurance** is meant to offer solace—and sometimes a little humor—to a weary soul. The **Weekly Examen** is adapted from the daily examen of Ignatius of Loyola. It can be done on your own, as a family, with a friend or prayer partner, or in a small group.

Again, choose what speaks to you; do not feel you need to engage every single section. The options in this book were designed to be used in different combinations to suit the needs of different readers, contexts, and schedules.

A few sections use slightly different formats:

Christmas Week. For this busy holiday time, a single week of reflections draws on the Scriptures from both Christmas and the Sunday after Christmas, since many of the readings and themes overlap and complement one another.

Weekday Holy Days. Five significant holy days always or usually fall on weekdays: Epiphany, Ash Wednesday, Holy Thursday, Good Friday, and Ascension of the Lord. Each has a separate, shortened entry (appearing before the start of the week leading up to the following Sunday) that includes Scripture quotes, excerpts from the commentary essays, a reflection question, and a prayer.

All Saints'. There is a full week of entries for All Saints' Day (November 1) or All Saints' Sunday (the first Sunday following November 1). Note that your congregation may celebrate Proper 26 or Proper 27 instead, depending on whether All Saints' is commemorated in your tradition or perhaps celebrated on November 1, proper, rather than the Sunday following.

May God bless you richly as you explore, study, connect, and pray your way through the pages of this book and God's Word as it is proclaimed in the lectionary cycle of Year A.

Heidi Haverkamp

Everyday
Connections

The Week Leading Up to the
First Sunday of Advent

Isaiah 2:1–5

Many peoples shall come and say,
"Come, let us go up to the mountain of the LORD,
    to the house of the God of Jacob;
that he may teach us his ways
    and that we may walk in his paths." (v. 3)

Psalm 122

For the sake of my relatives and friends
    I will say, "Peace be within you."
For the sake of the house of the LORD our God,
    I will seek your good. (vv. 8-9)

Romans 13:11–14

Besides this, you know what time it is, how it is now the moment for you to wake from sleep. For salvation is nearer to us now than when we became believers. (v. 11)

Matthew 24:36–44

"But about that day and hour no one knows, neither the angels of heaven, nor the Son, but only the Father." (v. 36)

LECTIO DIVINA

Underline a word or phrase that especially grabs your attention. Pray from that word or phrase and ask God to help you connect to its particular invitation for you this week.

Themes from This Week's Writers

THEME 1: *God's Future*

Isaiah 2:1–5

For many congregations and denominations that are declining in numbers, this is a genuine word of comfort and hope. God is not done with us yet. . . .

The promise of Isaiah 2:1–4, a text set immediately after a description of vast destruction, expands our understanding of hope.

LEANNE VAN DYK

Isaiah 2:1–5

This Advent question about "the days to come" strikes close to the heart for the followers of Jesus. It is that restless spirit that can be answered only by our hope in God. It is a longing that can be soothed only by the comfort of our future in God.

DAVID A. DAVIS

Psalm 122

These texts call us to see our faith not as the destination, but as an involved and continued journey, where we are always learning, always transforming our violent ways into instruments of peace, abundance, and provision.

MARCI AULD GLASS

THEME 2: *Staying Awake*

Romans 13:11–14

Staying awake or living in the divine light in the end times is not an individual or sectarian practice of spirituality. What is the life context in which today's Christians await the coming of Christ? Waiting is not passive but active resistance to darkness.

JIN YOUNG CHOI

Romans 13:11–14

The kingdom of God came into history in Jesus Christ, but we still wait for its final fulfillment.

Unhappily, the sense of the nearness of the end times can be a distraction from the task of living faithfully in the world. It can be and has been exploited.

JOHN M. BUCHANAN

Matthew 24:36–44

The preparedness of believers is judged by how they work for the benefit of others in the community rather than focusing solely on a future prize and, in the process, losing their souls. Believers are judged not so much by how well they are prepared to enter heaven but by how much they have been attending to the concerns of others in the community.

RAJ NADELLA

WHAT IS THE HOLY SPIRIT SAYING TO YOU THIS WEEK?

_____

_____

_____

_____

_____

A SPIRITUAL PRACTICE FOR THIS WEEK

Find a bare stick, branch, or twig. Write some words of intention on slips of paper for this Advent season (for instance: watch, awake, slow down, be ready, prepare, listen, repent, etc.) and attach them to the stick with tape, paper clips, or blue or purple ribbon, and use as a prayer focus this season.

First Reading

Isaiah 2:1–5

In days to come
    the mountain of the LORD's house
shall be established as the highest of the mountains,
    and shall be raised above the hills;
all the nations shall stream to it. (v. 2)

REFLECTION

Advent is a season boldly to lean into God's future unafraid. The
themes of Advent are as familiar as the liturgical decorations and the
congregational song. Advent is a kind of comfort food for those who
gather for worship, especially those for whom the church feels like home
this time of year.

The word of the Lord through the prophet Isaiah, then, can be
understood as a steady refrain in the season that proclaims and affirms
God's promise. Isaiah's portrayal of the divine hope strikes familiar notes
in the believer's ear about the days to come.

DAVID A. DAVIS

RESPONSE

What spiritual "comfort foods" do you enjoy in Advent worship?
Does church feel like home in this season for you? What other Advent
traditions or images are particularly hopeful or meaningful to you? What
does it mean to you, this year, to "lean into God's future, unafraid"?

PRAYER

God of promise, show me the way to your mountain that I may walk in
your paths and into your future, for your love's sake. Amen.

Canticle

Psalm 122

I was glad when they said to me,
  "Let us go to the house of the LORD!"
Our feet are standing
  within your gates, O Jerusalem. (vv. 1–2)

REFLECTION

The root of the word "advent" is the same root found in "adventure." Is Advent something we are excited to experience or something we need to "get through" as we survive the holiday season? These passages help us invite people into a journey that leads us through a season of peace toward the mystery of the nativity.

Our Advent journey is not without a destination. We do not wander in the wilderness with no goal. The mountain of the Lord (Isa. 2) and the house of the Lord (Ps. 122) give us imagery for our destination, as does a stable in Bethlehem.

MARCI AULD GLASS

RESPONSE

How is Advent a time of endurance for you? How could Advent be a time of adventure for you? How could it feel less like a wilderness and more like a journey? What imagery for your "destination" would be meaningful to you: a mountain? a house? something else?

PRAYER

Loving God, my feet are already standing within your gates even as I journey toward your coming again, here on earth and in the times to come. Amen.

Second Reading

Romans 13:11–14

The night is far gone, the day is near. Let us then lay aside the works of darkness and put on the armor of light, let us live honorably as in the day, not in reveling and drunkenness, not in debauchery and licentiousness, not in quarreling and jealousy. (vv. 12–13)

REFLECTION

Viktor Frankl . . . was a survivor of Nazi death camps. After the war he reflected on his experience . . . [concluding] that the prisoners who survived were those who somehow did not sink into despair but lived with hope. . . . "Only those who were oriented toward the future, toward a goal in the future, toward a meaning to fulfill in the future were likely to survive."[1]

There is a freedom that accompanies trust and confidence that in Jesus Christ ultimate issues have been resolved: that whatever chaos, suffering, and cruelty are happening in the world at the moment, history's final outcome remains safely in God's hands.

JOHN M. BUCHANAN

RESPONSE

How would you describe what it means to you to trust in Jesus Christ? Does it comfort you to imagine that "history's final outcome remains safely in God's hands"? How would you ask God or Jesus to give you hope for your goals, your purpose, or your future?

PRAYER

O Christ, as night turns to day, help me to set aside the works of darkness and put on the armor of light, so to live honorably and with hope in you. Amen.

1. Viktor Frankl, *The Unconscious God: Psychiatry and Theology* (New York: Simon & Schuster, 1975), 139.

Gospel

Matthew 24:36–44

"Keep awake therefore, for you do not know on what day your Lord is coming. But understand this: if the owner of the house had known in what part of the night the thief was coming, he would have stayed awake and would not have let his house be broken into." (vv. 42–43)

REFLECTION

The issue is not merely "eating and drinking" . . . but rather being uncaring in gluttonous overconsumption and focusing only on the things of this world. The point here is that "preparation" or "watchfulness" has nothing to do with obsessing over numbers, signs, and meanings. Rather, it has to do with living in the expectation that the teachings and example of Jesus are the norm! To "fear judgment" is surely another way of trying to live the right way.

DANIEL L. SMITH-CHRISTOPHER

RESPONSE

What do you think about Smith-Christopher's description of true watchfulness? What teachings and examples of Jesus are "the norm" in your life? What kinds of gluttony or overconsumption still get the upper hand? How would it help you to "fear judgment" in order to make changes? What changes do you most long for?

PRAYER

Gracious Lord, teach me how to stay awake: to watch for you but not to guard against you, that your love may break into my life and the world. Amen.

Weekend Reflections

FURTHER CONNECTION

Science tells us that there is nowhere where life can succeed in going on for ever. There will indeed be an End of the World.

. . . We shall die, and the cosmos will die, but the final word does not lie with death but with God. . . . This does not mean that death is not real, but it does mean that it is not the ultimate reality. Only God is ultimate, and that is a sufficient basis to enable us to embrace the Advent hope.

JOHN POLKINGHORNE (1930–2021), *LIVING WITH HOPE: A SCIENTIST LOOKS AT ADVENT, CHRISTMAS, AND EPIPHANY*

MAKING THE CONNECTIONS

Choose one or two questions for reflection:

1. What connections have you noticed between this week's texts and other passages in Scripture?

2. What connections have you made between this week's texts and the world beyond Scripture?

3. Does either of this week's two commentary themes speak especially to your life or the life of the world around you right now?

4. What is God saying to your congregation in particular through this week's readings and commentaries?

_____

_____

_____

_____

_____

_____

Sabbath Day

SCRIPTURE OF ASSURANCE

> I will sing of your steadfast love, O LORD, forever;
>> with my mouth I will proclaim your faithfulness to all
>> generations.
> I declare that your steadfast love is established forever;
>> your faithfulness is as firm as the heavens. (Psalm 89:1–2)

WEEKLY EXAMEN

- Take a quiet moment, seek out God's presence, and pray for the guidance of the Spirit.

- Consider the past week; recall specific moments and feelings that stand out to you.

- Choose one moment or feeling for deeper examination, thanksgiving, or repentance.

- Let go, breathe deeply, and invite Christ's love to surround and fill you in preparation for the week ahead.

- End with the Lord's Prayer.

The Week Leading Up to the
Second Sunday of Advent

Isaiah 11:1–10

The wolf shall live with the lamb,
    the leopard shall lie down with the kid,
the calf and the lion and the fatling together,
    and a little child shall lead them. (v. 6)

Psalm 72:1–7, 18–19

May he be like rain that falls on the mown grass,
    like showers that water the earth.
In his days may righteousness flourish
    and peace abound, until the moon is no more. (vv. 6–7)

Romans 15:4–13

May the God of steadfastness and encouragement grant you to live in harmony with one another, in accordance with Christ Jesus, so that together you may with one voice glorify the God and Father of our Lord Jesus Christ. (vv. 5–6)

Matthew 3:1–12

Then the people of Jerusalem and all Judea were going out to him, and all the region along the Jordan, and they were baptized by him in the river Jordan, confessing their sins. (vv. 5–6)

LECTIO DIVINA

Underline a word or phrase that especially grabs your attention. Pray from that word or phrase and ask God to help you connect to its particular invitation for you this week.

Themes from This Week's Writers

THEME 1: *The Peaceable Kingdom*

Isaiah 11:1–10

The peaceable kingdom portrays unlimited inbreaking of the kingdom of God and harmony between humans and animals. These are clearly images that reflect an expansive hope for justice, good order, and the well-being of the weakest and most vulnerable members of society.

LEANNE VAN DYK

Isaiah 11:1–10

Maybe this is not a bad definition of Advent . . . the peacefulness of God's new creation, which is yet to come, spilling into the here and now; the eternal hope of Christ's glorious kingdom inspiring, informing, and guiding the life of God's people in the present.

DAVID A. DAVIS

Romans 15:4–13

Worshiping God cannot be separated from welcoming others. These are essential components of Advent hope as Christians eagerly wait for the Day of the Lord when all the nations—usually translated as the "Gentiles" in English—will worship God together.

JIN YOUNG CHOI

THEME 2: *A New, Radical Way*

Romans 15:4–13

In her book *When in Romans*, Beverly Gaventa observes that "being members of one another means there is a relationship from which there is no exit plan."[1] Paul's radical ecclesiology, which claims the primacy

---

1. Beverly Roberts Gaventa, *When in Romans* (Grand Rapids: Baker Academic, 2016), 105.

of unity and community as Christ's gift to the church, . . . judges and challenges the contemporary churches, all of whom seem to reflect the profound divisions in American culture.

JOHN M. BUCHANAN

Matthew 3:1–12

John is not simply preparing the way for the Lord, as verse 3 seems to suggest. He is also showing the way. He is modeling for the many, especially the Judean elite, how to become a part of the new kingdom of God that is at hand. As John has demonstrated by example, participation in the new kingdom entails a radical change in one's lifestyle.

RAJ NADELLA

Matthew 3:1–12

It is important then to read these words with the appropriate joy in the hearing about coming judgment. . . . Do we imagine that "all Judea and the whole Jordan district" were streaming into the wilderness for fear of judgment or to celebrate the coming change? Clearly the latter.

DANIEL L. SMITH-CHRISTOPHER

WHAT IS THE HOLY SPIRIT SAYING TO YOU THIS WEEK?

_____

_____

_____

_____

_____

A SPIRITUAL PRACTICE FOR THIS WEEK

Seek out an empty, wilderness place to reread Matthew 3. You could choose a desert, a park, or a parking lot. If you met John the Baptist in a place like this, what would you talk with him about? How would he ask you to repent, and for what?

First Reading

Isaiah 11:1–10

A shoot shall come out from the stump of Jesse,
and a branch shall grow out of his roots.
The spirit of the LORD shall rest on him,
the spirit of wisdom and understanding,
the spirit of counsel and might,
the spirit of knowledge and the fear of the LORD. (vv. 1–2)

REFLECTION

The first verse refers to a shoot that emerges from a dead stump. A tender shoot is frail hope for new life. This evocative phrase reminds the reader of a similar image from Isaiah 42:3, referring to the Suffering Servant: "A bruised reed he will not break, and a dimly burning wick he will not quench." The images of frail shoot, a broken blade of grass, and a barely smoldering candle wick are all precarious signs of life. This image from Isaiah 11:1 demonstrates how much God can do with so little.

LEANNE VAN DYK

RESPONSE

What is it like to imagine God's kingdom as fragile or precarious as a tiny shoot, a broken grass blade, or a sputtering flame? What is happening in your life that might also resemble these images? If God can do "so much with so little," what might you dare to hope for?

PRAYER

Lord God of the tender shoot, give me a spirit of wisdom and understanding to see that new life is always springing from your spirit, even in my own life. Amen.

Canticle

Psalm 72:1–7, 18–19

Give the king your justice, O God,
and your righteousness to a king's son.
May he judge your people with righteousness,
and your poor with justice. (vv. 1–2)

REFLECTION

This branch from the tree of Jesse will be a ruler like the one described
in Psalm 72, girded with righteousness and faithfulness. The spirit of
the Lord will rest on this branch, which makes clear that this leader
is an agent of divine goodness, not the source of goodness and mercy.
It is human nature, perhaps, to bestow our hopes on, and credit our
successes to, human leaders. Both of these texts make clear that even the
most righteous rulers point us to the steadfast love, mercy, and justice of
God. Our praise is misdirected if it does not point toward God.

MARCI AULD GLASS

RESPONSE

How have you seen your community set hope or praise on a human
leader rather than God? How was this harmful? Who are some leaders in
your life who point beyond themselves to the "steadfast love, mercy, and
justice of God"? How have you seen this be life-giving?

PRAYER

Righteous God, teach me and all your leaders the justice and peace that
comes from you, that we may point all people to your love and your
kingdom. Amen.

Second Reading

Romans 15:4–13

Welcome one another, therefore, just as Christ has welcomed you, for the glory of God. (v. 7)

REFLECTION

Paul's argument is consistently that the purpose of the Scriptures is to encourage Christians to love one another as they hope for their salvation. Actually, the source of the endurance and comfort is God, and that gift is for us, again, to "live in harmony with [or be like-minded toward] one another" (v. 5). This "life together" involves glorifying God in unison, which is extended to this worshiping community's practice of welcome (vv. 6–7).

Paul uses Christ's example one more time to explain how this welcoming of one another serves the glory of God.

JIN YOUNG CHOI

RESPONSE

What do you think of Choi's statement that Scripture is meant to encourage us to love one another? What does it mean, in your congregation, to "welcome one another"? What does it mean to you that Christ has welcomed you, first? How are welcome and worship interconnected in your context?

PRAYER

O Christ, you have welcomed me with steadfastness and encouragement; teach me to welcome others and to allow them to welcome me, for the glory of God. Amen.

Gospel

Matthew 3:1–12

In those days John the Baptist appeared in the wilderness of Judea, proclaiming, "Repent, for the kingdom of heaven has come near." (vv. 1–2)

REFLECTION

John is not simply calling on people to join the new kingdom. He is also inviting them to a new space that he has embraced and made home: the wilderness. Several scholars have noted that wilderness functions as a liminal space in the history of Israel. It was where the Hebrew community spent a considerable amount of time after fleeing Egypt and before entering the promised land. . . . Within the context of Matthew's Gospel, wilderness is also an alternative space, one that espouses values that are diametrically different from the civilizational values of Roman cities.

RAJ NADELLA

RESPONSE

How is your church a liminal or alternative space for you, especially during this season of Advent? What it is like to consider your church as a wilderness in the midst of your wider community? What is a comfort for you in this? What is a challenge?

PRAYER

Merciful God, you invite me into the wilderness to glimpse my true self and the nearness of your kingdom. Teach me to repent, that I may know your kingdom more and more. Amen.

Weekend Reflections

FURTHER CONNECTION

When that primal fear of the dark—of the end—begins to slide over us, animals unselfconsciously and forthrightly offer unfearful responses. They take in the threat of dark and cold, and they adapt in amazing and ingenious ways. They shape themselves to life as it is given. . . .

The practice of Advent has always been about helping us to grasp the mystery of a new beginning out of what looks like death.

GAYLE BOSS (1957–), *ALL CREATION WAITS: THE ADVENT MYSTERY OF NEW BEGINNINGS*

MAKING THE CONNECTIONS

Choose one or two questions for reflection:

1. What connections have you noticed between this week's texts and other passages in Scripture?

2. What connections have you made between this week's texts and the world beyond Scripture?

3. Does either of this week's two commentary themes speak especially to your life or the life of the world around you right now?

4. What is God saying to your congregation in particular through this week's readings and commentaries?

_____

_____

_____

_____

_____

_____

Sabbath Day

SCRIPTURE OF ASSURANCE

"If you abide in me, and my words abide in you, ask for whatever you wish, and it will be done for you." (John 15:7)

WEEKLY EXAMEN

- Take a quiet moment, seek out God's presence, and pray for the guidance of the Spirit.

- Consider the past week; recall specific moments and feelings that stand out to you.

- Choose one moment or feeling for deeper examination, thanksgiving, or repentance.

- Let go, breathe deeply, and invite Christ's love to surround and fill you in preparation for the week ahead.

- End with the Lord's Prayer.

The Week Leading Up to the
Third Sunday of Advent

Isaiah 35:1–10

Say to those who are of a fearful heart,
    "Be strong, do not fear!
Here is your God.
    He will come with vengeance,
with terrible recompense.
    He will come and save you." (v. 4)

Psalm 146:5–10

The LORD sets the prisoners free;
    the LORD opens the eyes of the blind.
The LORD lifts up those who are bowed down;
    the LORD loves the righteous. (vv. 7b–8)

James 5:7–10

Be patient, therefore, beloved, until the coming of the Lord. The farmer waits for the precious crop from the earth, being patient with it until it receives the early and the late rains. (v. 7)

Matthew 11:2–11

Jesus answered them, "Go and tell John what you hear and see: the blind receive their sight, the lame walk, the lepers are cleansed, the deaf hear, the dead are raised, and the poor have good news brought to them." (vv. 4–5)

LECTIO DIVINA

Underline a word or phrase that especially grabs your attention. Pray from that word or phrase and ask God to help you connect to its particular invitation for you this week.

Themes from This Week's Writers

THEME 1: *Judgment and Salvation*

Isaiah 35:1–10

The dual insistence of the prophet can be seen concisely in 35:4b: "Here is your God. He will come with vengeance, with terrible recompense. He will come and save you." The paradox of punishment and salvation is deep in Isaiah. It is not an easy paradox to understand or resolve and stands as a perennial tension in the life of faith.

LEANNE VAN DYK

Isaiah 35:1–10

God's passion is on display in the intent to rescue; God's judgment is directed at all that threatens the coming kingdom. Here is your God. God will come and save you. It is the language of incarnation.

DAVID A. DAVIS

Matthew 11:2–11

What Jesus thus seems to be saying is that his revolution is neither a violent revolution of vengeful violence . . . nor an uprising of a powerful few. By telling the common people that "they" are as important, indeed just as powerful, as John is "in kingdom terms," Jesus is making a profoundly Gandhi-like call on "the masses."

DANIEL L. SMITH-CHRISTOPHER

THEME 2: *Prepare the Way*

James 5:7–10

Anyone who knows anything about farming knows that farmers do more than sit around and wait for rain. Farmers continue to work hard toward the ultimate goal of a robust crop. So it is an active waiting, preparing while waiting for the coming day of promised fulfillment.

JOHN M. BUCHANAN

Matthew 11:2–11

John's question at the beginning of the story pertains to Jesus' messianic identity. Jesus turns it into a question about his audience and about their ability, or lack thereof, to properly hear and see him and respond to the acts of God they have witnessed.

RAJ NADELLA

Matthew 11:2–11

It is crucial to take careful note of the evidence of the kingdom of God, according to Jesus. He does not merely say, "I'm here. That's all the proof you need!" For the evidence of the kingdom is justice and change—change for the blind, the lame, the poor, and even the dead. We see for whom the change is occurring: those who suffer.

DANIEL L. SMITH-CHRISTOPHER

WHAT IS THE HOLY SPIRIT SAYING TO YOU THIS WEEK?

_____

_____

_____

_____

_____

A SPIRITUAL PRACTICE FOR THIS WEEK

Reread James 5:7–10 and practice waiting as prayer this week. Notice whenever you are waiting (in line, at a traffic signal, for the microwave, on hold) and use that time to pause: say a mantra like "Be patient therefore, beloved, until the coming of the Lord," recall that you are beloved by God, or simply breathe deeply.

First Reading

Isaiah 35:1–10

And the ransomed of the LORD shall return,
and come to Zion with singing;
everlasting joy shall be upon their heads;
they shall obtain joy and gladness,
and sorrow and sighing shall flee away. (v. 10)

REFLECTION

About Baby Suggs's preaching, Morrison writes [in her novel *Beloved*], "She told them that the only grace they could have was the grace they could imagine."[1]

Serving as both preacher and prophet to her community, Baby Suggs nurtures the sacred imagination of God's people when brokenness, oppression, and suffering threaten to tear away at the collective sense of what it means to be created in the image of God. With an appeal to the imagination and the promise of grace, she is a prophet of hope. Similar to Baby Suggs, Isaiah offers a message of hope for a community surrounded by despair.

DAVID A. DAVIS

RESPONSE

What in your community's life right now is threatening to "tear away at the collective sense of what it means to be created in the image of God"? What is "the grace you can imagine"? What grace, do you think, could your community imagine? How could Isaiah offer comfort?

PRAYER

Lord of love, show me even in despair and exhaustion how to return to you with joy and singing, that my heart will not fear but trust in you. Amen.

1. Toni Morrison, *Beloved* (New York: Alfred A. Knopf, 1987), 88.

Canticle

Happy are those whose help is the God of Jacob,
  whose hope is in the LORD their God,
who made heaven and earth,
  the sea, and all that is in them;
who keeps faith forever;
  who executes justice for the oppressed;
  who gives food to the hungry. (v. 5–7)

REFLECTION

A Sunday of rejoicing is a good prescription for people overwhelmed by the news of the world, stressed by the crush of Christmas preparations, or feeling no reason at all to rejoice. These lectionary texts for the Third Sunday of Advent all lift up the depth of rejoicing that is deeper than feelings of fleeting happiness, emotions that may be nice in the moment, but are not grounded in deeper theological concepts of justice, healing, vision, and provision. The word translated "happy" in Psalm 146:5a . . . can also be translated "blessed."

MARCI AULD GLASS

RESPONSE

Write the word "rejoice" in large letters on a piece of paper. What does this word mean to you? Write some synonyms around the word. Then add: justice, healing, vision, provision. How do these words deepen the meaning of "rejoice" for you? What is God's good news, here?

PRAYER

Joyful God, I long for your hope and your justice; teach me to rejoice in all things because you are with me, my help and my strength. Amen.

Second Reading

James 5:7–10

Beloved, do not grumble against one another, so that you may not be judged. See, the Judge is standing at the doors! As an example of suffering and patience, beloved, take the prophets who spoke in the name of the Lord. (vv. 9–10)

REFLECTION

While the imagery of the judge standing at the doors highlights the nearness of the *parousia*, James is concerned primarily with the present trials that the Christians face. He describes such trials as "suffering and patience" and gives two examples, the prophets and Job, who suffered afflictions but showed their endurance (5:10–11).

. . . James's concern is not to explain the causes of suffering (theodicy), but to encourage the Christians to endure suffering. God does not test anyone because God is full of compassion and tender mercy (1:13–14; 5:11).

JIN YOUNG CHOI

RESPONSE

What trials or suffering are you facing in your own life right now? What does "endurance" mean to you? Do you ever feel God is testing you? How do you feel encouraged or comforted by your community in your endurance? How have you experienced God's mercy, here and now?

PRAYER

O God, teach me not to grumble but give me patience and endurance in suffering, just as you gave your prophets and your Son, Jesus Christ. Amen.

Gospel

Matthew 11:2–11

As they went away, Jesus began to speak to the crowds about John: "What did you go out into the wilderness to look at? A reed shaken by the wind? What then did you go out to see? Someone dressed in soft robes? Look, those who wear soft robes are in royal palaces." (vv. 7–8)

REFLECTION

Gil Scott-Heron . . . wrote a poem (and then song) titled "The Revolution Will Not Be Televised." One way of reading this often-quoted line is that social change is not something we can simply watch with little participation, like the evening news. It is not proffered by celebrities (political or media) on our behalf. . . . Jesus chides the masses who flock to see John, hoping that they will come to see something—something that will be done for them. . . . The Advent will not be televised! It will be lived out in the prophetic witness of the people of God through which oppressive power structures are resisted and reversed.

DANIEL L. SMITH-CHRISTOPHER

RESPONSE

In what ways are you watching Advent go by this year? In what ways are you actively (maybe overactively?) participating? In what ways are you standing back from prophetic promises of God? How can you, personally, live out God's prophetic witness in what you do this Advent?

PRAYER

God of action, you are always at work in and among your people; show me how to risk being part of your work and witness, in this season and times to come. Amen.

Weekend Reflections

FURTHER CONNECTION

God's coming isn't necessarily solely "joy to the world." It can also be "woe to the world." The promise of redemption also entails judgment. With judgment, the world, our world, as we know it, is torn apart, broken apart, to be made whole. It is a new world order created by God's presence. Just as [in the spiritual, "Oh Rocks, Don't Fall on Me,"] Jericho's walls came tumbling down, when God comes, worlds tumble and fall. The question is whether we will be left standing. Or will the rocks and mountains fall on us, crushing us? In other worlds, are we ready for the coming of God?

LUKE POWERY (1974–), *RISE UP, SHEPHERD! ADVENT REFLECTIONS ON THE SPIRITUALS*

MAKING THE CONNECTIONS

Choose one or two questions for reflection:

1. What connections have you noticed between this week's texts and other passages in Scripture?

2. What connections have you made between this week's texts and the world beyond Scripture?

3. Does either of this week's two commentary themes speak especially to your life or the life of the world around you right now?

4. What is God saying to your congregation in particular through this week's readings and commentaries?

MY CONNECTIONS

_____

_____

_____

_____

_____

_____

Sabbath Day

SCRIPTURE OF ASSURANCE

Knowledge puffs up, but love builds up. (1 Corinthians 8:1b)

WEEKLY EXAMEN

- Take a quiet moment, seek out God's presence, and pray for the guidance of the Spirit.

- Consider the past week; recall specific moments and feelings that stand out to you.

- Choose one moment or feeling for deeper examination, thanksgiving, or repentance.

- Let go, breathe deeply, and invite Christ's love to surround and fill you in preparation for the week ahead.

- End with the Lord's Prayer.

The Week Leading Up to the
Fourth Sunday of Advent

Isaiah 7:10–16

Again the LORD spoke to Ahaz, saying, Ask a sign of the LORD your God; let it be deep as Sheol or high as heaven. (vv. 10–11)

Psalm 80:1–7, 17–19

Restore us, O LORD God of hosts;
let your face shine, that we may be saved. (v. 19)

Romans 1:1–7

We have received grace and apostleship to bring about the obedience of faith among all the Gentiles for the sake of his name, including yourselves who are called to belong to Jesus Christ. (vv. 5–6)

Matthew 1:18–25

But just when he had resolved to do this, an angel of the Lord appeared to him in a dream and said, "Joseph, son of David, do not be afraid to take Mary as your wife, for the child conceived in her is from the Holy Spirit." (v. 20)

LECTIO DIVINA

Underline a word or phrase that especially grabs your attention. Pray from that word or phrase and ask God to help you connect to its particular invitation for you this week.

Themes from This Week's Writers

THEME 1: *God Sends Us a Sign and a Call*

Isaiah 7:10–16

Then the Lord . . . invites Ahaz to ask for a sign . . . , but Ahaz refuses with a hypocritically pious claim that he "will not put the LORD to the test" (v. 12). This is the context for the sign that Ahaz receives anyway: the sign of Immanuel, which means "God with us" (vv. 10–16).

SHARYN DOWD

Isaiah 7:10–16

Where God offers the divine will, Ahaz would rather invest in strategies and diplomacy to solve his problems. . . .

The church reaches its greatest clarity when it adheres to the will of its Creator . . . living in openness to what it believes God to be calling it to do, even at the risk of losing social prominence or cultural relevance.

JAMES D. FREEMAN

Matthew 1:18–25

[We might] sit with Joseph and be a bit more attentive to the vehicles—dreams or otherwise—with which God is calling to us. Of course, that attention is risky: if we listen for God, we might actually hear from God. Who among us is as willing as Joseph to receive a word that fundamentally alters the course of our life?

LAUREN F. WINNER

THEME 2: *A Gift for All the Nations*

Psalm 80:1–7, 17–19

Where is the good news for people in darkness during this Advent season? As God's face shines, are they able to see hope for restoration? As God's face shines, will they see how the birth of a child to a young woman can be a sign of God's faithfulness and power?

MARCI AULD GLASS

Romans 1:1–7

During . . . a season in which we wait and hope for God's coming into the world in human flesh, Paul's gospel for the ethnic other ("Gentile") reminds us that this gospel message is a message on behalf of the "other." . . . The contemporary challenge is whether our faith communities are prepared for the influx of the ethnic other (or economic or sexual other).

EMERSON B. POWERY

Romans 1:1–7

Paul spends time on many things in his letters, but rarely on cultural conversion. He is adamant that Gentiles can be adopted into the church without first becoming Jews. . . . Paul communicates the gospel by entering into others' mind-sets and experiences, rather than by critiquing or seeking to change them.

ANNA OLSON

WHAT IS THE HOLY SPIRIT SAYING TO YOU THIS WEEK?

_____

_____

_____

_____

_____

A SPIRITUAL PRACTICE FOR THIS WEEK

God is disappointed when Ahaz refuses to ask for a sign. This week, ask God to send you a sign. Keep an eye out for an object that gets your attention for any reason. It could be playful or serious. What is this thing a sign of, to you? Hang the item on your Christmas tree.

First Reading

Isaiah 7:10–16

Then Isaiah said: "Hear then, O house of David! Is it too little for you to weary mortals, that you weary my God also? Therefore the Lord himself will give you a sign." (vv. 13–14a)

REFLECTION

When the church veers off in a direction of its own choosing, when it puts even survival ahead of God's will, the path becomes murky.

Advent offers the church an opportunity to reflect on this course of direction, even as we prepare for the coming of God's reign in its fullness, . . . to welcome God's implicit offer of guidance and grace, while consciously turning from the desire to dictate our own future with programs and strategies designed to lead us to what the world might call success.

JAMES D. FREEMAN

RESPONSE

Do you think your congregation puts God's grace or its own survival at the center? How do you see God upholding the future of your church, even if that future is not "what the world might call success"? How is God offering your community guidance and grace right now?

PRAYER

Gracious God, guide me and my faith community to follow your grace and will, rather than survival or success, that the fullness of your kingdom may come in and through us. Amen.

Canticle

Psalm 80:1–7, 17–19

O Lᴏʀᴅ God of hosts,
  how long will you be angry with your people's prayers?
You have fed them with the bread of tears,
  and given them tears to drink in full measure. (vv. 4–5)

REFLECTION

During Advent, God asks us to ask God for a sign. Do we have the
courage to ask? Do we recognize God's signs as they appear, or do we
look past the young woman, pregnant with child, as we scan the crowds
for someone big and impressive?

The psalmist is willing to ask for a sign. In faith, he cries out for God
to "Stir up your might, and come to save us! Restore us, O God; let your
face shine, that we may be saved" (Ps. 80:2–3).

. . . The psalmist voices the people's cry for God's might to save them,
restore them.

MARCI AULD GLASS

RESPONSE

Do what God asks: write a prayer, psalm, or letter, asking God for
a sign. What do you long for? What signs do you already see? What
does the sign of Mary's pregnant belly mean for you this year? Cry out,
believing God is listening.

PRAYER

Hear me, O God: show me your word and your healing, that I might be
restored, fed, and saved by your grace. Amen.

Second Reading

Romans 1:1–7

To all God's beloved in Rome, who are called to be saints:
Grace to you and peace from God our Father and the Lord Jesus
Christ. (v. 7)

REFLECTION

As we prepare with our congregations to receive Christmas visitors, this
reading offers a chance to invite congregational reflection on the context
of the people who may not regularly grace our pews or chairs. The
preacher might introduce anecdotal or demographic information about
who is around in the neighborhood. Who are our neighbors, God's
beloved among us? What is their vocabulary? What are the longings of
their hearts that we might have a chance to meet with accessible words,
gestures, music, and offerings of beauty this Christmas?

ANNA OLSON

RESPONSE

What do you imagine the people who visit your church in the
Christmas season are longing for? Who are the neighbors of your
church, whether they come inside or not? How might God be inviting
you to notice, pray for, or welcome them?

PRAYER

Loving Jesus, teach me to see and greet each stranger and newcomer as
though I were encountering you before me, and to truly believe that we
are all called to belong to you. Amen.

Gospel

Matthew 1:18–25

Her husband Joseph, being a righteous man and unwilling to expose her to public disgrace, planned to dismiss her quietly. (v. 19)

REFLECTION

The Joseph story poses a fundamental ethical challenge . . . [to] pursue a course of action that is excessively good, excessively generous. . . . Joseph was poised to behave ethically. Because he wanted to protect Mary's reputation, he planned to "dismiss [Mary] quietly." This was a respectful and upright thing to do—but he was called by God to do something even more "righteous." He was called by God to an abundantly righteous act that required violating his culture's mores. He was called by God to go beyond his society's script for righteousness—in a way that risked bringing shame upon himself.

LAUREN F. WINNER

RESPONSE

What is a righteous act God has been calling you to consider recently? What if God is calling you to something more, even something beyond social boundaries? What could the Holy Spirit, through the story of Joseph and his excessive, outrageous generosity, be inviting you to risk this Christmas?

PRAYER

Spirit of righteousness, show me how to risk some excessive goodness and generosity this Advent, that I might not just be ethical, but radical. Amen.

Weekend Reflections

FURTHER CONNECTION

Often in life, things happen whose meaning we do not understand.
Our first reaction is frequently one of disappointment and rebellion.
Joseph set aside his own ideas in order to accept the course of events
and, mysterious as they seemed, to embrace them, take responsibility
for them and make them part of his own history. Unless we are
reconciled with our own history, we will be unable to take a single step
forward, for we will always remain hostage to our expectations and the
disappointments that follow.

> POPE FRANCIS (1936–), *"PATRIS CORDE*: ON THE 150TH
> ANNIVERSARY OF THE PROCLAMATION OF SAINT JOSEPH
> AS PATRON OF THE UNIVERSAL CHURCH"

MAKING THE CONNECTIONS

Choose one or two questions for reflection:

1. What connections have you noticed between this week's texts and
   other passages in Scripture?

2. What connections have you made between this week's texts and the
   world beyond Scripture?

3. Does either of this week's two commentary themes speak especially
   to your life or the life of the world around you right now?

4. What is God saying to your congregation in particular through this
   week's readings and commentaries?

_____

_____

_____

_____

_____

_____

Sabbath Day

SCRIPTURE OF ASSURANCE

> I will give thanks to the LORD with my whole heart;
> I will tell of all your wonderful deeds.
> I will be glad and exult in you;
> I will sing praise to your name, O Most High. (Psalm 9:1–2)

WEEKLY EXAMEN

- Take a quiet moment, seek out God's presence, and pray for the guidance of the Spirit.

- Consider the past week; recall specific moments and feelings that stand out to you.

- Choose one moment or feeling for deeper examination, thanksgiving, or repentance.

- Let go, breathe deeply, and invite Christ's love to surround and fill you in preparation for the week ahead.

- End with the Lord's Prayer.

Christmas Week

*Christmas Eve, Christmas Day, and the First
Sunday after Christmas Day*

Isaiah 52:7–10

How beautiful upon the mountains
    are the feet of the messenger who announces peace,
who brings good news,
    who announces salvation,
    who says to Zion, "Your God reigns." (v. 7)

Luke 2:1–20

But the angel said to them, "Do not be afraid; for see—I am bringing you good news of great joy for all the people: to you is born this day in the city of David a Savior, who is the Messiah, the Lord." (vv. 10–11)

John 1:1–14

And the Word became flesh and lived among us, and we have seen his glory, the glory as of a father's only son, full of grace and truth. (v. 14)

Matthew 2:13–23

Now after they had left, an angel of the Lord appeared to Joseph in a dream and said, "Get up, take the child and his mother, and flee to Egypt, and remain there until I tell you; for Herod is about to search for the child, to destroy him." (v. 13)

LECTIO DIVINA

Underline a word or phrase that especially grabs your attention. Pray from that word or phrase and ask God to help you connect to its particular invitation for you this week.

Themes from This Week's Writers

THEME 1: *To You Is Born, This Day*

Titus 3:4–7

This community may have been far away from the historical event of Christ's appearing, and they were no longer living in expectation of an imminent second coming. Nonetheless they experienced the reality of Jesus' appearing, and it transformed them.

PATRICIA J. CALAHAN

Luke 2:(1–7) 8–20

Elites in Rome looked down upon people living in Judea and Galilee. The orator Cicero once said that Judeans, among others, were "born to be slaves."[1] In the eyes of power, Mary, Joseph, and Jesus were "born to be slaves." So, too, were the shepherds. God says otherwise[:] . . . "to *you* is born this day in the city of David a Savior" (Luke 2:11).

ERICA KNISELY

Matthew 2:13–23

The shadow of the cross is already present as the Christ child threatens a powerful ruler and upends usual, hierarchical notions of authority. . . . Even in the midst of suffering and death we can remember signs of God's faithfulness . . . that hope is found in a child, God incarnate.

KRISTIN STROBLE

THEME 2: *The Wonder of the Incarnation*

Psalm 97

This God of power is also a God of tenderness. . . . Such a juxtaposition is seen in the Christ child, the infant Messiah, who in his very person is both divine power and human vulnerability.

CHRISTINE J. HONG

---

1. Cicero, *Epistulae ad Quintum Fratrem* 1.1.19; Cicero, *De Provinciis Consularibus* 10; cited in David Nystrom, "We Have No King but Caesar: Roman Imperial Ideology and the Imperial Cult," in *Jesus Is Lord, Caesar Is Not: Evaluating Empire in New Testament Studies*, ed. Scot McKnight and Joseph B. Modica (Downers Grove, IL: InterVarsity, 2013), 25.

John 1:1–14

No contradiction in human logic deters the author of John from confessing the divinity of the human Jesus Christ: Jesus as Logos is eternal spirit and wholly other and *at the same time* was flesh in the first century in Galilee, absolutely corporeal.

SALLY SMITH HOLT

Luke 2:1–14 (15–20)

On Christmas Eve, we need and want to hear the familiar Christmas story, and we need and want to hear the most basic theological gloss that story invites, which is also a commonplace: *God came from heaven and took on our human form because God loves us.*

LAUREN F. WINNER

WHAT IS THE HOLY SPIRIT SAYING TO YOU THIS WEEK?

_____

_____

_____

_____

_____

A SPIRITUAL PRACTICE FOR THIS WEEK

"To you, a child is born!" Schedule some time on your calendar this week to experience awe and wonder. Take a beautiful walk, sit still in a peaceful spot, take a drive down a scenic road, or find some other way to be intentionally amazed at the glory of God, incarnate among us.

Christmas Prophecy

Isaiah 52:7–10

Listen! Your sentinels lift up their voices,
  together they sing for joy;
for in plain sight they see
  the return of the LORD to Zion. (v. 8)

REFLECTION

This is a moment for revisiting the ancient Christian theological tension
between a realized and a future eschatology. Is the kingdom here, or
yet to come? . . . The world is still the world; the powers are still the
powers. Yet the testimony of Scripture is that there is a direct line from
the manger to the cross to the tomb to the mountaintop in Galilee to
the final consummation of the hope of salvation. The Christian liturgical
cycle has it right: the hope of Advent, birthed at Christmas, grows
through the ordinariness of things, until at year's end it blooms as Christ
the King, and then returns to hope again.

PAUL K. HOOKER

RESPONSE

Reflect on some connections you see, per Hooker's suggestion, between
the birth of Christ, the cross, the empty tomb, the ascension, and the
second coming. Or choose one or two of these. What do you notice?
How is the kingdom already here and yet also still to come?

PRAYER

O Alpha and Omega, your kingdom is already before me yet also still to
come; reveal to me how hope in Christ grows through the ordinariness
of things, in this season and through all times and places. Amen.

Christmas Epistle

Titus 3:4–7

But when the goodness and loving kindness of God our Savior appeared, he saved us, not because of any works of righteousness that we had done, but according to his mercy, through the water of rebirth and renewal by the Holy Spirit. (vv. 4–5)

REFLECTION

Titus brings [us] an opportunity to . . . experience Christmas not as a historical memory, but as the grace of Christ's living appearance in our own lives. Christ appeared for the people of this epistle. This appearance was experienced as a grace that enabled them to seek peace with a culture they perceived to be entirely opposed to their values. Christ also appears to us and changes us, freeing us from undue pride as we approach those with whom we are in conflict. The grace of Christ's appearance erases the false boundaries we create among people whom God loves.

PATRICIA J. CALAHAN

RESPONSE

How do you perceive the culture you live in to be opposed to your values? How could Christ's birth into your life "erase the false boundaries" you have erected? How could this be a rebirth or good news for you?

PRAYER

Lord of love, you do not love or save me because of any works of righteousness I have done, but because of your mercy and loving kindness. Help me to receive rebirth in Christ, as I learn to be the person you made me to be. Amen.

Christmas Gospel

Luke 2:1–20

And suddenly there was with the angel a multitude of the heavenly host, praising God and saying,
> "Glory to God in the highest heaven
> and on earth peace among those whom he favors!" (vv. 13–14)

REFLECTION

Since the shepherds are keeping guard at night over their flocks, the terrifying appearance of the glory of God creates an extraordinary image of light breaking through a dark, cold night, well before the invention of electricity (Luke 2:9). . . .

We should note that the light of divine glory shines not around the manger but around singing—celestial, articulate angels seen and heard through human fear and terror. . . . God's glory shines forth in the world, not in a private space or designated holy places like the Jerusalem temple or local synagogues, but in the open, boundless, dark fields at night.

DEIRDRE J. GOOD

RESPONSE

How is God's glory seeking you outside of private or churchy places, out in the fields and streets in your own life? Is there a glimpse of God's glory emerging in your life you are afraid to let yourself see?

PRAYER

God of glory, help me to see your light and your angels, not just around the manger, but out in the dark fields and lonely places of my life and my community. Amen.

Sunday Gospel

Matthew 2:13–23

When Herod saw that he had been tricked by the wise men, he was infuriated, and he sent and killed all the children in and around Bethlehem who were two years old or under, according to the time that he had learned from the wise men. (v. 16)

REFLECTION

This is a story of hope and joy mingled with bitter loss. The shadow of the cross is already present as the Christ child threatens a powerful ruler and upends usual, hierarchical notions of authority. Recalling the story of God's faithfulness toward Israel as well as the salvation found in Christ, . . . even in the midst of suffering and death we can remember signs of God's faithfulness, love, and humility; we can remember that hope is found in a child, God incarnate, and in the divine promise of ultimate restoration—not just for Israel but for the whole world.

KRISTIN STROBLE

RESPONSE

How have hope and joy been mingled with loss or danger for you this past year? Have you witnessed a massacre or made a "flight to Egypt" in any way? What does the hope of the Christ child mean for you this season? How does God's promise of restoration speak to you?

PRAYER

O God, you are with me in danger and go ahead of me to lead me to safety, even into exile; show me how to join in your work for the safety and restoration of your whole creation. Amen.

Weekend Reflections

Consider my Son, the gentle, loving Word born in a stable while Mary was on a journey. What does he show you? True pilgrims are constantly being born anew in the stable of self-knowledge. There by grace you will find Christ born within your soul. Look at baby Jesus lying there between the animals. He was so poor. Mary had nothing to cover him with and it was winter. The breath of animals and a blanket of hay kept him warm. Look again. The baby is the fire of Love, but he chose to endure the bitterest cold in his humanity.

The whole time my Son lived on earth, he chose to endure suffering.

CATHERINE OF SIENA (1347–80), *DIALOGUES*

MAKING THE CONNECTIONS

Choose one or two questions for reflection:

1. What connections have you noticed between this week's texts and other passages in Scripture?

2. What connections have you made between this week's texts and the world beyond Scripture?

3. Does either of this week's two commentary themes speak especially to your life or the life of the world around you right now?

4. What is God saying to your congregation in particular through this week's readings and commentaries?

_____

_____

_____

_____

_____

Sabbath Day

SCRIPTURE OF ASSURANCE

Now to him who by the power at work within us is able to accomplish abundantly far more than all we can ask or imagine, to him be glory in the church and in Christ Jesus to all generations, forever and ever. Amen. (Ephesians 3:20–21)

WEEKLY EXAMEN

- Take a quiet moment, seek out God's presence, and pray for the guidance of the Spirit.

- Consider the past week; recall specific moments and feelings that stand out to you.

- Choose one moment or feeling for deeper examination, thanksgiving, or repentance.

- Let go, breathe deeply, and invite Christ's love to surround and fill you in preparation for the week ahead.

- End with the Lord's Prayer.

The Week Leading Up to the
Second Sunday after Christmas Day

Jeremiah 31:7–14

See, I am going to bring them from the land of the north,
    and gather them from the farthest parts of the earth. (v. 8a)

Psalm 147:12–20

He sends out his word, and melts them;
    he makes his wind blow, and the waters flow.
He declares his word to Jacob,
    his statutes and ordinances to Israel. (vv. 18–19)

Ephesians 1:3–14

He destined us for adoption as his children through Jesus Christ, according to the good pleasure of his will, to the praise of his glorious grace that he freely bestowed on us in the Beloved. (vv. 5–6)

John 1:(1–9) 10–18

He came to what was his own, and his own people did not accept him. But to all who received him, who believed in his name, he gave power to become children of God, who were born, not of blood or of the will of the flesh or of the will of man, but of God. (vv. 11–13)

LECTIO DIVINA

Underline a word or phrase that especially grabs your attention. Pray from that word or phrase and ask God to help you connect to its particular invitation for you this week.

Themes from This Week's Writers

THEME 1: *Already, and Not Yet*

Jeremiah 31:7–14

Somehow even in exile, God would be present. Keeping this tension in mind, Jeremiah counsels God's people to build houses, plant gardens, marry, and bear children; they are to seek "the welfare of the city" even in Babylon (29:5–7).

MARK RALLS

Jeremiah 31:7–14

How do we, as the people of God, behave and believe authentically and faithfully in this space between partial fulfillment and full eschatological realization? A brave preacher might ponder the dissonance between our lives and the promises made in our tradition.

SONG-MI SUZIE PARK

John 1:(1–9) 10–18

Now that humans can see, hear, and know God, they must choose whether to participate in this new relationship or reject it and miss out on the life and light that are offered. . . . The light of Christ is seen, heard, and known when disciples heal, teach, preach, and love in the name of Christ.

KRISTIN STROBLE

THEME 2: *To Gather Up All in Christ*

Ephesians 1:3–14

Christ calls us to care not just for ourselves and our own; we are called to look across the gaps, to find folks of goodwill on the other side, and to take up our needles and thread and sew toward them. Christ calls us to mend the tears in the fabric of our communities, so as "to gather up all things in him" (1:10).

STEPHEN B. BOYD

Ephesians 1:3–14

The Ephesians and faithful communities like them are attempting to do something wonderful, but also something quite strange in the spiritual ecosystem of their time: they are forging a new kind of alternative and inclusive community that resists cultural divisions based on gender, race, national origins, or tribe.

RICHARD F. WARD

John 1:(1–9) 10–18

[We may] refuse to be children of God and therefore siblings to one another, and choose instead to be rivals, competitors, or even enemies. Lifting up the Word's relationship to God, creation, and humankind allows preachers to emphasize the call of followers of Jesus Christ also to be in loving relationship to God, creation, and one another.

JILL DUFFIELD

WHAT IS THE HOLY SPIRIT SAYING TO YOU THIS WEEK?

_____

_____

_____

_____

_____

A SPIRITUAL PRACTICE FOR THIS WEEK

One evening this week, stand outside of the place where you live, leaving as many lights on as you can. Take a photo or just look; imagine what it would be like to be exiled. Pray for refugees and consider making a financial gift to a charity that advocates for them.

First Reading

Jeremiah 31:7–14

I will turn their mourning into joy,
    I will comfort them, and give them gladness for sorrow.
I will give the priests their fill of fatness,
    and my people shall be satisfied with my bounty,
says the LORD. (v. 13b–14)

REFLECTION

No doubt this prophecy sounded absurd to the worried population of
Judah. Jeremiah's speech may sound bombastic to the modern listener.
Yet it is important to remember that Jeremiah is not talking about what
is, but what is possible through God. He affirms something for which
the Judeans yearn that has not yet occurred. Considering this hope
emanates from God's prophet, we should assume these wishes parallel
those of God. Stability, prosperity, and return: that is what God wants
for this beloved covenant people.

SONG-MI SUZIE PARK

RESPONSE

Write a prophecy, expressing your own hope in what is possible through
God for a group of which you are a part—nation, local community,
congregation, family, etc. Lean toward a hope that others might find
absurd, or even silly. What is it like to do this?

PRAYER

God of surprise, gather and lead me with your people from mourning
and anxiety to absurd hope, bountiful generosity, and joyful fatness.
Amen.

Canticle

Psalm 147:12–20

Praise the LORD, O Jerusalem!
　　Praise your God, O Zion!
For he strengthens the bars of your gates;
　　he blesses your children within you. (vv. 12–13)

REFLECTION

Seeing God in action, Israel now voices praise upon praise, for the God who rescues and restores is the very same God who administers creation: the world, the seasons, the cycles of fallowness and harvest. Praising YHWH is good, beautiful, and worthwhile; to praise YHWH is to participate in God's glorifying.

The psalmist names the reasons for praise: YHWH strengthens and blesses (v. 13), YHWH acts to assure peace, *shalom* (v. 14). YHWH fortifies the borders, protecting Israel from enemies, assuring that the city will be what it is meant to be, the home of a vital community where grace, mercy, and the power of God are evident.[1]

JOSEPH A. DONNELLA II

RESPONSE

What does "praise" or "praising God" mean in your spiritual life? Has it changed over time? What would you like it to mean, going forward? Write a list, poem, or prayer of things, large and small, you would like to praise God for this week.

PRAYER

Loving God, teach me to praise you with my whole heart, not only that I may know your glory and love but to know, in Christ, the glory and love within me. Amen.

---

1. Artur Weiser, *The Psalms: A Commentary*, trans. Herbert Hartwell (Philadelphia: Westminster Press, 1962), 837.

Second Reading

Ephesians 1:3–14

With all wisdom and insight he has made known to us the mystery of his will, according to his good pleasure that he set forth in Christ, as a plan for the fullness of time, to gather up all things in him, things in heaven and things on earth. (vv. 8b–10)

REFLECTION

"We are," Dr. Martin Luther King Jr. said, "caught in an inescapable network of mutuality, tied in a single garment of destiny."[1]

There is, however, a problem: that single garment has giant tears in the fabric. . . .

The work of reconciliation is far from complete, even within and between our churches. The "cosmic powers" are still at work tearing at the fabric of God's creation; there are many who believe that others, different from themselves, are enemies. The work to which God calls us in Christ is not easy, and it can be frightening to reach across these rips in the fabric of creation toward others who may view us as enemies.

STEPHEN B. BOYD

RESPONSE

Where have you particularly felt the mutuality of the "single garment" of God's creation lately? Where have you felt the gaps and tears? How do you feel called to reach across them? Where do you feel Christ, "who gathers up all things," woven into this garment?

PRAYER

Lord God, your will and plan for all things is woven into creation; show me how to more fully weave myself into this fabric and to reach across its gaps and tears with love and trust. Amen.

1. Martin Luther King Jr., "Letter from Birmingham Jail," in James Washington, ed., *A Testament of Hope: The Essential Writings and Speeches of Dr. Martin Luther King Jr.* (San Francisco: HarperSanFrancisco, 1991), 290.

Gospel

John 1:(1–9) 10–18

And the Word became flesh and lived among us, and we have seen his glory, the glory as of a father's only son, full of grace and truth. . . . From his fullness we have all received, grace upon grace. (vv. 14, 16)

REFLECTION

NASA invited witnesses to tell them what the eclipse [of 2017] meant to them in six words. Perhaps the preacher, in the run-up to this Second Sunday after Christmas, might ask the congregation to submit six words . . . describing what the birth of Jesus, the Word made flesh, means to them. . . .

. . . Given the timing of this text, a look back at various "words of the year"—contenders in 2017, for instance, were "complicit," "post-truth," "fake news," "resistance"—could provide a jumping-off point, allowing us to compare these words to the words of Scripture and to the Word made flesh.

JILL DUFFIELD

RESPONSE

Write out six words, as suggested, that describe what the Word becoming flesh in the birth of Jesus means to you. Then, look up Merriam-Webster's Words of the Year and compare lists. Can you make connections? Are there striking contrasts? Where do you find good news of God's love?

PRAYER

Word of God, you have pitched your tent among us; teach me to receive your grace and truth, alive and active all around me. Amen.

Weekend Reflections

FURTHER CONNECTION

I am sorry I ran from you. I am still running, running from that knowledge, that eye, that love from which there is no refuge. For you meant only love, and love, and I felt only fear, and pain. So once in Israel love came to us incarnate, stood in the doorway between two worlds, and we were all afraid.

ANNIE DILLARD (1945–), *TEACHING A STONE TO TALK: EXPEDITIONS AND ENCOUNTERS*

MAKING THE CONNECTIONS

Choose one or two questions for reflection:

1. What connections have you noticed between this week's texts and other passages in Scripture?

2. What connections have you made between this week's texts and the world beyond Scripture?

3. Does either of this week's two commentary themes speak especially to your life or the life of the world around you right now?

4. What is God saying to your congregation in particular through this week's readings and commentaries?

MY CONNECTIONS

_____

_____

_____

_____

_____

Sabbath Day

SCRIPTURE OF ASSURANCE

> Happy are those who find wisdom,
>   and those who get understanding,
> for her income is better than silver,
>   and her revenue better than gold. (Proverbs 3:13–14)

WEEKLY EXAMEN

- Take a quiet moment, seek out God's presence, and pray for the guidance of the Spirit.

- Consider the past week; recall specific moments and feelings that stand out to you.

- Choose one moment or feeling for deeper examination, thanksgiving, or repentance.

- Let go, breathe deeply, and invite Christ's love to surround and fill you in preparation for the week ahead.

- End with the Lord's Prayer.

Epiphany of the Lord

READINGS

Isaiah 60:1–6

Arise, shine; for your light has come,
　　and the glory of the Lord has risen upon you.
For darkness shall cover the earth,
　　and thick darkness the peoples;
but the Lord will arise upon you,
　　and his glory will appear over you. (vv. 1–2)

Psalm 72:1–7, 10–14

For he delivers the needy when they call,
　　the poor and those who have no helper.
He has pity on the weak and the needy,
　　and saves the lives of the needy. (vv. 12–13)

Ephesians 3:1–12

So that through the church the wisdom of God in its rich variety might now be made known to the rulers and authorities in the heavenly places. This was in accordance with the eternal purpose that he has carried out in Christ Jesus our Lord, in whom we have access to God in boldness and confidence through faith in him. (vv. 10–12)

Matthew 2:1–12

"Where is the child who has been born king of the Jews? For we observed his star at its rising, and have come to pay him homage." When King Herod heard this, he was frightened, and all Jerusalem with him; and calling together all the chief priests and scribes of the people, he inquired of them where the Messiah was to be born. (vv. 2–4)

Isaiah 60:1–6

If Epiphany is about revelation, who or what in the world has revealed God to us, and how can we, in turn, unveil and show God back to the world? How do we as the people of God respectfully live into our missional call to act as witnesses and bearers of God's transformation? In what ways have we, individually and as the church, obscured the revelation of God? What can we do to incarnate the Gospel more fully in the future?

SONGMI SUZIE PARK

Psalm 72:1–7, 10–14

What Herod did not and could not understand was that legitimacy of rule comes not from imperial domination, or the exercise of abusive power. Legitimate authority is derived from good and right relationships with God and God's people. The cultivation of grace and gladness brings patterns of justice and mercy, defense of the oppressed and needy. Rulers who banish the cruelty that has given sway to evil create a realm of peace, righteousness, and justice. Such shalom is the opposite of Herod's rule.

JOSEPH A. DONNELLA II

Ephesians 3:1–12

To transform the alienating and destructive aspects of our economic, political, and religious institutions by making known the wisdom of God, we must intentionally make places that welcome the rich diversity of God's creation. Creative practices that invite a variety of people to eat together, interpret the Scriptures together, and worship together might just do that work.

STEPHEN B. BOYD

Matthew 2:1–12

Herod is not the only one frightened by the star's indication of the birth of a "king of the Jews"; "all Jerusalem" fears as well (Matt. 2:3). An astrological phenomenon draws attention and causes anxiety. If the very heavens can change, if a new king has been born, what is next? The collapse of power, privilege, the status quo? Herod calls together the chief priests and scribes to confront this threat and figure out where the child will be born. In one room are gathered those who will continue to oppose Jesus and eventually hand him over to Pilate for crucifixion (27:1–2).

KRISTIN STROBLE

RESPONSE

Choose one of these four quotes that particularly gets your attention and write or reflect on how God might be speaking to you, to your experience or questions about the Epiphany this year, or to this time in your life.

PRAYER

O Jesus, you have been revealed to us, a light of mercy and justice for all peoples; teach us how we, in turn, may unveil and show you to all the world. Amen.

The Week Leading Up to the
Baptism of the Lord

Isaiah 42:1–9

Here is my servant, whom I uphold,
    my chosen, in whom my soul delights;
I have put my spirit upon him;
    he will bring forth justice to the nations. (v. 1)

Psalm 29

The LORD sits enthroned over the flood;
    the LORD sits enthroned as king forever. (v. 10)

Acts 10:34–43

"You know the message he sent to the people of Israel, preaching peace by Jesus Christ—he is Lord of all." (v. 36)

Matthew 3:13–17

And a voice from heaven said, "This is my Son, the Beloved, with whom I am well pleased." (v. 17)

LECTIO DIVINA

Underline a word or phrase that especially grabs your attention. Pray from that word or phrase and ask God to help you connect to its particular invitation for you this week.

Themes from This Week's Writers

THEME 1: *Baptism Calls Us to Join God's Mission*

Isaiah 42:1–9

It is the people, the community, who have the mission to open eyes that are blind, to free captives from prison, and to release from the dungeon those who sit in darkness. . . . The use of these words in Jesus' annunciation of his ministry are not to be understood as his personal mission but the mission of the community to whom he speaks.

JAMES H. EVANS JR.

Isaiah 42:1–9

We are not asked merely to admire the wonderful Servant of God; we are called to join the Servant in that work. . . . Christians were asked not only to wonder at the work of Jesus' life, death, and resurrection, but to join his work of reconciliation of the fractured world.

JOHN C. HOLBERT

Matthew 3:13–17

Baptism . . . gives public witness to God's saving grace, one's new birth in Christ, and incorporation into Christ's body. At the same time it is a commissioning for God's mission that we share with Christ. Baptism . . . is a marker of our being sent into the world to make disciples.

MARK ABBOTT

THEME 2: *God Is Doing a New Thing*

Acts 10:34–43

The translation of the beginning of Peter's speech, "I truly understand," is correct. . . . A livelier rendering might be "I am catching on." . . . Conversion is catching on to what God is doing around us and in us. What is true of an individual is also true for the church. Not only is conversion a matter of catching on to what God is doing. It may also be catching up to what God is doing.

STEPHEN FARRIS

Acts 10:34–43

In Jesus' baptism, the arrival of the Holy Spirit, and all the healing, liberation, and forgiveness of Jesus' ministry, we come to understand anew who God is, what God values, and what it means to be called into the people of God.

   . . . In Jesus we see God. . . . To see God's priorities in action, look to the activity of Jesus.

MATTHEW L. SKINNER

Matthew 3:13–17

If the Gospel is the book of the Genesis of Jesus the Christ, then the baptism scene marks formally a new stage in God's actions as Creator. A new creation is being brought forth, the realization of God's intentions not only for humankind, but for the whole of heaven and earth.

STANLEY P. SAUNDERS

WHAT IS THE HOLY SPIRIT SAYING TO YOU THIS WEEK?

_____

_____

_____

_____

_____

A SPIRITUAL PRACTICE FOR THIS WEEK

Make three Holy Spirit doves out of paper. Your doves can be basic, like a simple triangle cut-out, or complex, like folding an origami crane. Write a word or phrase on each dove that will call you to remember your baptism. Tape or hang where you will see them all week.

First Reading

I am the LORD, I have called you in righteousness,
    I have taken you by the hand and kept you;
I have given you as a covenant to the people,
    a light to the nations. (v. 6)

REFLECTION

For the next two full generations, the political and religious leaders of
the community lived in a suburb of one of the world's greatest cities and
attempted to survive in any way they could. . . .

. . . We too live in confusing and dispiriting times. . . . We are in
desperate need of a new infusion of optimism and intention, a clear
idea that God still has a plan for us, a plan beyond mere local goals,
but a plan that encompasses something far larger. In short, we need a
reminder that God has not given up on us, but calls us to the larger
purposes of God for the entire universe.

JOHN C. HOLBERT

RESPONSE

How are you longing to be reassured of God's plan or larger purposes at
this time in your life? What is dispiriting or confusing these days? Read
the above verse from Isaiah: how might God be speaking to you today?
What does remembering your baptism mean for you in this?

PRAYER

Lord God, you have called me in your righteousness; take me by the
hand, protect me, and give me as a light to my community—and even
to the whole world. Amen.

Canticle

Psalm 29

The voice of the LORD is over the waters;
    the God of glory thunders,
    the LORD, over mighty waters.
The voice of the LORD is powerful;
    the voice of the LORD is full of majesty. (vv. 3–4)

REFLECTION

There is a gentleness in God's voice that is heard again in Matthew, when Jesus emerges from the waters of the Jordan to the voice of God naming him as "Beloved." In the text from Acts, the voice of God is heard in the message that spread throughout Judea. Read in connection with Psalm 29, one can envision that message spreading out among people much as the voice of God is broadcast over the waters. . . .

. . . A preacher might explore the use of God's voice in these passages as God's self-disclosure to us.

ERIN KEYS

RESPONSE

What are some ways you have heard God's voice, recently? Has God sounded gentle? Thunderous? Or has God's voice been absent? If you were to ask God to speak and disclose something of Godself to you this week, what in particular might you be hoping to hear or understand?

PRAYER

Lord of glory, your voice is powerful, full of the strength, love, and beauty of your creation; send me your strength and your peace today and always. Amen.

Second Reading

Acts 10:34–43

Then Peter began to speak to them: "I truly understand that God shows no partiality, but in every nation anyone who fears him and does what is right is acceptable to him." (vv. 34–35)

REFLECTION

The big-picture good news in the story for the anxious church of the early twenty-first century may be simply that with God's help the early church got through its first great crisis. Acts shows us that the conversion of the church to a new sense of itself and a new sense of mission was not easy. It was not easy to reach out to Gentiles. They were different, after all, and it is always difficult to reach out to those who are different. The tensions of transition are manifest, even at the distance of two millennia. They did get through their crisis and perhaps, with God's good aid, so will we.

STEPHEN FARRIS

RESPONSE

What strains are most acute for you in being part of "the anxious church of the early twenty-first century"? How do you hear Peter striving to adjust to the new mission of the church in his time? How might Peter be a mentor for you or your congregation in your time?

PRAYER

God of all people, receive my anxiety, tension, and fear that, in you, I may journey through any transition or crisis. Amen.

Gospel

Matthew 3:13–17

And when Jesus had been baptized, just as he came up from the water, suddenly the heavens were opened to him and he saw the Spirit of God descending like a dove and alighting on him. (v. 16)

REFLECTION

Before we baptize a young person or adult, we usually put them through a process of study. A very natural question may arise from the baptismal candidate: "Will things be different for me after baptism?" Of course, the best response is with another question. "What would you expect to be different, and why?"

. . . In baptism we are affirmed and confirmed as children of God. Our union with God in Christ expressed in baptism anchors our identity in God's character and mission, particularly as these are revealed in Jesus Christ.

MARK ABBOTT

RESPONSE

What does your baptism mean to you at this point in your life? Does it mean something different now than it has in the past? How does it connect you to the life and revelation of Jesus? What does it mean to you to be a child of God—God's Beloved?

PRAYER

Spirit of God, descend upon my heart; teach me what baptism means and how beloved I truly am, a child of God in Christ. Amen.

Weekend Reflections

FURTHER CONNECTION

As dry flour cannot be united into a lump of dough, or a loaf, but needs water, so we who are many cannot be made one in Christ Jesus without the water that comes from heaven.

IRENAEUS OF LYONS (130–202), *AGAINST THE HERESIES*

MAKING THE CONNECTIONS

Choose one or two questions for reflection:

1. What connections have you noticed between this week's texts and other passages in Scripture?

2. What connections have you made between this week's texts and the world beyond Scripture?

3. Does either of this week's two commentary themes speak especially to your life or the life of the world around you right now?

4. What is God saying to your congregation in particular through this week's readings and commentaries?

MY CONNECTIONS

_____

_____

_____

_____

_____

_____

Sabbath Day

> But now thus says the LORD,
>> he who created you, O Jacob,
>> he who formed you, O Israel:
> Do not fear, for I have redeemed you;
>> I have called you by name, you are mine. (Isaiah 43:1)

WEEKLY EXAMEN

- Take a quiet moment, seek out God's presence, and pray for the guidance of the Spirit.

- Consider the past week; recall specific moments and feelings that stand out to you.

- Choose one moment or feeling for deeper examination, thanksgiving, or repentance.

- Let go, breathe deeply, and invite Christ's love to surround and fill you in preparation for the week ahead.

- End with the Lord's Prayer.

The Week Leading Up to the
Second Sunday
after the Epiphany

Isaiah 49:1–7

"It is too light a thing that you should be my servant
    to raise up the tribes of Jacob
    and to restore the survivors of Israel;
I will give you as a light to the nations,
    that my salvation may reach to the end of the earth." (v. 6)

Psalm 40:1–11

I have not hidden your saving help within my heart,
    I have spoken of your faithfulness and your salvation;
I have not concealed your steadfast love and your faithfulness
    from the great congregation. (v. 10)

1 Corinthians 1:1–9

I give thanks to my God always for you because of the grace of God that has
been given you in Christ Jesus, for in every way you have been enriched in
him, in speech and knowledge of every kind. (vv. 4–5)

John 1:29–42

The next day John again was standing with two of his disciples, and as he watched
Jesus walk by, he exclaimed, "Look, here is the Lamb of God!" (vv. 35–36)

LECTIO DIVINA

Underline a word or phrase that especially grabs your attention. Pray
from that word or phrase and ask God to help you connect to its
particular invitation for you this week.

Themes from This Week's Writers

THEME 1: *Be a Light to the Nations*

Isaiah 49:1–7

This theme of the restoration of Israel is quickly followed by the divine declaration to extend salvation to the ends of the earth. . . . Any temptation to understand the prophetic word as a call to a protonationalism is countered by the call to take this promise of God to all.

JAMES H. EVANS JR.

Isaiah 49:1–7

Like a thunderclap, YHWH shakes the despondent exiles out of their lethargy by giving to them the largest task they could ever conceive, nothing less than divine responsibility for the entire world. . . .

. . . In our time, it is crucial that we feel our work for Jesus is a part, however small, of that light for the world.

JOHN C. HOLBERT

John 1:29–42

We come to understand that identity is not primarily an egocentric discovery but a missional revelation. We are connected to Someone much bigger than us, and our lives take on meaning as we engage in God's mission. We find our true epiphany when we find our place in God's world.

MARK ABBOTT

THEME 2: *Called to Be Saints, as We Are*

1 Corinthians 1:1–9

To us a saint is a spiritual superstar, one who has achieved great things for God. Manifestly, the Corinthians are scrubs, not superstars—if they are defined by their own achievement. They are, however, saints because God has called them and sanctified them. The achievement belongs to God, not to them, and it is from God's call that their identity is derived.

STEPHEN FARRIS

1 Corinthians 1:1–9

Apparently, churches can grow unsteadily into their identity, manage disagreements, receive correction, and learn together what it means to live the Christian life in particular contexts without anyone having to call into doubt either the authenticity of someone else's commitment or the effectiveness of God's grace.

MATTHEW L. SKINNER

John 1:29–42

God uses us as witnesses not because we fit the right profile or have the right skill set. Seeing and naming what God is doing is about *God*, not about us, just as John's witness is not about himself, but about *Jesus*.

STANLEY P. SAUNDERS

WHAT IS THE HOLY SPIRIT SAYING TO YOU THIS WEEK?

_____

_____

_____

_____

_____

A SPIRITUAL PRACTICE FOR THIS WEEK

Spend some time reflecting on one or more of these questions: "What are you looking for?" "Where are you abiding?" "Where do you dwell?" "Where do you rest?" Notice what draws your energy or attention. What might Jesus be inviting you to "come and see"?

First Reading

Isaiah 49:1–7

Thus says the LORD,
    the Redeemer of Israel and his Holy One,
to one deeply despised, abhorred by the nations,
    the slave of rulers,
"Kings shall see and stand up,
    princes, and they shall prostrate themselves,
because of the LORD, who is faithful,
    the Holy One of Israel, who has chosen you." (v. 7)

REFLECTION

Here God is glorified as the prophet witnesses and embodies the power of the word. . . . The structures of power are confronted, . . . kings will stand and princes will bow down, because the prophet has been chosen by God. One of the critical insights of the African American understanding of this prophetic tradition is that praise and protest cannot be ultimately separated, and that the exaltation of the One who sends includes the elevation of the one who is sent. Theologically, this passage deepens our understanding of the prophetic task and provides clues to appropriating the task in our own time and place.

JAMES H. EVANS JR.

RESPONSE

How have praise and protest been related in churches you have been part of? Or kept separate? Have churches you have known elevated prophets or pushed them out? Write a prayer that expresses both protest and praise for a situation in your community and on your heart this week.

PRAYER

Redeemer God, teach me to praise and protest so even kings and princes, moguls and billionaires, will stand and bow before your wonderful justice and mercy. Amen.

Canticle

Psalm 40:1–11

Then I said, "Here I am;
   in the scroll of the book it is written of me.
I delight to do your will, O my God;
   your law is within my heart." (vv. 7–8)

REFLECTION

The psalmist remembers past deliverance with gratitude, and petitions God to help again. Neither the remembering nor the asking is passive, for the psalmist responds to God's salvific work by saying, "Here I am." Salvation from illness inspires the psalmist to declare her faithfulness to God not only with words (Ps. 40:9–10) but also with deeds. . . .

. . . In response to Psalm 40, worshipers might share their own stories of times when God saved them. This could take the form of a liturgy of remembrance that mirrors the psalm, allowing worshipers to give thanks and offer petitions, individually and corporately.

ERIN KEYS

RESPONSE

Reflect on a time God delivered or saved you. What was it like? What did it mean to you? Then, like the psalmist, declare to God in prayer: "Here I am." Where does this prayer seem to lead you? What would you like to say to God next?

PRAYER

O my God, lead me in delight to do your will. Your law is within my heart; here I am, send me. Amen.

Second Reading

To the church of God that is in Corinth, to those who are sanctified in Christ Jesus, called to be saints, together with all those who in every place call on the name of our Lord Jesus Christ, both their Lord and ours:

Grace to you and peace from God our Father and the Lord Jesus Christ. (vv. 2–3)

REFLECTION

To know who we are in Christ, we need one another.

As a result, there is a sacramental character to Christian community, which might sound astounding to the multitudes in the general population who have been burned by congregations and the sheer meanness of some communities. Nevertheless, each of us lives into the new self that God has freed us to be, not by retreating into ourselves, but by embracing our connections to others. . . . Perhaps ideals of the self-sufficient maverick and the isolated "spiritual" sojourner would compel Paul today to dash off more letters if he could.

MATTHEW L. SKINNER

RESPONSE

Do you tend to be a "self-sufficient maverick" or an "isolated spiritual sojourner"? How have your connections to Christian community, at church or elsewhere, and other Christians enriched your life? How have they hurt you? How might the Spirit be inviting you to deepen your spiritual relationships?

PRAYER

Christ Jesus, you call me to know who I am in you and also in the members of my community; give me grace and peace to know them and myself, more and more. Amen.

Gospel

John 1:29–42

When Jesus turned and saw them following, he said to them, "What are you looking for?" They said to him, "Rabbi" (which translated means Teacher), "where are you staying?" He said to them, "Come and see." They came and saw where he was staying, and they remained with him that day. (vv. 38–39)

REFLECTION

English translations typically render the Greek verb *menō* ("to remain, rest, stay, or abide"; used five times in 1:29–42) in two ways. . . . If, however, we translate *menō* consistently, then the Spirit "abides" or "dwells" with Jesus, and the disciples ask him not merely where he is staying but where he "abides." . . .

The one with whom the Spirit dwells has become the focal point of all the movement in the passage, the locus of abiding, rest, and remaining. This is, then, not only a story of calling and witness, but of seeking and abiding.

STANLEY P. SAUNDERS

RESPONSE

Reflect on this word, *menō*, and its many meanings. What does it mean to you to *menō* with Jesus, not just to follow him? Where does Jesus *menō* in your life? How is he inviting you to "come and see" this week?

PRAYER

Jesus the teacher, help me to follow where you are going and to stay with you, to come and see what you are doing in my life and all around me. Amen.

Weekend Reflections

FURTHER CONNECTION

I understand and I know from experience that: "The kingdom of God is within you." Jesus has no need of books or teachers to instruct souls; He teaches without the noise of words. Never have I heard Him speak, but I feel that He is within me at each moment; He is guiding and inspiring me with what I must say and do. I find just when I need them certain lights that I had not seen until then, and it isn't most frequently during my hours of prayer that these are most abundant but rather in the midst of my daily occupations.

THÉRÈSE OF LISIEUX (1873–97), *THE STORY OF A SOUL: THE AUTOBIOGRAPHY OF ST. THÉRÈSE OF LISIEUX*

MAKING THE CONNECTIONS

Choose one or two questions for reflection:

1. What connections have you noticed between this week's texts and other passages in Scripture?

2. What connections have you made between this week's texts and the world beyond Scripture?

3. Does either of this week's two commentary themes speak especially to your life or the life of the world around you right now?

4. What is God saying to your congregation in particular through this week's readings and commentaries?

_____

_____

_____

_____

_____

_____

Sabbath Day

SCRIPTURE OF ASSURANCE

> And you, child, will be called the prophet of the Most High;
>   for you will go before the Lord to prepare his ways,
> to give knowledge of salvation to his people
>   by the forgiveness of their sins. (Luke 1:76–77)

WEEKLY EXAMEN

- Take a quiet moment, seek out God's presence, and pray for the guidance of the Spirit.

- Consider the past week; recall specific moments and feelings that stand out to you.

- Choose one moment or feeling for deeper examination, thanksgiving, or repentance.

- Let go, breathe deeply, and invite Christ's love to surround and fill you in preparation for the week ahead.

- End with the Lord's Prayer.

The Week Leading Up to the
Third Sunday
after the Epiphany

Isaiah 9:1–4

The people who walked in darkness
    have seen a great light;
those who lived in a land of deep darkness—
    on them light has shined. (v. 2)

Psalm 27:1, 4–9

"Come," my heart says, "seek his face!"
    Your face, LORD, do I seek.
    Do not hide your face from me. (vv. 8–9a)

1 Corinthians 1:10–18

For the message about the cross is foolishness to those who are perishing, but to us who are being saved it is the power of God. (v. 18)

Matthew 4:12–23

"Land of Zebulun, land of Naphtali,
    on the road by the sea, across the Jordan, Galilee of the
        Gentiles—
the people who sat in darkness
    have seen a great light." (vv. 15–16a)

LECTIO DIVINA

Underline a word or phrase that especially grabs your attention. Pray from that word or phrase and ask God to help you connect to its particular invitation for you this week.

Themes from This Week's Writers

THEME 1: *Places of Struggle Become Places of Light*

Isaiah 9:1–4

The historical tropes of Zebulun and Naphtali, with their theological and cultic significations of both "home" and "struggle," established a bridge from the prophetic promise of God to the appearance of the fulfillment of that promise. Zebulun and Naphtali were among the first tribes from the northern kingdom of Israel carried away into captivity by the Assyrians.

JAMES H. EVANS JR.

Isaiah 9:1–4

It is all too easy to become cynical in the face of the centuries of wars, unrest, and suffering occurring in the name of the one who is supposedly the Prince of Peace. However, Christians who look always for the light of God in the darkness can never become cynical, because we trust in the God who always is bringing light.

JOHN C. HOLBERT

1 Corinthians 1:10–18

The new age that Christ has initiated demands altogether different systems of measurement and meaning, based on a cross-shaped understanding of God's ways of being in—and transforming—the world.

MATTHEW L. SKINNER

THEME 2: *"Follow Me"*

1 Corinthians 1:10–18

To be more contemporary, [Paul] does not say, "The real Christians in this church are behind me. The ones who want me out are fringe people." (This is not an invented quotation.) Amid church conflicts, the people who are behind us are also part of the problem if they are following us rather than Christ.

STEPHEN FARRIS

Matthew 4:12–23

The call to discipleship is thus presented not as something chosen by the disciples, but as the decisive, commanding act of Jesus. Because the kingdom of heaven has come near, there are no compromises to be made with the world as it is. This is unlike our modern notion of discipleship, in which "disciples" typically weigh, choose, and pursue their "calling" largely on their own terms.

STANLEY P. SAUNDERS

Matthew 4:12–23

Responding to Jesus' message of the kingdom of God is a keystone decision. This is one reason that repentance has to accompany it. The decision is life changing and requires deliberate life changes.

MARK ABBOTT

WHAT IS THE HOLY SPIRIT SAYING TO YOU THIS WEEK?

_____

_____

_____

_____

_____

A SPIRITUAL PRACTICE FOR THIS WEEK

All week, meditate on Jesus' invitation: "Follow me." Repeat it in prayer. Sing it to yourself. Draw, color, or doodle it. Write it on little pieces of paper and leave them in places you will see each day. At the end of the week, reflect on how its meaning may have opened up or changed for you.

First Reading

Isaiah 9:1–4

For the yoke of their burden,
and the bar across their shoulders,
the rod of their oppressor,
you have broken as on the day of Midian. (v. 4)

REFLECTION

This lectionary passage concludes by exhorting the hearers to remember God's actions "in the day of Midian's defeat" (v. 4 NIV). Midian's defeat was led by an insignificant and humble, if not reluctant, leader, Gideon. It reminds them that God's promises are already being fulfilled and that struggle is simply confirmation of such. . . .

Here, reconciliation is not primarily concerned with resolving the theological conundrums that have occupied Christian thinkers for centuries, but with reuniting a people with their past. A people whose alienation is symbolized by significant names long forgotten are now called upon to remember who God is.

JAMES H. EVANS JR.

RESPONSE

Reflect on significant struggles and leaders in your past; or, if it seems more relevant, in the past of your congregation. How might God be calling you to remember ways God's promises have already been fulfilled? How could this help you "to remember who God is"?

PRAYER

O God, you walk with me through the darkness and struggles I face now; help me to see how you have already fulfilled your promises to me and to your people. Amen.

Canticle

Psalm 27:1, 4–9

The LORD is my light and my salvation;
whom shall I fear?
The LORD is the stronghold of my life;
of whom shall I be afraid? (v. 1)

REFLECTION

Within the Bible there are nearly three hundred admonitions of "Do not be afraid," but are we to take that phrase literally as many often do? It is possible that to "Do not be afraid" is not to eradicate the emotion of fear, but rather to echo the psalmist and Isaiah, expressing our faith in the midst of our fear, thus demonstrating a greater confidence than one born of no fear at all. . . . Which is a more powerful declaration of faith: to say one has no fear, or to say one has fear but believes anyway?

ERIN KEYS

RESPONSE

Make a list of at least three, maybe more, active fears you are carrying right now. Do you ever feel pressure not to be afraid, to eliminate fear in your life? This week, how could you express faith in a loving God even from the midst of your fears?

PRAYER

Lord of light, be with me in my fear, for you are my salvation and my stronghold; I believe, help my unbelief. Amen.

Second Reading

1 Corinthians 1:10–18

What I mean is that each of you says, "I belong to Paul," or "I belong to Apollos," or "I belong to Cephas," or "I belong to Christ." Has Christ been divided? Was Paul crucified for you? Or were you baptized in the name of Paul? (vv. 12–13)

REFLECTION

A unity that celebrates otherness and repents of past domineering and oppression requires intentional activity; it cannot come from promises and slogans. The sinister habits we have grown used to perpetuating and suffering are persistent. They make it difficult for communities to progress beyond anemic truces based on mutual tolerance, which masquerades as unity. As the social damages of racial tension, economic disparity, political polarization, misogyny, homophobia, and shoddy hospitality continue to show their corrosive effects, distinctively Christian values and practices concerning authentic unity become all the more vital for congregations' self-understanding and patterns of behavior.

MATTHEW L. SKINNER

RESPONSE

What does unity look like in your congregation? How have you felt unity in your congregation or community that also "celebrates otherness"? Where have you felt unity to be superficial? What would it mean for your congregation to grow further into being "one in Christ"?

PRAYER

Christ of all people, I belong to you; help me grow as one with all the members of your body, that we may not just tolerate, but love and learn from one another, even through tension and fracture. Amen.

Gospel

Matthew 4:12–23

As he walked by the Sea of Galilee, he saw two brothers, Simon, who is called Peter, and Andrew his brother, casting a net into the sea—for they were fishermen. And he said to them, "Follow me, and I will make you fish for people." (vv. 18–19)

REFLECTION

In both Isaiah and Matthew, the redemption of the people in darkness entails liberation *from* the nations, but . . . the mission *to* the nations, with which the Gospel will culminate (28:16–20), is also ever on the horizon. The redemption that Jesus here announces and inaugurates is not just for Judeans or Galilean Jews, nor even just for the twelve restored tribes of Israel . . . but also ultimately for those who held them captive. Here is a reminder that the church's mission is not just for people like us, but for all, even for our enemies (5:43–48).

STANLEY P. SAUNDERS

RESPONSE

Who would you consider to be your or your community's "captors" or "enemies"? What is it like to consider that Jesus' and the church's mission is also for them? What redemption might Jesus have in mind for them, do you think? How are you called to be part of it?

PRAYER

Redeemer Jesus, you love me and you love my enemies; help me hear your call to follow you, not only for my own good, but for the good of my enemies, too. Amen.

Weekend Reflections

FURTHER CONNECTION

On a certain time, an impressive silence fell upon me, and I stood as if some one was about to speak to me, yet I had no such thought in my heart. —But to my utter surprise there seemed to sound a voice which I thought I distinctly heard, and most certainly understand, which said to me, "Go preach the Gospel!" I immediately replied aloud, "No one will believe me." Again I listened, and again the same voice seemed to say—"Preach the Gospel; I will put words in your mouth, and will turn your enemies to become your friends."

JARENA LEE (1783-1864), *THE LIFE AND RELIGIOUS EXPERIENCE OF JARENA LEE*, FIRST AUTHORIZED FEMALE PREACHER IN THE AFRICAN METHODIST EPISCOPAL CHURCH

MAKING THE CONNECTIONS

Choose one or two questions for reflection:

1. What connections have you noticed between this week's texts and other passages in Scripture?

2. What connections have you made between this week's texts and the world beyond Scripture?

3. Does either of this week's two commentary themes speak especially to your life or the life of the world around you right now?

4. What is God saying to your congregation in particular through this week's readings and commentaries?

_____

_____

_____

_____

_____

Sabbath Day

SCRIPTURE OF ASSURANCE

Have nothing to do with stupid and senseless controversies; you know that they breed quarrels. (2 Timothy 2:23)

WEEKLY EXAMEN

- Take a quiet moment, seek out God's presence, and pray for the guidance of the Spirit.

- Consider the past week; recall specific moments and feelings that stand out to you.

- Choose one moment or feeling for deeper examination, thanksgiving, or repentance.

- Let go, breathe deeply, and invite Christ's love to surround and fill you in preparation for the week ahead.

- End with the Lord's Prayer.

The Week Leading Up to the
Fourth Sunday after the Epiphany

Micah 6:1–8

He has told you, O mortal, what is good;
  and what does the LORD require of you
but to do justice, and to love kindness,
  and to walk humbly with your God? (v. 8)

Psalm 15

O LORD, who may abide in your tent?
  Who may dwell on your holy hill? (v. 1)

1 Corinthians 1:18–31

Consider your own call, brothers and sisters: not many of you were wise by human standards, not many were powerful, not many were of noble birth. (v. 26)

Matthew 5:1–12

"Blessed are the poor in spirit, for theirs is the kingdom of heaven.
  "Blessed are those who mourn, for they will be comforted." (vv. 3–4)

LECTIO DIVINA

Underline a word or phrase that especially grabs your attention. Pray from that word or phrase and ask God to help you connect to its particular invitation for you this week.

Themes from This Week's Writers

Micah 6:1–8

Ten thousand oily rivers belong to the realm of fantasy—or arch
sarcasm. . . .

. . . Bitter sarcasm erupts in the human's frustrated recognition of the
human condition. Everything we return to God came first as a gift to us.

PATRICIA K. TULL

Micah 6:1–8

What is required? Only justice, kindness, and love are necessary—
precisely the opposite of what one would expect from an overly legalistic
faith. In an era when white supremacists have openly chanted anti-
Semitic slogans like "blood and soil," it is more important than ever that
the church honor our Jewish roots.

KEN EVERS-HOOD

Psalm 15

If we are honest, we must confess that we do not make the cut; though
we may try, we fail time and time again in living a blameless life.
Certainly, it is only by God's mercy that we are welcomed in the tent or
invited to ascend the holy hill where we may join with others in praise
of our God.

ERIC TODD MYERS

THEME 2: *Blessed Are the Lowly*

1 Corinthians 1:18–31

Paul exhorts them to humility based on the foolishness of the cross
and God's choice of them for the mission of the church. . . . Just as one
cannot access the foolishness of God's plan of salvation through the

cross, so one cannot discern the blessing of the poor in spirit by human wisdom. God reveals this blessing.

CHARLES L. AARON JR.

1 Corinthians 1:18–31

We gain power only when we know we lack it; we preach Christ only when we are no longer on display for our giftedness.

The Unlikely becoming Somebody, the invisible becoming visible, and the lowly becoming exalted and God's free choice over against human selection runs right through our texts.

SCOT MCKNIGHT

Matthew 5:1–12

It is not those in positions of power or prestige who are identified as blessed but those on the margins. . . . God's favor on those who exist precariously on the underbelly of social, religious, and economic power structures connects with Paul's statement about the wisdom of the cross.

CHRISTOPHER T. HOLMES

WHAT IS THE HOLY SPIRIT SAYING TO YOU THIS WEEK?

_____

_____

_____

_____

_____

A SPIRITUAL PRACTICE FOR THIS WEEK

Do a walking meditation on Micah 6:8: walk outdoors in a struggling neighborhood, an affluent neighborhood, a strip mall, or a shopping corridor. Or indoors, in a hospital, a mall, a big-box store, or an airport. What does God invite you to see, through Micah, in this particular place?

First Reading

Micah 6:1–8

Hear, you mountains, the controversy of the LORD,
    and you enduring foundations of the earth;
for the LORD has a controversy with his people,
    and he will contend with Israel. (v. 2)

REFLECTION

God appears to be playing the role of the plaintiff bringing a complaint against Israel, acting the role of the defendant. Acting as judge are the mountains, hills, and foundations of the earth. Perhaps the mountains and hills serve as judge because they have been there long enough to watch how God has acted in Israel's life over the eons.

How evocative, to imagine humanity arguing our case for justice before the environment itself! . . . Preachers could take what is a very familiar text in a new direction here, pairing Micah 6:8 with creation care and justice for the marginalized.

KEN EVERS-HOOD

RESPONSE

Imagine mountains, hills, waters, and earth in your local geography as the judges of human activity. What might they have to teach or say to you and your neighbors? What do they hope for? What might God be trying to say to you and your community through them?

PRAYER

Loving God, show me how to do justice and love kindness, not only for other human beings but for all of creation. Amen.

Canticle

Psalm 15

Those who walk blamelessly, and do what is right,
    and speak the truth from their heart;
who do not slander with their tongue,
    and do no evil to their friends,
    nor take up a reproach against their neighbors. (vv. 2–3)

REFLECTION

Once, while driving down a country road, I saw a sign in a front yard:
"It's hard to walk humbly with God when you're still running with the
Devil." Whether one believes in a personification of evil complete with
red tights, horns, and pitchfork is not important. What is important
is that following the way of God means living in a different way than
you did before, a constant turning from evil and a continuous turning
to following the way of the Lord. Those who walk humbly with God
live a different life that can be seen in the actions of doing, loving, and
walking.

ERIC TODD MYERS

RESPONSE

What may be making it hard in your own life, lately, to "walk humbly
with God"? How might God be inviting you to turn and change? How
might you be longing, yourself, to live a different life? What is God
inviting you to hear in Psalm 15 this week?

PRAYER

Gracious God, I long to abide with you and in you; teach me to live a
life and to walk a walk that turns always toward you, and away from sin
and the evil one. Amen.

Second Reading

1 Corinthians 1:18–31

God chose what is low and despised in the world, things that are not, to reduce to nothing things that are, so that no one might boast in the presence of God. (vv. 28–29)

REFLECTION

The Beatitudes then are not a list of would-be virtues for high-status people but a countercultural list of people least likely to be valued for God's ultimate kingdom mission. These, Jesus announces for all to hear, are kingdom people. The most common reaction to Jesus' list had to be, "What about me? Why didn't you mention me?" Exactly.

Our text offers the uncommon commonness of a biblical trajectory that values all, great or small. This devaluing of what we value highlights the Bible's incongruity of grace and radical democratization of a status rooted in a different kind of spirituality.

SCOT MCKNIGHT

RESPONSE

Make a list of traits and qualities you most value in the leaders of your church. Then, in yourself. Place them alongside the Beatitudes or reread Paul's words in this passage. What if God values what is foolish and weak in you as much as what is strong and wise? In your church's leaders?

PRAYER

God of the lowly, bless me in my strengths and in my weaknesses, that I may see your wisdom in human foolishness; that I may boast about your strength and love, not my own. Amen.

Gospel

Matthew 5:1–12

"Blessed are the meek, for they will inherit the earth.
"Blessed are those who hunger and thirst for righteousness, for they will be filled." (vv. 5–6)

REFLECTION

Meekness does not mean cowardliness. Women, like men, are not called to be victims of abuse. Too often, this text has been used to keep people "in their place" so that others could do with them as they please. Meekness and the promise that such will inherit the earth do not equal, for instance, a kind of "manifest destiny" that justifies enslavement and the displacement of people groups. It does not assume or appropriate its reward. The Gandhis, Martin Luther King Jrs., Cesar Chavezes, the Malala Yousafzais, and Tegla Loroupes know this all too well. In short, meekness does not preclude the courage to be peacemakers, justice seekers, or prophets (Matt. 5:12); it is a prerequisite for it.

ZAIDA MALDONADO PÉREZ

RESPONSE

What is your relationship with your own meekness? How have you seen meekness draw abuse? How have you seen it as an asset? How is meekness a prerequisite for making change in the world? For ensuring spiritual health and personal wholeness?

PRAYER

Jesus, you saw the crowds and told them how blessed they were; teach me to see my own blessedness and to rejoice in the upside-down power of meekness, peacemaking, grief, and hunger. Amen.

Weekend Reflections

FURTHER CONNECTION

> Her full nature . . . spent itself in channels which had no great name
> on the earth. But the effect of her being on those around her was
> incalculably diffusive: for the growing good of the world is partly
> dependent on unhistoric acts; and that things are not so ill with you
> and me as they might have been, is half owing to the number who lived
> faithfully a hidden life, and rest in unvisited tombs.
>
> GEORGE ELIOT (1819–80), *MIDDLEMARCH*

MAKING THE CONNECTIONS

Choose one or two questions for reflection:

1. What connections have you noticed between this week's texts and other passages in Scripture?

2. What connections have you made between this week's texts and the world beyond Scripture?

3. Does either of this week's two commentary themes speak especially to your life or the life of the world around you right now?

4. What is God saying to your congregation in particular through this week's readings and commentaries?

MY CONNECTIONS

_____

_____

_____

_____

_____

Sabbath Day

SCRIPTURE OF ASSURANCE

Lead me to the rock
   that is higher than I;
for you are my refuge,
   a strong tower against the enemy. (Psalm 61:2b–3)

WEEKLY EXAMEN

- Take a quiet moment, seek out God's presence, and pray for the guidance of the Spirit.

- Consider the past week; recall specific moments and feelings that stand out to you.

- Choose one moment or feeling for deeper examination, thanksgiving, or repentance.

- Let go, breathe deeply, and invite Christ's love to surround and fill you in preparation for the week ahead.

- End with the Lord's Prayer.

The Week Leading Up to the

Fifth Sunday
after the Epiphany

Isaiah 58:1–9a (9b–12)

If you offer your food to the hungry
  and satisfy the needs of the afflicted,
then your light shall rise in the darkness
  and your gloom be like the noonday. (v. 10)

Psalm 112:1–9 (10)

Praise the LORD!
  Happy are those who fear the LORD,
  who greatly delight in his commandments. (v. 1)

1 Corinthians 2:1–12 (13–16)

My speech and my proclamation were not with plausible words of wisdom, but with a demonstration of the Spirit and of power, so that your faith might rest not on human wisdom but on the power of God. (vv. 4–5)

Matthew 5:13–20

No one after lighting a lamp puts it under the bushel basket, but on the lampstand, and it gives light to all in the house. In the same way, let your light shine before others, so that they may see your good works and give glory to your Father in heaven. (vv. 15–16)

LECTIO DIVINA

Underline a word or phrase that especially grabs your attention. Pray from that word or phrase and ask God to help you connect to its particular invitation for you this week.

Themes from This Week's Writers

THEME 1: *Awe and Humility before God*

Psalm 112:1–9 (10)

For the English reader, the word "fear" gives reason to pause. What does it mean to fear the Lord? Fear (*yare*) can mean to be scared or terrified. . . . Fear (*yare*) can also mean to revere, to stand in awe, to honor or respect someone.

ERIC TODD MYERS

1 Corinthians 2:1–12 (13–16)

Perhaps Paul would call the reader to approach the revelation of the Spirit with the same humility that he has encouraged thus far in the letter, as well as the fear and trembling that he himself experienced. That humility would enable one to appreciate that God has revealed something of the divine self through the Spirit.

CHARLES L. AARON JR.

1 Corinthians 2:1–12 (13–16)

Wisdom, then, for Paul is not about knowledge, study, expertise, technology, and mastery. . . . Wisdom is to live in God's world in God's way, and God's way is Christ, and Christ's way is the cross.

SCOT MCKNIGHT

THEME 2: *Let Your Light Shine before Others*

Isaiah 58:1–9a (9b–12)

Instead of a season predicated on the economics of gift giving . . . this focus on the light might prod us to wonder how we cared for one another with our language, fed the hungry, and cared for the poor.

KEN EVERS-HOOD

Matthew 5:13–20

Reference to the disciples' light (vv. 14, 16) frames the identification of the disciples as a city on a hill and as a light set on a stand. The metaphor of the disciples as a city on a hill highlights the visible, conspicuous nature of their existence. Their distinctiveness cannot or should not be hidden.

CHRISTOPHER T. HOLMES

Matthew 5:13–20

[Light's] rays reach unlikely places and welcome *all* to its benefits. This too is a reflection of God's reign. Like a city built on a hill, the light of followers *around the world* and throughout history is to shine for all to see. It (i.e., their good works) is to be a natural and grateful expression of the light of God in them.

ZAIDA MALDONADO PÉREZ

WHAT IS THE HOLY SPIRIT SAYING TO YOU THIS WEEK?

_____

_____

_____

_____

_____

A SPIRITUAL PRACTICE FOR THIS WEEK

This week, set a dish of salt or saltshaker on your desk, prayer altar, or another place you will see it every day. If you can, make a food, like oatmeal or loaf of bread, both with salt and without salt and notice the difference. Reflect on salt and what it is like. What does the Spirit invite you to see, or taste?

First Reading

Isaiah 58:1–9a (9b–12)

Is not this the fast that I choose:
  to loose the bonds of injustice,
  to undo the thongs of the yoke,
to let the oppressed go free,
  and to break every yoke? (v. 6)

REFLECTION

True repentance is indeed a journey inward for self-examination, as the worshipers in Isaiah 58 seem to intend. It is also a journey outward, adopting practices that mend the world, just as God had done on their ancestors' behalf. Worship alone, unaccompanied by righteous habits, cannot bring reconciliation with God.

Knowing that criticism can only discourage if it lacks a vision of alternatives, the poet then presents what he imagines could be. A just society is a healed one. Reconciliation with neighbors brings holiness.

PATRICIA K. TULL

RESPONSE

What past act of injury or neglect might your congregation need to repent for? How might God be inviting your congregation (or just you, as a start) to do so? What "righteous habits" or alternative vision for your neighborhood could you or your congregation adopt to help bring reconciliation?

PRAYER

God of righteousness, guide my community to repent and be transformed in you, that we may learn your ways of justice, service, and reconciliation and help to heal our world. Amen.

Canticle

Psalm 112:1–9 (10)

[The righteous] have distributed freely, they have given to the
poor;
their righteousness endures forever;
their horn is exalted in honor.
The wicked see it and are angry;
they gnash their teeth and melt away;
the desire of the wicked comes to nothing. (vv. 9–10)

REFLECTION

The psalm's concluding verse addresses the status of "the wicked," those
who do not revere the Lord. Who are the wicked? They are the ones
who do not trust in God and who do not live out their lives following
God's commandments. We are not told that they are punished for not
following the commandments. They see the life of the happy ones and
are angry. Instead of fearing the Lord, the wicked ones are full of rage.
They gnash their teeth. Their lives are miserable at best. The psalm ends
with their miserable lives amounting to nothing.

ERIC TODD MYERS

RESPONSE

What if we all are susceptible to being "the wicked"? When was a time
you found yourself angry at people who were happy? Or "full of rage"
because you felt miserable? How could following the psalmist's advice—
to trust in God and follow the commandments—be useful advice to you
on this front?

PRAYER

Merciful God, help me to transform my anger to compassion for my
neighbor and for myself, and to turn my fear to generosity and freedom.
Amen.

Second Reading

1 Corinthians 2:1–12 (13–16)

Now we have received not the spirit of the world, but the Spirit that is from God, so that we may understand the gifts bestowed on us by God. And we speak of these things in words not taught by human wisdom but taught by the Spirit, interpreting spiritual things to those who are spiritual. (vv. 12–13)

REFLECTION

Paul's message that God has revealed mysteries and part of God's very self can produce an experience of awe and wonder. The highest learning and the deepest thinking, although helpful to the church, cannot plumb the depths of the mysteries of God. If God has chosen to reveal such mysteries, can the church not work together despite its differences to appreciate the gift God has bequeathed to it?

. . . The church seeks a deeper understanding of God and the mind of Christ. The church offers more than just advice for daily living. It offers a sense of awe at God's revelation.

CHARLES L. AARON JR.

RESPONSE

What about "God's very self" fills you with awe and wonder? How have you felt the deep mysteries of God revealed to you, recently—even the tiniest peek? How could a church like yours offer more experiences of awe and wonder? How could you be part of that?

PRAYER

Spirit of wonder, you stir in us awe and delight at the depths of the presence of God and the mind of Christ; teach us to teach others about your divine mystery so that our faith may rest not on human wisdom but on the power of God. Amen.

Gospel

Matthew 5:13–20

"You are the salt of the earth; but if salt has lost its taste, how can its saltiness be restored? It is no longer good for anything, but is thrown out and trampled under foot.

"You are the light of the world. A city built on a hill cannot be hid." (vv. 13–14)

REFLECTION

While it is critical to consider the implications of our call for daily life and ministry, it is just as critical to reconsider the audience Jesus is addressing. The "you" (*hymeis*, second person plural) in the discourse are the "meek," the "poor in spirit," "peacemakers," those who "mourn," those who are "merciful" and "hunger and thirst for righteousness" (Matt. 5:3–9). People used to being singled out (or singling themselves out) as the center and paragon of all that is good and right in the world often, and all too easily, equate such passages with themselves and with their nation.

ZAIDA MALDONADO PÉREZ

RESPONSE

Think of a particular group of people who are outsiders or an underclass in your context, or a particular group of international refugees. Imagine that Jesus is speaking this passage to them. How does it sound different? What is Jesus inviting you to notice about them? About yourself? About Jesus?

PRAYER

God of the meek, teach me to see your kingdom in the salt, light, and gifts of the least of my brothers and sisters. Amen.

Weekend Reflections

I ask you to reach down inside yourself, and find the truth your life
is compelling you to see. That is your road to true peace, and it is the
beginning of the evolution of humankind. Because every change in the
world starts within. It begins with one individual who envisions his
or her micro-universe the way it can be, and settles for nothing less.
And as one individual moves towards the light, that light ignites more
individual flames and eventually the revolutionary inner work becomes
a transformative outer work that builds into a bonfire of light, the
kind of light that can change the world. It starts from within, with one
individual who seeks the way of peace. Will you be that person?

JOHN LEWIS (1940–2020), *ACROSS THAT BRIDGE: A VISION
FOR CHANGE AND THE FUTURE OF AMERICA*

MAKING THE CONNECTIONS

Choose one or two questions for reflection:

1. What connections have you noticed between this week's texts and
   other passages in Scripture?

2. What connections have you made between this week's texts and the
   world beyond Scripture?

3. Does either of this week's two commentary themes speak especially
   to your life or the life of the world around you right now?

4. What is God saying to your congregation in particular through this
   week's readings and commentaries?

_____

_____

_____

_____

_____

_____

Sabbath Day

SCRIPTURE OF ASSURANCE

> Thus says the LORD:
> Maintain justice, and do what is right,
> for soon my salvation will come,
> and my deliverance be revealed. (Isaiah 56:1)

WEEKLY EXAMEN

- Take a quiet moment, seek out God's presence, and pray for the guidance of the Spirit.

- Consider the past week; recall specific moments and feelings that stand out to you.

- Choose one moment or feeling for deeper examination, thanksgiving, or repentance.

- Let go, breathe deeply, and invite Christ's love to surround and fill you in preparation for the week ahead.

- End with the Lord's Prayer.

The Week Leading Up to the
Sixth Sunday
after the Epiphany

Deuteronomy 30:15–20

See, I have set before you today life and prosperity, death and adversity. If you obey the commandments of the LORD your God that I am commanding you today, by loving the LORD your God, walking in his ways, and observing his commandments, decrees, and ordinances, then you shall live and become numerous, and the LORD your God will bless you in the land that you are entering to possess. (vv. 15–16)

Psalm 119:1–8

I will praise you with an upright heart,
    when I learn your righteous ordinances.
I will observe your statutes;
    do not utterly forsake me. (vv. 7–8)

1 Corinthians 3:1–9

And so, brothers and sisters, I could not speak to you as spiritual people, but rather as people of the flesh, as infants in Christ. (v. 1)

Matthew 5:21–37

And if your right hand causes you to sin, cut it off and throw it away; it is better for you to lose one of your members than for your whole body to go into hell. (v. 30)

LECTIO DIVINA

Underline a word or phrase that especially grabs your attention. Pray from that word or phrase and ask God to help you connect to its particular invitation for you this week.

Themes from This Week's Writers

THEME 1: *Choosing the Way of God*

Deuteronomy 30:15–20

We humans do actually have a say in things that matter to us. . . . As we choose our own actions and allegiances, these decisions over a lifetime define the distinctiveness of our path. The encouragement to choose life reminds us that we do have options.

PATRICIA K. TULL

Deuteronomy 30:15–20

While it can feel comforting to talk about God's unconditional grace and love, when this unconditionality begins to imply God is on our side no matter what, power easily eclipses justice, and the church can lose its ability to remind the state that God is God and we are not. . . . Our choices are real, and our choices matter.

KEN EVERS-HOOD

Psalm 119:1–8

Because we are in relationship with God, we seek to follow the commandments. Because we are people of the covenant, we strive to keep Torah. Following God's way guides how we parent, how we vote, the manner in which we conduct business, how the church is the church, and even how we pastor and preach.

ERIC TODD MYERS

THEME 2: *What Are the Sins of the "Flesh"?*

1 Corinthians 3:1–9

Paul does not write as though the body itself is inherently evil. For Paul, "flesh" refers to human weakness and sinfulness. . . . Accusing the Corinthians of "fleshiness" confronts them with the underlying condition that has led to their divisions.

CHARLES L. AARON JR.

1 Corinthians 3:1–9

Flesh is self-centered egoism and power mongering, fighting off compassion for others, resisting justice and sustaining injustice, and finding ways to divide one person from another because Flesh hates peace. Flesh wants power in the way of the empire. Flesh coerces, teams up against others, brags about its accomplishments, and touts only its own line.

SCOT MCKNIGHT

Matthew 5:21–37

We can affirm that the desire prohibited by Jesus, whether understood in a possessive or sexual way, is wrong because it objectifies another person. . . . Anything that causes us to objectify or commodify others must be cut away and discarded.

CHRISTOPHER T. HOLMES

WHAT IS THE HOLY SPIRIT SAYING TO YOU THIS WEEK?

_____

_____

_____

_____

_____

A SPIRITUAL PRACTICE FOR THIS WEEK

Reflecting on Matthew 5:21–37, write five or six things that are common knowledge or advice in your community, and imagine what Jesus would say instead: "You have heard it said that _____, but Jesus says to you _____." Are any of them especially surprising or challenging?

First Reading

Deuteronomy 30:15–20

I call heaven and earth to witness against you today that I have set before you life and death, blessings and curses. (v. 19a)

REFLECTION

Who would not choose life over death, if we could see clearly where diverging paths led, and if we could overcome our own resistance to sensible choices? Whether as youths deciding how far to take risks, middle-aged adults reconsidering unhealthy habits, or elders finding our way to gratitude over bitterness, we would be helped by recognizing how these choices improve or even save our lives. If choosing life is so rational, one might ask, why do we often choose badly? Is the mantra "Choose life" a sufficient guide? Can we win the will to choose life only through encountering the alternatives?

PATRICIA K. TULL

RESPONSE

Think of some life-giving decisions you have made in the past few years. Think of some decisions that were not life-giving. When has "choosing life" been a rational decision for you? When has it been slippery? Compare with Paul's take: "I do not do the good I want" (Romans 7:19).

PRAYER

Gracious God, you invite us to make free choices in this life you have given us; help us to choose life and wholeness—and when we cannot, give us grace to know and share your love all the same. Amen.

Canticle

Psalm 119:1–8

Happy are those whose way is blameless,
  who walk in the law of the Lord.
Happy are those who keep his decrees,
  who seek him with their whole heart. (vv. 1–2)

REFLECTION

[This] is a worthy response to the first reading from Deuteronomy, part
of Moses' farewell speech to the people of Israel. Moses' speech uses an
"if . . . then" method of argument: "If you do such and such, then such
and such will happen." Here Moses outlines the covenant to the people:
live according to God's commandments, and the Lord will bless you.
The Torah serves as instruction on how to live out God's desire for God's
people. In this way, the Torah is not a heavy burden but rather direction
as to how to live in joy following God's way.

ERIC TODD MYERS

RESPONSE

Rules can be rigid and burdensome, and religious rules have often hurt
people. But is the root intention of God's law different, somehow? How,
in your experience, has following God's commandments or keeping a
religious way of life offered you freedom or joy?

PRAYER

God of the law, you offer us rules and guidelines to shape our lives, not
as a burden but as a guide and a trellis for happiness and wholeness;
direct me in my relationship to your law that I may find blessing and
joy. Amen.

Second Reading

1 Corinthians 3:1–9

Even now you are still not ready, for you are still of the flesh. For as long as there is jealousy and quarreling among you, are you not of the flesh, and behaving according to human inclinations? For when one says, "I belong to Paul," and another, "I belong to Apollos," are you not merely human? (vv. 2b–4)

REFLECTION

Pastors who work with other pastors create churches that work with other churches, and when pastors and churches work together in a given community, the church becomes a witness against the divisiveness of the empire, the power mongering of the personality cults, and the evil one's operation in the Flesh that wants more than anything to keep us apart.

. . . In the personifying force called Flesh, we discover what sociologist Korie Edwards describes as the invisibility of white privilege and white power.[1] Whiteness is about power in the deepest structures of American society, and it is sadly mirrored in white American churches.

SCOT MCKNIGHT

RESPONSE

How do the pastors and churches in your community work together? What kind of cross-cultural and cross-racial relationships are active and fruitful? How might white privilege be at work between pastors and congregations, keeping people from becoming, together, "a witness against the divisiveness of the empire"?

PRAYER

Christ of all, teach me to know that I am merely human, that I belong to you and to my brothers and sisters; show us how to subvert and unlearn white supremacy, that working together, we may become your field, your building. Amen.

1. Korie L. Edwards, *The Elusive Dream: The Power of Race in Interracial Churches* (New York: Oxford University Press, 2008).

Gospel

Matthew 5:21–37

"You have heard that it was said to those of ancient times, 'You shall not murder'; and 'whoever murders shall be liable to judgment.' But I say to you that if you are angry with a brother or sister, you will be liable to judgment; and if you insult a brother or sister, you will be liable to the council; and if you say, 'You fool,' you will be liable to the hell of fire." (vv. 21–22)

REFLECTION

[These] antitheses of Jesus focus on interpersonal relationships. Each can be understood as an elaboration of the love command. . . . Jesus' teachings do not only elaborate or expand the love command; they also radicalize and internalize it. Elsewhere, Jesus indicates that sinful behaviors like murder, adultery, fornication, theft, false witness, and slander originate in the heart (Matt. 15:19; Mark 7:21). . . .

The antitheses connect in important ways with the Old Testament readings for this week as well; they, too, identify the heart as the control center for right action (Deut. 30:17; Ps. 119:2, 4, 7).

CHRISTOPHER T. HOLMES

RESPONSE

When you take an oath, what kinds of things do you say? How have you seen what is inside yourself influence your external behaviors? When you think about changing behaviors in yourself you do not like, do you think of changing your heart first, or something else? What do you make of Jesus' harsh tone about all this?

PRAYER

Jesus the teacher, show my heart and mind how to form themselves to you, to turn first to compassion, curiosity, and grace, not anger or passion, that my inner spirit may feel more like your kingdom than a hell or prison. Amen.

Weekend Reflections

FURTHER CONNECTION

Jesus' message focused on the urgency of a radical change in the inner attitude of the people. He recognized fully that out of the heart are the issues of life and that no external force, however great and overwhelming, can at long last destroy a people if it does not first win the victory of the spirit against them. . . . Again and again he came back to the inner life of the individual. With increasing insight and startling accuracy he placed his finger on the "inward center" as the crucial arena where the issues would determine the destiny of his people.

HOWARD THURMAN (1898–1981), *JESUS AND THE DISINHERITED*

MAKING THE CONNECTIONS

Choose one or two questions for reflection:

1. What connections have you noticed between this week's texts and other passages in Scripture?

2. What connections have you made between this week's texts and the world beyond Scripture?

3. Does either of this week's two commentary themes speak especially to your life or the life of the world around you right now?

4. What is God saying to your congregation in particular through this week's readings and commentaries?

_____

_____

_____

_____

_____

Sabbath Day

SCRIPTURE OF ASSURANCE

> The LORD is gracious and merciful,
> slow to anger and abounding in steadfast love. (Psalm 145:8)

WEEKLY EXAMEN

- Take a quiet moment, seek out God's presence, and pray for the guidance of the Spirit.

- Consider the past week; recall specific moments and feelings that stand out to you.

- Choose one moment or feeling for deeper examination, thanksgiving, or repentance.

- Let go, breathe deeply, and invite Christ's love to surround and fill you in preparation for the week ahead.

- End with the Lord's Prayer.

The Week Leading Up to the
Seventh Sunday
after the Epiphany

Leviticus 19:1–2, 9–18

The LORD spoke to Moses, saying:
    Speak to all the congregation of the people of Israel and say to them: You shall be holy, for I the LORD your God am holy. (vv. 1–2)

Psalm 119:33–40

Teach me, O LORD, the way of your statutes,
    and I will observe it to the end.
Give me understanding, that I may keep your law
    and observe it with my whole heart. (vv. 33–34)

1 Corinthians 3:10–11, 16–23

For God's temple is holy, and you are that temple.
    Do not deceive yourselves. If you think that you are wise in this age, you should become fools so that you may become wise. (vv. 17b–18)

Matthew 5:38–48

"And if you greet only your brothers and sisters, what more are you doing than others? Do not even the Gentiles do the same? Be perfect, therefore, as your heavenly Father is perfect." (vv. 47–48)

LECTIO DIVINA

Underline a word or phrase that especially grabs your attention. Pray from that word or phrase and ask God to help you connect to its particular invitation for you this week.

Themes from This Week's Writers

THEME 1: *Called to Be a Holy People*

Leviticus 19:1–2, 9–18

Leviticus insists that God's people not only pray for neighbors, but provide for the most basic needs of neighbors. . . . A holy life, therefore, has concrete economic consequence and is always lived with a view toward the most vulnerable neighbor.

GARY W. CHARLES

Leviticus 19:1–2, 9–18

The call to be holy, as the Lord is holy, is itself an overwhelming task. Perhaps remembering the final verse of this text, loving your neighbor as you love yourself, can remind us to take time to care for ourselves in the midst of pursuing personal and social holiness.

CAROLYN BROWNING HELSEL

1 Corinthians 3:10–11, 16–23

They are failing in their calling to become, collectively, the temple of God's Spirit or, in another of Paul's images, Christ's body (11:29; 12:12–27). Such failure is a betrayal of God's desire for a holy people to represent God and embody God's purposes in the world.

MICHAEL LODAHL

THEME 2: *Can We Be Perfect, as God Is Perfect?*

1 Corinthians 3:10–11, 16–23

Paul identifies the church—both the particular church at Corinth and the church universal—as the temple raised in the resurrection of Jesus Christ. We are God's temple because God's Spirit dwells within us, the Spirit of Jesus. This requires a kind of exercise in attending to Jesus' Spirit in our midst, embodying Jesus' Spirit in our congregation, and living Jesus' Spirit in the world.

SHANNON CRAIGO-SNELL

Matthew 5:38–48

Thus, being children of God as Father is to live and to love a certain way. It is not a status or a sentiment but an activity, a behavior. It is to be perfect as our heavenly Father is perfect (v. 48), that is, perfectly promiscuous in the love of neighbors, transgressing parochial security by extending love generously, even to enemies.

TOMMY GIVENS

Matthew 5:38–48

Our highest aspiration is nothing short of seeking to return to our identity in the image of God: to be perfect, that is, complete (*telos*), even as God is perfect/complete (Matt. 5:48). Jesus himself models this for us in his choice not to destroy his enemies, but to love them, even by laying down his life for them.

CHRISTINE CHAKOIAN

WHAT IS THE HOLY SPIRIT SAYING TO YOU THIS WEEK?

_____

_____

_____

_____

_____

A SPIRITUAL PRACTICE FOR THIS WEEK

Choose an enemy to pray for this week. Write their name on a piece of paper and place it somewhere you will see it regularly. You might use this prayer: "May [name] have enough. May [name] love and be loved. May [name] know and be known by God."

First Reading

Leviticus 19:1–2, 9–18

You shall not hate in your heart anyone of your kin; you shall reprove your neighbor, or you will incur guilt yourself. You shall not take vengeance or bear a grudge against any of your people, but you shall love your neighbor as yourself: I am the Lord. (vv. 17–18)

REFLECTION

The concept of holiness is an infrequent visitor to Christian pulpits. Even when this text is considered on a Sunday morning, it is often dismissed as being a part of the archaic Old Testament. Too many Christians believe with the heretic Marcion of the second century that Jesus arrived to delete the first half of what we know as the Bible, especially to delete such tedious and often arcane books as Leviticus. The problem with that hermeneutic of Scripture is that Leviticus 19 was one of the favorite chapters of Jesus.

GARY W. CHARLES

RESPONSE

How do you feel about the Old Testament? How do you feel about Leviticus? What have you heard others in your congregation say about them? What do you think Leviticus 19 can still teach us about living a holy life? What can Leviticus 19 teach us about Jesus?

PRAYER

Holy God, your Word is living and active; guide me to know you and Christ Jesus more and more as I read, study, and reflect on Holy Scripture, even its most difficult passages. Amen.

Canticle

Lead me in the path of your commandments,
    for I delight in it.
Turn my heart to your decrees,
    and not to selfish gain. (vv. 35–36)

REFLECTION

Much of our culture finds quite alien the notion of delighting in
law. Thus our first task as interpreters of this word may be to suggest
examples of gratitude for law. . . . Christians who are formed by Paul's
criticism of Torah and Americans who define freedom as the absence of
laws are ill prepared to understand how the psalmist rejoices in God's
commandments.

For this psalmist, God's law is the gift that brings order and beauty
to the chaos and selfishness of normal human life. The ordinances of
God are good, and only by living in such righteousness can there be
wholesome life.

GAIL RAMSHAW

RESPONSE

What are some laws you "delight in," in the Bible or the Constitution?
What do "God's law" or "God's decrees" connote for you? Are there
certain religious practices, morals, rules, or ethics that particularly shape
your everyday choices? How do they bring freedom, order, or beauty to
your life?

PRAYER

Lead me, O Lord, in the path of your commandments; teach me
gratitude and understanding, that I may keep your law with my whole
heart. Amen.

Second Reading

1 Corinthians 3:10–11, 16–23

Do you not know that you are God's temple and that God's Spirit dwells in you? If anyone destroys God's temple, God will destroy that person. For God's temple is holy, and you are that temple. (vv. 16–17)

REFLECTION

The Gospels image Jesus as the temple. . . . When asked for a sign, Jesus responds, "Destroy this temple, and in three days I will raise it up" (John 2:19).

[But] Paul identifies the church—both the particular church at Corinth and the church universal—as the temple raised in the resurrection of Jesus Christ. We are God's temple because God's Spirit dwells within us, the Spirit of Jesus. This requires a kind of exercise in attending to Jesus' Spirit in our midst, embodying Jesus' Spirit in our congregation, and living Jesus' Spirit in the world.

SHANNON CRAIGO-SNELL

RESPONSE

In this passage, "you" is plural. What is it like to think of God's temple not as the self or Jesus, but as a group of people gathered in the Spirit? How is your congregation a temple where people can meet God? How do you meet God in the midst of your congregation?

PRAYER

Spirit of God, your temple is holy and we, your church, are that temple; show us how to become holy fools so that we may become wise in Christ. Amen.

Gospel

Matthew 5:38–48

"You have heard that it was said, 'An eye for an eye and a tooth for a tooth.' But I say to you, Do not resist an evildoer. But if anyone strikes you on the right cheek, turn the other also; and if anyone wants to sue you and take your coat, give your cloak as well." (vv. 38–40)

REFLECTION

Revenge is a natural reaction to harm. Jesus reminds us that it is not our only option. We can instead choose love. When Judas betrayed him with a kiss, Jesus called him "friend." . . .

In our political climate, which celebrates disdain and disparagement, what if we practiced the "still more excellent way" of love (1 Cor. 12:31)? In our culture, which rewards vitriol on social media and sports events, what if we chose to "speak the truth in love" (Eph. 4:15)? Imagine the shocking surprise of kindness. Revenge is sweet; but sweeter still is the reign of God.

CHRISTINE CHAKOIAN

RESPONSE

Think of someone who has offended you recently, who you tend to make snarky comments about to your friends. What would it be like to practice empathy, compassion, and kindness toward this person? What are other ways you could move away from disdain and disparagement in your life?

PRAYER

Brother Jesus, teach me to speak the truth in love, but also to love my enemies and pray for those who persecute me, that I may not seek the sweetness of revenge but the sweeter joy of the reign of God. Amen.

Weekend Reflections

Abbot Lot came to Abbot Joseph and said: "Father, according as I am able, I keep my little rule, and my little fast, my prayer, meditation and contemplative silence; and according as I am able I strive to cleanse my heart of thoughts: now what more should I do?"

The elder rose up in reply and stretched out his hands to heaven, and his fingers became like ten lamps of fire. He said: "Why not be totally changed into fire?"

TRADITIONAL SAYING OF THE DESERT FATHERS, FOURTH CENTURY

MAKING THE CONNECTIONS

Choose one or two questions for reflection:

1. What connections have you noticed between this week's texts and other passages in Scripture?

2. What connections have you made between this week's texts and the world beyond Scripture?

3. Does either of this week's two commentary themes speak especially to your life or the life of the world around you right now?

4. What is God saying to your congregation in particular through this week's readings and commentaries?

_____

_____

_____

_____

_____

_____

Sabbath Day

SCRIPTURE OF ASSURANCE

Our competence is from God, who has made us competent to be ministers of a new covenant, not of letter but of spirit; for the letter kills, but the Spirit gives life. (2 Corinthians 3:5b–6)

WEEKLY EXAMEN

- Take a quiet moment, seek out God's presence, and pray for the guidance of the Spirit.

- Consider the past week; recall specific moments and feelings that stand out to you.

- Choose one moment or feeling for deeper examination, thanksgiving, or repentance.

- Let go, breathe deeply, and invite Christ's love to surround and fill you in preparation for the week ahead.

- End with the Lord's Prayer.

The Week Leading Up to the
Eighth Sunday
after the Epiphany

Isaiah 49:8–16a

They shall feed along the ways,
    on all the bare heights shall be their pasture;
they shall not hunger or thirst,
    neither scorching wind nor sun shall strike them down,
for he who has pity on them will lead them,
    and by springs of water will guide them. (vv. 9b–10)

Psalm 131

O LORD, my heart is not lifted up,
    my eyes are not raised too high;
I do not occupy myself with things
    too great and too marvelous for me. (v. 1)

1 Corinthians 4:1–5

Think of us in this way, as servants of Christ and stewards of God's mysteries.
Moreover, it is required of stewards that they be found trustworthy. (vv. 1–2)

Matthew 6:24–34

"No one can serve two masters; for a slave will either hate the one and love
the other, or be devoted to the one and despise the other. You cannot serve
God and wealth." (v. 24)

LECTIO DIVINA

Underline a word or phrase that especially grabs your attention. Pray
from that word or phrase and ask God to help you connect to its
particular invitation for you this week.

Themes from This Week's Writers

THEME 1: *Humble before God's Mysteries*

Psalm 131

The authoritative voice we usually encounter in the psalms—the speaker as a monarch, a warrior, a priest, a shepherd responsible for a large flock, a knowledgeable historian—is absent here. Rather, the speaker is small, lowly, without a significant role to play in the community, and is accepting of this status.

GAIL RAMSHAW

1 Corinthians 4:1–5

The character of God is such that if any person is certain they know exactly who God is, they are wrong. What they imagine to be God is an idol or an illusion. God cannot be fully known in certainty like a script or a diagram. . . . Christian faith involves learning all we possibly can about God, and realizing that God is more than that.

SHANNON CRAIGO-SNELL

1 Corinthians 4:1–5

What is meant by mysteries? At the very least, this term indicates truth that cannot be arrived at by human effort alone. God's mysteries cannot be discovered by humanity; they must be revealed by God. Paul and his colleagues are thereby stewarding God's mysteries when they preserve and pass on the good news of Jesus' birth, life, death, and resurrection.

SHANNON CRAIGO-SNELL

THEME 2: *Trust in God, Not Wealth or Property*

Isaiah 49:8–16a

The Servant dares people who are returning from exile or have recently returned to a devastated Jerusalem to trust that God will be with them in their rebuilding and that their time of desolation is over (v. 16). God holds the future of God's people in the palm of God's hand; their future is no longer in doubt.

GARY W. CHARLES

Matthew 6:24–34

Our shared and embodied life will be directed by the illuminating vision of God, or by the opaque guide of corruptible goods, which fills us with anxiety and acquisitiveness rather than hope and hospitality. Our eye, and therefore our body and its appetites, is always being formed by one over the other.

TOMMY GIVENS

Matthew 6:24–34

Whom will we serve, God or wealth? . . . Among many options, we are encouraged to pursue happiness, fame, pleasure, achievement, power, and, especially for women, beauty. . . . The problem is that *wherever* our treasure is, Jesus warns us, there our heart will be also (v. 21)—*either* in heaven *or* on earth, but not both.

CHRISTINE CHAKOIAN

WHAT IS THE HOLY SPIRIT SAYING TO YOU THIS WEEK?

_____

_____

_____

_____

_____

A SPIRITUAL PRACTICE FOR THIS WEEK

Most Westerners have a lot of choices in what we wear and eat, every day. Challenge yourself to make fewer choices this week about your clothes and your meals. Make a plan to help you do this as seems best in your context. What do you notice? How does Matthew 6:24–34 speak to you differently?

First Reading

Isaiah 49:8–16a

Can a woman forget her nursing child,
    or show no compassion for the child of her womb?
Even these may forget,
    yet I will not forget you.
See, I have inscribed you on the palms of my hands. (vv. 15–16)

REFLECTION

As highly unlikely as it would be for a nursing mother to forget her
child, the text suggests that even if they did forget, God would not
forget, since God's love is even more intense than that of a mother for
her child. The final verse in this selection reiterates this tender love,
describing God as having inscribed Israel's name on God's hands, like a
tattoo, permanently demonstrating God's care for the people. Though
the people have been in exile and feel forgotten by God, these words
proclaim that God could never forget those whom God loves so dearly.

CAROLYN BROWNING HELSEL

RESPONSE

Draw an image, even a very basic one, of God's hands with your name
tattooed on God's palms. What is it like to make this drawing? Have
you ever been afraid God might forget about you? Is there something
you would like to ask for, in particular, from God this week?

PRAYER

Mother God, you have inscribed me on the palms of your hands
and you will not forget me; help me to know and trust in my eternal
belovedness in you. Amen.

Canticle

Psalm 131

But I have calmed and quieted my soul,
    like a weaned child with its mother;
    my soul is like the weaned child that is with me.

Israel, hope in the Lord
    from this time on and forevermore. (vv. 2–3)

REFLECTION

When as Christians we hear the closing line of the first reading—"See, I have inscribed you on the palms of my hands"—we inevitably picture the crucifixion. The divine compassion of Christ our mother is seen in the wounds of Jesus on the cross. In these wounds, we place our hope. On her crowded lap, we sing our praise. In the final verse of the psalm, we borrow our forebears' language and call ourselves "Israel" (v. 3), the people chosen by God to live in covenant. Together we calm ourselves, accepting the embrace of God's benevolent care.

GAIL RAMSHAW

RESPONSE

Have you ever thought of or prayed to Christ as our mother? What is it like to imagine a mother who has been crucified? Reread the psalm with this image of our Lord in mind. What do you notice? Draw or write a prayerful response.

PRAYER

Christ, our mother, you tend my weary soul as a weaned child, quiet and calm at your breast; help me to rest in humility and hope. Amen.

Second Reading

1 Corinthians 4:1–5

Therefore do not pronounce judgment before the time, before the Lord comes, who will bring to light the things now hidden in darkness and will disclose the purposes of the heart. Then each one will receive commendation from God. (v. 5)

REFLECTION

What we do as bodies, in every moment given us . . . matters because God is the Creator of all things, and "the LORD's compassion is over all that [God] has made" (Ps. 145:9). . . . We are called to give an account to the One before whom "no creature is hidden," this One who is "a consuming fire" (Heb. 4:13; 12:29).

Such sobering considerations should be taken seriously but should also be seasoned with the gracious description of our divine judge as the God of deep compassion, in the palms of whose hands our lives are inscribed (Isa. 49:16).

MICHAEL LODAHL

RESPONSE

Imagine you are being called to give God an account of your life today, a God who is fierce but compassionate. What are you proud of? What do you feel sheepish about? What needs God's mercy? What would you like to cast off into God's consuming fire?

PRAYER

God of holy fire, you will bring to light what is hidden in darkness in me; no one can be my true judge but you. Teach me to be a trustworthy servant of Christ and steward of your mysteries. Amen.

Gospel

Matthew 6:24–34

"Therefore do not worry, saying, 'What will we eat?' or 'What will we drink?' or 'What will we wear?' For it is the Gentiles who strive for all these things; and indeed your heavenly Father knows that you need all these things. But strive first for the kingdom of God and his righteousness, and all these things will be given to you as well." (vv. 31–33)

REFLECTION

We must envision our life together without being controlled by anxious questions about how to guarantee the future of our embodied life, about where the supposedly scarce provisions for that life will come from (v. 31). Living by such faithless questions drives us to serve not God but mammon, the god of apparent security, prosperity, and unassailable stability. This anxious drive starves our trustful bonds of sharing and healthy interdependence. . . . It blinds us to the light of God's justice, and living by such worry fills our bodies with the darkness of greed, suspicion, and rivalry.

TOMMY GIVENS

RESPONSE

What are some significant worries you carry for your or your family's embodied life right now? How are you feeling scarcity? How is this affecting your relationship with God? Your neighbor? How might you move into more trust and comfort in "the kingdom of God and his righteousness"?

PRAYER

Gracious God, you know everything I need—food, drink, clothing, shelter. I want to depend on you above all things; show me how to reject wealth as a master and strive first for your kingdom. Amen.

Weekend Reflections

I asked participants who claimed to be "strong followers of Jesus" whether Jesus spent time with the poor. Nearly 80 percent said yes. Later in the survey, I sneaked in another question, I asked this same group of strong followers whether they spent time with the poor, and less than 2 percent said they did. I learned a powerful lesson: We can admire and worship Jesus without doing what he did. We can applaud what he preached and stood for without caring about the same things. We can adore his cross without taking up ours. I had come to see that the great tragedy of the church is not that rich Christians do not care about the poor but that rich Christians do not know the poor.

SHANE CLAIBORNE (1975–), *THE IRRESISTIBLE REVOLUTION: LIVING AS AN ORDINARY RADICAL*

MAKING THE CONNECTIONS

Choose one or two questions for reflection:

1. What connections have you noticed between this week's texts and other passages in Scripture?

2. What connections have you made between this week's texts and the world beyond Scripture?

3. Does either of this week's two commentary themes speak especially to your life or the life of the world around you right now?

4. What is God saying to your congregation in particular through this week's readings and commentaries?

_____

_____

_____

_____

_____

_____

Sabbath Day

SCRIPTURE OF ASSURANCE

> Let the words of my mouth and the meditation of my heart
> be acceptable to you,
> O LORD, my rock and my redeemer. (Psalm 19:14)

WEEKLY EXAMEN

- Take a quiet moment, seek out God's presence, and pray for the guidance of the Spirit.

- Consider the past week; recall specific moments and feelings that stand out to you.

- Choose one moment or feeling for deeper examination, thanksgiving, or repentance.

- Let go, breathe deeply, and invite Christ's love to surround and fill you in preparation for the week ahead.

- End with the Lord's Prayer.

The Week Leading Up to the
Ninth Sunday
after the Epiphany

Deuteronomy 11:18–21, 26–28

You shall put these words of mine in your heart and soul, and you shall bind them as a sign on your hand, and fix them as an emblem on your forehead. Teach them to your children, talking about them when you are at home and when you are away, when you lie down and when you rise. (vv. 18–19)

Psalm 31:1–5, 19–24

Incline your ear to me;
    rescue me speedily.
Be a rock of refuge for me,
    a strong fortress to save me. (v. 2)

Romans 1:16–17; 3:22b–28 (29–31)

For there is no distinction, since all have sinned and fall short of the glory of God; they are now justified by his grace as a gift, through the redemption that is in Christ Jesus. (3:22–24)

Matthew 7:21–29

"Not everyone who says to me, 'Lord, Lord,' will enter the kingdom of heaven, but only the one who does the will of my Father in heaven." (v. 21)

LECTIO DIVINA

Underline a word or phrase that especially grabs your attention. Pray from that word or phrase and ask God to help you connect to its particular invitation for you this week.

Themes from This Week's Writers

THEME 1: *God's Gift of Grace*

Psalm 31:1–5, 19–24

As a response to the Deuteronomy reading, this psalm stanza acknowledges that we have indeed not made the right choices. . . . We cannot trust to ourselves for any standing before God. Rather, we require a rock that is greater than any we can construct on our own.

GAIL RAMSHAW

Romans 1:16–17; 3:22b–28 (29–31)

Because grace is a gift, we cannot earn it, deserve it, or somehow manipulate God into handing it over. Paul has again reframed the conversation so it is not about us—our embarrassments, inadequacies, or accomplishments—but about God's power.

SHANNON CRAIGO-SNELL

Matthew 7:21–29

Walking ahead of his people, Jesus will open for them not a way around judgment but through it; not blessing instead of curse but blessing that absorbs and depletes the curse; not life rather than death but life through death.

TOMMY GIVENS

THEME 2: *God Is Faithful and Asks Us to Be Faithful, Too*

Deuteronomy 11:18–21, 26–28

These visual reminders will serve as prompts to a fickle, and often faithless, people that the choice to live in obedience to God's law is not a one-time choice, but must be made with each new day and by each new generation.

GARY W. CHARLES

Romans 1:16–17; 3:22b–28 (29–31)

It is true that Jesus Christ is our Redeemer, but it is equally important that redemption is always for, or toward, the divine purpose of creating and sustaining a faithful people who will not only proclaim, but also embody, God's own faithfulness toward creation.

MICHAEL LODAHL

Matthew 7:21–29

Why does Jesus press us again and again to listen to him, and to seek the will of God alone? Because we will always be vulnerable to the siren call of other voices. Though they change shape and form, they will never go away.

CHRISTINE CHAKOIAN

WHAT IS THE HOLY SPIRIT SAYING TO YOU THIS WEEK?

_____

_____

_____

_____

_____

A SPIRITUAL PRACTICE FOR THIS WEEK

Is there any Scripture "written on your gates" or otherwise displayed in your home, as Deuteronomy instructs? Why or why not? What verses that are important to you might be missing?

First Reading

Deuteronomy 11:18–21, 26–28

See, I am setting before you today a blessing and a curse: the blessing, if you obey the commandments of the LORD your God that I am commanding you today; and the curse, if you do not obey the commandments of the LORD your God. (vv. 26–28a)

REFLECTION

The "blessing-curse" motif . . . does not always track with human experience and religious observance (see Job). At times, the people of God are faithful, and despite their faithfulness, life is accursed. At the same time, sometimes the people of God live under the curse of chasing other gods, and yet they prosper. Surely Jesus was faithful to God and yet suffered the curse of the cross. Preaching from this text is to emphasize the importance of choosing a life of faithfulness, while also recognizing that God's grace is not a reward for our faithfulness, but what inspires it in us.

GARY W. CHARLES

RESPONSE

What was a time you benefited from turning away from God? What was a time you were punished or cursed for being faithful? What reasons do you have for choosing a life of faithfulness with God, even when it is not a guarantee of happiness or prosperity?

PRAYER

O Lord my God, put your words in my heart and soul that I may grow in faithfulness to you, not to gain any reward but to belong to you, and so be guided by your love and purpose for me. Amen.

Canticle

Psalm 31:1–5, 19–24

You are indeed my rock and my fortress;
  for your name's sake lead me and guide me,
take me out of the net that is hidden for me,
  for you are my refuge. (vv. 3–4)

REFLECTION

What would it mean for us to see Christ as our rock of refuge? . . .
Not only personally, God, my private rock, during the struggles of my
individual life; but also ecclesially, God as refuge for all the baptized;
and culturally, God as the fortress for my community of choice; and
politically, God as the courthouse of a just society. "Be strong," calls out
verse 24. If you are close to despair, hang on, and receive the comfort
proclaimed in today's Gospel: it is Christ who is our strong rock, the
fortress that keeps us safe, the foundation of our house.

GAIL RAMSHAW

RESPONSE

Have you felt the need for a refuge lately? Where have you been trying
to find safety? How is it for you to imagine Christ as a rock or fortress?
What kind of safety, foundation, and refuge does Christ offer, in
contrast to other sources, for you?

PRAYER

O Christ the rock and fortress, for your name's sake lead me and guide
me, take me out of the net that is hidden for me. Give me and all your
church strength and comfort, that we may find refuge in you. Amen.

Second Reading

Romans 1:16–17; 3:22b–28 (29–31)

Then what becomes of boasting? It is excluded. By what law? By that of works? No, but by the law of faith. For we hold that a person is justified by faith apart from works prescribed by the law. (3:27–28)

REFLECTION

As individuals and as communities, we are so deeply formed by our broken world that we cannot imagine or enact an entirely new way of being that does not repeat fractured patterns. We cannot enact our own salvation. . . .

The good news is that God, out of God's own righteousness, offers us grace as a gift. This grace justifies us, putting us right with God, and calls us to participate in God's establishment of right relationships on Earth. It does not immediately eliminate injustice in human societies, but it is the basis out of which we can participate with God in that work.

SHANNON CRAIGO-SNELL

RESPONSE

Reflect on what it means to you to be an individual formed by a broken world; then, a church community formed by a broken world. What "fractured patterns" have you noticed, lately? What does it mean to know we have been granted God's grace to begin again, anyway?

PRAYER

Loving Christ, all have sinned and fallen short of the glory of God; help us to learn to believe in your grace and redemption, that we are justified in you by our faith, not our works. Amen.

Gospel

Matthew 7:21–29

"Everyone then who hears these words of mine and acts on them will be like a wise man who built his house on rock. The rain fell, the floods came, and the winds blew and beat on that house, but it did not fall, because it had been founded on rock. And everyone who hears these words of mine and does not act on them will be like a foolish man who built his house on sand." (vv. 24–26)

REFLECTION

The difference between the wise and the foolish is not that one undergoes judgment and the other does not. They both undergo judgment. The difference between them is not that one hears Jesus' words and the other does not. They both hear Jesus' words. The difference is that one hears Jesus' words, obeys them, and so builds a house that weathers the coming storm, while the other hears Jesus' words, does not do them, and so builds a house that is swept away by the same storm.

TOMMY GIVENS

RESPONSE

What was a time when you built "a house on sand," and paid the price during a storm? What are some ways you might still be on sand? What are some ways you are building on rock, now? What words of Jesus do you resist obeying most?

PRAYER

Lord Jesus, show me how to call on your name but also to do your will, building the house of my faith on rock, not on the sand. Amen.

Weekend Reflections

FURTHER CONNECTION

Instead of this bewildering and exhausting rushing from one thing to another monastic stability means accepting this particular community, this place and these people, this and no other, as the way to God. The man or woman who voluntarily limits himself or herself to one building and a few acres of ground for the rest of life is saying that contentment and fulfilment do not consist in constant change, that true happiness cannot necessarily be found anywhere other than this place and this time.

ESTHER DE WAAL (1930–), *SEEKING GOD: THE WAY OF ST. BENEDICT*

MAKING THE CONNECTIONS

Choose one or two questions for reflection:

1. What connections have you noticed between this week's texts and other passages in Scripture?

2. What connections have you made between this week's texts and the world beyond Scripture?

3. Does either of this week's two commentary themes speak especially to your life or the life of the world around you right now?

4. What is God saying to your congregation in particular through this week's readings and commentaries?

_____

_____

_____

_____

_____

_____

Sabbath Day

SCRIPTURE OF ASSURANCE

And the peace of God, which surpasses all understanding, will guard your hearts and your minds in Christ Jesus. (Philippians 4:7)

WEEKLY EXAMEN

- Take a quiet moment, seek out God's presence, and pray for the guidance of the Spirit.

- Consider the past week; recall specific moments and feelings that stand out to you.

- Choose one moment or feeling for deeper examination, thanksgiving, or repentance.

- Let go, breathe deeply, and invite Christ's love to surround and fill you in preparation for the week ahead.

- End with the Lord's Prayer.

The Week Leading Up to
Transfiguration Sunday

Exodus 24:12–18

Then Moses went up on the mountain, and the cloud covered the mountain. The glory of the LORD settled on Mount Sinai, and the cloud covered it for six days; on the seventh day he called to Moses out of the cloud. (vv. 15–16)

Psalm 99

Extol the LORD our God,
and worship at his holy mountain;
for the LORD our God is holy. (v. 9)

2 Peter 1:16–21

For we did not follow cleverly devised myths when we made known to you the power and coming of our Lord Jesus Christ, but we had been eyewitnesses of his majesty. For he received honor and glory from God the Father when that voice was conveyed to him by the Majestic Glory, saying, "This is my Son, my Beloved, with whom I am well pleased." (vv. 16–17)

Matthew 17:1–9

And he was transfigured before them, and his face shone like the sun, and his clothes became dazzling white. Suddenly there appeared to them Moses and Elijah, talking with him. . . . From the cloud a voice said, "This is my Son, the Beloved; with him I am well pleased; listen to him!" (vv. 2–3, 5b)

LECTIO DIVINA

Underline a word or phrase that especially grabs your attention. Pray from that word or phrase and ask God to help you connect to its particular invitation for you this week.

Themes from This Week's Writers

THEME 1: *God Is Mystery*

Exodus 24:12–18

In our modern era, which elevates frenzy to the level of an idol, these awe-filled verses in Exodus 24 invite readers to do nothing but sit quietly in the awesome presence of God.

GARY W. CHARLES

Exodus 24:12–18

God is mysterious, beautiful, confounding, and reassuring. Clouds in the sky can be beautiful and awe inspiring. Dark clouds can elicit fear of bad weather or excitement for coming rain. . . .

. . . *The Cloud of Unknowing*, written anonymously in the fourteenth century, advises Christians to seek God by *not* seeking God, knowing God by allowing oneself to begin *unknowing* God.

CAROLYN BROWNING HELSEL

Psalm 2 and Psalm 99

"Holy" in verse 9 is not—as is common in English usage—about sinlessness, but about almighty presence, otherness from what is common, beyond what we know. It reiterates the otherness described in the Exodus 24 narrative of the cloud and fire of "the glory of the Lord."

GAIL RAMSHAW

THEME 2: *We Are Changed When God Comes Near*

2 Peter 1:16–21

While the transfiguration is richly meaningful in different ways in each Gospel, here it is used as a stamp of authority on a particular kind of knowledge the author is claiming: eyewitness experience of the glory of God. This is different than book learning, no matter how sacred the book. It is a different way of knowing to experience something firsthand.

SHANNON CRAIGO-SNELL

Matthew 17:1–9

Disciples must allow Jesus to teach them who Jesus is and what is involved in following him together. This path of disturbing formation, so that we learn to see by the light of Jesus as we have not yet seen, is thematic to the Gospel of Matthew.

TOMMY GIVENS

Matthew 17:1–9

The transfiguration reminds us that when God comes near to us, it changes everything. Suddenly, the disciples saw Jesus not only as a wise teacher or courageous leader, but as the fulfillment of God's messianic promise. . . . The transfiguration changed not only their view of Jesus; it transformed them. So it is with us.

CHRISTINE CHAKOIAN

WHAT IS THE HOLY SPIRIT SAYING TO YOU THIS WEEK?

_____

_____

_____

_____

_____

A SPIRITUAL PRACTICE FOR THIS WEEK

Begin to reflect on what your Lenten practice might be, whether giving something up, taking something on, fasts, almsgiving, prayers, changes in your home, or a book you will read. Ask the Holy Spirit to guide you. Find a balance between challenge and joy in whatever you choose.

First Reading

Exodus 24:12–18

Now the appearance of the glory of the LORD was like a devouring fire on the top of the mountain in the sight of the people of Israel. Moses entered the cloud, and went up on the mountain. Moses was on the mountain for forty days and forty nights. (vv. 17–18)

REFLECTION

Whereas Peter cannot be still in the midst of God's glory, the text from Exodus pictures Moses in quiet awe before the living God. In the Gospel text for the day, Moses appears atop a mountain silently, not to speak to the disciples or a crowd, but to witness the glory of God; he arrives not to speak but to listen, the same emphasis made in Exodus 24 when Moses is summoned up the mountain by God.

. . . What would it mean for churches to resist Peter's urge to "build booths" and to learn the wisdom of Moses, and in the words of the psalmist, to "Be still, and know that I am God" (Ps. 46:10)?

GARY W. CHARLES

RESPONSE

How do you recognize yourself in Peter? In Moses? How does your congregation worry about "building booths"? How does your congregation long to be still? What would it look like for you to spend some time with God on the mountain this week?

PRAYER

God of glory, you invite me to enter the cloud of your mystery and stand with you on the mountain; show me how to listen, to witness, to be still in you, or just to be. Amen.

Canticle

Psalm 2

I will tell of the decree of the LORD:
He said to me, "You are my son;
    today I have begotten you.
Ask of me, and I will make the nations your heritage,
    and the ends of the earth your possession." (vv. 7–8)

REFLECTION

In Psalm 2, then, God has set the king—and Jesus Christ—on a holy
hill. Jerusalem, the hill of Zion, is both the city of the Israelite king and
the place of Jesus' crucifixion. In verse 7, God claims the king as son,
and Christians hear those words spoken of Jesus at his transfiguration.
In verse 8, God gives power to the king, and Christians believe that all
authority has been given to Christ. . . . Christians give to Jesus Christ
the obeisance that ancient peoples were to grant their monarch.

GAIL RAMSHAW

RESPONSE

When you hear Jesus described as a king, what do you imagine? What
do his power and kingship mean to you, spiritually? How is Jesus
powerful in your life? What does it mean to you that, like the hill of
Zion, his kingship is interconnected with his crucifixion?

PRAYER

King Jesus, son of God, help me to know the true power you have in my
life and in your world, that I may belong to you and to love, not to the
powers of hate and fear. Amen.

Second Reading

2 Peter 1:16–21

We ourselves heard this voice come from heaven, while we were with him on the holy mountain.

So we have the prophetic message more fully confirmed. You will do well to be attentive to this as to a lamp shining in a dark place, until the day dawns and the morning star rises in your hearts. (vv. 18–19)

REFLECTION

We long for the undeniable confirmation of hearing God's voice from heaven and seeing a familiar face limned with glory. Karl Rahner, a twentieth-century Roman Catholic theologian, argued that in modern times, being a Christian could not be a matter of merely accepting a particular theory of how the world works or even a narrative of particular events. . . .

. . . Christian faith—perhaps now more than ever—relies on an everyday mysticism, in which we who have been formed by the stories and rituals of the church are able to see the holy light of God in the world around us.

SHANNON CRAIGO-SNELL

RESPONSE

Have you ever encountered God in a mystical way? Do you experience a sense of "the holy light of God" or God's presence in the world around you? Is a sense of the experience of God's presence important to your faith, or are other things more important?

PRAYER

Holy God, reveal yourself to me—as a lamp shining in a dark place, as a great and holy mountain—as I wait for your day to dawn, your morning star to rise in my heart. Amen.

Gospel

When the disciples heard this, they fell to the ground and were overcome by fear. But Jesus came and touched them, saying, "Get up and do not be afraid." And when they looked up, they saw no one except Jesus himself alone. (vv. 6–8)

REFLECTION

Like Peter, we are often unaware of which visions we are able to see. Scientists point out that our physical vision is limited, not just by farsightedness or nearsightedness, but by our brain's selective interpretation of what we perceive. . . .

So also our spiritual vision can be unreliable, as Peter's was. His embrace of the transfiguration is surrounded by multiple equivocations. He declares Jesus the Messiah, then rebukes Jesus for naming the suffering ahead. . . . Selective sight is not new. How much we will miss if we close our eyes to revelation, both of welcomed blessings and needed correction!

CHRISTINE CHAKOIAN

RESPONSE

How do you see Christ or experience "spiritual vision" in everyday life? How do you define "spiritual vision"? How can it be unreliable? What might blur this vision or keep you from seeing certain blessings or "needed corrections" sometimes? How might the Spirit be inviting you to open your eyes even more?

PRAYER

O Jesus Christ, open my eyes to see you as you reveal yourself to me, that I may not be blinded by apathy or overcome by fear, but look up, and so meet you, who calls me friend. Amen.

Weekend Reflections

It has seemed to me sometimes as though the Lord breathes on this poor gray ember of Creation and it turns to radiance—for a moment or a year or the span of a life. And then it sinks back into itself again, and to look at it no one would know it had anything to do with fire, or light. . . . But the Lord is more constant and far more extravagant than it seems to imply. Wherever you turn your eyes the world can shine like transfiguration. You don't have to bring a thing to it except a little willingness to see. Only, who could have the courage to see it?

MARILYNNE ROBINSON (1943–), PASTOR JOHN AMES IN *GILEAD*

MAKING THE CONNECTIONS

Choose one or two questions for reflection:

1. What connections have you noticed between this week's texts and other passages in Scripture?

2. What connections have you made between this week's texts and the world beyond Scripture?

3. Does either of this week's two commentary themes speak especially to your life or the life of the world around you right now?

4. What is God saying to your congregation in particular through this week's readings and commentaries?

_____

_____

_____

_____

_____

Sabbath Day

SCRIPTURE OF ASSURANCE

> For you shall go out in joy,
>   and be led back in peace;
> the mountains and the hills before you
>   shall burst into song,
>   and all the trees of the field shall clap their hands.
>   (Isaiah 55:12)

WEEKLY EXAMEN

- Take a quiet moment, seek out God's presence, and pray for the guidance of the Spirit.

- Consider the past week; recall specific moments and feelings that stand out to you.

- Choose one moment or feeling for deeper examination, thanksgiving, or repentance.

- Let go, breathe deeply, and invite Christ's love to surround and fill you in preparation for the week ahead.

- End with the Lord's Prayer.

Ash Wednesday

Isaiah 58:1–12

If you offer your food to the hungry
   and satisfy the needs of the afflicted,
then your light shall rise in the darkness
   and your gloom be like the noonday.
The LORD will guide you continually,
   and satisfy your needs in parched places,
   and make your bones strong. (vv. 10–11a)

Psalm 51:1–17

The sacrifice acceptable to God is a broken spirit;
   a broken and contrite heart, O God, you will not despise.
   (v. 17)

2 Corinthians 5:20b–6:10

We are treated as impostors, and yet are true; as unknown, and yet are well known; as dying, and see—we are alive; as punished, and yet not killed; as sorrowful, yet always rejoicing; as poor, yet making many rich; as having nothing, and yet possessing everything. (6:8b–10)

Matthew 6:1–6, 16–21

"Beware of practicing your piety before others in order to be seen by them; for then you have no reward from your Father in heaven." (v. 1)

Isaiah 58:1–12

Far from portraying a strict dichotomy between the privileged and the oppressed, the Isaiah text acknowledges that *all* people long for God, even as the ways in which they seek access to God may differ. . . . At the same time, the prophet does not claim that sincere spiritual need replaces the obligation to pursue social justice; instead, enacting social justice is itself a salve for the weary power broker's soul and a manifestation of a deep spiritual connection with the Divine.

CAMERON B. R. HOWARD

Psalm 51:1–17

Ash Wednesday is the door that leads into Lent. Psalm 51 is not only the key to that door; it is also a map of the journey we will walk with Jesus from here to the cross and onward to the empty tomb.

LEIGH CAMPBELL-TAYLOR

2 Corinthians 5:20b–6:10

Paul closes with particularly striking contradictions. . . . These tensions are characteristic of Paul's ministry. Resolving them would oversimplify the gospel. Choosing one or another of a binary pair would leave us poorer still.

A sermon might invite a community to name the living tensions that characterize them, to claim the ways they are living here and in between, and to embrace an interstitial reality.

ERIC D. BARRETO

Matthew 6:1–6, 16–21

It is not others whom we need to impress. It is only God who is to confirm our fulfillment of the commandments—unto excess, unto perfection. Jesus seems to want it both ways: "Fast, but wash your face, show no discomfort," and God will reward you; but also, "Do your good works openly so that others may bear witness and give God glory." Just here we must study our own intentions and attitudes, the why and the how of our Lenten disciplines.

W. SCOTT HALDEMAN

Joel 2:1–2, 12–17

To "repent and believe the gospel," is to accept death itself as a servant of life in oneness with a merciful God who leaves a grain offering in a loaf of bread and a drink offering in a cup of wine. Symbols of a broken and bloody body become the doorway to new life rather than to life's end.

WM. LOYD ALLEN

RESPONSE

Choose one of these four quotes that particularly gets your attention and write or reflect on how God might be speaking to you, to your experience or questions about Ash Wednesday and Lent this year, or to this time in your life.

PRAYER

Have mercy on me and sustain in me a willing spirit, O God, as I begin this season of Lent. Amen.

The Week Leading Up to the
First Sunday in Lent

Genesis 2:15–17; 3:1–7

But the serpent said to the woman, "You will not die; for God knows that when you eat of it your eyes will be opened, and you will be like God, knowing good and evil." (3:4–5)

Psalm 32

Then I acknowledged my sin to you,
    and I did not hide my iniquity;
I said, "I will confess my transgressions to the LORD,"
    and you forgave the guilt of my sin. (v. 5)

Romans 5:12–19

If, because of the one man's trespass, death exercised dominion through that one, much more surely will those who receive the abundance of grace and the free gift of righteousness exercise dominion in life through the one man, Jesus Christ. (v. 17)

Matthew 4:1–11

Then Jesus was led up by the Spirit into the wilderness to be tempted by the devil. He fasted forty days and forty nights, and afterwards he was famished. (vv. 1–2)

LECTIO DIVINA

Underline a word or phrase that especially grabs your attention. Pray from that word or phrase and ask God to help you connect to its particular invitation for you this week.

Themes from This Week's Writers

THEME 1: *Sin and Death*

Genesis 2:15–17; 3:1–7

While we know that the first humans did not die immediately, they did suffer many allegorical deaths. . . .

. . . At the beginning of Lent, the text invites us to contemplate these "deaths" that result from our decisions.

DAVID G. GARBER JR.

Romans 5:12–19

Death and Sin need to be capitalized, for they represent personified forces.[1] They are the names of those who afflict us but whom Jesus defeats. They are leading actors in the narrative Paul is recounting, not just bit characters.

ERIC D. BARRETO

Romans 5:12–19

Jesus' forgiving, redeeming love is mightier than Adam's sin. Where Adam's sin held onto us, Jesus' gift of love releases humanity from bondage, once and for all.

SARAH BIRMINGHAM DRUMMOND

THEME 2: *What Is Lent For?*

Psalm 32

Follow the outline of Christian salvation history, moving from the despair of leaving Eden behind to the glory of leaving the tomb behind. Every Lent is a miniaturized version of that transformative arc: through the journey of Lenten penitence, we leave behind the solemnity of Ash

---

1. See Katherine Grieb, *The Story of Romans: A Narrative Defense of God's Righteousness* (Louisville, KY: Westminster John Knox, 2002), 56–84.

Wednesday and move toward celebrating the joy of Easter Sunday. Psalm 32 offers welcome signposts.

LEIGH CAMPBELL-TAYLOR

Matthew 4:1–11

The wisest people among us have always chosen times of aloneness. They have chosen aloneness in order to open themselves to prayer, to letting go, to making choices.

MIKEAL C. PARSONS

Matthew 4:1–11

Jesus, like Moses, like Elijah, must fast. The excursion into the wilderness is Spirit-led. Forty days, like Noah, like Moses, like the years of wandering, speaks of fullness. Enough! He is famished. Emmanuel is weak with hunger. Right on time, the tempter arrives. It is better to remain hungry than to take the bait.

W. SCOTT HALDEMAN

WHAT IS THE HOLY SPIRIT SAYING TO YOU THIS WEEK?

_____

_____

_____

_____

_____

A SPIRITUAL PRACTICE FOR THIS WEEK

Choose a particular way to fast on Ash Wednesday. You might abstain from meat, or alcohol, or skip lunch or dinner. Drink hot tea or water to calm a hungry stomach. Attend a service, spend time in prayer or spiritual reading, or take a walk to accompany your fast.

First Reading

The Lord God took the man and put him in the garden of Eden to till it and keep it. And the Lord God commanded the man, "You may freely eat of every tree of the garden; but of the tree of the knowledge of good and evil you shall not eat, for in the day that you eat of it you shall die." (2:15–17)

REFLECTION

So often today our work is at odds with an Edenic vision of stewardship. We produce goods in ways that exploit the earth rather than care for it. We value the things produced more than the people who produce them. . . . We tend to value the *pain* of work rather than the primordial joy of the work itself. We "humble-brag" about how busy we are, . . . forgetting all the while that we human beings are part of God's creation, and thus in stewarding creation, we must also take care of ourselves.

CAMERON B. R. HOWARD

RESPONSE

Do you value the "pain of work"? Have you ever valued it in a way that was harmful to yourself, other people, or other creatures? In contrast, when would you say you have felt the "primordial joy" of work? What would it mean to steward yourself as part of God's creation, in work and play?

PRAYER

Lord God, you have given us the earth to till and keep; teach us to care for and steward all creation in your name, even our own minds and bodies. Amen.

Canticle

Psalm 32

Many are the torments of the wicked,
  but steadfast love surrounds those who trust in the LORD.
Be glad in the LORD and rejoice, O righteous,
  and shout for joy, all you upright in heart. (vv. 10–11)

REFLECTION

While the Genesis text makes clear that God will not abide human efforts to make ourselves godlike, the psalm makes clear that God is also ready to forgive us (vv. 1, 5), to preserve us (v. 7), and to surround us with "steadfast love" (v. 10).

This image of God "surrounding" (vv. 7b, 10b) us "with glad cries of deliverance" (v. 7b) as well as with "steadfast love" (v. 10) is an especially potent and poignant contrast to the idea of God exiling people from God's presence. Even in the wasteland of sin, we are never beyond God's gracious reclamation.

LEIGH CAMPBELL-TAYLOR

RESPONSE

Is there an exile from God, or "wasteland of sin" you feel in your own life? Or in the life of someone you love? What has it meant to you in the past to trust in God? What do you hear Psalm 32 inviting you to do, in your own situation?

PRAYER

Lord of love, you have promised that your steadfast love, grace, and joy will surround those who trust in you; open my heart to seek this trust, and keep your eye always upon me, I pray. Amen.

Second Reading

Romans 5:12–19

Therefore, just as sin came into the world through one man, and death came through sin, and so death spread to all because all have sinned. (v. 12)

REFLECTION

Thinking of Death and Sin as personified forces helps bring additional exegetical clarity to verses 12–14. Sin is an invading force, an impostor smuggling itself into a law meant to bring life and grace. Sin's interference has distorted the law from within, and Sin draws Death in its wake. Death here certainly includes when we draw our last breath; but also every instance of harm, oppression, injustice. Death breaks God's good world; but the power of Sin and Death, while widespread, even universal, is not absolute. Death has had dominion, but something has changed.

ERIC D. BARRETO

RESPONSE

How does imagining sin and death as personified forces, Sin and Death, change this passage for you? What is it like to think of sin as something larger than a personal experience? Death as something more universal than a personal life event?

PRAYER

God of life, you stand with me and all Creation against Sin and Death in the person of Jesus Christ; may I embody and share this abundance of grace and free gift of righteousness you give to all in Christ. Amen.

Gospel

Matthew 4:1–11

Jesus said to him, "Away with you, Satan! for it is written,
 'Worship the Lord your God,
  and serve only him.'"
Then the devil left him, and suddenly angels came and waited on him.
(vv. 10–11)

REFLECTION

Empty and vulnerable by choice, Jesus was brought face-to-face with the dark options of another path. In those moments, he remembered who he was, who God declared him to be at the river just days before: "My Son." "My Beloved." When the seducer came, Jesus could speak from the deep wellspring of knowing who he was—God's Beloved Son—and say, "No." However vast the difference between Jesus' relationship with God and ours, we too are daughters and sons of God. We too are God's Beloved—and we do the work of aloneness to confirm, clarify, and sustain that identity.

MIKEAL C. PARSONS

RESPONSE

How deeply do you know and feel, at this time in your life, that you are God's Beloved? What is the deep wellspring of your knowing who you are? How do you feel called, in this season, to confirm, clarify, and sustain that identity?

PRAYER

Beloved Jesus, in you and with you I am God's Beloved; strengthen me to claim this name so I may worship and serve only God, and send the devil packing. Amen.

Weekend Reflections

The kiva is a square or circular underground chamber, covered by a roof of wooden beams with an opening in the center. You enter a kiva the same way you enter a submarine: by descending the ladder. Once inside the packed earth chamber of the kiva, you are in darkness. . . .

. . . While a cathedral's soaring arches or a mosque's great domes are designed to point us upward, the kiva is intended to point us downward. The spiritual focal point is not above us, but below. We are not to look up, but down. What we seek is not in the sky, but in the earth.

STEVEN CHARLESTON (1949–), *LADDER TO THE LIGHT:*
AN INDIGENOUS ELDER'S MEDITATIONS ON HOPE AND COURAGE

MAKING THE CONNECTIONS

Choose one or two questions for reflection:

1. What connections have you noticed between this week's texts and other passages in Scripture?

2. What connections have you made between this week's texts and the world beyond Scripture?

3. Does either of this week's two commentary themes speak especially to your life or the life of the world around you right now?

4. What is God saying to your congregation in particular through this week's readings and commentaries?

_____

_____

_____

_____

_____

_____

Sabbath Day

SCRIPTURE OF ASSURANCE

We always give thanks to God for all of you and mention you in our prayers, constantly remembering before our God and Father your work of faith and labor of love and steadfastness of hope in our Lord Jesus Christ. (1 Thessalonians 1:2–3)

WEEKLY EXAMEN

- Take a quiet moment, seek out God's presence, and pray for the guidance of the Spirit.

- Consider the past week; recall specific moments and feelings that stand out to you.

- Choose one moment or feeling for deeper examination, thanksgiving, or repentance.

- Let go, breathe deeply, and invite Christ's love to surround and fill you in preparation for the week ahead.

- End with the Lord's Prayer.

The Week Leading Up to the
Second Sunday in Lent

Genesis 12:1–4a

Now the LORD said to Abram, "Go from your country and your kindred and your father's house to the land that I will show you. I will make of you a great nation, and I will bless you, and make your name great, so that you will be a blessing." (vv. 1–2)

Psalm 121

The LORD will keep you from all evil;
　　he will keep your life.
The LORD will keep
　　your going out and your coming in
　　from this time on and forevermore. (vv. 7–8)

Romans 4:1–5, 13–17

For the promise that he would inherit the world did not come to Abraham or to his descendants through the law but through the righteousness of faith. (v. 13)

John 3:1–17

[Nicodemus] came to Jesus by night and said to him, "Rabbi, we know that you are a teacher who has come from God; for no one can do these signs that you do apart from the presence of God." Jesus answered him, "Very truly, I tell you, no one can see the kingdom of God without being born from above." (vv. 2–3)

LECTIO DIVINA

Underline a word or phrase that especially grabs your attention. Pray from that word or phrase and ask God to help you connect to its particular invitation for you this week.

Themes from This Week's Writers

THEME 1: *Faith and Trust in God*

Genesis 12:1–4a

We know from the rest of Abram's story that his confidence in God's promises falters time and again, and yet God's faithfulness to the promise persists. . . . God can draw out infinite blessings from the life of one person, or one community, simply trying to respond faithfully to God's call.

CAMERON B. R. HOWARD

Romans 4:1–5, 13–17

Faith rides on the waves of life, rising and falling. Faith is not just a matter of individual belief, of *my* certainty in times of trouble. Faith is nurtured and held by our neighbors, our siblings in faith. "Hoping against hope" may mean that sometimes I need someone else to hold my trust in God for me when my trust is slipping.

ERIC D. BARRETO

Romans 4:1–5, 13–17

[Abraham] was righteous by trusting God, not trusted by God for being righteous. Therefore, Paul makes a strong argument in this passage that trusting God is in itself good, and it is the beginning of good things that can happen to those who trust God.

SARAH BIRMINGHAM DRUMMOND

THEME 2: *God Calls Us to the Unknown*

Psalm 121

Whether the journey in question is Abram's journey to an unknown land, or a pilgrim's journey to Jerusalem, or a congregation's journey through Lent, what better reassurance can there be than that our eternal God cares for us eternally?

Lent helps us hear God's call to leave behind the sin that we know and to travel toward new life in God.

LEIGH CAMPBELL-TAYLOR

John 3:1–17

Jesus speaks nonsense and yet tells us not to be astonished. We have little enough to do with being born the first time. To be born again is an impossibility. There is nothing any of us can do. It is completely up to the whimsy of Spirit—this Spirit that is as unpredictable as wind.

W. SCOTT HALDEMAN

John 3:1–17

Too often we give in to our base inclinations to build walls, real and metaphorical, between ourselves and others. . . . God's love transgresses all human barriers placed in the way, embracing and enveloping persons for who they are—God's children formed in God's image.

MIKEAL C. PARSONS

WHAT IS THE HOLY SPIRIT SAYING TO YOU THIS WEEK?

_____

_____

_____

_____

_____

A SPIRITUAL PRACTICE FOR THIS WEEK

Nicodemus left home to talk to Jesus. God told Abraham, "*Lech lecha!*"—get going and go to a new place! Leave home or your comfort zone this week: set aside time to go on a retreat, even for just an hour or two, in a new place, or schedule a couple days at a retreat center sometime in the weeks to come.

First Reading

Genesis 12:1–4a

So Abram went, as the LORD had told him; and Lot went with him. (v. 4)

REFLECTION

On the Second Sunday in Lent, the Old Testament passage . . . reminds us of the God who makes promises and who wishes to bless humanity. This same God, however, makes difficult demands of Abram, asking him to break with his past—his homeland—and travel to a new land of promise. This faithful immigrant, in turn, will become the agent of blessing for all nations. . . . In this simple introduction to Abram's story, we do not hear from Abram himself. All the narrative tells us is that Abram followed God's call and embarked on the journey at seventy-five years of age.

DAVID G. GARBER JR.

RESPONSE

Is there a difficult demand or new journey that God is asking you to consider right now? What are the challenges? What blessings could emerge, for you, others, or even successive generations? What do you understand God's promises to be for you, no matter where you are?

PRAYER

God of promise, you ask me to leave home and the places I know to seek you in a new land, a land that you will show me; help me trust that you will bless me so that I will be a blessing, no matter where you lead me. Amen.

Canticle

Psalm 121

I lift up my eyes to the hills—
 from where will my help come?
My help comes from the LORD,
 who made heaven and earth. (vv. 1–2)

REFLECTION

Known as a Song of Ascent—songs that may have been sung by pilgrims journeying up to Jerusalem—Psalm 121 is recognized as a psalm of trust. From start to finish, it exudes a serenely rooted trust in God's power and in God's loving care.

 . . . Immediately acknowledging the human need for help and the divine capacity to give that help creates a sense of relationship: the trustworthiness of God enables us to live in trusting reliance on God. Perhaps that is how Abram was able to leave behind all he knew.

LEIGH CAMPBELL-TAYLOR

RESPONSE

Write these two verses out in your own handwriting on a piece of paper. (Or write the entire psalm.) Pray as you write, really hearing the words as if they were spoken about your own life. What does trusting in God mean for you, right now?

PRAYER

O Lord who keeps Israel, you neither slumber nor sleep; you will keep my going out and my coming in from this time on and forevermore. Amen.

Second Reading

Romans 4:1–5, 13–17

Now to one who works, wages are not reckoned as a gift but as something due. But to one who without works trusts him who justifies the ungodly, such faith is reckoned as righteousness. (vv. 4–5)

REFLECTION

Many give up bad habits during Lent, with the hope that God will help them work on their character and improve as human beings. Others take on new spiritual practices, including a generalized seriousness and restraint that make them less fun to be around. Whereas these observances surely provide opportunities for reflection and spiritual growth, it is a mistake to understand them in any transactional way. We do not give things up, or take things on, during Lent in an effort to bring God closer to us. Our efforts at faithfulness have no earning power.

SARAH BIRMINGHAM DRUMMOND

RESPONSE

Are you observing Lent this year with new spiritual practices? Have you in the past? What has been your motivation for doing so? Have you ever noticed in yourself a belief that you could "earn" God's closeness or blessing? What did that look like?

PRAYER

God of Abraham, you are close to me no matter what my works, practices, fasts, prayers, almsgiving, or spiritual growth may be; teach me the blessings of faith as a gift, not a transaction. Amen.

Gospel

John 3:1–17

"Do not be astonished that I said to you, 'You must be born from above.' The wind blows where it chooses, and you hear the sound of it, but you do not know where it comes from or where it goes. So it is with everyone who is born of the Spirit." (vv. 7–8)

REFLECTION

Gusting winds bear away debris but also branches, roofs, sometimes even cars and boats. What if those who are being borne by Spirit are actually being carried away—perhaps to "come 'round right," as the old Shaker hymn puts it. Now free of "the way things are" we can see, we can enter this "kingdom of God," this alternative reality where justice reigns and mercy abounds, where all are fed and satisfied, where every tear is wiped away and death is no more. This is Jesus' perplexing invitation to Nicodemus . . . and to us.

W. SCOTT HALDEMAN

RESPONSE

What might it mean this week for you or your congregation to let yourselves be blown around by the Spirit? To be carried away, lose some control, get free of the "way things are"? To risk some destruction? What might Jesus be inviting you to?

PRAYER

Holy Spirit, you blow where you choose, and I do not know where you come from or where you are going; help me to hear you—inviting me to be born anew in you, through Christ. Amen.

Weekend Reflections

FURTHER CONNECTION

The speech of God to this barren family, then, is a call to abandonment, renunciation, and relinquishment. It is a call for a dangerous departure from the presumed world of norms and security. . . . Such renunciation, of course, is exceedingly difficult to speak of in our culture which focuses on self-indulgence because "you owe yourself this." But notice, the summons is not law or discipline, but promise. The narrative knows that such departure from securities is the only way out of barrenness. The whole of the Abrahamic narrative is premised on this seeming contradiction: to stay in safety is to remain barren; to leave in risk is to have hope.

WALTER BRUEGGEMANN (1933–), *GENESIS: A BIBLE COMMENTARY FOR PREACHING AND TEACHING*

MAKING THE CONNECTIONS

Choose one or two questions for reflection:

1. What connections have you noticed between this week's texts and other passages in Scripture?

2. What connections have you made between this week's texts and the world beyond Scripture?

3. Does either of this week's two commentary themes speak especially to your life or the life of the world around you right now?

4. What is God saying to your congregation in particular through this week's readings and commentaries?

_____

_____

_____

_____

_____

_____

Sabbath Day

SCRIPTURE OF ASSURANCE

> Save me, O LORD, from my enemies;
> I have fled to you for refuge.
> . . . .
> Let your good spirit lead me
> on a level path. (Psalm 143:9, 10b)

WEEKLY EXAMEN

- Take a quiet moment, seek out God's presence, and pray for the guidance of the Spirit.

- Consider the past week; recall specific moments and feelings that stand out to you.

- Choose one moment or feeling for deeper examination, thanksgiving, or repentance.

- Let go, breathe deeply, and invite Christ's love to surround and fill you in preparation for the week ahead.

- End with the Lord's Prayer.

The Week Leading Up to the
Third Sunday in Lent

Exodus 17:1–7

[Moses] called the place Massah and Meribah, because the Israelites quarreled and tested the LORD, saying, "Is the LORD among us or not?" (v. 7)

Psalm 95

O that today you would listen to his voice!
  Do not harden your hearts, as at Meribah,
  as on the day at Massah in the wilderness. (vv. 7b–8)

Romans 5:1–11

For if while we were enemies, we were reconciled to God through the death of his Son, much more surely, having been reconciled, will we be saved by his life. But more than that, we even boast in God through our Lord Jesus Christ, through whom we have now received reconciliation. (vv. 10–11)

John 4:5–42

A Samaritan woman came to draw water, and Jesus said to her, "Give me a drink." (His disciples had gone to the city to buy food.) The Samaritan woman said to him, "How is it that you, a Jew, ask a drink of me, a woman of Samaria?" (Jews do not share things in common with Samaritans.) (vv. 7–9)

LECTIO DIVINA

Underline a word or phrase that especially grabs your attention. Pray from that word or phrase and ask God to help you connect to its particular invitation for you this week.

Themes from This Week's Writers

THEME 1: *Is God with Us or Not?*

Exodus 17:1–7

The Lord's presence seems to them to be primarily as a dispenser of good things. If they do not have what they want at a particular moment, then they question whether the Lord is actually present with them. Presumably if they had all they thought they needed or wanted, they would not ask this question.

REBECCA ABTS WRIGHT

Exodus 17:1–7

The Hebrew people in the desert saw God through the lens of fear and blame. They assumed that God was out to get them. Yet God, in steadfast love and faithfulness, responds to their complaints and doubts in the midst of their fear with water to keep them alive.

JANE ANNE FERGUSON

Psalm 95

When we—like the wilderness generation long ago—ask, "Is the Lord among us or not?" (Exod. 17:7), Psalm 95 flips the question to demand, "Are we properly attentive to the Lord among us or not?" In the wilderness of our Lenten journey, we are cared for by the sovereign God who creates, redeems, and sustains us.

LEIGH CAMPBELL-TAYLOR

THEME 2: *Reconciliation with God Is a Gift Freely Offered*

Romans 5:1–11

Regardless of how we read the sacrificial language, the notion that God in Romans 5:1–11 must be appeased so as to vent divine wrath is off base. . . . God proves love for us by the death of Christ. . . . Far from being full of wrath that must be appeased, God actively sought a way for us to be reconciled.

JEROME F. D. CREACH

Romans 5:1–11

Baptism is not a seal against eternal damnation but a public communal acknowledgment that we are all beloved children of God to be embraced by the love of Christian community. The "peace with God through our Lord Jesus Christ" of which Paul writes (Rom. 5:1) is ours now and forever merely because we are human.

SALLY B. PURVIS

John 4:5–42

Both the woman herself and Jesus' disciples are astonished that he touches a cup she has touched and then—even more incredibly—actually speaks to her. John notes in an aside, perhaps for the sake of Gentile readers, that "Jews do not share things in common with Samaritans." Jesus' defiance of racial, ethnic, and gender boundaries in this story is shot through all four Gospels.

MICHAEL L. LINDVALL

WHAT IS THE HOLY SPIRIT SAYING TO YOU THIS WEEK?

_____

_____

_____

_____

_____

A SPIRITUAL PRACTICE FOR THIS WEEK

Consider something from your past that you regret or do not like to think about. Write a prayer or confession to Jesus about this. Then, read Jesus' words to the Samaritan woman. What grace or accountability do you hear God inviting you to consider? If needed, seek out a trusted friend, pastor, or advisor for more conversation.

First Reading

Exodus 17:1–7

But the people thirsted there for water; and the people complained against Moses and said, "Why did you bring us out of Egypt, to kill us and our children and livestock with thirst?" So Moses cried out to the LORD, "What shall I do with this people? They are almost ready to stone me." (vv. 3–4)

REFLECTION

How can we nurture faith in authentic ways in the midst of complaint and bitterness? Moses is at his wit's end in this story. Pastors, lay leaders, fearful parishioners often feel at their wits' ends in the midst of change. What does Moses do? He cries out to God in desperation and frustration, possibly some anger. In that cry he *relinquishes* the people's complaints to God, lets them go. Moses does not try to fix the situation on his own power. Whether out of pure faith or the weariness of despair, Moses throws up his hands, trusts, and stops to listen.

JANE ANNE FERGUSON

RESPONSE

What kind of complaining or bitterness is there in your life or congregation lately? How could you "cry out," like Moses, and relinquish these complaints to God? How would God respond? What would it look like to trust God instead of your own power?

PRAYER

Lord God, please listen to my cries, my complaints, and my anger, that I may feel your love and care for me, and continue this my journey, trusting in you. Amen.

Canticle

Psalm 95

O come, let us worship and bow down,
  let us kneel before the LORD, our Maker!
For he is our God,
  and we are the people of his pasture,
  and the sheep of his hand. (vv. 6–7a)

REFLECTION

Look at Psalm 95's opening section as a step-by-step depiction of the proper relationship between God and God's people. First, we are to approach God with joyful, thankful praise (vv. 1–2). Why? Because God created all that is, and no other god is worthy of consideration (vv. 3–5). Next, we are humbly to worship God (v. 6). Why? Because God is our God, and we are God's own (v. 7a). It is then, while we are reverently focused on the rightly sovereign God, that the psalmist exhorts us to listen to God's voice (v. 7b). Such worshipful attentiveness to God is the correct attitude for faithful people.

LEIGH CAMPBELL-TAYLOR

RESPONSE

What are some sources of joy in God's creation in your life? Praise God for these things. What does it mean to you that "God is our God," and you are God's own? Offer God humility and worship for this reality. Then, reflect: Today, how can I seek to listen for God's voice?

PRAYER

O Lord, maker of all creation, teach me to praise you, worship you, and listen to your voice, because you are my God, and I belong to you. Amen.

Second Reading

But God proves his love for us in that while we still were sinners Christ died for us. Much more surely then, now that we have been justified by his blood, will we be saved through him from the wrath of God. (vv. 8–9)

REFLECTION

What I observed in my sixteen years of being a pastor to someone on death row is that an emerging sense of being forgiven preceded acknowledgment of sin. In a long, slow process . . . the person on death row began to believe she was forgiven, accepted, loved by God. . . .
. . . The deeper the message of God's love could penetrate her heart and soul, the more she was able to acknowledge the horror of what she had done, and the more she was able to acknowledge that horror, the more she could embrace God's love and acceptance.

SALLY B. PURVIS

RESPONSE

How is it, do you think, that love and grace could help a person claim a wrong or "horror" they had committed after accusation, judgment, or punishment failed? This week, reflect on how you might first approach a sin of your own or of another person with love and forgiveness.

PRAYER

Loving God, we are reconciled to you by the death of Jesus Christ your Son; show us how to forgive others as you have forgiven us, that we might be saved from wrath, both yours and ours. Amen.

Gospel

John 4:5–42

Many Samaritans from that city believed in him because of the woman's testimony, "He told me everything I have ever done." So when the Samaritans came to him, they asked him to stay with them; and he stayed there two days. (vv. 39–40)

REFLECTION

A *Samaritan* apostle? A Samaritan *woman* apostle? This passage responds to these questions with a resounding *Yes*. To place the unnamed Samaritan woman in the saintly company of Peter, Philip, and Nathanael is to watch long-standing barriers of race and gender fall and the reconciling message of Christ rise.

We might, upon our first reading of this text, wonder why Jesus decides to go through Samaria. . . . Jesus is not merely trying to make good time to Galilee. He is much more intent on revealing his divine nature and helping us see that something good can come out of Samaria.

ANDREW NAGY-BENSON

RESPONSE

If Jesus were to head into a shocking area of your community to recruit disciples, where would it be? What shocking sort of person might he seek out there, for conversation and a drink of water? Are you called, in some way, to seek out this same place or person?

PRAYER

O Jesus, you sought out women, foreigners, and underdogs and called them to be your apostles; lead me to places and people that will surprise me with the good news of your living water. Amen.

Weekend Reflections

FURTHER CONNECTION

The Samaritan woman would become one of the most popular figures in early Christian art. She appeared in the mid-third-century Dura Europas baptistry, in the Roman catacombs, and in early church mosaics. Usually wearing a striped dress, she stood at the well, bucket in hand, while Jesus sat nearby, speaking to her. Her boldness in disputation suggests that one way paradise flows into the world as living water is through those who raise questions, probe answers, and stay in the conversation.

RITA NAKASHIMA BROCK (1950–) AND REBECCA ANN PARKER
(1953–), *SAVING PARADISE: HOW CHRISTIANITY TRADED
LOVE OF THIS WORLD FOR CRUCIFIXION AND EMPIRE*

MAKING THE CONNECTIONS

Choose one or two questions for reflection:

1. What connections have you noticed between this week's texts and other passages in Scripture?

2. What connections have you made between this week's texts and the world beyond Scripture?

3. Does either of this week's two commentary themes speak especially to your life or the life of the world around you right now?

4. What is God saying to your congregation in particular through this week's readings and commentaries?

_____

_____

_____

_____

_____

_____

Sabbath Day

SCRIPTURE OF ASSURANCE

> My house shall be called a house of prayer
>   for all peoples.
> Thus says the Lord GOD,
>   who gathers the outcasts of Israel. (Isaiah 56:7b–8a)

WEEKLY EXAMEN

- Take a quiet moment, seek out God's presence, and pray for the guidance of the Spirit.

- Consider the past week; recall specific moments and feelings that stand out to you.

- Choose one moment or feeling for deeper examination, thanksgiving, or repentance.

- Let go, breathe deeply, and invite Christ's love to surround and fill you in preparation for the week ahead.

- End with the Lord's Prayer.

The Week Leading Up to the
Fourth Sunday in Lent

1 Samuel 16:1–13

But the LORD said to Samuel, "Do not look on his appearance or on the height of his stature, because I have rejected him; for the LORD does not see as mortals see; they look on the outward appearance, but the LORD looks on the heart." (v. 7)

Psalm 23

Even though I walk through the darkest valley,
  I fear no evil;
for you are with me;
  your rod and your staff—
    they comfort me. (v. 4)

Ephesians 5:8–14

For once you were darkness, but now in the Lord you are light. Live as children of light—for the fruit of the light is found in all that is good and right and true. Try to find out what is pleasing to the Lord. (vv. 8–10).

John 9:1–41

So for the second time they called the man who had been blind, and they said to him, "Give glory to God! We know that this man is a sinner." He answered, "I do not know whether he is a sinner. One thing I do know, that though I was blind, now I see." (vv. 24–25)

LECTIO DIVINA

Underline a word or phrase that especially grabs your attention. Pray from that word or phrase and ask God to help you connect to its particular invitation for you this week.

Themes from This Week's Writers

THEME 1: *God Does Not See as Mortals See*

1 Samuel 16:1–13

None of the people whom God chooses in the Bible from Abram/ Abraham onward is said to be chosen because of a set of sterling inner qualities that only God can see. Undoubtedly God does know a person's "true inner self," but we are never told that it is on such basis that any person is selected for any task.

REBECCA ABTS WRIGHT

1 Samuel 16:1–13

David is the Cinderella leader coming from the margins of the tribe rather than the mainstream. . . . He is young, maybe naive, not as acquainted with the ways of society, because he has been in the fields with his harp and the sheep for company.

JANE ANNE FERGUSON

Psalm 23

There is no obvious reason for what the psalmist receives. The psalmist lists no accomplishments or credits. God's favor has come apart from whatever the psalmist has done or left undone. . . . God's motivations are generous and mysterious, beyond expectation and calculation.

JOHN W. WURSTER

THEME 2: *How Does Knowing Christ Transform Us?*

Ephesians 5:8–14

[Ephesians] commands Christians to have a pure life because God has transformed them. . . . Other NT letters also . . . have a section on ethical behavior that gives concrete examples of actions Christians should engage in or avoid because of their new life in Christ (Rom. 12–14; Col. 3–4; 1 Thess. 4:1–12).

JEROME F. D. CREACH

Ephesians 5:8–14

Ephesians 5:8 is a succinct statement of the dynamics of conversion: the change has happened, now live out the change. The instructional tone of the verse's context reminds new converts that though they can claim the new life God offers them in the gospel of Jesus Christ, they can do so only if they live it out.

SALLY B. PURVIS

John 9:1–41

Jesus is absent from this story for far longer than in any other episode in the Gospels, from verse 8 through verse 34! In a sense, the blind man becomes a disciple as he gradually "sees" who Jesus is and testifies through a progression of professions: from "the man called Jesus" (9:11) to "a prophet" (v. 17) to a man "from God" (v. 33).

ANDREW NAGY-BENSON

WHAT IS THE HOLY SPIRIT SAYING TO YOU THIS WEEK?

_____

_____

_____

_____

_____

A SPIRITUAL PRACTICE FOR THIS WEEK

Choose an image or icon of Jesus to focus on this week. Reflect on what you see in this image, and then, on what you cannot see. How does Jesus invite you to see? What does it mean to you to see and know Jesus at this time in your life?

First Reading

1 Samuel 16:1–13

When they came, he looked on Eliab and thought, "Surely the LORD's anointed is now before the LORD." . . . Jesse made seven of his sons pass before Samuel, and Samuel said to Jesse, "The LORD has not chosen any of these." (vv. 6, 10)

REFLECTION

Samuel is not to rely on outward appearance in making the choice for Saul's successor, but to think carefully about the choice. Actually, in this case, the Lord has already said that Samuel is to rely on God's pointing out the chosen son, and not to make a hasty decision on his own. As a more general maxim, the saying would seem to commend thought, pondering, consultation with God, in place of quick conclusions at first sight. (Pairing this lection with the Gospel appointed from John 9 is another indication that sight/insight is a major theme of the day.)

REBECCA ABTS WRIGHT

RESPONSE

Are you discerning an important decision or new hire? What would it be like to rely, not on sight or your own judgment, but on God's choice and consultation? How might God see differently than you do? How might you be called, at this time in your life, to see as God sees?

PRAYER

God of surprises, you do not see as I see. Teach me to encounter my fellow human beings as you do; help me not look on outward appearances, but on the heart. Amen.

Canticle

Psalm 23

Surely goodness and mercy shall follow me
    all the days of my life,
and I shall dwell in the house of the LORD
    my whole life long. (v. 6)

REFLECTION

Beloved and familiar, Psalm 23 affirms the shepherding activity of
God with a series of short phrases in which God is the subject and the
psalmist is the object of God's care. God is the one who "makes me
lie down in green pastures," who "leads me beside still waters," who
"restores my soul," and who "leads me in right paths" (Ps. 23:2–3). As
the psalm continues, the relationship between the subject (God) and the
object (psalmist) deepens, as indicated by the more intimate second-
person point of view.

JOHN W. WURSTER

RESPONSE

Reread Psalm 23, noticing the way the language changes from first
person to second person. What do you notice about this increasing
intimacy? Do you hear an invitation to deepen your own relationship
with God? How might you be longing for God to shepherd you this
week?

PRAYER

O God my shepherd, you want to lead me, always, to waters, pastures,
and paths alongside you; help me to see that no matter what is around
me, I will dwell in your house all the days of my life. Amen.

Second Reading

Ephesians 5:8–14

Take no part in the unfruitful works of darkness, but instead expose them. For it is shameful even to mention what such people do secretly; but everything exposed by the light becomes visible, for everything that becomes visible is light. (vv. 11–14a)

REFLECTION

Ephesians 5:6–7 implores the reader to dissociate from the disobedient. Verses 8–9 tell why. "You are light," and the "fruit of the light" is found in good actions, not in the dark actions listed in 4:25–5:5. Verses 10–14 take this reasoning further. They hint that acts done in secret are by nature acts contrary to God. Therefore, the believer must bring all things into the light. Verses 13–14 suggest that anything visible, that can stand being exposed to the light and done openly, is by nature of God.

JEROME F. D. CREACH

RESPONSE

What have you noticed about the feelings and actions you keep secret and those you share, even just with a person you trust? What would it mean to you to bring *all* things into the light? Is there a particular thing God might be inviting you to expose to light this week?

PRAYER

God who sees, everything exposed to your light becomes visible; teach me to live as a child of this light and to bring forth fruits that are good, right, true, and pleasing to you. Amen.

Gospel

John 9:1–41

As he walked along, he saw a man blind from birth. His disciples asked him, "Rabbi, who sinned, this man or his parents, that he was born blind?" Jesus answered, "Neither this man nor his parents sinned; he was born blind so that God's works might be revealed in him." (vv. 1–3)

REFLECTION

I have often counseled people facing loss or tragedy to try to avoid asking the "why?" question and, rather, to struggle to ask the "how?" question. Asking *why* a death has come too early or *why* suffering has suddenly enveloped a good life are questions that usually lead nowhere. Asking *how*—*how* one might find a way through the pain to a strong and vibrant life in spite of it all—is a question with answers. . . . Remember the familiar but jolting statement attributed to Helen Keller: "I thank God for my handicaps. For through them I have found myself, my work, and my God."

MICHAEL L. LINDVALL

RESPONSE

Reflect on a recent loss, tragedy, or handicap in your life. How might Christ be offering you a way, through the pain or grief, to persist in a "vibrant life"? To a new way of seeing? What do Helen Keller's words, here, say to you?

PRAYER

Gracious Christ, you invite me to see that my losses, limits, and handicaps are not a punishment; help me to find your way of life through my pain and to see and behold you, beside and within me. Amen.

Weekend Reflections

FURTHER CONNECTION

Have you ever been at sea in a dense fog, when it seemed as if a tangible white darkness shut you in, and the great ship, tense and anxious, groped her way toward the shore with plummet and sounding-line, and you waited with beating heart for something to happen? I was like that ship before my education began, only I was without compass or sounding-line, and had no way of knowing how near the harbour was. "Light! give me light!" was the wordless cry of my soul, and the light of love shone on me in that very hour.

HELEN KELLER (1880–1968), *THE STORY OF MY LIFE*

MAKING THE CONNECTIONS

Choose one or two questions for reflection:

1. What connections have you noticed between this week's texts and other passages in Scripture?

2. What connections have you made between this week's texts and the world beyond Scripture?

3. Does either of this week's two commentary themes speak especially to your life or the life of the world around you right now?

4. What is God saying to your congregation in particular through this week's readings and commentaries?

_____

_____

_____

_____

_____

_____

Sabbath Day

SCRIPTURE OF ASSURANCE

> Your words were found, and I ate them,
> and your words became to me a joy
> and the delight of my heart;
> for I am called by your name,
> O LORD, God of hosts. (Jeremiah 15:16)

WEEKLY EXAMEN

- Take a quiet moment, seek out God's presence, and pray for the guidance of the Spirit.

- Consider the past week; recall specific moments and feelings that stand out to you.

- Choose one moment or feeling for deeper examination, thanksgiving, or repentance.

- Let go, breathe deeply, and invite Christ's love to surround and fill you in preparation for the week ahead.

- End with the Lord's Prayer.

The Week Leading Up to the
Fifth Sunday in Lent

Ezekiel 37:1–14

He led me all around them; there were very many lying in the valley, and they were very dry. He said to me, "Mortal, can these bones live?" I answered, "O Lord God, you know." (vv. 2–3)

Psalm 130

I wait for the Lord, my soul waits,
    and in his word I hope;
my soul waits for the Lord
      more than those who watch for the morning,
      more than those who watch for the morning. (vv. 5–6)

Romans 8:6–11

To set the mind on the flesh is death, but to set the mind on the Spirit is life and peace. For this reason the mind that is set on the flesh is hostile to God; it does not submit to God's law—indeed it cannot, and those who are in the flesh cannot please God. (vv. 6–8)

John 11:1–45

"I knew that you always hear me, but I have said this for the sake of the crowd standing here, so that they may believe that you sent me." When he had said this, he cried with a loud voice, "Lazarus, come out!" The dead man came out. (vv. 42–44a)

LECTIO DIVINA

Underline a word or phrase that especially grabs your attention. Pray from that word or phrase and ask God to help you connect to its particular invitation for you this week.

Themes from This Week's Writers

THEME 1: *Can These Dry Bones Live?*

Ezekiel 37:1–14

Perhaps Ezekiel said this with robust confidence. "O God, you know that you can do all things. If you want these bones to live, then of course they will." Ezekiel may not have been able to rouse more than a tired whisper: "O God, I don't know anything anymore. Everything seems bleak. Do you not see how bad off we are? But if anyone knows, you do."

REBECCA ABTS WRIGHT

Ezekiel 37:1–14

I wonder if one of the prophet's first responses to Spirit's question, "Can these bones live?" is, instinctively, "I certainly hope not!" . . . Before we ask for new life, perhaps we too can simply sit with our bones. Get to know them. Grieve with them. Let Spirit teach us.

JANE ANNE FERGUSON

Psalm 130

Even in that place, the psalm urges us to voice our prayer to God and to cry for deliverance. For as lonely as that valley may feel, God is still present in it. As high as the dry bones are stacked, God insists on life. As tightly as the tomb is sealed, God refuses to let death have the last word.

JOHN W. WURSTER

THEME 2: *Those Who Believe in Me, Even Though They Die, Will Live*

Romans 8:6–11

The spirit of God who raised Jesus from the dead dwells within those who have accepted the saving power of Christ's death. The result is that those who were once "dead" because of sin now have life because of God's righteousness (v. 10). This is the culmination of what Paul celebrates in Romans 8:1–11: believers now have life, because the Spirit of God lives within them.

JEROME F. D. CREACH

John 11:1–45

In essence, Jesus brings the promise of future resurrection into the present; death has no power, today or tomorrow, over those who believe in him (John 5:28–29; 6:39–40, 44, 54). He also brings eternal life into the here and now; abundant life is given to those who believe in him (3:16, 36; 5:24; 6:47; 10:28; 17:2).

ANDREW NAGY-BENSON

John 11:1–45

The core theme of the lection—even more than Jesus' love, compassion, and vulnerability—is the defiance of death. Jesus does not just raise Lazarus from the grave; he mocks the grave in his almost blasé attitude toward the last enemy. He . . . waits two days before setting out for Bethany, refusing to let death set his agenda.

MICHAEL L. LINDVALL

WHAT IS THE HOLY SPIRIT SAYING TO YOU THIS WEEK?

_____

_____

_____

_____

_____

A SPIRITUAL PRACTICE FOR THIS WEEK

Find a piece of bone or an image of a skull or skeleton to use as a focus for prayer this week. What is it like to imagine your own death? How has death been present in your life in recent years? What is it like to imagine new life in Christ, in this life and in the life to come?

First Reading

Ezekiel 37:1–14

Then he said to me, "Prophesy to the breath, prophesy, mortal, and say to the breath: Thus says the Lord GOD: Come from the four winds, O breath, and breathe upon these slain, that they may live." (v. 9)

REFLECTION

Why does God make such a request? Could the Lord not have revived those bones without Ezekiel's help? Well, yes and no. Here we are at a major message of this lection. First, God desires an interactive, cooperative relationship with human beings. This relational nature seems to be so much a part of the definition of the biblical God that an aloof or absolutely separated "God" would be as impossible for the prophets to conceive as a notion of dry rain or frigid fire. Of course the sovereign God could act alone, but God chooses instead to act in concert with human beings.

REBECCA ABTS WRIGHT

RESPONSE

Reflect on the image of God as aloof and separate. How is this image familiar to you? Then, reflect on the image of God seeking a cooperative relationship with humans. How is this image familiar to you? How may God be inviting you into cooperation, now?

PRAYER

God of the breath, teach me to prophesy to bones and to people, that we may come to new life in you, together. Amen.

Canticle

Psalm 130

Out of the depths I cry to you, O Lord.
   Lord, hear my voice!
Let your ears be attentive
   to the voice of my supplications! (vv. 1–2)

REFLECTION

The psalmist has descended to a point where there is no one to help but
God. Described as "the depths" (Ps. 130:1), it is a dark and bleak place
in which resources have been exhausted. The way forward is unclear.
Fear is close; despair looms. Mustering faith, the psalmist cries to God,
begging to be heard. In a reflective way that seems to boost confidence,
the psalmist remembers God's persistent mercy (vv. 3–4). Memories of
God's past faithfulness build hope for the present. Though still in the
depths, the psalmist adopts a posture of anticipation of how God will
respond to the cries for help.

JOHN W. WURSTER

RESPONSE

When was the last time you felt in "the depths"? Maybe you feel that
way now? What are ways you cry out to God? How have you longed to
be heard? What are your memories of God's past faithfulness? How have
you experienced resurrection? How are you still hoping to receive it?

PRAYER

God of help, please listen to me and hear what I long to tell you; I wait
for you, and in your word, I hope. Amen.

Second Reading

Romans 8:6–11

But if Christ is in you, though the body is dead because of sin, the Spirit is life because of righteousness. If the Spirit of him who raised Jesus from the dead dwells in you, he who raised Christ from the dead will give life to your mortal bodies also through his Spirit that dwells in you. (vv. 10–11)

REFLECTION

Let us pause here and ask ourselves what it might mean to "have the Spirit of Christ," or to have "Christ in you," or to have God's Spirit indwelling Christian believers. Paul is pointing us to a mystery here, but what mystery? . . . I read this as Paul's suggestions of a mystical connection between believers and God, a sense of being overtaken, of being filled with the Spirit of Christ such that there can be no other passion. It is as though intimacy with Christ, with God, leaves no room, no spiritual space, for that which is not of God.

SALLY B. PURVIS

RESPONSE

What does it mean to you to "have the Spirit of Christ," would you say? How have you felt the Spirit dwelling within you? What is the mystery of God, for you? (Or is it, in fact, a mystery?) How would you describe your passion or love for God?

PRAYER

Loving Christ, if you are in me, your Spirit dwells in me, even if I do not always understand how; give life to my body and soul, that I may set my mind on you and live in your love and your law. Amen.

Gospel

John 11:1–45

Martha said to Jesus, "Lord, if you had been here, my brother would not have died. But even now I know that God will give you whatever you ask of him." (vv. 21–22)

REFLECTION

Throughout the Gospel of John, Jesus demonstrates power to give life. From the opening verses of the prologue, Jesus (the Word) is the source of all creation (John 1:3). He also brings into the world "eternal life"—a life-force stronger than death and the wellspring of abundant living. For John, eternal life is given, here and now, to those who believe "that Jesus is the Messiah, the Son of God" (John 20:31). At the heart of our Gospel passage lies the miracle of life given.

ANDREW NAGY-BENSON

RESPONSE

How have you seen the power of Jesus to give life in your own faith journey? What is this power, do you think? Do you find it hard to believe in? How do you see it at work in your life now? How do you hope to respond?

PRAYER

Jesus, you are my friend, my brother, and my God. You have the power of eternal life; come with me to the places of death in my life, for I know you are stronger than death. Amen.

Weekend Reflections

The cross is not the terrible end to an otherwise god-fearing and happy life, but it meets us at the beginning of our communion with Christ. When Christ calls a man, he bids him come and die. It may be a death like that of the first disciples who had to leave home and work to follow him, or it may be a death like Luther's, who had to leave the monastery and go out into the world. But it is the same death every time—death in Jesus Christ, the death of the old man at his call.

DIETRICH BONHOEFFER (1906-45), *THE COST OF DISCIPLESHIP*

MAKING THE CONNECTIONS

Choose one or two questions for reflection:

1. What connections have you noticed between this week's texts and other passages in Scripture?

2. What connections have you made between this week's texts and the world beyond Scripture?

3. Does either of this week's two commentary themes speak especially to your life or the life of the world around you right now?

4. What is God saying to your congregation in particular through this week's readings and commentaries?

_____

_____

_____

_____

_____

_____

Sabbath Day

SCRIPTURE OF ASSURANCE

Help me, O LORD my God!
Save me according to your steadfast love.
Let them know that this is your hand;
you, O LORD, have done it. (Psalm 109:26–27)

WEEKLY EXAMEN

- Take a quiet moment, seek out God's presence, and pray for the guidance of the Spirit.

- Consider the past week; recall specific moments and feelings that stand out to you.

- Choose one moment or feeling for deeper examination, thanksgiving, or repentance.

- Let go, breathe deeply, and invite Christ's love to surround and fill you in preparation for the week ahead.

- End with the Lord's Prayer.

The Week Leading Up to
Palm/Passion Sunday

Matthew 21:1–11

When he entered Jerusalem, the whole city was in turmoil, asking, "Who is this?" The crowds were saying, "This is the prophet Jesus from Nazareth in Galilee." (vv. 10–11)

Isaiah 50:4–9a

I gave my back to those who struck me,
    and my cheeks to those who pulled out the beard;
I did not hide my face
    from insult and spitting. (v. 6)

Philippians 2:5–11

And being found in human form,
    he humbled himself
    and became obedient to the point of death—
    even death on a cross. (vv. 7b–8)

Matthew 26:14–27:66

Pilate said to them, "Then what should I do with Jesus who is called the Messiah?" All of them said, "Let him be crucified!" Then he asked, "Why, what evil has he done?" But they shouted all the more, "Let him be crucified!" (27:22–23)

LECTIO DIVINA

Underline a word or phrase that especially grabs your attention. Pray from that word or phrase and ask God to help you connect to its particular invitation for you this week.

Themes from This Week's Writers

THEME 1: *Jesus Challenges and Disrupts*

Psalm 118:1–2, 19–29

This verse ("the stone that the builders rejected has become the chief cornerstone") . . . is quoted by Jesus as part of a stinging attack on the religious authorities (21:42). . . .
Matthew, however, seizes upon this verse as crucially reflective of God's amazing work, which is inherently disruptive.

JOHN W. WURSTER

Matthew 21:1–11

The coronation parade into Jerusalem, however, is an unmistakable challenge to Caesar. Jesus enters Jerusalem, which was the former capital of Israel and Judah and the current regional capital from which Caesar's representative, the prefect Pontius Pilate, governs. Jesus enters the city as if he is claiming it as his own.

O. WESLEY ALLEN JR.

Matthew 21:1–11

"Lowly pomp" is an oxymoron in the world's calculation. Jesus' triumph emerged from shame and suffering. Jesus' vision and interpretation of his entry into Jerusalem, a place both of death and of exaltation, must be embraced through eyes of faith and hearts of hope.

DIANE G. CHEN

THEME 2: *The Suffering Servant*

Isaiah 50:4–9a

Both the Servant in Isaiah and the apostle Paul faced harsh opposition. Both, however, also proclaimed faith in the God whose grace enabled them to follow where God's call led them.

KATHRYN SCHIFFERDECKER

Philippians 2:5–11

Slaves were at the bottom of the social pyramid. The slave was obedient to the master. At another level, most people in the ancient world believed that everyone served a deity (or deities). Jesus was obedient to God, which meant being obedient to the divine purpose of effecting the transition from the old age to the new.

RONALD J. ALLEN

Matthew 26:14–27:66

One should note that the actual act of crucifying Jesus is told in very little detail. There is no depiction of nailing or bleeding. . . . Humanity's obsession with the morbid and grotesque should not be entertained in a sermon on the cross. It is *the fact* that Jesus was crucified and died that is important to the Gospel writers, not the horrific details of that death.

O. WESLEY ALLEN JR.

WHAT IS THE HOLY SPIRIT SAYING TO YOU THIS WEEK?

_____

_____

_____

_____

_____

A SPIRITUAL PRACTICE FOR THIS WEEK

Read Psalm 31:9–16, aloud or silently. Then, take an old bowl, mug, or flowerpot and smash it. What do you feel and think as you look at the broken pot? Choose some words from the psalm and write them on the broken pieces with a permanent marker. Use as your prayer focus this week.

First Reading

Isaiah 50:4–9a

The Lord GOD helps me;
    therefore I have not been disgraced;
therefore I have set my face like flint,
    and I know that I shall not be put to shame. (v. 7)

REFLECTION

It is not unusual to associate Jesus' life and ministry with suffering, especially during Holy Week—even suffering that is on behalf of others. . . . Nowadays, the majority of human energy goes to minimize suffering as much as possible. Medicine and technology are only two of the most powerful ways we do that. The impression, if not explicit message, of those attempts is that suffering is altogether bad, an evil to avoid at all costs. As for suffering intentionally for someone else? Simply unbelievable (cf. Rom. 5:7–8). Then again, there is Isaiah 50:4–9a, and there is Jesus in Holy Week.

BRENT A. STRAWN

RESPONSE

What are the most common ways you see people in your community minimizing or numbing their suffering? How do you avoid suffering in your own life? Have you seen people willing to suffer for their neighbor? Are you willing to suffer for someone else? How and how not?

PRAYER

O Lord God, you are my help in suffering—not to deny or erase it but to walk through it with me, bearing the pain, humiliation, and shame alongside me so that, like Jesus in his passion, I will not be alone. Amen.

Palm Canticle

Psalm 118:1–2, 19–29

O give thanks to the Lord, for he is good;
   his steadfast love endures forever!

Let Israel say,
   "His steadfast love endures forever." (vv. 1–2)

REFLECTION

God's faithful love through the ages takes a particular shape as a
congregation gathers on Palm Sunday. Psalm 118 almost functions as a
script as Matthew describes Jesus' triumphal entry into Jerusalem in this
day's Gospel lesson. The love of God expressed through the generations
is present and vital as Jesus enters the city. God's deliverance is at hand
again. *Let us give thanks for what God is doing this day. Let us give thanks
for God is good this day.* Jesus enfleshes God's goodness, and the crowds
respond to Jesus with shouts of praise.

JOHN W. WURSTER

RESPONSE

This year, how could you begin Holy Week with a sense of thankfulness
and joy, like the crowds on Palm Sunday? Inspired by Psalm 118, you
might reflect on the faithful love of God "through the ages" in your
congregation, your extended family, your city or town, or even all
humanity.

PRAYER

O Lord, your steadfast love endures forever; I give thanks to you, for
you are good. Remind me of your faithfulness through the ages and lead
me to praise and joy as I prepare for this Holy Week. Amen.

Second Reading

Philippians 2:5–11

Let the same mind be in you that was in Christ Jesus,
who, though he was in the form of God,
    did not regard equality with God
    as something to be exploited,
but emptied himself,
    taking the form of a slave. (vv. 5–7a)

REFLECTION

Sooner or later life will empty us: the phone call in the middle of the
night, the serious look on the surgeon's face, the note left on the kitchen
counter. Emptying can consist of the long, slow diminishing of joy and
purpose, or it can crash upon us in an instant. Faith communities also
experience seasons of great loss and grief. Acknowledging Jesus' own
emptying can be a welcome reminder that we are never alone in such
times.

JULIE PEEPLES

RESPONSE

What was a time when life emptied you? How has life emptied you,
or your congregation, recently? As you enter Holy Week, how could
acknowledging Jesus' emptying help you through your own?

PRAYER

O God, receive me in my emptiness as I seek to follow your Son, who
emptied himself for me, into Holy Week, that the pain of love may be
something I share with you, in Christ. Amen.

Palm Gospel

Matthew 21:1–11

The disciples went and did as Jesus had directed them; they brought the donkey and the colt, and put their cloaks on them, and he sat on them. A very large crowd spread their cloaks on the road, and others cut branches from the trees and spread them on the road. (vv. 6–8)

REFLECTION

In 2015, Pope Francis visited Philadelphia for the World Meeting of Families. Much to the curiosity and delight of the public, the Holy Father chose to ride in a tiny Fiat for a pope-mobile, rather than a fancy limousine or large protected vehicle worthy of an honored dignitary. . . . Indeed, a ruler on a beast of burden and a pope in a compact car challenged the status quo and invited self-reflection on one's definition of greatness. It is in the relinquishing of the world's trappings of greatness that true greatness is embodied (Matt. 20:26).

DIANE G. CHEN

RESPONSE

What are some "trappings of greatness" you have found yourself attracted to, whether in your work or personal life? What is appealing about those things? More deeply, what do you believe truly embodies greatness and goodness? How do the leaders you most admire demonstrate these things?

PRAYER

Jesus, son of David, show me how to follow you, not as though I were in a parade but on a walk with you and with the neediest of my neighbors. Amen.

Passion Gospel

Matthew 26:14–27:66

And when they had crucified him, they divided his clothes among themselves by casting lots; then they sat down there and kept watch over him. Over his head they put the charge against him, which read, "This is Jesus, the King of the Jews." (27:35–37)

REFLECTION

In [He Qi's] 1999 work . . . *The Crucifixion*, Jesus is positioned at the center. . . . [But the] painting highlights the characters around Jesus . . . [in] a range of skin tones, from light to yellow to brown and dark. It is this motley crew, not Jesus' own disciples, who hold vigil under the cross. All of them carry the shame of low status in Jesus' day. They represent sinners, tax collectors, the blind, the lame, women, children, and Gentiles. Jesus was nailed to the cross because of his politically radical mission to restore these nameless and powerless people to physical, spiritual, and communal wholeness.

DIANE G. CHEN

RESPONSE

What would it mean to make the people keeping vigil, as described by Chen, the focus of your Holy Week this year? Do you identify more with the disciples who hid or the motley crew at the cross? What motley crew might Jesus be inviting you to see in your own community?

PRAYER

Jesus, show me how to look for you on the cross, crucified, but also in the crowd gathered around the cross; help me to witness with you this week, and to be a witness and a servant to all my neighbors who are nameless and powerless. Amen.

Weekend Reflections

FURTHER CONNECTION

We hope that love is stronger than death. And if not, well . . . not a bad way to die, trying.

PÁDRAIG Ó TUAMA (1975–), "STATIONS OF THE CROSS,
A REFLECTION FOR GOOD FRIDAY 2020"

MAKING THE CONNECTIONS

Choose one or two questions for reflection:

1. What connections have you noticed between this week's texts and other passages in Scripture?

2. What connections have you made between this week's texts and the world beyond Scripture?

3. Does either of this week's two commentary themes speak especially to your life or the life of the world around you right now?

4. What is God saying to your congregation in particular through this week's readings and commentaries?

MY CONNECTIONS

_____

_____

_____

_____

_____

_____

Sabbath Day

> O send out your light and your truth;
>   let them lead me;
> let them bring me to your holy hill
>   and to your dwelling. (Psalm 43:3)

WEEKLY EXAMEN

- Take a quiet moment, seek out God's presence, and pray for the guidance of the Spirit.

- Consider the past week; recall specific moments and feelings that stand out to you.

- Choose one moment or feeling for deeper examination, thanksgiving, or repentance.

- Let go, breathe deeply, and invite Christ's love to surround and fill you in preparation for the week ahead.

- End with the Lord's Prayer.

Holy Thursday

Exodus 12:1–4 (5–10), 11–14

This is how you shall eat it: your loins girded, your sandals on your feet, and your staff in your hand; and you shall eat it hurriedly. It is the passover of the LORD. (v. 11)

Psalm 116:1–2, 12–19

I will offer to you a thanksgiving sacrifice
   and call on the name of the LORD.
I will pay my vows to the LORD
   in the presence of all his people. (vv. 17–18)

1 Corinthians 11:23–26

For as often as you eat this bread and drink the cup, you proclaim the Lord's death until he comes. (v. 26)

John 13:1–17, 31b–35

Now before the festival of the Passover, Jesus knew that his hour had come to depart from this world and go to the Father. Having loved his own who were in the world, he loved them to the end. (v. 1)

REFLECTIONS

Exodus 12:1–4 (5–10), 11–14

Both Israel and the church thus commemorate and celebrate God's ultimate victory *before* experiencing it. Therefore, the futuristic or eschatological aspects of the meal are just as important as the past, memorializing ones, if not more important. Liturgy is indeed a way the past is made present, but it is also a way to make the future present. . . . How could this be true for local Christian communions?

BRENT A. STRAWN

Psalm 116:1–2, 12–19

[These verses] point to three applications: . . . How might we share in God's work of delivering the oppressed and setting captives free? . . . How might we fulfill Jesus' call to "do this" in remembrance of him, devoting ourselves to others? . . . How might we demonstrate to the world that we are Christ's disciples?

DAVID GAMBRELL

1 Corinthians 11:23–26

Communion can happen in all sorts of places; no white linens are required. Anxious family members and strangers crowding in a small hospital waiting room pass around the cookies someone brought; a thermos or two of coffee appears. A place of stressful waiting becomes sacred space. A table is set up under a city bridge where men and women dealing with homelessness often camp out. Sandwiches and lemonade take the place of white bread and grape juice as volunteers and guests break bread together.

JULIE PEEPLES

John 13:1–17, 31b–35

Now, the hour has come. . . . Jesus did not get crucified because he suddenly ran out of luck and ran out of time. He gave his life as a gift (10:18), and his "hour" had come to fulfillment. He had accomplished that which he was sent to do, and "having loved his own who were in the world, he loved them to the end" (13:1b). . . . In other words, Jesus loved them both until his hour had come and until his love was filled to the brim.

THOMAS G. LONG

RESPONSE

Choose one of these four quotes that particularly gets your attention and write or reflect on how God might be speaking to you, to your experience or questions about Holy Week this year, or to this time in your life.

PRAYER

O Jesus, as often as we eat this bread and drink the cup, as often as we wash one another's feet, we proclaim your death until you come again. Now, the hour has come. Amen.

Good Friday

Isaiah 52:13–53:12

Yet it was the will of the LORD to crush him with pain.
When you make his life an offering for sin,
   he shall see his offspring, and shall prolong his days;
through him the will of the LORD shall prosper. (53:10)

Psalm 22

To him, indeed, shall all who sleep in the earth bow down;
   before him shall bow all who go down to the dust,
   and I shall live for him. (v. 29)

Hebrews 4:14–16; 5:7–9

For we do not have a high priest who is unable to sympathize with our weaknesses, but we have one who in every respect has been tested as we are, yet without sin. Let us therefore approach the throne of grace with boldness, so that we may receive mercy and find grace to help in time of need. (4:15–16)

John 18:1–19:42

So they took Jesus; and carrying the cross by himself, he went out to what is called The Place of the Skull, which in Hebrew is called Golgotha. There they crucified him, and with him two others, one on either side, with Jesus between them. (19:16b–18)

REFLECTIONS

Isaiah 52:13–53:12

The text is not about us, except as the beneficiaries of God's extraordinary mercy and curious power, which bring redemption through another's suffering. There is no takeaway except awe. . . . We get our best glimpse into the heart of the Creator, whose ongoing determination is to bring a broken, sinful humanity, and even creation itself, to God's good end.

JAMES C. HOWELL

Psalm 22

Could it be that, while Matthew and Mark recognized Jesus' voice in the desperate cry at the opening of Psalm 22, John heard the Word of the Lord in its confident conclusion? This would be consistent with the image of Jesus throughout the Fourth Gospel: clear in purpose, authoritative, and in control—even as he died on the cross.

DAVID GAMBRELL

Hebrews 4:14–16; 5:7–9

For all who have suffered persecution, abuse, rejection, discrimination, here is a word of promise: Jesus identifies with our pain. Jesus our "high priest" has "passed through the heavens" in order to walk this world with humanity. . . . Instead of highlighting the cross and the cruelty it represents, the author invites the reader to turn around and face the "throne of grace," where Christ's healing may be found.

CATHY CALDWELL HOOP

John 18:1–19:42

The term "Good Friday" seems counterintuitive. . . . Fear, dread, violence, pain, suffering, and death are a few of the terms that depict Jesus' crucifixion. Soldiers arrest Jesus, his disciples flee, Roman officials condemn him, his followers deny him, and Jesus dies a painful death while nailed to a cross. Nothing about this series of events is "good." Yet one archaic definition of good was "holy."

JONATHAN L. WALTON

RESPONSE

Choose one of these four quotes that particularly gets your attention and write or reflect on how God might be speaking to you, to your experience or questions about Holy Week this year, or to this time in your life.

PRAYER

Lord Jesus, we stand and face your cross, your throne of grace, with boldness. Show us how to stand nearby, close to you and your friends, until all is finished. Amen.

The Week Leading Up to

Easter Day/Resurrection of the Lord

Jeremiah 31:1–6

Again I will build you, and you shall be built,
  O virgin Israel!
Again you shall take your tambourines,
  and go forth in the dance of the merrymakers. (v. 4)

Colossians 3:1–4

So if you have been raised with Christ, seek the things that are above, where Christ is, seated at the right hand of God. (v. 1)

John 20:1–18

So [Mary Magdalene] ran and went to Simon Peter and the other disciple, the one whom Jesus loved, and said to them, "They have taken the Lord out of the tomb, and we do not know where they have laid him." Then Peter and the other disciple set out and went toward the tomb. (vv. 2–3)

Matthew 28:1–10

And suddenly there was a great earthquake; for an angel of the Lord, descending from heaven, came and rolled back the stone and sat on it. His appearance was like lightning, and his clothing white as snow. For fear of him the guards shook and became like dead men. (vv. 2–4)

LECTIO DIVINA

Underline a word or phrase that especially grabs your attention. Pray from that word or phrase and ask God to help you connect to its particular invitation for you this week.

Themes from This Week's Writers

THEME 1: *In Christ, Love Overcomes Death*

Jeremiah 31:1–6

Eternal life is not a reward for a life well lived or faith properly declared. Rather, God forges a relationship of love with us that is so strong even death cannot cancel it out. Notice the way "again" recurs three times in verse 4. God's is a determined love.

JAMES C. HOWELL

Psalm 118:1–2, 14–24

From hosanna to hallelujah, Psalm 118 encompasses the mystery of our faith. On the first Sunday of Easter, this psalm helps us to proclaim that the risen Lord is the Alpha and the Omega, and that death will never have the last word.

DAVID GAMBRELL

John 20:1–18

Just as God raised Jesus from the dead, Jesus lifts Mary's broken spirit. Resurrection Sunday represents renewal and revival. Those things that appear inconceivable can become plausible, and the unimaginable becomes tenable. . . . Those things that we thought were dead were brought back to life.

JONATHAN L. WALTON

THEME 2: *Resurrection Leads Us Not Only to Heaven Above But to Earthly Justice*

Colossians 3:1–4

We are called to act, to set our minds on Christ. All of Paul's letters, including Colossians, move from teaching the gospel to encouraging us to act in its light: this is who you are, so live like it! We set our minds on Christ; yet we should not be so "heavenly minded" that we are of "no earthly use."

EDITH M. HUMPHREY

Acts 10:34–43

Peter's message takes the worshiper beyond the garden tomb, beyond the upper room, and beyond the road to Emmaus. Peter's message, with its minimalist description of Easter, boils this holy day's message down to its essence: God desires to redeem all of creation. God loves all of creation, in all its amazing diversity. "I truly understand that God shows no partiality," Peter preaches.

CATHY CALDWELL HOOP

Matthew 28:1–10

Roman imperial agents killed him.

They cannot keep him dead. They cannot prevail against God's determined commitment to life and justice for all the bodies of the world. . . .

. . . It displays how much the just treatment of bodies and their interactions with other bodies matter in God's workings in the world.

WARREN CARTER

WHAT IS THE HOLY SPIRIT SAYING TO YOU THIS WEEK?

_____

_____

_____

_____

_____

A SPIRITUAL PRACTICE FOR THIS WEEK

This week, strive to be as present to the readings and services of Holy Week as you can. Consider fasting in some way on Good Friday; abstain from meat or alcohol, or skip lunch or dinner entirely. Drink hot tea or water to ease a hungry stomach.

First Reading

Jeremiah 31:1–6

I have loved you with an everlasting love;
therefore I have continued my faithfulness to you.
Again I will build you, and you shall be built. (vv. 3b–4a)

REFLECTION

"I have loved you with an everlasting love; that is why I have continued
my *hesed* to you" (v. 3, my trans.).

That wonderful Hebrew word is nearly untranslatable. NRSV reads
"faithfulness," which is surely not wrong, but the word contains a world
of power in it. Its basic meaning, when used as an attribute of God, is
"unbreakable connection." It announces that there is finally nothing we
can do that can separate us from this love of God. . . .

God's *hesed* is the foundation of our relationship with God.

JOHN C. HOLBERT

RESPONSE

We may think of Holy Week first as a commemoration of Jesus'
suffering. This week, reflect on the readings and rituals as evidence of
God's *hesed*, God's unbreakable connection to us. What does it mean
to you this Holy Week that nothing you can do can separate you from
God's love?

PRAYER

Risen Christ, your love is everlasting and your faithfulness to me is
unbreakable; nothing I can do can separate me from you. Again, you
will build me, and again, I will be built. Alleluia! Amen.

Canticle

Psalm 118:1–2, 14–24

I shall not die, but I shall live,
    and recount the deeds of the LORD.
The LORD has punished me severely,
    but he did not give me over to death. (vv. 17–18)

REFLECTION

Psalm 118 offers several valuable insights for preaching on the Resurrection of the Lord. First, the gift of new life is no garden-variety miracle, no springtime bud or chrysalis; Psalm 118 depicts resurrection as a hard-fought battle with the powers of evil and death (vv. 5–18). Second, the work of resurrection is not something we can accomplish through our own best efforts and intentions; it is always the Lord's doing, and it is "marvelous in our eyes" (v. 23). . . . Finally, our primary response to the gift of life redeemed and restored is that of gratitude: "O give thanks to the LORD."

DAVID GAMBRELL

RESPONSE

How often have you associated the resurrection with new leaves or spring buds? How often have you associated it with a battle? What kind of battle against death or what "work of resurrection" is happening in your life or your congregation, lately? How is it "the Lord's doing"?

PRAYER

Risen Christ, your resurrection is not just sweetness and lilies, but a fierce victory overcoming death and evil; this is the Lord's doing, and it is marvelous. Alleluia! Amen.

Second Reading

Colossians 3:1–4

Set your minds on things that are above, not on things that are on earth, for you have died, and your life is hidden with Christ in God. When Christ who is your life is revealed, then you also will be revealed with him in glory. (vv. 2–4)

REFLECTION

Even when playing a game, hiding alone can be unsettling. There is the fear of never being found. With Christ as our hiding companion, we do not have to fear being alone. He is our companion on this life journey, and God is our hiding place. Expand upon this idea of God as our hiding place, a source of shelter. If we are hidden in God, then we may also say that God is never hidden from us. God is ever accessible to us.

The paradox here is this: though we are hidden in God, we do not hide from the world.

CATHY CALDWELL HOOP

RESPONSE

Have you ever felt you were hiding alone, in life? What does it mean to you to be "hidden with Christ in God" instead? How is God a shelter for you? How might Christ be your "hiding companion"? How could taking shelter in God help you to not hide from the world?

PRAYER

Risen Christ, hide me with you in God; not so I escape from this world, but so I may die and shelter with you and then rise and be revealed with you, as the person you call me to be. Alleluia! Amen.

Second Reading

Acts 10:34–43

That message spread throughout Judea, beginning in Galilee after the baptism that John announced: how God anointed Jesus of Nazareth with the Holy Spirit and with power; how he went about doing good and healing all who were oppressed by the devil, for God was with him. (vv. 37–38)

REFLECTION

The very same one who "went about Judea and Galilee" and died also rose from the dead, eating and drinking anew with the apostles. Even more, it is he who will come, finally, at the last judgment. Peter's sermon fills out the meaning of Hebrews 13:8, that Jesus is the same yesterday, today, and forever. Some today divide the "Jesus of history" from the "Christ of faith." The preacher can correct this by showing how Peter's words depict Jesus as one who took on everything it is to be human, and yet who truly embodied (and embodies) our merciful and just God.

EDITH M. HUMPHREY

RESPONSE

Do you separate the "Jesus of history" from the "Christ of faith"? Or, did you at one time? When you hear the phrase "Jesus is the same yesterday, today, and forever," what does it mean to you? How is it important to you this Easter that Jesus truly embodied (and embodies) God?

PRAYER

Holy Spirit, lead me in the way of the risen Christ, both the Jesus of history and Christ of faith, that I may share his love and good news with all. Alleluia! Amen.

Gospel

John 20:1–18

Jesus said to her, "Woman, why are you weeping? Whom are you looking for?" Supposing him to be the gardener, she said to him, "Sir, if you have carried him away, tell me where you have laid him, and I will take him away." (v. 15)

REFLECTION

So, it is "still dark" when Mary Magdalene goes to the tomb of Jesus. The rest of the scene is a mixture, misunderstanding intertwined with profound belief. Here Mary Magdalene represents the confusion and bewilderment the resurrection creates, and the beloved disciple embodies the deep faith called for by that event. Mary sees that . . . Jesus has already been raised . . . but Mary does not yet comprehend. . . . Mary's own awakening to faith will happen later (20:11–18). The preacher may wish to explore how faith often moves slowly from disorientation to deep conviction.

THOMAS G. LONG

RESPONSE

We do not often believe that misunderstanding or confusion are compatible with true faith. Have you ever experienced this? This Easter, do you identify more in this reading with Mary Magdalene and her bewilderment or with John, the beloved disciple, and his deep faith?

PRAYER

Risen Christ, you come to meet me whether I feel bewilderment or certainty, seeking to confound my doubts and confirm my faith. Alleluia! Amen.

Gospel

Matthew 28:1–10

Suddenly Jesus met them and said, "Greetings!" And they came to him, took hold of his feet, and worshiped him. Then Jesus said to them, "Do not be afraid; go and tell my brothers to go to Galilee; there they will see me." (vv. 9–10)

REFLECTION

In George Bernard Shaw's 1923 play *Saint Joan*, Robert de Baudricourt tells Joan that the voices she hears come from her own imagination. She answers, "Of course. That is how the messages of God come to us." Easter calls us to imagine reality reborn. Imagine beings who exist only in two dimensions, like a living square drawn on a flat sheet of paper. If a three-dimensional sphere floated into the square's reality, it would appear to the square as an inexplicable ever-widening circle. Humans are three-dimensional beings whose spiritual experiences introduce another dimension. The idea is to point beyond the current horizon.

WM. LOYD ALLEN

RESPONSE

When have you had a spiritual experience where a glimpse of another dimension of reality peeked through? What do you hear in these words of Joan of Arc? How is Easter inviting you, in this season of your life, to see beyond the current horizon? To "imagine reality reborn"?

PRAYER

Gracious God, your messages come to me through the pathways of my imagination; help me to listen even to what may seem unreal or ridiculous, to not be afraid of new life or resurrection, and to meet the risen Christ in my heart and in your people. Amen.

Weekend Reflections

FURTHER CONNECTION

Through the resurrection, God responds to the violence of the cross—the violence of the world—in a nonviolent but forceful manner. It is important to understand that nonviolence is not the same as passivity or accommodation to violence. Rather it is a forceful response that protects the integrity of life. Violence seeks to do another harm, while nonviolence seeks to rescue others from harm. It seeks to break the very cycle of violence itself. . . . That God could defeat the unmitigated violence of the cross reveals the consummate power of the nonviolent, life-giving force that is God.

KELLY BROWN DOUGLAS (1958–), *STAND YOUR GROUND: BLACK BODIES AND THE JUSTICE OF GOD*

MAKING THE CONNECTIONS

Choose one or two questions for reflection:

1. What connections have you noticed between this week's texts and other passages in Scripture?

2. What connections have you made between this week's texts and the world beyond Scripture?

3. Does either of this week's two commentary themes speak especially to your life or the life of the world around you right now?

4. What is God saying to your congregation in particular through this week's readings and commentaries?

_____

_____

_____

_____

_____

_____

Sabbath Day

SCRIPTURE OF ASSURANCE

Therefore, since we are justified by faith, we have peace with God through our Lord Jesus Christ, through whom we have obtained access to this grace in which we stand; and we boast in our hope of sharing the glory of God. (Romans 5:1–2)

WEEKLY EXAMEN

- Take a quiet moment, seek out God's presence, and pray for the guidance of the Spirit.

- Consider the past week; recall specific moments and feelings that stand out to you.

- Choose one moment or feeling for deeper examination, thanksgiving, or repentance.

- Let go, breathe deeply, and invite Christ's love to surround and fill you in preparation for the week ahead.

- End with the Lord's Prayer.

The Week Leading Up to the
Second Sunday of Easter

Acts 2:14a, 22–32

"This man, handed over to you according to the definite plan and foreknowledge of God, you crucified and killed by the hands of those outside the law. But God raised him up, having freed him from death, because it was impossible for him to be held in its power." (vv. 23–24)

Psalm 16

Therefore my heart is glad, and my soul rejoices;
    my body also rests secure.
For you do not give me up to Sheol,
    or let your faithful one see the Pit. (vv. 9–10)

1 Peter 1:3–9

Although you have not seen him, you love him; and even though you do not see him now, you believe in him and rejoice with an indescribable and glorious joy, for you are receiving the outcome of your faith, the salvation of your souls. (vv. 8–9)

John 20:19–31

Jesus said to them again, "Peace be with you. As the Father has sent me, so I send you." When he had said this, he breathed on them and said to them, "Receive the Holy Spirit." (vv. 21–22)

LECTIO DIVINA

Underline a word or phrase that especially grabs your attention. Pray from that word or phrase and ask God to help you connect to its particular invitation for you this week.

Themes from This Week's Writers

THEME 1: *Believing without Seeing*

Acts 2:14a, 22–32

The import of Peter's use of Psalm 16 in this reading is to remind us that even though the gospel comes to us through the witness of other human beings, the object of our faith is never other people, even the apostles themselves, but the God who certainly raised Jesus from the dead.

IAN A. MCFARLAND

Acts 2:14a, 22–32

This is not proof by human standards, proof that demands evidence and argument. God is above such proof, but that is the very point of Peter's proclamation.

KAROLINE M. LEWIS

John 20:19–31

Some self-righteous Christians even use this very Gospel story as a condemnation of doubt. . . . "Blessed are those who have not seen and yet have come to believe" (v. 29). This is proof-texting at its worst. After all, the story is not about judgment and condemnation. It is about *reassuring* Thomas in the midst of his doubt *so that* he can come to faith.

RUBÉN ROSARIO RODRÍGUEZ

THEME 2: *Jesus' Wounds and Our Wounds*

1 Peter 1:3–9

[These] Christians . . . are caught in a tension commonly experienced by followers of Jesus: they are reveling in the glory of their "new birth" (1 Pet. 1:3), while at the same time suffering affliction as a consequence of their identification with the resurrected Christ. . . . Their hope for an inheritance that is "imperishable, undefiled, and unfading" (v. 4) allows them to survive, and even see the benefit of, their suffering in the here and now.

CYNTHIA L. RIGBY

1 Peter 1:3–9

No matter our life circumstances, trials will come along that will challenge our faith. Those trials may come *because of* our witness—the kinds of trials Peter is addressing—or they may become *an occasion for* our witness.

BEVERLY ZINK-SAWYER

John 20:19–31

There, Jesus gives them a gift that counters the very fear the disciples are experiencing in 20:19. Jesus then shows the disciples his wounds, not "the father" as Philip had requested (14:8–9). Is it perhaps possible to see God only by looking upon Jesus' wounds?

MARGARET P. AYMER

WHAT IS THE HOLY SPIRIT SAYING TO YOU THIS WEEK?

_____

_____

_____

_____

_____

A SPIRITUAL PRACTICE FOR THIS WEEK

Make feasting your spiritual discipline as Easter season begins. Make this week festive and find ways to celebrate resurrection: plan a favorite meal, buy flowers, treat yourself to a special something, wear colorful clothes, schedule a massage, or whatever else creates a sense of new life or delight.

First Reading

Acts 2:14a, 22–32

"You that are Israelites, listen to what I have to say: Jesus of Nazareth, a man attested to you by God with deeds of power, wonders, and signs that God did through him among you, as you yourselves know. . . . This Jesus God raised up, and of that all of us are witnesses." (vv. 22, 32)

REFLECTION

If Pentecost cannot be connected to Jesus' resurrection, to say we have missed the point might very well be the biggest understatement of the last two millennia. . . . Here is where Peter's sermon is an ecclesial necessity and most vital. Peter here reminds us that the pouring out of the Spirit was never and could never be a onetime event. It is this constancy of the Spirit as God's presence and power at work to which we give witness. We give witness to this truth whenever and wherever we see the world's powers being toppled by God's power.

KAROLINE M. LEWIS

RESPONSE

Pentecost is still weeks away, but the Spirit is always at work. How have you seen the pouring out of the Holy Spirit, alive and ongoing, happening in your life or your congregation? How have you felt called to give witness and a nudge to the toppling of the world's powers in your community?

PRAYER

Holy Spirit, after the resurrection, you formed a church of witnesses and seekers through your constancy and power; continue to work among us, that we may also bear witness and push against the unjust powers in this world. Amen.

Canticle

Psalm 16

Protect me, O God, for in you I take refuge.
I say to the LORD, "You are my Lord;
    I have no good apart from you." (vv. 1–2)

REFLECTION

This plea for refuge and protection, with which the psalm begins, can
be seen as a response to Peter's accusation in Acts 2:23 that "this man
[Jesus], you crucified and killed by the hands of those outside the law."
The Good Friday memories of violence are here used to evoke repentance
and a new beginning. Peter invites the crowd to join him in his own
movement from the denials of Good Friday to hope in the resurrection.
God will protect those who cry out to God even, and especially, when
they cry out in repentance for the evil that they have done.

RHODORA E. BEATON

RESPONSE

This Easter season, how are you feeling invited to make a new beginning
or to repentance? How are you longing for refuge or protection through
an upcoming change, risk, or challenge? How do you find yourself
longing to cry out to God this week?

PRAYER

O God, in you I take refuge; show me the path of life so that in your
presence I might find and share the fullness of your joy. Amen.

Second Reading

1 Peter 1:3–9

In this you rejoice, even if now for a little while you have had to suffer various trials. . . . Although you have not seen him, you love him; and even though you do not see him now, you believe in him and rejoice with an indescribable and glorious joy. (vv. 6, 8)

REFLECTION

Their Christian faith had alienated them from their neighbors, giving rise to a sense of cultural ostracism at best and more severe persecution at worst. That predicament bears striking similarity to the situation in which many Christian communities find themselves today, yielding a clear connection between this text and the contemporary church. Like them we ask, What does it mean to live as Easter people? What does it mean to profess Christian faith decades, even centuries removed from the resurrection? What does it mean to continue to "believe in [Christ]" . . . when we might be mocked or ignored for our efforts?

BEVERLY ZINK-SAWYER

RESPONSE

What are some ways you feel alienated from the wider culture because of your Christian faith or church affiliation? What does it mean to you to be a Christian in modern society? How do you hear Peter speaking to you and your congregation today, in this letter from two millennia ago?

PRAYER

Gracious God, even if I must suffer various trials for my faith for a little while, I rejoice because although I have not seen you, I love you. Amen.

Gospel

John 20:19–31

Then he said to Thomas, "Put your finger here and see my hands. Reach out your hand and put it in my side. Do not doubt but believe." Thomas answered him, "My Lord and my God!" (vv. 27–28)

REFLECTION

The Protestant Reformation was founded on the belief that all we need is grace, *sola gratia*. What if many Protestants have turned faith into a "work"? What if too many Protestants are all too quick to condemn those who find some aspect of our Christian faith hard to believe? Doubt is not a sin. Yes, Jesus praises those who are able to believe without benefit of incontrovertible evidence, but he does not reject Thomas because of his doubt. Instead he embraces Thomas, takes him by the hand, and provides Thomas with all the evidence he needs to come to faith. *This* is grace in action.

RUBÉN ROSARIO RODRÍGUEZ

RESPONSE

Have you ever found yourself thinking of doubt as a weakness, or even a sin? What are some doubts about God, Jesus, or religion you are carrying right now? What would it be like to imagine yourself as Thomas, receiving Jesus' embrace—and even evidence and proofs—nonetheless?

PRAYER

My Lord and my God, you met Thomas with acceptance and grace; thank you for receiving both my doubts and my prayers with love. Amen.

Weekend Reflections

> Our wounds are hurting us; where is the balm?
> Lord Jesus, by Thy Scars, we claim Thy grace.
> If, when the doors are shut, Thou drawest near,
> Only reveal those hands, that side of Thine;
> We know today what wounds are, have no fear,
> Show us Thy Scars, we know the countersign.
> The other gods were strong; but Thou wast weak;
> They rode, but Thou didst stumble to a throne;
> But to our wounds only God's wounds can speak,
> And not a god has wounds, but Thou alone.
>
> EDWARD SHILLITO (1872–1948), "JESUS OF THE SCARS"

MAKING THE CONNECTIONS

Choose one or two questions for reflection:

1. What connections have you noticed between this week's texts and other passages in Scripture?

2. What connections have you made between this week's texts and the world beyond Scripture?

3. Does either of this week's two commentary themes speak especially to your life or the life of the world around you right now?

4. What is God saying to your congregation in particular through this week's readings and commentaries?

_____

_____

_____

_____

_____

_____

Sabbath Day

SCRIPTURE OF ASSURANCE

You hem me in, behind and before,
and lay your hand upon me.
Such knowledge is too wonderful for me;
it is so high that I cannot attain it. (Psalm 139:5–6)

WEEKLY EXAMEN

- Take a quiet moment, seek out God's presence, and pray for the guidance of the Spirit.

- Consider the past week; recall specific moments and feelings that stand out to you.

- Choose one moment or feeling for deeper examination, thanksgiving, or repentance.

- Let go, breathe deeply, and invite Christ's love to surround and fill you in preparation for the week ahead.

- End with the Lord's Prayer.

The Week Leading Up to the
Third Sunday of Easter

Acts 2:14a, 36–41

But Peter, standing with the eleven, raised his voice and addressed them, . . .
"Therefore let the entire house of Israel know with certainty that God has
made him both Lord and Messiah, this Jesus whom you crucified."
Now when they heard this, they were cut to the heart and said to Peter and
to the other apostles, "Brothers, what should we do?" (vv. 14, 36–37)

Psalm 116:1–4, 12–19

What shall I return to the Lord
for all his bounty to me?
I will lift up the cup of salvation
and call on the name of the Lord. (vv. 12–13)

1 Peter 1:17–23

Through him you have come to trust in God, who raised him from the dead
and gave him glory, so that your faith and hope are set on God. (v. 21)

Luke 24:13–35

Then their eyes were opened, and they recognized him; and he vanished from
their sight. They said to each other, "Were not our hearts burning within us
while he was talking to us on the road, while he was opening the scriptures
to us?" (vv. 31–32)

LECTIO DIVINA

Underline a word or phrase that especially grabs your attention. Pray
from that word or phrase and ask God to help you connect to its
particular invitation for you this week.

Themes from This Week's Writers

THEME 1: *Conversion and New Life in Christ*

Acts 2:14a, 36–41

Peter's injunctions to his audience are not the orders of a dictator, but rather appeals made in the name of a loving God to receive a new life that is offered freely. They should thus be taken in the same vein as those other imperatives, "Take, eat," and "Drink from it, all of you."

IAN A. MCFARLAND

Acts 2:14a, 36–41

"What should we do?" (v. 37) is exactly the question we should ask, not once or twice over the course of our Christian life, but every single day. . . . What should we do? Perhaps put on a new set of glasses so as to see the world in all its resurrected splendor.

KAROLINE M. LEWIS

1 Peter 1:17–23

The metaphor of "seed" serves as a reminder that . . . what we *are* and *do* has lasting consequences. The "genuine mutual love" (v. 22) we show for one another and for all of God's creation, along with other dimensions of our holy living, enable the church to plant "seed" that will take root and spread.

BEVERLY ZINK-SAWYER

THEME 2: *Knowledge of God Is by the Grace of God*

Psalm 116:1–4, 12–19

In Peter's preaching, it is not the human, but "the Lord our God" who calls (Acts 2:40) and promises, inviting sinners to seek baptism and salvation. The human beings listen to God's voice and . . . begin a new way of life with God that day. They, and we, can now express the words of the psalmist with increasing confidence: "I love the LORD, because he has heard my voice and my supplications."

RHODORA E. BEATON

Luke 24:13–35

The Emmaus disciples' eyes were "seized" (NRSV "kept from recognizing," Gk. *krateō*), suggesting perhaps a divine action that is reversed when their eyes are later opened during the breaking of the bread (24:16, 31).

MARGARET P. AYMER

Luke 24:13–35

Paradoxically, it takes the risen Jesus to explain this hidden message contained in the sacred Scriptures of Israel. Furthermore, it is the risen Jesus who then teaches the church how to read and understand the whole of Scripture through the lens of his earthly life and ministry.

RUBÉN ROSARIO RODRÍGUEZ

WHAT IS THE HOLY SPIRIT SAYING TO YOU THIS WEEK?

_____

_____

_____

_____

_____

A SPIRITUAL PRACTICE FOR THIS WEEK

Jesus was often made known to his disciples over a meal. This week, for as many of your meals as possible, light a candle, begin with grace or a silent pause, or read one or two verses from Luke 24:13–35. When eating with others, look for Jesus in the faces of your dining companions.

First Reading

Acts 2:14a, 36–41

Peter said to them, "Repent, and be baptized every one of you in the name of Jesus Christ so that your sins may be forgiven; and you will receive the gift of the Holy Spirit. For the promise is for you, for your children, and for all who are far away, everyone whom the Lord our God calls to him." (vv. 38–39)

REFLECTION

What becomes of those who ignore or actively reject the good news? . . . There is at least the suggestion that for all Peter's efforts, not everyone who was present went on to be baptized that day. . . . Even if some that day ignored the message, the promise remains for them and their children, as well as "for all who are far away." If Peter is to be taken at his word here, "everyone whom the Lord our God calls to him" includes simply *everyone:* the promise is for all, without exception.

IAN A. MCFARLAND

RESPONSE

Is there someone you love who ignores or has rejected the good news? How has that felt? What is it like to imagine that God's "promise remains for them and their children"? That God always welcomes? That God is always calling us in love, even in ways we might not see?

PRAYER

Loving God, your promise is for all people in all places and all generations; send your Holy Spirit to those who may be waiting for your nudge, so they too might receive your gift of faith. Amen.

Canticle

Psalm 116:1–4, 12–19

I love the LORD, because he has heard
  my voice and my supplications.
Because he inclined his ear to me,
  therefore I will call on him as long as I live. (vv. 1–2)

REFLECTION

Psalm 116's unusual opening sets the stage for the themes of loving
dialogue that develop in the pairing of psalm and first reading. As
J. Clinton McCann points out, the Psalms in general rarely mention
humans who explicitly express love for God.[1] Psalm 116 is the
exception, beginning with a proclamation of love. The speaker explains
this love with reference to the claim that God "has heard my voice and
my supplications" (Ps. 116:1). The psalmist loves because he or she
has been heard. This is the invitation to a lifelong, loving relationship:
"I will call on [God] as long as I live" (v. 2).

RHODORA E. BEATON

RESPONSE

What would it be like to offer the prayer "I love you" to God in your
own prayer life this week? How does this feel? Then, reflect on feeling
heard by God. Is there more you want to say this week, in particular?
Write out your "supplications" and offer them to God.

PRAYER

Holy God, I love you; what can I give you in return for all the bounty
you have given to me? I will call on you as long as I live. Amen.

---

1. J. Clinton McCann, "Psalms," in *The New Interpreter's Bible* (Nashville: Abingdon, 1996), 6:1148.

Second Reading

1 Peter 1:17–23

Now that you have purified your souls by your obedience to the truth so that you have genuine mutual love, love one another deeply from the heart. You have been born anew, not of perishable but of imperishable seed, through the living and enduring word of God. (vv. 22–23)

REFLECTION

Both Acts 2:14a, 36–41 and Luke 24:13–35 describe changes to the "heart" that come with recognizing one's relationship to the death and resurrection of Jesus Christ. Those listening to Peter are "cut to the heart" when they realize they have crucified the Messiah (Acts 2:37); the disciples feel their "hearts burning within [them]" when supping with the risen Lord (Luke 24:32). Like our passage in 1 Peter, these texts communicate that a change takes place at the core of those who are "born anew" (1 Pet. 1:23) as they recognize their relationship to Jesus Christ.

CYNTHIA L. RIGBY

RESPONSE

Draw a picture of your own heart. What does it carry? How is it hurting? How does it love? Does it ever burn within you? How would you like the risen Christ to change or heal it? Draw or write some reflections on these questions.

PRAYER

Loving Christ, descend upon my heart; teach me to love deeply, to feel cut to the heart by my part in your death and any injustice, to feel my heart burning within me, born anew and filled with hope. Amen.

Gospel

Luke 24:13–35

But they urged him strongly, saying, "Stay with us, because it is almost evening and the day is now nearly over." So he went in to stay with them. When he was at the table with them, he took bread, blessed and broke it, and gave it to them. Then their eyes were opened, and they recognized him; and he vanished from their sight. (vv. 29–31)

REFLECTION

Calvin describes the communion as "a spiritual mystery . . ." yet in the bread and the wine "we may say that Jesus Christ is there offered to us that we may possess Him."[1]

. . . [This] passage recalls Jesus feeding the five thousand as well as the Last Supper with his disciples, so the comparison to the Lord's Supper is easily and naturally made. In fact, the pacing of the scene, in which there is act of table fellowship (v. 30) that leads to an act of revelation (v. 31) echoes the earliest liturgical form of the communion recorded in 1 Corinthians 11:23–26.

RUBÉN ROSARIO RODRÍGUEZ

RESPONSE

When you receive communion, how would you describe your experience of Jesus, revealed and offered to you? What details of the Emmaus story echo or deepen the meaning of the Lord's Supper for you most?

PRAYER

Jesus, friend, you reveal yourself to me and all your people in the eating of broken bread that is shared around a table; open my eyes so I may recognize and receive you with all my heart. Amen.

---

1. John Calvin, "A Short Treatise on the Lord's Supper," in *John Calvin: Writings on Pastoral Piety*, ed. and with trans. by Elsie Anne McKee (New York: Paulist, 2001), 106–8.

Weekend Reflections

We cannot love God unless we love each other, and to love we must know each other. We know Him in the breaking of bread, and we know each other in the breaking of bread, and we are not alone anymore. Heaven is a banquet and life is a banquet, too, even with a crust, where there is companionship.

DOROTHY DAY (1897–1980), *THE LONG LONELINESS: THE AUTOBIOGRAPHY OF THE LEGENDARY CATHOLIC SOCIAL ACTIVIST*

MAKING THE CONNECTIONS

Choose one or two questions for reflection:

1. What connections have you noticed between this week's texts and other passages in Scripture?

2. What connections have you made between this week's texts and the world beyond Scripture?

3. Does either of this week's two commentary themes speak especially to your life or the life of the world around you right now?

4. What is God saying to your congregation in particular through this week's readings and commentaries?

_____

_____

_____

_____

_____

_____

Sabbath Day

SCRIPTURE OF ASSURANCE

> I will thank you forever,
> because of what you have done.
> In the presence of the faithful
> I will proclaim your name, for it is good. (Psalm 52:9)

WEEKLY EXAMEN

- Take a quiet moment, seek out God's presence, and pray for the guidance of the Spirit.

- Consider the past week; recall specific moments and feelings that stand out to you.

- Choose one moment or feeling for deeper examination, thanksgiving, or repentance.

- Let go, breathe deeply, and invite Christ's love to surround and fill you in preparation for the week ahead.

- End with the Lord's Prayer.

The Week Leading Up to the
Fourth Sunday of Easter

Acts 2:42–47

Awe came upon everyone, because many wonders and signs were being done by the apostles. All who believed were together and had all things in common; they would sell their possessions and goods and distribute the proceeds to all, as any had need. (vv. 43–45)

Psalm 23

Surely goodness and mercy shall follow me
    all the days of my life,
and I shall dwell in the house of the LORD
    my whole life long. (v. 6)

1 Peter 2:19–25

He himself bore our sins in his body on the cross, so that, free from sins, we might live for righteousness; by his wounds you have been healed. For you were going astray like sheep, but now you have returned to the shepherd and guardian of your souls. (vv. 24–25)

John 10:1–10

The one who enters by the gate is the shepherd of the sheep. The gatekeeper opens the gate for him, and the sheep hear his voice. He calls his own sheep by name and leads them out. (vv. 2–3)

LECTIO DIVINA

Underline a word or phrase that especially grabs your attention. Pray from that word or phrase and ask God to help you connect to its particular invitation for you this week.

Themes from This Week's Writers

THEME 1: *Christian Life in Community*

Acts 2:42–47

Luke's description of the serene existence of the first community, dwelling at peace with one another and those about them, parallels the psalmist's calm assurance that God will provide what we need. . . .

By contrast, the other two lessons are more suggestive of the tensions that will accompany the growth of the church.

IAN A. MCFARLAND

Acts 2:42–47

On our own, left to our own devices, achieving such ideals is impossible. However, with the power of the Holy Spirit, we are at the very least called to lean into this kind of community. Moreover, the Spirit might just teach us how to expect it.

KAROLINE M. LEWIS

Psalm 23

No one will want for anything, because it is clear that the people "had all things in common" and distributed "to all, as any had need" (Acts 2:44–45). Those in the Acts community are depicted as being as happy as the metaphorical sheep in Psalm 23.

RHODORA E. BEATON

THEME 2: *Jesus Is the Good Shepherd*

1 Peter 2:19–25

The theme of sheep and shepherds appears at the end of the passage and reappears in the final chapter . . . with Jesus, the "chief shepherd" (5:4). The reader is not yet any kind of assistant shepherd, but a sheep who has "gone astray" (1 Pet. 2:25; also Isa. 53:6) and been found by Jesus, the "guardian" (1 Pet. 2:25).

CYNTHIA L. RIGBY

1 Peter 2:19–25

This text from 1 Peter begins with the acknowledgment of painful suffering but ends with the pastoral depiction of a guardian shepherd. For us, that juxtaposition is a powerful reminder that no matter what we experience as we hold fast to our faith in Jesus Christ and risk our lives for what is right, we are always brought back into the fold and guarded by the grace of the Good Shepherd.

BEVERLY ZINK-SAWYER

John 10:1–10

The text also makes clear that while the church must employ capable women and men to shepherd God's "flock," ultimately, there is only one shepherd: Jesus Christ, our Lord and Savior . . . , and the task of God's appointed shepherds here on earth is to lead the flock to its one true Lord, in whom we find abundant life (v. 10).

RUBÉN ROSARIO RODRÍGUEZ

WHAT IS THE HOLY SPIRIT SAYING TO YOU THIS WEEK?

_____

_____

_____

_____

_____

A SPIRITUAL PRACTICE FOR THIS WEEK

Spread some praise, goodwill, and abundant life this week. Each day, give at least one person a compliment or appreciation, whether a family member, friend, coworker, or stranger. Be specific, simple, and sincere; try not to fib or exaggerate. This can also be a practice of gratitude.

First Reading

Acts 2:42–47

Day by day, as they spent much time together in the temple, they broke bread at home and ate their food with glad and generous hearts, praising God and having the goodwill of all the people. And day by day the Lord added to their number those who were being saved. (vv. 46–47)

REFLECTION

Resurrection is not simply a personal claim that secures your after-death reality. Resurrection brings you into a community that follows Jesus in order to live as Easter people. We need the community so as not to forget who we truly are. It is too easy these days to individualize our faith confessions, as if they did not make a difference for how we move about in the world and how we view the other. Resurrection, fundamentally, is a communal affair, a promise that directs a way of living now and determines a community in our future.

KAROLINE M. LEWIS

RESPONSE

Is your church congregation your primary "Easter people" community? In what ways does being part of a community, at your church or elsewhere, inform your faith journey? What does it mean in your life that "Resurrection, fundamentally, is a communal affair"?

PRAYER

Christ of all people, gather me in your resurrection into a sense of community, so that I may remember who I am, in you. Amen.

Canticle

Psalm 23

You prepare a table before me
   in the presence of my enemies;
you anoint my head with oil;
   my cup overflows. (v. 5)

REFLECTION

What does it mean for God to "restore my soul"? . . .

The reading from the Acts of the Apostles can help to answer this
question. . . . Rather than having "a table [set] before" them (Ps. 23:5),
"they broke bread at home" (Acts 22:46). Instead of an overflowing
cup (Ps. 23:5), they eat "with glad and generous hearts" (Acts 22:46).
Their companionship (bread sharing) protects, comforts, nourishes,
and restores them. . . . Community members place their confidence in
God's "goodness and mercy" (Ps. 23:6), which have called together a
community of generous people who care about one another.

RHODORA E. BEATON

RESPONSE

What does "restore my soul" mean for you? How has God restored you,
in the past or recently, through the hearts and hands of a community?
How have you been part of a community that restored others,
particularly those neglected or rejected by their community at large?

PRAYER

Shepherding God, open my soul to be restored in the love and caring
of community, trusting in the goodness and healing of companionship
with other people. Amen.

Second Reading

1 Peter 2:19–25

For it is a credit to you if, being aware of God, you endure pain while suffering unjustly. If you endure when you are beaten for doing wrong, what credit is that? But if you endure when you do right and suffer for it, you have God's approval. (vv. 19–20)

REFLECTION

Peter here addresses . . . the reality of suffering for those who claim Christian faith. Peter makes clear not only *why* we must accept the reality of suffering as part of our Christian identity ("because Christ also suffered" for us, 1 Pet. 2:21), but also *how* we must suffer (without returning abuse or threat, entrusting ourselves instead "to the one who judges justly," v. 23). Christian suffering in light of Christ's suffering on our behalf then becomes both a necessary part of the holy living to which we are called in the previous chapter and a witness to those who would persecute us.

BEVERLY ZINK-SAWYER

RESPONSE

What was a time in your life that you endured some kind of suffering because of your faith, practice, or identity? How is suffering a part of "holy living" or a life in Christ for you, now? Have you ever thought of suffering as a form of witness to those who would persecute you?

PRAYER

Christ of suffering, be with me in my pain and struggle, that I may not be overwhelmed but find you by my side, and a sense of witness, hope, and new life in my suffering. Amen.

Gospel

John 10:1–10

"I am the gate. Whoever enters by me will be saved, and will come in and go out and find pasture. The thief comes only to steal and kill and destroy. I came that they may have life, and have it abundantly." (vv. 9–10)

REFLECTION

The proverb Jesus tells first describes the difference between a thief and a shepherd. . . . Verses 3–5 describe the familiarity between the shepherd and sheep: they know his voice, and the shepherd knows their names. A second distinction then emerges between the shepherd and a stranger whose voice the sheep do not know and whom they will not follow (v. 5). The stranger may not be a bandit, but neither is the stranger the shepherd. Thus, this proverb explains how to be a good shepherd: enter correctly, know the doorkeeper, and get to know each sheep by name.

MARGARET P. AYMER

RESPONSE

If Jesus is the gate, are human beings the shepherds, sheep, and thieves? Who is acting as a shepherd in your life, right now? Who or what might be acting like a thief? How are you called to act more as a shepherd, according to the descriptions of the Gospel of John and Aymer, here?

PRAYER

Jesus, holy gate, you came that we might have life; make me your shepherd that I will know your voice and guide others—and also myself—to your abundant pastures. Amen.

Weekend Reflections

FURTHER CONNECTION

Jesus says he is the gate, the gate of the sheepfold, of the corral (John 10:9–16). So why are we often tempted to be the gate ourselves? Besides the true gate—which is Christ—we also set ourselves up as a gate. Everyone's got to go through our gate, ours: our ideologies, our definitions, our ways of doing things. This won't do! Christ is enough. One gate is enough—Christ. . . .

. . . It is a terrible temptation to shut the shepherd up inside our sheepfold, behind our own gate.

DOM HELDER CAMARA (1909–99), *THROUGH THE GOSPELS WITH DOM HELDER CAMARA*

MAKING THE CONNECTIONS

Choose one or two questions for reflection:

1. What connections have you noticed between this week's texts and other passages in Scripture?

2. What connections have you made between this week's texts and the world beyond Scripture?

3. Does either of this week's two commentary themes speak especially to your life or the life of the world around you right now?

4. What is God saying to your congregation in particular through this week's readings and commentaries?

_____

_____

_____

_____

_____

_____

Sabbath Day

SCRIPTURE OF ASSURANCE

So let us not grow weary in doing what is right, for we will reap at harvest time, if we do not give up. So then, whenever we have an opportunity, let us work for the good of all, and especially for those of the family of faith. (Galatians 6:9–10)

WEEKLY EXAMEN

- Take a quiet moment, seek out God's presence, and pray for the guidance of the Spirit.

- Consider the past week; recall specific moments and feelings that stand out to you.

- Choose one moment or feeling for deeper examination, thanksgiving, or repentance.

- Let go, breathe deeply, and invite Christ's love to surround and fill you in preparation for the week ahead.

- End with the Lord's Prayer.

The Week Leading Up to the
Fifth Sunday of Easter

Acts 7:55–60

"Look," [Stephen] said, "I see the heavens opened and the Son of Man standing at the right hand of God!" But they covered their ears, and with a loud shout all rushed together against him. (vv. 56–57)

Psalm 31:1–5, 15–16

You are indeed my rock and my fortress;
for your name's sake lead me and guide me,
take me out of the net that is hidden for me,
for you are my refuge. (vv. 3–4)

1 Peter 2:2–10

Come to him, a living stone, though rejected by mortals yet chosen and precious in God's sight, and like living stones, let yourselves be built into a spiritual house, to be a holy priesthood, to offer spiritual sacrifices acceptable to God through Jesus Christ. (vv. 4–5)

John 14:1–14

"Do not let your hearts be troubled. Believe in God, believe also in me. In my Father's house there are many dwelling places. If it were not so, would I have told you that I go to prepare a place for you?" (vv. 1–2)

LECTIO DIVINA

Underline a word or phrase that especially grabs your attention. Pray from that word or phrase and ask God to help you connect to its particular invitation for you this week.

Themes from This Week's Writers

THEME 1: *Confronting the Powers of Death and Sin*

Acts 7:55–60

The resurrection of Jesus is no "happily ever after." . . . His "overcoming" of death entails continual confrontation by his followers against death-dealing actions, dispositions, behavior patterns, and systemic structures from traditions, religious and secular alike, that repudiate the prospect and reject the challenge of resurrection life.

DAVID J. SCHLAFER

Acts 7:55–60

Jesus stands as one in agreement with Stephen and the audacity with which he speaks. . . . Stephen stands at the edge of life because he has confronted the local leaders about their opposition to God's will and purpose. His bravery is a model for the church to do likewise.

BRIDGETT A. GREEN

John 14:1–14

Jesus . . . asks us to focus on what is next. A sermon might do the same, pointing beyond Jesus' death and resurrection. It might direct disciples to the future and . . . to the resurrection power Jesus lets loose in this world, shattering the power of death in its many forms.

LINDSAY P. ARMSTRONG

THEME 2: *Trust in God*

Psalm 31:1–5, 15–16

The overwhelming emphasis in Acts is on trust in God and generosity of spirit. Like the psalmist, Stephen can say, "My times are in your hand" (Ps. 31:15), even as he realizes that his deliverance from "the hand of my enemies and persecutors" (v. 15) will be an eschatological one.

RHODORA E. BEATON

1 Peter 2:2–10

Like many other NT texts, [1 Peter] must help its recipients understand persecution. It must convince them that it is not an indication that they have displeased God and not an indication that they have chosen the wrong god.

JERRY L. SUMNEY

John 14:1–14

Jesus invites us to trust in him in spite of troubling times. . . . In the midst of uncertainty, he asks the disciples to follow him. Even as Jesus is announcing his death, he insists that he is the way, the truth, and the life, and they can continue to trust in him.

PHILIP WINGEIER-RAYO

WHAT IS THE HOLY SPIRIT SAYING TO YOU THIS WEEK?

_____

_____

_____

_____

_____

A SPIRITUAL PRACTICE FOR THIS WEEK

Scan the news and find a story about a person who has been killed, like Stephen, for their beliefs. Write out what happened, briefly, in your own words, or draw a picture. Pray for this person and their family this week. How does this person's story open your mind differently to the Acts reading?

First Reading

Acts 7:55–60

Then they dragged him out of the city and began to stone him; and the witnesses laid their coats at the feet of a young man named Saul. While they were stoning Stephen, he prayed, "Lord Jesus, receive my spirit." (vv. 58–59)

REFLECTION

Stephen's execution was not a consequence of his care for widows (Acts 6:1–6) or even his miraculous works (6:8). He died because he told a hard truth to the council about their disregard of God's prophetic word through the ages. In the wait for the eschaton, the Christian church is called to be like Stephen and tell hard truths to society's leaders, especially other Christian leaders, who profess to care for the welfare of others and to follow God, while their rhetoric and actions remain antithetical to God's prophetic word and the examples of Jesus.

BRIDGETT A. GREEN

RESPONSE

Is there a hard truth you feel your congregation is being called to tell at this time? Who would this message be for, and how would it best be given? What risks are involved? How could telling a hard truth be, in fact, a way of caring for others?

PRAYER

Lord Jesus, give me and all your church courage to tell the hard truth of your prophetic word to powers and principalities, having faith that you are with us through risk and danger. Amen.

Canticle

Psalm 31:1–5, 15–16

My times are in your hand;
> deliver me from the hand of my enemies and persecutors.
Let your face shine upon your servant;
> save me in your steadfast love. (vv. 15–16)

REFLECTION

In the midst of the Easter season, Psalm 31 and the martyrdom of
Stephen serve as reminders that the paschal mystery continues. Violence
and death persist in the world. Like Stephen, some members of the
assembly may have wondered how a situation could go from "just
talking" to a violent argument. Like the psalmist, some may fear "the net
that is hidden for me" (Ps. 31:4) or the shame that lingers in a long-kept
secret. . . . The good news is that the hand of God is indeed a refuge,
even though chaos remains present.

RHODORA E. BEATON

RESPONSE

The "paschal mystery" is the interdependence of Christ's death and
resurrection. How would you describe the interdependence between
death and new life in your own journey? What fears do you carry, now,
about persecutors or lurking dangers? How could this resurrection
season or the "hand of God" feel like a refuge for you?

PRAYER

God of resurrection, my times are in your hand; let your face shine upon
me despite my fears and my enemies, and save me with your steadfast
love. Amen.

Second Reading

1 Peter 2:2–10

But you are a chosen race, a royal priesthood, a holy nation, God's own people, in order that you may proclaim the mighty acts of him who called you out of darkness into his marvelous light.

> Once you were not a people,
> but now you are God's people (vv. 9–10a)

REFLECTION

Despite the inclination of Western Christians to view themselves as rejected or ostracized, we rarely face situations today in which our own congregation is our exclusive source of community and positive participation in the world.

Certainly, some Christian communities, especially in other parts of the world, find themselves in situations like those addressed by 1 Peter: scorned and in precarious social and political positions. However, many of us live with a vastly different experience, in which our status in our political environments is secure and our identification with Jesus and Christianity more broadly empowers rather than endangers our status.

BRIAN S. POWERS

RESPONSE

How do you feel rejected or ostracized as a Christian in your context? How do you feel part of the majority? How does your faith identity influence your social status? How do you hear 1 Peter speaking to you and your congregation at this time?

PRAYER

Jesus of the outsider, you call me to be chosen, but also to be rejected, to be built into a house of love and welcome, but also of spiritual sacrifices, for your love's sake. Amen.

Gospel

John 14:1–14

Jesus said to him, "I am the way, and the truth, and the life. No one comes to the Father except through me. If you know me, you will know my Father also. From now on you do know him and have seen him." (vv. 6–7)

REFLECTION

It has been made to sound as if Jesus suddenly stopped his private conversation with friends and issued a worldwide proclamation to all people, demanding explicit, universal, unequivocal belief in him. . . .

If Jesus had aimed for his disciples to embody a narrow exclusivity, he might have said, "My Father's house has just a few reserved rooms, so get your act together and command the world to do the same." Instead, in his last hours, Jesus teaches his disciples to live as he lived, revealing the stunning abundance and welcome of God.

LINDSAY P. ARMSTRONG

RESPONSE

How do you understand Jesus' words in John 14? What is Jesus inviting his disciples to know and do? What is Jesus inviting you to know and do? What does it mean, do you think, that Jesus says, "I am the way," rather than, "This is the way"?

PRAYER

Risen Jesus, I want to know you and your Father, and to see you; I believe that you are the way, and that you have prepared a place for me and for all people. Amen.

Weekend Reflections

FURTHER CONNECTION

Imagine that this Lord Himself is at your side and see how lovingly and how humbly He is teaching you—and, believe me, you should stay with so good a Friend for as long as you can before you leave Him. If you become accustomed to having Him at your side, and if He sees that you love Him to be there and are always trying to please Him, you will never be able to send Him away, nor will He ever fail you. He will help you in all your trials and you will have Him everywhere. Do you think it is a small thing to have such a Friend as that beside you?

TERESA OF ÁVILA (1515–82), *THE WAY OF PERFECTION*

MAKING THE CONNECTIONS

Choose one or two questions for reflection:

1. What connections have you noticed between this week's texts and other passages in Scripture?

2. What connections have you made between this week's texts and the world beyond Scripture?

3. Does either of this week's two commentary themes speak especially to your life or the life of the world around you right now?

4. What is God saying to your congregation in particular through this week's readings and commentaries?

_____

_____

_____

_____

_____

_____

Sabbath Day

SCRIPTURE OF ASSURANCE

Therefore we ourselves boast of you among the churches of God for your steadfastness and faith during all your persecutions and the afflictions that you are enduring. (2 Thessalonians 1:4)

WEEKLY EXAMEN

- Take a quiet moment, seek out God's presence, and pray for the guidance of the Spirit.

- Consider the past week; recall specific moments and feelings that stand out to you.

- Choose one moment or feeling for deeper examination, thanksgiving, or repentance.

- Let go, breathe deeply, and invite Christ's love to surround and fill you in preparation for the week ahead.

- End with the Lord's Prayer.

The Week Leading Up to the
Sixth Sunday of Easter

Acts 17:22–31

Then Paul stood in front of the Areopagus and said, "Athenians, I see how extremely religious you are in every way. For as I went through the city and looked carefully at the objects of your worship, I found among them an altar with the inscription, 'To an unknown god.' What therefore you worship as unknown, this I proclaim to you." (vv. 22–23)

Psalm 66:8–20

Come and hear, all you who fear God,
and I will tell what he has done for me. (v. 16)

1 Peter 3:13–22

Always be ready to make your defense to anyone who demands from you an accounting for the hope that is in you; yet do it with gentleness and reverence. Keep your conscience clear, so that, when you are maligned, those who abuse you for your good conduct in Christ may be put to shame. (vv. 15b–16)

John 14:15–21

"They who have my commandments and keep them are those who love me; and those who love me will be loved by my Father, and I will love them and reveal myself to them." (v. 21)

LECTIO DIVINA

Underline a word or phrase that especially grabs your attention. Pray from that word or phrase and ask God to help you connect to its particular invitation for you this week.

Themes from This Week's Writers

THEME 1: *A Call to Gentle and Generous Evangelism*

Psalm 66:8–20

As we sing the psalm, we are joining with Paul, who is preaching to the polytheists and intellectuals of Athens. "Come and hear," we call out, appealing as did Paul especially to "God-fearers," persons outside of the faith community who are nevertheless seeking God.

GAIL RAMSHAW

Acts 17:22–31

God's plan is expansive and does not rely on our ability to articulate it fully. Our constant searching and groping for divine revelation is evidence of God's commitment to draw near to us (v. 27).

. . . Paul's speech reassures believers that God's power transcends human power and human-made edifices.

BRIDGETT A. GREEN

Acts 17:22–31

Paul is "deeply distressed" to see that the city is full of idols. Yet, rather than retreating from the scene or undertaking a frontal attack, he engages what he finds, respectfully and dialogically. . . . Paul tries to assist his listeners to see both *through* and *beyond* those idols.

DAVID J. SCHLAFER

THEME 2: *Serving Others as Christ Serves Us*

1 Peter 3:13–22

This text offers us . . . a call for the church to be a community that models putting the good of others ahead of one's own good. This is a call particularly to those among us who hold significant status: we must be sure to privilege the needs of those of lesser status, just as Christ gave up status by coming to earth and dying on the cross for us.

JERRY L. SUMNEY

1 Peter 3:13–22

The passage roots itself in the idea that we should "not fear what they fear" (v. 14). . . . the fear of looking foolish, of not accumulating wealth, of being scorned. . . . Our behavior as committed Christians must be different, full of the grace and patience reflected in God's actions in Christ.

BRIAN S. POWERS

John 14:15–21

Such love is more than emotion or sentiment. As Jesus was sent by the Father, so we are sent. . . . We need to be loved as much as we need to share love. What it means to be people of God is to be people who, thanks to the love of God we know in Jesus, actively share and receive love.

LINDSAY P. ARMSTRONG

WHAT IS THE HOLY SPIRIT SAYING TO YOU THIS WEEK?

_____

_____

_____

_____

_____

A SPIRITUAL PRACTICE FOR THIS WEEK

Use Jesus' words as your focus for prayer this week: "Because I live, you also will live." Write out these words on sticky notes and place where you will see them, use as a meditation mantra, journal on them each day, or write out and illuminate the words as a drawing prayer. Where does the Spirit lead you?

First Reading

Acts 17:22–31

The God who made the world and everything in it, he who is Lord of heaven and earth, does not live in shrines made by human hands, nor is he served by human hands, as though he needed anything, since he himself gives to all mortals life and breath and all things. (vv. 24–25)

REFLECTION

Going into his preaching encounter with the Athenians, Paul is "deeply distressed" to see that the city is full of idols. Yet, rather than retreating from the scene or undertaking a frontal attack, he engages what he finds, respectfully and dialogically. . . . Paul tries to assist his listeners to see both *through* and *beyond* those idols. . . . What contemporary idols do preachers and parishioners encounter in contemporary cultural settings? How can Easter preaching acts be analogously framed? The prospects are as provocative and wide as the preacher's perception and imagination.

DAVID J. SCHLAFER

RESPONSE

What are some contemporary idols you have noticed people in your community may be attached to? What are some idols in your own life, would you say? How would you invite yourself to see "both through and beyond" them, to the living God of love?

PRAYER

O God, you do not live in places made by human hands; help me to see through the idols of my own creation that I may worship only you, who made the world and everything in it. Amen.

Canticle

Psalm 66:8–20

Bless our God, O peoples,
    let the sound of his praise be heard,
who has kept us among the living,
    and has not let our feet slip. (vv. 8–9)

REFLECTION

Some verses of this psalm are cast in the plural, as if all the members
of Israel are at praise, and some verses are cast in the singular, as if the
author is offering a personal song of gratitude. This alternation between
plural and singular is common in the Psalms, and indeed is a mark of
Christian worship, in which the individual and the assembly weave
in and out of one another. So it is that if this is a Sunday on which
it is difficult for me to praise God, I trust to the rest of the baptized
community to carry me along with their song.

GAIL RAMSHAW

RESPONSE

How has it felt for you to praise God, lately? To lament? To pray? What
is it like to allow the worship community to praise for you when you
cannot praise? To lament for you when you cannot lament? Or to pray
for you when you cannot pray?

PRAYER

O God, you listen to the words of my prayers, whether they praise or
lament or say nothing much; when I cannot pray, please send your Spirit
to pray for me. Amen.

Second Reading

1 Peter 3:13–22

Now who will harm you if you are eager to do what is good? But even if you do suffer for doing what is right, you are blessed. Do not fear what they fear, and do not be intimidated, but in your hearts sanctify Christ as Lord. (vv. 13–15a)

REFLECTION

This passage seeks to strengthen believers who are experiencing unjust suffering by assuring them of God's vindication, mediated to them through the exalted Christ. They are encouraged to see their suffering as an imitation of Christ's willingness to suffer for others. While this can be great comfort to those trapped in unjust suffering, it is also very dangerous. Such passages have been used to encourage wives to remain with abusive husbands and to tell the oppressed or enslaved to accept their suffering as an imitation of Christ. This is certainly an illegitimate use of what this text says.

JERRY L. SUMNEY

RESPONSE

Was there ever a time you thought God was asking you to suffer? Have you ever been told, or known of someone else who was told, that enduring unjust suffering is an imitation of Christ somehow? How can we know when suffering is Christlike and when it is needless or abusive?

PRAYER

Christ of love, you were put to death in the flesh, but made alive in the spirit; if I must also walk through pain and death, I have faith that you will go with me. Amen.

Gospel

John 14:15–21

In a little while the world will no longer see me, but you will see me; because I live, you also will live. On that day you will know that I am in my Father, and you in me, and I in you. (vv. 19–20)

REFLECTION

An understanding of the Holy Spirit as the consoler can be especially profound for those who have suffered a loss or face anxiety about an uncertain future. . . .

. . . Sometimes people feel tired and struggle to continue on. . . . The Gospel of John offers food for Christians on the journey stating that "the world will no longer see me, but you will see me" (John 14:19). In other words, although it may seem that Jesus has abandoned us or is not in sight, he is with us, accompanying us, and will reward us.

PHILIP WINGEIER-RAYO

RESPONSE

Make a list of the ways you feel tired or struggling this week. Has Jesus felt absent? As you read Jesus' words, what do you hear him inviting you to notice or feel? How might the Holy Spirit carry or console you this week?

PRAYER

Holy Spirit, you are my consoler and comforter; show me how to feel and see the presence of Christ in you—to feel you in me, and me in you. Amen.

Weekend Reflections

God doesn't know very much about math, because when you give to others, it should be that you are subtracting from yourself. But in this incredible kind of way . . . in fact you are making space for more to be given to you.

. . . The Dead Sea in the Middle East receives fresh water, but it has no outlet, so it doesn't pass the water out. It receives beautiful water from the rivers, and the water goes dank. I mean, it just goes bad. And that's why it is the Dead Sea. It receives and does not give.

DESMOND TUTU (1931–2021), *THE BOOK OF JOY:*
LASTING HAPPINESS IN A CHANGING WORLD

MAKING THE CONNECTIONS

Choose one or two questions for reflection:

1. What connections have you noticed between this week's texts and other passages in Scripture?

2. What connections have you made between this week's texts and the world beyond Scripture?

3. Does either of this week's two commentary themes speak especially to your life or the life of the world around you right now?

4. What is God saying to your congregation in particular through this week's readings and commentaries?

_____

_____

_____

_____

_____

_____

Sabbath Day

SCRIPTURE OF ASSURANCE

> Your word is a lamp to my feet
> and a light to my path. (Psalm 119:105)

WEEKLY EXAMEN

- Take a quiet moment, seek out God's presence, and pray for the guidance of the Spirit.

- Consider the past week; recall specific moments and feelings that stand out to you.

- Choose one moment or feeling for deeper examination, thanksgiving, or repentance.

- Let go, breathe deeply, and invite Christ's love to surround and fill you in preparation for the week ahead.

- End with the Lord's Prayer.

Ascension of the Lord

Acts 1:1–11

"But you will receive power when the Holy Spirit has come upon you; and you will be my witnesses in Jerusalem, in all Judea and Samaria, and to the ends of the earth." (v. 8)

Psalm 93

More majestic than the thunders of mighty waters,
  more majestic than the waves of the sea,
  majestic on high is the LORD! (v. 4)

Ephesians 1:15–23

God put this power to work in Christ when he raised him from the dead and seated him at his right hand in the heavenly places, far above all rule and authority and power and dominion, and above every name that is named, not only in this age but also in the age to come. (vv. 20–21)

Luke 24:44–53

"You are witnesses of these things. And see, I am sending upon you what my Father promised; so stay here in the city until you have been clothed with power from on high." (vv. 48–49)

Acts 1:1–11

Jesus prepares the apostles for the unexpected nature of God's plan. Human vision cannot comprehend the scale and scope of the divine project. God's salvation extends to all people from Jerusalem to the ends of the earth, disrupting and penetrating boundaries, whether political, cultural, or ethnic. God's sovereignty supersedes any earthly claims, imperial power, or political ambitions, even those of the apostles (cf. Luke 1:52).

BRIDGETT A. GREEN

Psalm 93

When Christians hear of God's water, we think of baptism, in which the terrifying otherness of raging seas has been contained by God, as if God said to the seas, "Thus far shall you come, and no farther" (Job 38:11). Likewise, in baptism, the power of water to drown is turned by the mercy of God into a sweet washing, the horror of the sinking of the *Titanic* into our regularly marking our foreheads with water from the font.

GAIL RAMSHAW

Ephesians 1:15–23

The ascension of Jesus is a demonstration of God's power that intends to draw all people into the blessings God offers in Christ. Those blessings exceed our imaginations and are so abundant that they spill over into the whole world. That eschatological act of taking Christ into heaven is an irreplaceable part of God's plan to be recognized as the God of the whole world, whose intentions to save will not be thwarted by our divisions.

JERRY L. SUMNEY

Luke 24:44–53

Interim times teach, change, and prepare us. . . . In-between times can forge in us a skill that the faithful of all ages have to learn: the art of waiting. When those rare moments of closure and new beginnings actually occur and then wear off, God is in the in-between time, teaching and reforming us once again, helping us rejoice in the reality that we are neither stagnant nor completed.

LINDSAY P. ARMSTRONG

RESPONSE

Choose one of these four quotes that particularly gets your attention and write or reflect on how God might be speaking to you, to your experience or questions about Christ's resurrection or ascension, or to this time in your life.

PRAYER

O Jesus Christ, you have gone from the earth but are with me and go before me. Fill me with your power and blessing that I might be your witness and disciple. Amen.

The Week Leading Up to the
Seventh Sunday of Easter

Acts 1:6–14

"But you will receive power when the Holy Spirit has come upon you; and you will be my witnesses in Jerusalem, in all Judea and Samaria, and to the ends of the earth." When he had said this, as they were watching, he was lifted up, and a cloud took him out of their sight. (vv. 8–9)

Psalm 68:1–10, 32–35

Sing to God, sing praises to his name;
  lift up a song to him who rides upon the clouds—
his name is the LORD—
  be exultant before him. (v. 4)

1 Peter 4:12–14; 5:6–11

But rejoice insofar as you are sharing Christ's sufferings, so that you may also be glad and shout for joy when his glory is revealed. If you are reviled for the name of Christ, you are blessed, because the spirit of glory, which is the Spirit of God, is resting on you. (4:13–14)

John 17:1–11

"All mine are yours, and yours are mine; and I have been glorified in them. And now I am no longer in the world, but they are in the world, and I am coming to you. Holy Father, protect them in your name that you have given me, so that they may be one, as we are one." (vv. 10–11)

LECTIO DIVINA

Underline a word or phrase that especially grabs your attention. Pray from that word or phrase and ask God to help you connect to its particular invitation for you this week.

Themes from This Week's Writers

THEME 1: *"You Will Be My Witnesses"*

Acts 1:6–14

"You will be my witnesses" becomes the true hinge in the story. All along, Luke has been hinting that the followers of Jesus are more than observers. . . . Luke is moving us into a next generation, from those who were with Jesus to those who have an encounter with the resurrected Jesus through the Holy Spirit. The ascension narrative sets up the disciples—and us—to be ready for an outpouring of power from on high.

BRADLEY E. SCHMELING

Acts 1:6–14

The preacher can help a congregation reflect on how it understands itself as a missionary community rather than a collection of individuals, and that none of our congregations stand on their own. We are part of the global company of Spirit-infused witnesses to the reestablishment of the reign of God.

JENNIFER L. LORD

1 Peter 4:12–14; 5:6–11

We must not hide inside our own heads, congregations, or neighborhoods so that our view of reality gets distorted, thinking we are alone in our pain or safer inside ourselves than connected in community. We are not "the only ones." We are not alone. We have one another and God, who has promised always to be with us (Isa. 41:10; Matt. 28:20).

HEIDI HAVERKAMP

THEME 2: *That We All May Be One in Christ*

1 Peter 4:12–14; 5:6–11

First Peter 4:13 points to "sharing Christ's sufferings," using a word that connotes communion and fellowship in Christ's "suffering," which is repeated twice in this lectionary passage (5:9, 10). This recalls that Christ was not only resurrected. He suffered first. In all this, the promise is that the "Spirit of God is resting on you" (4:14).

GREG COOTSONA

John 17:1–11

Jesus reaches across the boundaries of time to unite us with him in his glory, a glory that comes through suffering (vv. 20–23). With the disciples, we too listen in on the prayer; we too are its beneficiaries.

MARTHA C. HIGHSMITH

John 17:1–11

To be one as Jesus and the Father are one is to be unified but also distinct. Frankly, as the church, we have little problem with distinction and more struggles with unity. . . . That very unity is a gift and a grace from God that we strive to live into as our Christian vocation.

KIRA AUSTIN-YOUNG

WHAT IS THE HOLY SPIRIT SAYING TO YOU THIS WEEK?

_____

_____

_____

_____

_____

A SPIRITUAL PRACTICE FOR THIS WEEK

After the ascension, the disciples locked themselves in a room to pray. This week, schedule some time to do the same, even just a short time: meditate, pray, journal, or read a book. Savor the stillness and prepare yourself for the Holy Spirit to come into your life in unpredictable ways.

First Reading

Acts 1:6–14

While he was going and they were gazing up toward heaven, suddenly two men in white robes stood by them. They said, "Men of Galilee, why do you stand looking up toward heaven? This Jesus, who has been taken up from you into heaven, will come in the same way as you saw him go into heaven." (vv. 10–11)

REFLECTION

The Acts passage and the account of the ascension speak to Christ's ongoing presence and power in the lives of believers, and throughout the earth. Those who believe Christ's present-tense presence shape worship language, songs, and rites that proclaim Christ's presence and work in our midst. We trust his promises to be with us. Some sermons play with the language of ascension: Jesus neither is absent nor has he absconded, but he has ascended to the place of glorification and authority (John 17). He ascends to a different place and way of being present.

JENNIFER L. LORD

RESPONSE

How do you experience the ongoing presence and power of Christ in the worship at your church? How does worship invite you to trust Christ's promise to be with you? With the whole church community? Does your church seem to feel it must go it alone sometimes, that God is absent? Do you?

PRAYER

Eternal Christ, why do I stand looking up to heaven for you? Even when you seem absent, you are in the midst of my heart and my community. Amen.

Canticle

Psalm 68:1–10, 32–35

Ascribe power to God,
  whose majesty is over Israel;
  and whose power is in the skies.
Awesome is God in his sanctuary,
  the God of Israel;
  he gives power and strength to his people. (vv. 34–35)

REFLECTION

The emotion that fills the psalm is exuberant joy. One might imagine
that when the Savior leaves the scene, the community is sorrowful.
The Psalms, though, the first hymnbook of Christians, call us to exult,
to be jubilant, to praise the majesty of an awesome protector. At the
ascension, it is not that Jesus leaves us, but that—using the poetic phrase
of the Scriptures—Christ is now at the right hand of divine authority,
dispensing power and strength to all the people.

GAIL RAMSHAW

RESPONSE

There are many artistic renditions of Christ in glory, at the right hand
of God. Using your imagination and indulging in a sense of play, create
a rendition of Christ, ascended, in words or a drawing that feels more
alive and relevant to your context and life. Have fun and indulge some
"exuberant joy"!

PRAYER

Joyful God, you are awesome and majestic, powerful and playful; give
me strength and a light heart to live in your ways, now and always.
Amen.

Second Reading

1 Peter 4:12–14; 5:6–11

Discipline yourselves, keep alert. Like a roaring lion your adversary the devil prowls around, looking for someone to devour. Resist him, steadfast in your faith, for you know that your brothers and sisters in all the world are undergoing the same kinds of suffering. (5:8–9)

REFLECTION

The final command moves to the devil and the Christians' need to stay alert. Why? The "slanderer" or "backbiter" (the literal meaning of the Greek word for "devil") is a "lion" (5:8). To first-century ears, this would not be a zoo animal behind the bars of a cage, but a frightening predator in the wild. So Christians were to "keep alert" (5:8). Verse 9 is not actually a command ("resist the devil"), but an epithet of the devil as "whom you resist," as if this is simply a fact.

GREG COOTSONA

RESPONSE

How do you conceive of the devil? Which of these terms stands out to you, perhaps offering a new perspective or understanding? Are there ways you are aware that you are consciously working to "resist evil" in your life right now? How could these words encourage you?

PRAYER

Almighty God, help me to stay alert to the reality of evil, prowling near, that I may be steadfast in faith, honesty, and goodness. I cast all my anxiety on you, because I know you care for me. Amen.

Gospel

John 17:1–11

"I have made your name known to those whom you gave me from the world. They were yours, and you gave them to me, and they have kept your word. Now they know that everything you have given me is from you." (vv. 6–7)

REFLECTION

As Eastertide draws to a close, the Gospel reading for the Seventh Sunday of Easter focuses on the end of Jesus' time on earth. In prayer, he looks back on his life and ministry. This retrospective also provides a glimpse of what lies ahead as Jesus anticipates the new reality of resurrection and what it will mean for his relationship with his followers. Notions of glory shine through . . . both fully realized in God and God's Son, and a promised glory yet to be fulfilled. This tension is evident in the lack of understanding about Jesus and his ministry from those he encounters, his disciples, and others.

MARTHA C. HIGHSMITH

RESPONSE

Even Jesus struggled with transitions. As he looks back on his human life and ahead to what will come, what words speak especially to you about your own relationship to Christ? How do you relate to standing in a place of change that others may fear or not understand?

PRAYER

God of all, you have given me to Jesus, and everything Jesus has given me is from you. Jesus is no longer in the world, but I am. Protect and guide me so that I and all your people may be one in you: Creator, Christ, and Holy Spirit. Amen.

Weekend Reflections

FURTHER CONNECTION

The *telos* or "divine endgame," for racial reconciliation is not restored relationship between Whites and people of color. It is not . . . the image of "a Big Black dude and a White dude on a stage, hugging it out with a single tear rolling down their cheeks." It is the establishment of a just world, one in which racial inequities have been abolished. . . .

All sectors of society, including the church, must undertake the task of building beloved community.

CHANEQUA WALKER-BARNES (1972–), *I BRING THE VOICES OF MY PEOPLE: A WOMANIST VISION FOR RACIAL RECONCILIATION*

MAKING THE CONNECTIONS

Choose one or two questions for reflection:

1. What connections have you noticed between this week's texts and other passages in Scripture?

2. What connections have you made between this week's texts and the world beyond Scripture?

3. Does either of this week's two commentary themes speak especially to your life or the life of the world around you right now?

4. What is God saying to your congregation in particular through this week's readings and commentaries?

_____

_____

_____

_____

_____

_____

Sabbath Day

SCRIPTURE OF ASSURANCE

Proclaim the message; be persistent whether the time is favorable or unfavorable; convince, rebuke, and encourage, with the utmost patience in teaching. (2 Timothy 4:2)

WEEKLY EXAMEN

- Take a quiet moment, seek out God's presence, and pray for the guidance of the Spirit.

- Consider the past week; recall specific moments and feelings that stand out to you.

- Choose one moment or feeling for deeper examination, thanksgiving, or repentance.

- Let go, breathe deeply, and invite Christ's love to surround and fill you in preparation for the week ahead.

- End with the Lord's Prayer.

The Week Leading Up to the
Day of Pentecost

Numbers 11:24–30

Two men remained in the camp, one named Eldad, and the other named Medad, and the spirit rested on them; they were among those registered, but they had not gone out to the tent, and so they prophesied in the camp. (v. 26)

1 Corinthians 12:3b–13

For in the one Spirit we were all baptized into one body—Jews or Greeks, slaves or free—and we were all made to drink of one Spirit. (v. 13)

Acts 2:1–21

Divided tongues, as of fire, appeared among them, and a tongue rested on each of them. All of them were filled with the Holy Spirit and began to speak in other languages, as the Spirit gave them ability. (vv. 3–4)

John 20:19–23

Jesus said to them again, "Peace be with you. As the Father has sent me, so I send you." When he had said this, he breathed on them and said to them, "Receive the Holy Spirit." (vv. 21–22)

LECTIO DIVINA

Underline a word or phrase that especially grabs your attention. Pray from that word or phrase and ask God to help you connect to its particular invitation for you this week.

Themes from This Week's Writers

THEME 1: *Gifts of the Spirit*

Numbers 11:24–30

Some persons are gifted with spirited speech and can raise their voice in public and private forums, influencing others' return to God. Others may prophesy by actions, God's Spirit working in them as they write or parent or even shop in ways that beg for attention to God's intentions.

JENNIFER L. LORD

1 Corinthians 12:3b–13

Paul takes up the topic of God's power and reminds his hearers that the principal outworking of the Spirit is the unity of God's people. . . . Paul dislikes intensely any divisions among Christ's people.

GREG COOTSONA

Acts 2:1–21

In each of our readings the Spirit comes upon believers, empowering them to be the living water, which Jesus has promised. Indeed, the promised gift made to the disciples by the risen Lord in John 20:22, when he exhorts them to "receive the Holy Spirit," is extended at Pentecost and continues to be manifest now.

L. SHANNON JUNG

THEME 2: *The Spirit Crosses Human Barriers*

Numbers 11:24–30

God regularly speaks outside the boundaries of even the most sacrosanct and approved "camp." The young Joshua is bothered by this breach of order, but Moses . . . sees the bigger picture, wishing that all of God's people would be captured by the Spirit's prophetic power.

BRADLEY E. SCHMELING

John 20:19–23

The Spirit breaks through barriers: locked doors; language; individualism; fear; racial, ethnic, and social divisions. The Spirit transforms, renews, unites, and sends us into the world to carry on the work both begun and fulfilled in the life of Jesus.

MARTHA C. HIGHSMITH

Acts 2:1–21

God's Spirit is empowering God's servants to speak God's message across all human barriers, as promised in Luke 24:47–49 and Acts 1:8. Although this promise was first and foremost for Jesus' first disciples, it is quite clear that it extends to all of Jesus' followers for all generations (2:38–39).

CRAIG S. KEENER

WHAT IS THE HOLY SPIRIT SAYING TO YOU THIS WEEK?

_____

_____

_____

_____

_____

A SPIRITUAL PRACTICE FOR THIS WEEK

Celebrate Pentecost with wind and fire! You could wear red, make wind chimes, fly a kite, blow bubbles, toast with a bubbly drink, sit with friends around a fire, make a cake with red frosting, say "Peace be with you" in a new language, or draw flames and doves in chalk on your sidewalk or driveway.

First Reading

Numbers 11:24–30

And a young man ran and told Moses, "Eldad and Medad are prophesying in the camp." And Joshua son of Nun, the assistant of Moses, one of his chosen men, said, "My lord Moses, stop them!" But Moses said to him, "Are you jealous for my sake? Would that all the LORD's people were prophets, and that the LORD would put his spirit on them!" (vv. 27–29)

REFLECTION

Eldad and Medad become signs that God's Spirit can blow in directions not predicted or even acceptable according to tradition or sacred text. The Spirit, breathing between the Lord and Moses, breathing between Moses and the seventy, eventually breathing between Jesus and the disciples on Pentecost, always breathes across boundaries to include other prophets who are among the people. These texts teach us to look beyond the regular people and places to find prophetic utterance. God is always at work both in the center and at the edge, among people we have not expected.

BRADLEY E. SCHMELING

RESPONSE

Were you ever a tattletale as a kid? Have you tattled on someone as an adult—or wanted to? What have you seen at risk when traditional boundaries are broken? What have you seen get lost when they are rigid? How might the Holy Spirit be working around the boundaries of your community now?

PRAYER

God of justice, you are always calling all your people to be prophets; teach me not to be afraid and put your Spirit upon me, that I too may declare your justice and grace to your people. Amen.

Canticle

Psalm 104:24–34, 35b

Yonder is the sea, great and wide,
 creeping things innumerable are there,
 living things both small and great.
There go the ships,
 and Leviathan that you formed to sport in it. (vv. 25–26)

REFLECTION

For a landed people like the ancient Canaanites, the sea represented unbounded chaos, the terror of existence outside of human civilization, and in verses 25–26 the psalmist dismisses any fear of the sea by praising God for its wonder. It would be helpful if the service folder for this Sunday included a picture of the Leviathan of verse 26, so that the assembly catches the meaning of this fascinating Israelite claim, that the ancient Near Eastern sea monster, who churns up the waters and swallows drowned sailors, is in reality only a grand sea creature that God created for sheer enjoyment.

GAIL RAMSHAW

RESPONSE

When you imagine the vastness of the ocean, what do you see? What else in God's creation strikes you with its grandeur, unknowability, or danger? What do you imagine God enjoys about these things? Do you have a favorite "monster" or fantastical part of creation you believe God especially enjoys?

PRAYER

Fantastic God, you sent forth your spirit and creation emerged: great and wide, abundant and varied, majestic and playful; I want to enjoy and delight in it, as you do. Amen.

Second Reading

1 Corinthians 12:3b–13

Now there are varieties of gifts, but the same Spirit; and there are varieties of services, but the same Lord; and there are varieties of activities, but it is the same God who activates all of them in everyone. (vv. 4–6)

REFLECTION

We may measure Christian worthiness in exterior signs like Sunday attendance, "good" behavior, Bible study, or volunteer work. We may even judge our own worthiness more harshly than others', discounting our right to belong, participate, or even pray, because we believe our spiritual merits do not measure up. Christian community and faith are gifts of the Spirit, not something to be earned. They are gifts not only to us as individuals, but to our entire communities, both inside and outside the church. Paul emphasizes that our gifts work together, each particular and unique, but none better or less worthy than another.

HEIDI HAVERKAMP

RESPONSE

How do you tend to measure "Christian worthiness"? Reflect on a way you have felt you do not measure up spiritually, as a member, leader, pastor, or Christian. What if your worthiness is a gift from God? What is the gift God gives to others in you, just being yourself?

PRAYER

Holy Spirit, you have given your children a vast variety of gifts and talents, interests and loves; teach me to rejoice that it is you, the same God, who calls forth and activates all of them in everyone, for the good of all your world. Amen.

Second Reading

Acts 2:1–21

"In our own languages we hear them speaking about God's deeds of power." All were amazed and perplexed, saying to one another, "What does this mean?" But others sneered and said, "They are filled with new wine." (vv. 11b–13)

REFLECTION

Although an early witness to the Azusa Street revival celebrated that "the color line is washed away in the blood," human depravity soon enough reared its head. Accustomed to a range of worship styles, including that of his own African American community, [William] Seymour welcomed loud and joyful worship (often evident in the Psalms), as well as quiet. Seymour's key mentor on the matter of tongues, however, was accustomed only to a quiet experience of the Spirit. Thus he rejected this worship; further, he reportedly derided the revival in racist terms.

CRAIG S. KEENER

RESPONSE

Make a list of some worship styles, otherwise foreign to you, that you have enjoyed or admired from afar. Then, make a list of worship styles that you find puzzling, disturbing, or ridiculous. Do you notice ways that race may play a part in these lists? Or class? Or education level?

PRAYER

Holy Spirit, you inspire, as a gift, faithful and devout worship in your people in many ways, forms, and languages; show me how to respect and honor the worship of others, even when it perplexes or shocks me. Amen.

Gospel

John 20:19–23

After he said this, he showed them his hands and his side. Then the disciples rejoiced when they saw the Lord. Jesus said to them again, "Peace be with you. As the Father has sent me, so I send you." (vv. 20–21)

REFLECTION

Greeting one another with the peace of Christ is an action and event that is full of hope and gravitas when we can encourage one another to proclaim the gospel without fear or anxiety. Jesus' second greeting of "peace be with you" in 20:21 is directly linked to his sending of the disciples into the world. Instead of catching up on the latest gossip or trading compliments on apparel, exchanging the peace of Christ with one another could be a reminder that, whatever our fears and anxieties, the risen Christ is present among us and sends us out in the world to bear witness.

KIRA AUSTIN-YOUNG

RESPONSE

Do you "pass the peace" at your church? How do you feel about the practice? How does recalling that these words were first said by Jesus deepen or change your feelings? Imagine Jesus saying it to you now: what do you hear him saying in particular to you, this week?

PRAYER

Risen Christ, you greeted your apostles with a word of peace; send me as God sent you, and show me how to greet all I meet with this peace. Amen.

Weekend Reflections

The miracle of Pentecost isn't that divided people learn to speak one lingua franca—the dream of every Empire. It's that we learn to speak and understand languages that aren't our own—the joy and struggle of Beloved Community.

JONATHAN WILSON-HARTGROVE (1980–),
TWITTER POST ON MAY 22, 2021

MAKING THE CONNECTIONS

Choose one or two questions for reflection:

1. What connections have you noticed between this week's texts and other passages in Scripture?

2. What connections have you made between this week's texts and the world beyond Scripture?

3. Does either of this week's two commentary themes speak especially to your life or the life of the world around you right now?

4. What is God saying to your congregation in particular through this week's readings and commentaries?

_____

_____

_____

_____

_____

_____

Sabbath Day

SCRIPTURE OF ASSURANCE

First of all you must understand this, that no prophecy of scripture is a matter of one's own interpretation, because no prophecy ever came by human will, but men and women moved by the Holy Spirit spoke from God. (2 Peter 1:20–21)

WEEKLY EXAMEN

- Take a quiet moment, seek out God's presence, and pray for the guidance of the Spirit.

- Consider the past week; recall specific moments and feelings that stand out to you.

- Choose one moment or feeling for deeper examination, thanksgiving, or repentance.

- Let go, breathe deeply, and invite Christ's love to surround and fill you in preparation for the week ahead.

- End with the Lord's Prayer.

The Week Leading Up to
Trinity Sunday

Genesis 1:1–2:4a

So God created humankind in his image
  in the image of God he created them;
  male and female he created them.
God blessed them, and God said to them, "Be fruitful and multi-
  ply, and fill the earth and subdue it." (vv. 27–28)

Psalm 8

What are human beings that you are mindful of them,
  mortals that you care for them?

Yet you have made them a little lower than God,
  and crowned them with glory and honor. (vv. 4–5)

2 Corinthians 13:11–13

The grace of the Lord Jesus Christ, the love of God, and the communion of
the Holy Spirit be with all of you. (v. 13)

Matthew 28:16–20

"Go therefore and make disciples of all nations, baptizing them in the name
of the Father and of the Son and of the Holy Spirit, and teaching them to
obey everything that I have commanded you. And remember, I am with you
always, to the end of the age." (vv. 19–20)

LECTIO DIVINA

Underline a word or phrase that especially grabs your attention. Pray
from that word or phrase and ask God to help you connect to its
particular invitation for you this week.

Themes from This Week's Writers

THEME 1: *Created in God's Image*

Genesis 1:1–2:4a

Creation in God's image does not simply mean that humans are rational or spiritual, but that they are called to imitate God in the care and nurture of creation. All people, whatever their race or gender or class, are created in God's image.

LYNN JAPINGA

Psalm 8

Humans are created last, on the sixth day, in the image of God (Gen. 1:26). So they represent the Deity in the world, as a proxy for God's cosmic governance. In both Psalm 8 and the Priestly creation account, humans do not have dominion on their own merit, but because of God's overarching authority.

JOEL MARCUS LEMON

Genesis 1:1–2:4a

God creates humanity male and female, but male and female seem to be contained within *adam*, within "the earthling." . . . The text emphasizes humanity's shared connection between genders reflective of our origin from and connection with the earth.

ANDREW FOSTER CONNORS

THEME 2: *The Interrelational Nature of the Divine*

2 Corinthians 13:11–13

God promises peace; even in situations where reconciliation seems humanly impossible, it becomes possible by the power of God. Certainly we are called to participate in the work of peace, but it is a work that God inspires, God effects, and God concludes.

PAUL T. NIMMO

2 Corinthians 13:11–13

Paul knows something very important: without God's Holy Spirit, our koinonia—community, communion, fellowship—is impossible. In the power of God's Holy Spirit, it is possible for us to live together in our differences. Indeed, it strengthens and grows us as Christ's body to live together in our differences.

SARAH S. HENRICH

Matthew 28:16–20

This conclusion to Matthew's Gospel serves as a powerful word for Trinity Sunday. . . . [Churches] acknowledge both the intrarelational nature of the Divine and the relational nature of God's interaction with the community of faith. The name Emmanuel emphasizes that God is with *us*, and Jesus' presence is made known where "two or three are gathered" in his name (18:20).

MARY F. FOSKETT

WHAT IS THE HOLY SPIRIT SAYING TO YOU THIS WEEK?

_____

_____

_____

_____

_____

A SPIRITUAL PRACTICE FOR THIS WEEK

To which person of the Trinity do you most often address your prayers? Or feel closest to? What is it about the Creator, Christ, or Holy Spirit that draws you most? This week, pray to a more unfamiliar person of the Trinity. What is this like? Is anything new about the mystery and diversity of God revealed to you?

First Reading

God saw everything that he had made, and indeed, it was very good. And there was evening and there was morning, the sixth day. (1:31)

REFLECTION

Some geologists have proposed that the first nuclear explosion (code-named "Trinity") marked a new period in geologic time, the Anthropocene Epoch, meaning the "new human" epoch, characterized by human dominion of the earth. As the selection for Trinity Sunday, Genesis 1 therefore compels us to compare and contrast God's creative powers with our own. . . . How might we contrast the unquestionably good fruits of God's creation with our own? Perhaps Genesis 1 . . . not only elucidates the contrast between God's idea of good with that of humans, but also provides a foundational definition for "good" from which all other notions can be judged.

ANDREW FOSTER CONNORS

RESPONSE

Human creativity can be both life-giving and deadly. What are some ways you see human creativity now dominating life on earth? What is God's creativity like? How could you relate this to the nature of the Trinity? What has God defined as "good," would you say? Where do you find hope?

PRAYER

Holy Trinity, you create humankind in your image and invite us to join you in creativity; teach me to create, as you do, with care, stewardship, and goodness. Amen.

Canticle

You have set your glory above the heavens.
   Out of the mouths of babes and infants
you have founded a bulwark because of your foes,
   to silence the enemy and the avenger. (vv. 1b–2)

REFLECTION

For God's glory to reside "above the heavens" (v. 1) suggests that
the scale of God's majesty exceeds humans' ability to comprehend
it. It stands outside our ability to observe it. . . . It is invisible, but
nevertheless palpable within the world, for God protects God's
people (v. 2). This paradox of God's glory as both powerful and
incomprehensible is expressed through a unique literary image. The
sounds of babbling infants are associated with the strength of a fortress
(v. 2). For the psalmist, God's glory is ultimately unknowable, like the
meaning of baby talk, but also strong enough to repulse an enemy.

JOEL MARCUS LEMON

RESPONSE

How is God like a fortress? Like the burbling of an infant? What
connections do you see between these? (What kind of bulwark is baby
babble?) How is it good news, do you think, that God is unknowable
and incomprehensible? What is the good news of this for you this week?

PRAYER

Holy Trinity, your majesty is like a fortress, like the chatter of babies,
like the vastness of the cosmos; may the mystery of your glory inspire
and comfort me. Amen.

Second Reading

2 Corinthians 13:11–13

Finally, brothers and sisters, farewell. Put things in order, listen to my appeal, agree with one another, live in peace; and the God of love and peace will be with you. (v. 11)

REFLECTION

A string of present imperative verbs reminds the Corinthians and us that much continues to be required of us. The verbs carry the weight of urging folks to continue to rejoice, to continue to put themselves in order as if God's Holy Spirit served as a metaphysical chiropractor to realign this out-of-sync group. They are to continue to be either comforted or admonished by Paul, or both. They are called to share the ethos of Christ and to live in peace. The triune blessing is not somehow to fall upon them, but rather to infuse them and empower all they will yet become.

SARAH S. HENRICH

RESPONSE

If you were to write a brief, loving message of encouragement and admonishment to your own community, what would you say? Mirror these verses closely, if you like, or do something very different. What is the Spirit inviting you to understand about your membership or leadership in your community at this time?

PRAYER

Holy Trinity, may your threefold name bless me and your church, to infuse and empower all we will yet become. Amen.

Gospel

Matthew 28:16–20

Now the eleven disciples went to Galilee, to the mountain to which Jesus had directed them. When they saw him, they worshiped him; but some doubted. (vv. 16–17)

REFLECTION

Signficantly, in all of these passages Jesus encourages those of little faith; he does not belittle them. Later the disciples who doubted when they saw the resurrected Jesus were among the disciples who were sent to make disciples. Thus, it should be reassuring for both the preacher and the congregation that worshiping on Trinity Sunday does not require full understanding of Trinitarian theology. Worship that recognizes the grace, love, and communion that define the triune God is more than enough to sustain us both to be and to make disciples.

OLIVER LARRY YARBROUGH

RESPONSE

What are some of your doubts about the concept of the Trinity? What is it like to hear that Jesus appeared to all his disciples, even those who doubted? That even those who doubted felt the freedom to worship Jesus? What is important for you, this week, in this?

PRAYER

Holy Trinity, you shelter me always, earnest or puzzled, grounded or confused, in the shelter of your grace, glory, and love; teach me to worship in the space of freedom between doubt and faith. Amen.

Weekend Reflections

FURTHER CONNECTION

All theological language is an approximation, offered tentatively in holy awe. That's the best human language can achieve. We can say, "It's like—it's similar to . . . ," but we can never say, "It is . . ." because we are in the realm of beyond, of transcendence, of mystery. And we must—absolutely must—maintain a fundamental humility before the Great Mystery. If we do not, religion always worships itself and its formulations and never God.

RICHARD ROHR (1943–), *THE DIVINE DANCE: THE TRINITY AND YOUR TRANSFORMATION*

MAKING THE CONNECTIONS

Choose one or two questions for reflection:

1. What connections have you noticed between this week's texts and other passages in Scripture?

2. What connections have you made between this week's texts and the world beyond Scripture?

3. Does either of this week's two commentary themes speak especially to your life or the life of the world around you right now?

4. What is God saying to your congregation in particular through this week's readings and commentaries?

MY CONNECTIONS

_____

_____

_____

_____

_____

_____

Sabbath Day

SCRIPTURE OF ASSURANCE

Have nothing to do with profane myths and old wives' tales. (1 Timothy 4:7a)

WEEKLY EXAMEN

- Take a quiet moment, seek out God's presence, and pray for the guidance of the Spirit.

- Consider the past week; recall specific moments and feelings that stand out to you.

- Choose one moment or feeling for deeper examination, thanksgiving, or repentance.

- Let go, breathe deeply, and invite Christ's love to surround and fill you in preparation for the week ahead.

- End with the Lord's Prayer.

The Week Leading Up to
Proper 3
(Sunday between May 22 and May 28)

Isaiah 49:8–16a

Thus says the LORD:
In a time of favor I have answered you,
  on a day of salvation I have helped you;
I have kept you and given you
  as a covenant to the people,
to establish the land,
  to apportion the desolate heritages. (v. 8)

Psalm 131

O Israel, hope in the LORD
  from this time on and forevermore. (v. 3)

1 Corinthians 4:1–5

But with me it is a very small thing that I should be judged by you or by any human court. I do not even judge myself. I am not aware of anything against myself, but I am not thereby acquitted. It is the Lord who judges me. (vv. 3–4)

Matthew 6:24–34

"But strive first for the kingdom of God and his righteousness, and all these things will be given to you as well.

"So do not worry about tomorrow, for tomorrow will bring worries of its own. Today's trouble is enough for today." (vv. 33–34)

LECTIO DIVINA

Underline a word or phrase that especially grabs your attention. Pray from that word or phrase and ask God to help you connect to its particular invitation for you this week.

Themes from This Week's Writers

THEME 1: *Do Not Fear God's Judgment*

Isaiah 49:8–16a

[The Israelites] lost their land and their homes. Their temple was destroyed. They assumed that God had abandoned them as punishment for their failure to obey the covenant. The prophet, however, announces otherwise. God has not left them.

LYNN JAPINGA

1 Corinthians 4:1–5

We will be judged only by the one who sends us and whom we serve. The judgments of others—whether our congregations, colleagues, friends, or families—are only penultimate. Moreover, we will not ultimately be judged *by ourselves.* We can be our own worst advocates and our own worst critics, and neither is salutary or helpful in the Christian life.

PAUL T. NIMMO

1 Corinthians 4:1–5

"Whose judgment matters to us?" we should always be asking. If it is God's judgment that matters—not because we are frightened of it but because we are in a relationship of love and respect with God—that love and respect is at the center of our lives in a complex and diverse world.

SARAH S. HENRICH

THEME 2: *Strive First for the Kingdom of God*

Isaiah 49:8–16a

The volume of human activity certainly pales in comparison to God's movement in the text. . . . Even so, . . . human activity is essential to Isaiah's vision, precisely because God calls forth human proclamation and compassionate leadership.

ANDREW FOSTER CONNORS

Matthew 6:24–34

Jesus says basic needs will be given to those who strive first for the kingdom of God and his righteousness. He does not say God will provide "the abundance of possessions." Similarly, the day's Gospel ends with a matter-of-fact acknowledgment that both today and tomorrow will have a sufficiency of troubles. . . . There is no suggestion that striving first for the kingdom of God and his righteousness will change that.

OLIVER LARRY YARBROUGH

Matthew 6:24–34

As Christian discipleship is about imitating Jesus, so is it also about recognizing and living out the way of the kingdom that he teaches and embodies. Discipleship involves more than following specific instructions. . . . Discipleship for Matthew is the practice of life itself.

MARY F. FOSKETT

WHAT IS THE HOLY SPIRIT SAYING TO YOU THIS WEEK?

_____

_____

_____

_____

_____

A SPIRITUAL PRACTICE FOR THIS WEEK

Most Westerners have a lot of choices in what we wear and eat, every day. Challenge yourself to make fewer choices this week about your clothes and your meals. Make a plan to help you do this as seems best in your context. What do you notice? How does Matthew 6:24–34 speak to you differently?

First Reading

Isaiah 49:8–16a

Can a woman forget her nursing child,
   or show no compassion for the child of her womb?
Even these may forget,
   yet I will not forget you.
See, I have inscribed you on the palms of my hands. (vv. 15–16)

REFLECTION

Envisioning God as a mother as Isaiah does here offers a profoundly
intimate picture of the Divine as sheltering, nurturing, and giving birth
to a child, then feeding and caring for it. It goes against our assumption
of a distant, mysterious, demanding, and punishing God. . . . The
distant God may ironically seem safer and more familiar. A God who is
too close for comfort brings her own challenges. We may find that she
is as fiercely protective as a dangerous mother bear (Hos. 13:8). We may
find that we cannot escape the intensity of her love (Ps. 139:1–18).

LYNN JAPINGA

RESPONSE

Does a distant God seem safer and more familiar to you than a
nurturing, mothering God? How might this be related to your
relationship with your own mother or father? What kind of mothering
do you long for from God at this time in your life?

PRAYER

Mother God, you have inscribed me on the palms of your hands
and you will not forget me; help me to know and trust in my eternal
belovedness in you. Amen.

Canticle

Psalm 131

But I have calmed and quieted my soul,
    like a weaned child with its mother;
    my soul is like the weaned child that is with me. (v. 2)

REFLECTION

Some have suggested that the words of the psalm come from a mother's mouth.[1] Other translations do not go so far in identifying the psalmist as the mother of "the weaned child." Despite these challenges, most scholars agree that this psalm does in fact give us access to a woman's voice in prayer, however fleeting and incomplete.

. . . This quiet, reserved woman lifts her voice to address the whole assembly of Israel in verse 3. She encourages everyone to wait on Yahweh, to hope (*yahel*) in God day in and day out.

JOEL MARCUS LEMON

RESPONSE

Read this psalm, aloud or to yourself, imagining that a woman's voice is praying. What is this like? What do you notice? What is the power of a mother's prophetic voice?

PRAYER

Christ, our mother, you tend my weary soul as a weaned child, quiet and calm at your breast; help me to rest in humility and hope. Amen.

1. Brent A. Strawn, "A Woman at Prayer (Psalm 131:2b) and Arguments 'from Parallelism,'" *Zeitschrift für die Alttestamentliche Wissenschaft* 124 (2012): 421. See Marianne Grohmann, "The Imagery of the 'Weaned Child' in Psalm 131," *The Composition of the Book of Psalms*, ed. Erich Zenger, Bibliotheca ephemeridum theologicarum lovaniensium 238 (Leuven: Peeters, 2010), 513–22.

Second Reading

1 Corinthians 4:1–5

Therefore do not pronounce judgment before the time, before the Lord comes, who will bring to light the things now hidden in darkness and will disclose the purposes of the heart. Then each one will receive commendation from God. (v. 5)

REFLECTION

The judgments of others—whether our congregations, colleagues, friends, or families—are only penultimate. Moreover, we will not ultimately be judged *by ourselves*. We can be our own worst advocates and our own worst critics, and neither is salutary or helpful in the Christian life. There is, of course, a place for self-reflection—just as there is for friendly or collegial evaluation!—but it is neither the first place nor the last place.

. . . Instead, we will be judged by the one who gave himself for us, and who justifies us so that we do not need to justify ourselves.

PAUL T. NIMMO

RESPONSE

What are some of the ways you judge yourself most harshly? In what ways are you sensitive to the judgments of others? How might the judgments of Jesus Christ be different from these? What does it mean to you that ultimately, only Jesus will judge us? Justify us?

PRAYER

Lord Jesus, you will bring to light what is hidden in darkness in me; no one can be my true judge but you. Teach me to be a trustworthy servant of God and steward of your mysteries. Amen.

Gospel

Matthew 6:24–34

"No one can serve two masters; for a slave will either hate the one and love the other, or be devoted to the one and despise the other. You cannot serve God and wealth." (v. 24)

REFLECTION

By suggesting to his hearers that they must choose between "two masters," Jesus makes use of the metaphor of enslavement, well known in antiquity and utilized by the apostle Paul. Here the metaphor deftly illustrates how we are owned by what we most value and serve. As Matthew's parables of the Hidden Treasure (13:44) and the Pearl of Great Price (13:45–46) suggest, the things to which we devote ourselves indicate a lot about who we are.

Acquiring wealth takes time, intention, and sustained energy. What we possess and how we spend our time over the years reveals our deepest commitments and values.

MARY F. FOSKETT

RESPONSE

How are you "owned" or consumed by your financial security, these days? Or the things you buy and consume? What are the ways that you value and serve your spiritual life? What would it look like to invest in your spiritual future the way that many invest in their financial future?

PRAYER

Gracious God, you know everything I need—food, drink, clothing, shelter. I want to depend on you above all things; show me how to reject wealth as a master and strive first for your kingdom. Amen.

Weekend Reflections

FURTHER CONNECTION

I asked participants who claimed to be "strong followers of Jesus" whether Jesus spent time with the poor. Nearly 80 percent said yes. Later in the survey, I sneaked in another question, I asked this same group of strong followers whether they spent time with the poor, and less than 2 percent said they did. I learned a powerful lesson: We can admire and worship Jesus without doing what he did. We can applaud what he preached and stood for without caring about the same things. We can adore his cross without taking up ours. I had come to see that the great tragedy of the church is not that rich Christians do not care about the poor but that rich Christians do not know the poor.

SHANE CLAIBORNE (1975–), *THE IRRESISTIBLE REVOLUTION: LIVING AS AN ORDINARY RADICAL*

MAKING THE CONNECTIONS

Choose one or two questions for reflection:

1. What connections have you noticed between this week's texts and other passages in Scripture?

2. What connections have you made between this week's texts and the world beyond Scripture?

3. Does either of this week's two commentary themes speak especially to your life or the life of the world around you right now?

4. What is God saying to your congregation in particular through this week's readings and commentaries?

_____

_____

_____

_____

_____

_____

Sabbath Day

SCRIPTURE OF ASSURANCE

> Let the words of my mouth and the meditation of my heart
> be acceptable to you,
> O LORD, my rock and my redeemer. (Psalm 19:14)

WEEKLY EXAMEN

- Take a quiet moment, seek out God's presence, and pray for the guidance of the Spirit.

- Consider the past week; recall specific moments and feelings that stand out to you.

- Choose one moment or feeling for deeper examination, thanksgiving, or repentance.

- Let go, breathe deeply, and invite Christ's love to surround and fill you in preparation for the week ahead.

- End with the Lord's Prayer.

The Week Leading Up to
Proper 4

(Sunday between May 29 and June 4)

Deuteronomy 11:18–21, 26–28

You shall put these words of mine in your heart and soul, and you shall bind them as a sign on your hand, and fix them as an emblem on your forehead. (v. 18)

Genesis 6:9–22; 7:24; 8:14–19

And God said to Noah, "I have determined to make an end of all flesh, for the earth is filled with violence because of them; now I am going to destroy them along with the earth." (6:13)

Romans 1:16–17; 3:22b–28

For there is no distinction, since all have sinned and fall short of the glory of God; they are now justified by his grace as a gift, through the redemption that is in Christ Jesus, whom God put forward as a sacrifice of atonement by his blood, effective through faith. (3:22b–25a)

Matthew 7:21–29

"Not everyone who says to me, 'Lord, Lord,' will enter the kingdom of heaven, but only the one who does the will of my Father in heaven. . . .

"Everyone then who hears these words of mine and acts on them will be like a wise man who built his house on rock." (vv. 21, 24)

LECTIO DIVINA

> Underline a word or phrase that especially grabs your attention. Pray from that word or phrase and ask God to help you connect to its particular invitation for you this week.

Themes from This Week's Writers

THEME 1: *What Kind of God Destroys the Earth?*

Genesis 6:9–22; 7:24; 8:14–19

God does not give up on the world. Instead, God continually finds new ways to engage with God's people. After the flood, God will make a covenant with Abraham, give the law, and send the prophets. Finally, God will take human flesh and transform the world, not through destruction, but through vulnerability, suffering, and resurrection.

LYNN JAPINGA

Genesis 6:9–22; 7:24; 8:14–19

This disturbing portrayal of God compels us to reflect on violence and abuse done in the name of religion. . . . Perhaps God's promise at the end of the flood that God will never attempt to destroy humanity again (Gen. 8:21) hints that this text, rather than serving as authorization for God-ordained violence against humanity, really is a prohibition.

ANDREW FOSTER CONNORS

Psalm 46

Likewise, in the Genesis flood account, water obliterates the world and also provides a means by which God creates the world anew. Water brings death and life. The richness of this image is alive in the sacrament of baptism, by which one dies with Christ and is raised to new life through God's saving actions.

JOEL MARCUS LEMON

THEME 2: *Build Your House on Rock*

Romans 1:16–17; 3:22b–28

All of us are beset daily by warnings of catastrophic consequences if we make the "wrong" choices. . . . Paul reminds us here: we do not make the future. Of course, we can impact it, especially our own, but God continues to care and patiently to bring God's own future to us.

SARAH S. HENRICH

Matthew 7:21–29

[Jesus is preaching against] the quest for public reward, which in Matthew is as much of (if not more of) a danger for disciples as it is for the scribes and Pharisees. Thus, like the rest of the Sermon on the Mount, the concluding segments of the sermon summarize true discipleship as requiring both saying and doing *from one's heart.*

OLIVER LARRY YARBROUGH

Matthew 7:21–29

It is easy to feel irrelevant and to start looking anxiously for ways to show that church matters. In these situations, Jesus' words remind us that the gospel calls the church only to be faithful to God's vision for the world.

MARY F. FOSKETT

WHAT IS THE HOLY SPIRIT SAYING TO YOU THIS WEEK?

_____

_____

_____

_____

_____

A SPIRITUAL PRACTICE FOR THIS WEEK

Is there any Scripture "written on your gates" or otherwise displayed in your home, as Deuteronomy instructs? Why or why not? What verses that are important to you might be missing? How could you display them in a way that is meaningful to you?

First Reading

Deuteronomy 11:18–21, 26–28

See, I am setting before you today a blessing and a curse: the blessing, if you obey the commandments of the LORD your God that I am commanding you today; and the curse, if you do not obey the commandments of the LORD your God. (vv. 26–28a)

REFLECTION

People do not always get what they deserve. Blessings and curses are not always distributed in ways that seem connected to behavior. . . .

. . . Moses encourages the people to obey God because he thinks obedience will lead them to a better life. It was and is good advice, but no single lecture can anticipate and include all the nuances of life and theology. This is not the last word in Moses' theology, or a definitive statement of how the world always works. Good behavior often leads to a happier life, but there is no guarantee.

LYNN JAPINGA

RESPONSE

What was a time, recently, when you did not feel you received what you deserved? Were you disappointed or surprised by grace? How has "good behavior" made your life happier? How has it made your life less happy? What does God want for us, here, do you think?

PRAYER

O Lord my God, put your words in my heart and soul that I may grow in faithfulness to you, not to gain any reward but to belong to you, and so be guided by your love and purpose for me. Amen.

Canticle

Psalm 46

He makes wars cease to the end of the earth;
    he breaks the bow, and shatters the spear;
    he burns the shields with fire.
"Be still, and know that I am God!
    I am exalted among the nations,
    I am exalted in the earth." (vv. 9–10)

REFLECTION

It is common to hear "Be still and know that I am God" (Ps. 46:10) set
musically as a call for one to stop worrying and focus on one's spiritual
life. Such an individualistic and interiorized reading is at odds with the
immediate context of the psalm. The verse is, in fact, a stern address to
the whole world, a command from God's very mouth, for the nations
to stop their destructive raging. God ensures his claim of sovereignty by
putting an end to all such violence.

JOEL MARCUS LEMON

RESPONSE

What it is like to hear God speak this verse as a demand for justice and
peace? Who are some of the leaders, nations, or groups you see causing
destruction and violence right now? Write out Psalm 46:10, as you pray
for these people and places.

PRAYER

Almighty God, you command us to be still and know that you, alone,
are God; show me how I can be a part of your justice and peacemaking
here on earth. Amen.

Second Reading

Romans 1:16–17; 3:22b–28

Then what becomes of boasting? It is excluded. By what law? By that of works? No, but by the law of faith. For we hold that a person is justified by faith apart from works prescribed by the law. (3:27–28)

REFLECTION

Our salvation is a matter of sheer gift—of *grace*.

In turn, this means that boasting is no longer a possibility, for we have no righteousness of our own of which we can boast. Instead, we are called only to receive. That passivity, that quietism at the heart of the first movement of salvation, can be profoundly countercultural in a world that measures the value of people by what they do and what they achieve. It can also be slightly disorienting in a world where we seem to have to fight for everything we have. Yet it is the calm at the center of Christian faith.

PAUL T. NIMMO

RESPONSE

How do you tend to feel about your own righteousness? Do you ever lean toward boasting? Toward denial? What does it mean to you at this time in your life that, according to Nimmo's interpretation, faith is a free gift from God, and the first step of salvation is a passive quietism?

PRAYER

Loving Christ, all have sinned and fallen short of the glory of God; help us to learn to believe in your grace and redemption, and that we are justified in you by our faith, not our works. Amen.

Gospel

Matthew 7:21–29

"On that day many will say to me, 'Lord, Lord, did we not prophesy in your name, and cast out demons in your name, and do many deeds of power in your name?' Then I will declare to them, 'I never knew you; go away from me, you evildoers.'" (vv. 22–23)

REFLECTION

When the passage is read in the context of the Gospel's understanding of the kingdom of heaven, it takes on new meaning. . . . Even as the story undermines the false equivalence of deeds of power with the doing of God's will, it also overturns the assumption that in order to be aligned with God's purposes, churches must enact visible and dramatic change, or initiate headline-catching ministries. For the transformation to which Matthew's Gospel points does not depend on great displays of power or public acclaim. The persons in Jesus' illustration who said, "Lord, Lord," mistakenly assumed that it did.

MARY F. FOSKETT

RESPONSE

Are there deeds of power you have wished your congregation was capable of? Or, have deeds of power ever been done that have caused you concern? If transformation in Christ does not depend on dramatic, visible change or headline-catching ministry, then what does it depend on, according to Jesus, do you think?

PRAYER

Lord Jesus, show me how to call on your name but also to do your will, building the house of my faith on rock, not on the sand. Amen.

Weekend Reflections

FURTHER CONNECTION

Instead of this bewildering and exhausting rushing from one thing to another monastic stability means accepting this particular community, this place and these people, this and no other, as the way to God. The man or woman who voluntarily limits himself or herself to one building and a few acres of ground for the rest of life is saying that contentment and fulfilment do not consist in constant change, that true happiness cannot necessarily be found anywhere other than this place and this time.

ESTHER DE WAAL (1930–), *SEEKING GOD: THE WAY OF ST. BENEDICT*

MAKING THE CONNECTIONS

Choose one or two questions for reflection:

1. What connections have you noticed between this week's texts and other passages in Scripture?

2. What connections have you made between this week's texts and the world beyond Scripture?

3. Does either of this week's two commentary themes speak especially to your life or the life of the world around you right now?

4. What is God saying to your congregation in particular through this week's readings and commentaries?

_____

_____

_____

_____

_____

_____

Sabbath Day

SCRIPTURE OF ASSURANCE

And the peace of God, which surpasses all understanding, will guard your hearts and your minds in Christ Jesus. (Philippians 4:7)

WEEKLY EXAMEN

- Take a quiet moment, seek out God's presence, and pray for the guidance of the Spirit.

- Consider the past week; recall specific moments and feelings that stand out to you.

- Choose one moment or feeling for deeper examination, thanksgiving, or repentance.

- Let go, breathe deeply, and invite Christ's love to surround and fill you in preparation for the week ahead.

- End with the Lord's Prayer.

The Week Leading Up to
Proper 5
(Sunday between June 5 and June 11)

Hosea 5:15–6:6

"Let us know, let us press on to know the LORD;
his appearing is as sure as the dawn;
he will come to us like the showers,
like the spring rains that water the earth." (6:3)

Genesis 12:1–9

So Abram went, as the LORD had told him; and Lot went with him. Abram was seventy-five years old when he departed from Haran. (v. 4)

Romans 4:13–25

No distrust made [Abraham] waver concerning the promise of God, but he grew strong in his faith as he gave glory to God, being fully convinced that God was able to do what he had promised. (vv. 20–21)

Matthew 9:9–13, 18–26

When the Pharisees saw this, they said to his disciples, "Why does your teacher eat with tax collectors and sinners?" But when he heard this, he said, "Those who are well have no need of a physician, but those who are sick." (vv. 11–12)

LECTIO DIVINA

Underline a word or phrase that especially grabs your attention. Pray from that word or phrase and ask God to help you connect to its particular invitation for you this week.

Themes from This Week's Writers

THEME 1: *Faith in God Leads Us to Action*

Genesis 12:1–9

It is telling that God calls on two senior citizens (12:4) to undertake the first journey toward the promised land. As the story indicates, no one is ever too old or too anything to receive God's call. Lastly, this narrative shows us that it is not simply belief or faith, but following God's commandments, that is of true importance.

SONG-MI SUZIE PARK

Genesis 12:1–9

This affirmation is not "everything is fine, so go your way." God's voice—this holy voice of foundation and permanence—always challenges and confronts as it moves us to a new place. That is the point: God is our stability, not a program for renewal or a new, shiny idea.

MARK RAMSEY

Romans 4:13–25

This lectionary text does not suggest that Abraham and Sarah had more faith, were more pious, or prayed harder. Faith is not a magic potion that solves our disappointments and dashed expectations. Faith is predicated on God's faithfulness to us. We share in the faith of Sarah and Abraham by moving forward even in disappointment and unfilled hopes and dreams.

WYNDY CORBIN REUSCHLING

THEME 2: *Keeping Faith while We Are Suffering*

Romans 4:13–25

As happened with Abraham in the book of Genesis, Paul tells us, it is easy to lose faith in a promise when time and physical weariness set in. Paul interprets the narratives about Abraham and Sarah and their difficulty in having children at such advanced ages (Gen. 17:15–22) as instructive for the need to have ongoing faith in the face of evidence to the contrary.

EFRAÍN AGOSTO

Matthew 9:9–13, 18–26

The lectionary version says that she believes that she will be "made well" but the verb is more particularly "saved." As a woman with an unclean condition, being healed is a broader salvation from her personal and social suffering.

SONIA E. WATERS

Matthew 9:9–13, 18–26

[Jesus] eats with tax collectors and shows up for those who need him. All of us need him. He shows up for all of us. He comes not for the righteous, but for the sinners. He beckons *all* of us to glance up from our tiny tax booths and cubicles, our interminable suffering and exhaustion, even our piercing, life-shattering grief—to follow him.

DENISE THORPE

WHAT IS THE HOLY SPIRIT SAYING TO YOU THIS WEEK?

_____

_____

_____

_____

_____

A SPIRITUAL PRACTICE FOR THIS WEEK

Approach the presence of Jesus through Christian music this week—but as a foreigner. Choose a genre that is unfamiliar or even distasteful to you: pop, rap, country, gospel choir, plainchant, another language. Choose an album or artist and listen all week. What do you notice about Jesus, from this cultural perspective outside of your own?

First Reading

Hosea 5:15–6:6

For I desire steadfast love and not sacrifice,
the knowledge of God rather than burnt offerings. (6:6)

REFLECTION

This verse has been deliberately misread as God disparaging action, especially ritual action, and elevating belief and right emotions. However, as Hosea's list of charges clearly shows, actions reflect belief; hence, when God demands steadfast love and knowledge, God is calling for right and ethical action. It is not actions per se but empty actions that are declared to be displeasing to God. In essence, God is saying, What use is going to church every Sunday if you cheat, lie, and rob people during the week?

SONG-MI SUZIE PARK

RESPONSE

Does your practice of Sunday worship tend to feel like a ritual action or habit rather than a way to grow in love? Is it ever a source of self-righteousness or pride? How is attending worship helping you grow into a wiser, more compassionate person? What might those around you say?

PRAYER

Lord of the Sabbath, I want to know you and live in your ways; teach me to worship in such a way that I grow both in steadfast love for my neighbor and into an expansive sense of your presence. Amen.

Canticle

Psalm 50:7–15

For every wild animal of the forest is mine,
    the cattle on a thousand hills.
I know all the birds of the air,
    and all that moves in the field is mine. (vv. 10–11)

REFLECTION

Consider nature, which figures centrally in both the first reading and
the psalm. . . . Hosea equates divine steadfastness with the constancy of
cosmic rhythms, and erratic human devotion with morning mist. How
does our understanding of the fragility and complexity of ecological
and cosmic phenomena illuminate such metaphors today? Further,
the prophetic passage ends with burnt offerings, lifeless animal bodies.
The psalmist widens the lens to focus on both domestic and untamed
species, on birds, and on blood. God has no need of such offerings. Yet
mass extinction reigns.

W. SCOTT HALDEMAN

RESPONSE

Name some ways that humans injure and sacrifice the lives of animals
for gain, greed, and pleasure. Even if not made in God's image, animals
are clearly beloved of God. Reading this psalm, how might God be
inviting us to be more like God in our relationship with animals?

PRAYER

Loving God, you do not look kindly on the careless killing of animals;
give me a sense of care and fellowship with my fellow creatures, that I
may see them as yours first, not mine. Amen.

Second Reading

Romans 4:13–25

Therefore [Abraham's] faith "was reckoned to him as righteousness." Now the words, "it was reckoned to him," were written not for his sake alone, but for ours also. It will be reckoned to us who believe in him who raised Jesus our Lord from the dead. (vv. 22–24)

REFLECTION

Paul writes about the "reckoning" or "logic" that comes from believing in God's promises (4:22–25). The "logic" (the root word for "reckoning" is *logos*) of faith is that trusting in the God who fulfills promises leads to one's designation as a "righteous" one. Abraham's faith led, logically in God's reckoning, to his righteousness (*dikaiosynē*). Such reckoning works not only for Abraham, "the father of faith," but for all who believe similarly in the promises of God. The previous experiences of the people Israel, beginning with Abraham, foreshadowed Paul's current day and that of future generations of the faithful.

EFRAÍN AGOSTO

RESPONSE

How easy or difficult has it been for you lately to trust in God's promises? What does that look like in your life right now? How would you describe the state of your faith this week? What does it mean to you to be assured of your righteousness in Christ?

PRAYER

God of Abraham, show me how to have faith in your promise of life and love; help me to know that it is not what I say, do, or accomplish but my ability to trust in you that grounds my faith. Amen.

Gospel

Matthew 9:9–13, 18–26

Then suddenly a woman who had been suffering from hemorrhages for twelve years came up behind him and touched the fringe of his cloak, for she said to herself, "If I only touch his cloak, I will be made well." (vv. 20–21)

REFLECTION

Some of us [like the leader of the synagogue] receive the good news only when we reach a moment of all-encompassing, visceral pain and grief—kneeling before Jesus, desperately begging for his touch of resurrection, for the restoration of relationship. . . . Others of us journey with the bleeding woman: worn down, depleted, isolated, reaching from within the fog of vulnerability and pain to grab onto the garment of the One whose presence can make us well. Whether by means of high drama or ordinary tenacity, we hear a voice saying, "Follow me," . . . an invitation to a shared table where Jesus welcomes sinners.

DENISE THORPE

RESPONSE

How do you resemble the leader of the synagogue? The woman pulling at Jesus' cloak? What pain in you needs the healing of Christ this week? How is Jesus inviting you toward healing? And then, to "follow me"?

PRAYER

Brother Jesus, you welcomed both the leader of the synagogue and the bleeding woman to ask for your healing and then to follow you; you invite me to do the same, whatever my suffering or fears. Amen.

Weekend Reflections

FURTHER CONNECTION

"Can it cure the one spiritual disease?" asked Father Brown, with a serious curiosity.

"And what is the one spiritual disease?" asked Flambeau, smiling.

"Oh, thinking one is quite well," said his friend.

G.K. CHESTERTON (1874–1936), "THE EYE OF
APOLLO," A FATHER BROWN MYSTERY

MAKING THE CONNECTIONS

Choose one or two questions for reflection:

1. What connections have you noticed between this week's texts and other passages in Scripture?

2. What connections have you made between this week's texts and the world beyond Scripture?

3. Does either of this week's two commentary themes speak especially to your life or the life of the world around you right now?

4. What is God saying to your congregation in particular through this week's readings and commentaries?

_____

_____

_____

_____

_____

_____

Sabbath Day

SCRIPTURE OF ASSURANCE

> But I will sing of your might;
> I will sing aloud of your steadfast love in the morning.
> For you have been a fortress for me
> and a refuge in the day of my distress. (Psalm 59:16)

WEEKLY EXAMEN

- Take a quiet moment, seek out God's presence, and pray for the guidance of the Spirit.

- Consider the past week; recall specific moments and feelings that stand out to you.

- Choose one moment or feeling for deeper examination, thanksgiving, or repentance.

- Let go, breathe deeply, and invite Christ's love to surround and fill you in preparation for the week ahead.

- End with the Lord's Prayer.

The Week Leading Up to
Proper 6
(Sunday between June 12 and June 18)

Exodus 19:2–8a

"You have seen what I did to the Egyptians, and how I bore you on eagles' wings and brought you to myself. Now therefore, if you obey my voice and keep my covenant, you shall be my treasured possession out of all the peoples." (vv. 4–5a)

Genesis 18:1–15 (21:1–7)

The LORD said to Abraham, "Why did Sarah laugh, and say, 'Shall I indeed bear a child, now that I am old?' Is anything too wonderful for the LORD? At the set time I will return to you, in due season, and Sarah shall have a son." (18:13–14)

Romans 5:1–8

And not only that, but we also boast in our sufferings, knowing that suffering produces endurance, and endurance produces character, and character produces hope. (vv. 3–4a)

Matthew 9:35–10:8 (9–23)

"And you will be hated by all because of my name. But the one who endures to the end will be saved. When they persecute you in one town, flee to the next; for truly I tell you, you will not have gone through all the towns of Israel before the Son of Man comes." (10:22–23)

LECTIO DIVINA

Underline a word or phrase that especially grabs your attention. Pray from that word or phrase and ask God to help you connect to its particular invitation for you this week.

Themes from This Week's Writers

THEME 1: *Is Anything Too Wonderful for the Lord?*

Genesis 18:1–15 (21:1–7)

Such stories about miraculous pregnancies can provide hope, but can also mislead struggling women into thinking that their infertility is the result of a lack of faith. . . . A discussion about how the biblical narratives, especially stories about miracles, can help and also hurt the people of God, is worthy of the pulpit.

SONG-MI SUZIE PARK

Exodus 19:2–8a and Genesis 18:1–15 (21:1–7)

So many people come to worship each week having been marinated in dull, despairing, or distracting conventional wisdom about everything that is perceived as not possible. Liturgically, these texts of promise and covenant yearn for an hour of joyful prayer, holy surprise, heartfelt praise, deep nurture, and a feeling of soaring on eagles' wings.

MARK RAMSEY

Romans 5:1–8

In effect, "hope" completes the chain, and so the main point is that suffering in this life, just like the death of Jesus, does not end there. Come what may, there is always hope, just as the death of Jesus issues in resurrection, the ultimate hope. Thus this type of hope "does not disappoint" (v. 5a).

EFRAÍN AGOSTO

THEME 2: *The Cost of Discipleship*

Romans 5:1–8

The passage assumes there will be suffering for those who follow Christ's way and share in his life.

Paul suggests that suffering may produce certain character traits (vv. 3–5). However, these are not guaranteed results. Suffering takes an enormous toll on persons, and its effects are often unpredictable.

WYNDY CORBIN REUSCHLING

Matthew 9:35–10:8 (9–23)

Controversy and persecution are not a sign that the mission has failed. Instead, the believers are told to keep their wits about them, using persecutions strategically for public witness.

SONIA E. WATERS

Matthew 9:35–10:8 (9–23)

Given the church's proclivity to indulge wretched behavior in the name of being nice and then to suck people dry with committees, duties, obligations, and moral demands, this Gospel word on boundaries and limits bears attention. Inherent to the authority Jesus vests in his disciples is an admonition to trust and to give—and then to set limits when the gift is not received or is abused.

DENISE THORPE

WHAT IS THE HOLY SPIRIT SAYING TO YOU THIS WEEK?

_____

_____

_____

_____

_____

A SPIRITUAL PRACTICE FOR THIS WEEK

Reflect on Romans 5:1–8 by writing it out, slowly, by hand. Have fun and be creative or keep it simple. How does writing a text change how you experience it? What stands out to you? If you have time, write it out more than once and see how this influences your understanding.

First Reading

Exodus 19:2–8a or Genesis 18:1–15 (21:1–7)

Indeed, the whole earth is mine, but you shall be for me a priestly kingdom and a holy nation. (Exodus 19:5b–6a)

And she said, "Who would ever have said to Abraham that Sarah would nurse children? Yet I have borne him a son in his old age." (Genesis 21:7)

REFLECTION

Flannery O'Connor . . . was fond of saying "mystery is the great embarrassment to the modern mind." . . . This is precisely why these texts of God's covenant and God's audacious promise of a child, cloaked as they are in the mystery of holiness, are so needed to our modern minds. Stories of God's activity that would lead us to exclaim, "Is anything too wonderful for the Lord?"—this is something we need to draw close to, not to dismantle for examination. These words allow us to give ourselves over in awe and wonder to experience what it is to be treasured by the living God.

MARK RAMSEY

RESPONSE

How do you feel embarrassed by mystery? How do you feel a need for it? What longings in yourself seem too audacious or ridiculous to contemplate? How might God be inviting you to give yourself over to awe, wonder, or radical expectation this week?

PRAYER

Gracious Lord, is anything too wonderful for you? Open my heart to the power of your mystery that I may give myself over to awe, and wonder at how deeply I am treasured by you, the living God. Amen.

Canticle

Psalm 116:1–2, 12–19

O Lord, I am your servant;
    I am your servant, the child of your serving girl.
    You have loosed my bonds.
I will offer to you a thanksgiving sacrifice
    and call on the name of the Lord. (vv. 16–17)

REFLECTION

Hagar too might have declared, "O Lord, I am your servant; . . . you have loosed my bonds" (v. 16). . . . Yet, it is Ishmael (is it not?) who is "child of a servant girl," who is servant of the Lord, whose bonds have been loosed and who will make his vows to the Lord (vv. 16, 18). The psalmist might point [you] to a rereading of the story of the promise of Isaac and then his birth and circumcision through the eyes of a character left unmentioned: Ishmael, Isaac's half brother, who is also a child of promise but slave and outcast and refugee.

W. SCOTT HALDEMAN

RESPONSE

Reread this psalm twice, imagining first that Sarah is speaking, then Ishmael. (You may want to reread his birth story in Genesis 16.) Which perspective do you identify with most? What gaps or connections might the Spirit be inviting you to notice in your own family, congregation, or community, through these varying perspectives?

PRAYER

O El Roi: God who sees, teach me to see and have compassion for my own needs, but also to see the ways my needs may cause others to suffer, that I may live into your wholeness and righteousness. Amen.

Second Reading

Romans 5:1–8

And hope does not disappoint us, because God's love has been poured into our hearts through the Holy Spirit that has been given to us.

For while we were still weak, at the right time Christ died for the ungodly. (vv. 5–6)

REFLECTION

The hope that God gives, one that does not disappoint, keeps us from the futility and despair that characterizes so much of human suffering. Hope is not just wanting things to be better or different. Hope is not a form of denial about how bad things might be. Rather, hope is a gift from God and a Christian virtue that helps us trust God and God's ability to bring about meaning and life, even in our most dire circumstances. It is God who can bring life out of suffering, as God brought life out of Christ's suffering.

WYNDY CORBIN REUSCHLING

RESPONSE

How does it make a difference to understand hope, not as a wishing that things were different or denying how bad they really are, but as trust that God can bring new life and meaning out of suffering? How is this speaking to your life this week? To this week's headlines?

PRAYER

God of hope, your love has been poured into our hearts through the Holy Spirit; teach us to trust your ability to bring about meaning and life, even out of suffering and despair. Amen.

Gospel

Matthew 9:35–10:8 (9–23)

Take no gold, or silver, or copper in your belts, no bag for your journey, or two tunics, or sandals, or a staff; for laborers deserve their food. Whatever town or village you enter, find out who in it is worthy, and stay there until you leave. (vv. 9–11)

REFLECTION

This wandering life is also another way to live as Jesus did, for he was an itinerant preacher with nowhere to lay his head (Matt. 8:20). It is possible that Matthew's community was started by such preachers or that it sent poor itinerant preachers in mission. Certainly the call to wander for God reaches all the way back to Abraham, and today's reading from Genesis 18 also suggests themes of surprising provision and promise when all hope seemed lost. [You] could reflect on how Jesus calls believers to minister in vulnerability, depend on God's provision, and follow God's call even when the way seems unclear.

SONIA E. WATERS

RESPONSE

How have you felt like a wanderer in your life, recently or in the past? Did it feel like a call from God, in some way? How has God provided for you or surprised you, in wandering? What has the vulnerability of wandering taught you about following God? Depending on God?

PRAYER

Jesus the wanderer, you had nowhere to lay your head; guide me in the journey of my life and work, that I may not hide in self-sufficiency but depend on you and my neighbors. Amen.

Weekend Reflections

FURTHER CONNECTION

My name was Isabella; but when I left the house of bondage, I left
everything behind. I wa'n't goin' to keep nothin' of Egypt on me, an'
so I went to the Lord an' asked Him to give me a new name. And the
Lord gave me Sojourner, because I was to travel up an' down the land,
showing the people their sins, an' bein' a sign unto them. Afterwards
I told the Lord I wanted another name, 'cause everybody else had two
names; and the Lord gave me Truth, because I was to declare the truth
to the people.

SOJOURNER TRUTH (1797–1883), *ATLANTIC MONTHLY*, APRIL 1863

MAKING THE CONNECTIONS

Choose one or two questions for reflection:

1. What connections have you noticed between this week's texts and
   other passages in Scripture?

2. What connections have you made between this week's texts and the
   world beyond Scripture?

3. Does either of this week's two commentary themes speak especially
   to your life or the life of the world around you right now?

4. What is God saying to your congregation in particular through this
   week's readings and commentaries?

_____

_____

_____

_____

_____

_____

Sabbath Day

SCRIPTURE OF ASSURANCE

Now the LORD came and stood there, calling as before, "Samuel! Samuel!" And Samuel said, "Speak, for your servant is listening." (1 Samuel 3:10)

WEEKLY EXAMEN

- Take a quiet moment, seek out God's presence, and pray for the guidance of the Spirit.

- Consider the past week; recall specific moments and feelings that stand out to you.

- Choose one moment or feeling for deeper examination, thanksgiving, or repentance.

- Let go, breathe deeply, and invite Christ's love to surround and fill you in preparation for the week ahead.

- End with the Lord's Prayer.

The Week Leading Up to
Proper 7
(Sunday between June 19 and June 25)

Jeremiah 20:7–13

If I say, "I will not mention him,
    or speak any more in his name,"
then within me there is something like a burning fire
    shut up in my bones;
I am weary with holding it in,
    and I cannot. (v. 9)

Genesis 21:8–21

But Sarah saw the son of Hagar the Egyptian, whom she had borne to Abraham, playing with her son Isaac. So she said to Abraham, "Cast out this slave woman with her son; for the son of this slave woman shall not inherit along with my son Isaac." The matter was very distressing to Abraham on account of his son. (vv. 9–11)

Romans 6:1b–11

But if we have died with Christ, we believe that we will also live with him. We know that Christ, being raised from the dead, will never die again; death no longer has dominion over him. (vv. 8–9)

Matthew 10:24–39

Are not two sparrows sold for a penny? Yet not one of them will fall to the ground apart from your Father. And even the hairs of your head are all counted. So do not be afraid; you are of more value than many sparrows. (vv. 29–31)

LECTIO DIVINA

Underline a word or phrase that especially grabs your attention. Pray from that word or phrase and ask God to help you connect to its particular invitation for you this week.

Themes from This Week's Writers

THEME 1: *Those Who Lose Their Life for My Sake Will Find It*

Jeremiah 20:7–13

As is evident from Jeremiah's example, being faithful to God can lead to ridicule and ill-treatment from the community, even from friends. . . .

Jeremiah's lament opens up space for a discussion of difficulties faced by those who currently are called by God to speak and work for moral transformation in society.

SONG-MI SUZIE PARK

Jeremiah 20:7–13

That Jeremiah was both called, affirmed, faithful, *and* in great pain is a theme that a sermon could embrace: the difficulty of holding all those things together in one life.

MARK RAMSEY

Romans 6:1b–11

The crucifixion and death that Paul describes are actions that have already been done to Christ. . . . We are not commanded to crucify ourselves or to ask others to do the same. Using examples from popular devotional books that refer to "dying to self" and "crucifying one's self" may be ways to help congregants see the harmful ways in which this language is used.

WYNDY CORBIN REUSCHLING

THEME 2: *Facing Fear*

Romans 6:1b–11

We may sin again as frail human beings, but our goal lies in being more and more like Christ each and every day. Death has no power over Christ (v. 9), nor should it over us. Even though our mortal body will pass away, death does not have the last word.

EFRAÍN AGOSTO

Matthew 10:24–39

For the early church, tribulations occur because Jesus does not usher in the peaceable kingdom but the beginning chaos of the end times. . . . Persecution, family discord, and the destruction of social ties are the expected suffering before the messianic age. The new family gathered together by this shepherd is prioritized over earthly loyalties.

SONIA E. WATERS

Matthew 10:24–39

The snapshot of Christian living [Matthew] offers is the life of Jesus himself: Jesus suffered; he was falsely accused, persecuted, run out of town, backed to the edge of a cliff, questioned by authorities, and eventually killed. We should expect no less. Our suffering does not mean that we are not beloved by God. It simply means that the power of a life drenched in God's love threatens the powers and principalities of this world.

DENISE THORPE

WHAT IS THE HOLY SPIRIT SAYING TO YOU THIS WEEK?

_____

_____

_____

_____

_____

A SPIRITUAL PRACTICE FOR THIS WEEK

Find the closest domestic violence or homeless shelter for women and children. Learn about its mission. Pray for its leaders and clients each day this week. At the end of the week, as you are able, make a generous donation.

First Reading

Genesis 21:8–21

And God heard the voice of the boy; and the angel of God called to Hagar from heaven, and said to her, "What troubles you, Hagar? Do not be afraid; for God has heard the voice of the boy where he is. Come, lift up the boy and hold him fast with your hand, for I will make a great nation of him." (vv. 17–18)

REFLECTION

That Hagar is rescued twice by God, who twice promises her that her descendants will thrive, hints that God has particular regard for those who, like Hagar, are oppressed, powerless, and marginalized. . . . How have we, like Sarah and Abraham, thrown out the Hagars and Ishmaels to fend for themselves in the desert? How can we instead act on behalf of the Hagars and Ishmaels by calling out and challenging society when it mistreats the marginalized and powerless? After all, as these stories remind us, the God of Hagar watches and sees the oppression of her descendants (21:17).

SONG-MI SUZIE PARK

RESPONSE

Who are the "Hagars and Ishmaels" in your community? How has your church acted on their behalf? Neglected to act? Or perhaps actively abandoned or excluded them? How might God be calling you or your congregation to serve, reach out, or advocate for them, now?

PRAYER

El Roi: God who sees, you see the struggle and hear the voice of the powerless; teach me to see, listen to, and serve the people my congregation or community has forgotten or abandoned. Amen.

Canticle

Psalm 69:7–10 (11–15), 16–18

Do not hide your face from your servant,
  for I am in distress—make haste to answer me.
Draw near to me, redeem me,
  set me free because of my enemies. (vv. 17–18)

REFLECTION

The psalmist is among the captives, surrounded by those who wish harm
to the people, mocked by those who deny the power and concern of
their God. Distress is all around; death seems imminent. . . .
  . . . Are we to preach comfort to those in distress, perhaps as their
privilege is eroded? Are we to announce destruction based either on
divine judgment of the nation's faithlessness or because of divine
abandonment? Should we, because we reside as captives in foreign
territory, try to sustain the hope—both our own and that of our
people—that our cities and our fortunes will be reclaimed?

W. SCOTT HALDEMAN

RESPONSE

How might you or your congregation be residing "as captives in foreign
territory"? Do you feel called to announce God's judgment this week, or
do you long for God's comfort? Or both? How can you pray, this week,
for your city to be reclaimed by God's love and justice?

PRAYER

Loving God, do not hide your face from me or any who are in distress;
give me your comfort and strengthen me to listen to your judgments, to
be willing to be changed, that I may be set free. Amen.

Second Reading

Romans 6:1b–11

The death he died, he died to sin, once for all; but the life he lives, he lives to God. So you also must consider yourselves dead to sin and alive to God in Christ Jesus. (vv. 10–11)

REFLECTION

It may be tempting in congregations to assume that persons already know the gospel of Christ, or once they have accepted the gospel, they need not be reminded of its power in their own lives. A wise friend once said there were parts of his life that remained sadly untouched by the good news, and that the gospel of Christ still needed to be preached to him. Persons in our congregations need to hear again and again the good news that is offered in this passage. . . . We cannot hear this good news enough.

WYNDY CORBIN REUSCHLING

RESPONSE

What would it look like for you to feel alive to God in Christ Jesus? What parts of your life, would you say, remain "sadly untouched by the good news"? How do you need to hear, again and again, the gospel of Christ preached to you?

PRAYER

Christ Jesus, preach to me the message of your good news, that all of my body, my heart, and my life may truly receive it. Amen.

Gospel

Matthew 10:24–39

"Whoever loves father or mother more than me is not worthy of me; and whoever loves son or daughter more than me is not worthy of me; and whoever does not take up the cross and follow me is not worthy of me. Those who find their life will lose it, and those who lose their life for my sake will find it." (vv. 37–39)

REFLECTION

It is awe inspiring to imagine the personal and social losses that Matthew's community must have experienced in order to make this teaching an encouraging word for them. It is debated whether they were still a part of the synagogue or had been expelled, though the constant clashes with religious leaders in this Gospel would suggest that a breach had already occurred. They also held the traumatic memory of the fall of the temple in 70 CE, and would have been vulnerable to waves of Roman persecution. It is a community that is embattled and somewhat defenseless, like sparrows.

SONIA E. WATERS

RESPONSE

Reflect on a traumatic event that has had a significant effect on your life or the life of your congregation. When have you felt embattled or defenseless? Persecuted or expelled? How does reading this passage from the perspective of a traumatized community change the words and how you hear them?

PRAYER

O God, you are with us through trauma, violence, and persecution; preserve us in your love that we do not become embittered but remain compassionate and hopeful, through your Son Jesus Christ. Amen.

Weekend Reflections

Hagar has "spoken" to generation after generation of black women because her story has been validated as true by suffering black people. She and Ishmael together, as family, model many black American families in which a lone woman/mother struggles to hold the family together in spite of the poverty to which ruling class economics consign it. Hagar, like many black women, goes into the wide world to make a living for herself and her child, with only God by her side.

DELORES WILLIAMS (1937–), *SISTERS IN THE WILDERNESS: THE CHALLENGE OF WOMANIST GOD-TALK*

MAKING THE CONNECTIONS

Choose one or two questions for reflection:

1. What connections have you noticed between this week's texts and other passages in Scripture?

2. What connections have you made between this week's texts and the world beyond Scripture?

3. Does either of this week's two commentary themes speak especially to your life or the life of the world around you right now?

4. What is God saying to your congregation in particular through this week's readings and commentaries?

_____

_____

_____

_____

_____

_____

Sabbath Day

SCRIPTURE OF ASSURANCE

Jesus said to them again, "Peace be with you. As the Father has sent me, so I send you." When he had said this, he breathed on them and said to them, "Receive the Holy Spirit." (John 20:21–22)

WEEKLY EXAMEN

- Take a quiet moment, seek out God's presence, and pray for the guidance of the Spirit.

- Consider the past week; recall specific moments and feelings that stand out to you.

- Choose one moment or feeling for deeper examination, thanksgiving, or repentance.

- Let go, breathe deeply, and invite Christ's love to surround and fill you in preparation for the week ahead.

- End with the Lord's Prayer.

The Week Leading Up to
Proper 8
(Sunday between June 26 and July 2)

Jeremiah 28:5–9

"As for the prophet who prophesies peace, when the word of that prophet comes true, then it will be known that the Lord has truly sent the prophet." (v. 9)

Genesis 22:1–14

After these things God tested Abraham. He said to him, "Abraham!" And he said, "Here I am." He said, "Take your son, your only son Isaac, whom you love, and go to the land of Moriah, and offer him there as a burnt offering on one of the mountains that I shall show you." (vv. 1–2)

Romans 6:12–23

Do you not know that if you present yourselves to anyone as obedient slaves, you are slaves of the one whom you obey, either of sin, which leads to death, or of obedience, which leads to righteousness? (v. 16)

Matthew 10:40–42

"Whoever welcomes a prophet in the name of a prophet will receive a prophet's reward; and whoever welcomes a righteous person in the name of a righteous person will receive the reward of the righteous." (v. 41)

LECTIO DIVINA

> Underline a word or phrase that especially grabs your attention. Pray from that word or phrase and ask God to help you connect to its particular invitation for you this week.

Themes from This Week's Writers

THEME 1: *Are We Welcoming Prophets in Our Midst, or Not?*

Jeremiah 28:5–9

[Jeremiah] wished that his opponent's prophesy could be true, but his word from God meant that it was not. . . . It is not easy to distinguish true prophets from false ones; in the press of the current prophets, no one carries a sign distinguishing the true from the false.

STEPHEN BRECK REID

Psalm 89:1–4, 15–18

Consider the possibility that prophecy is more complex than predicting the future. Instead of thinking of prophets as persons who predict the future, we should think of them as persons who attempt to shape the future that God intends. Prophecy becomes a dynamic process, rather than the prediction of a single event that either happens or does not.

J. CLINTON MCCANN JR.

Matthew 10:40–42

When God sent emissaries and prophets into our midst to tell us a new way, a way of justice and equity and mercy, we heard this as bad news, not good news. We offered no welcome, no hospitality, and no cold cup of water. Instead we denied and rejected and expelled, and we still have received no reward, because we did not know the time of our visitation.

NIBS STROUPE

THEME 2: *How Does Our Discipleship Shape Our Lives?*

Romans 6:12–23

Today's reading . . . focuses on living out the reality of justification by choosing which dominion, God or sin, rules and shapes daily life. . . . Paul does not use the term "slave" to advocate for social change, but to illustrate the polarity between a life surrendered to sin and a life surrendered to God.

RENATA FURST

Romans 6:12–23

Powerful sin will not remain powerful enough to rule us and have controlling dominion over our lives, as we are enabled to live under the liberating rule of grace. This transforming movement from serving our own idolatries to serving righteousness infuses the heart and soul of our personhood with sanctifying hope and possibility.

DEAN K. THOMPSON

Matthew 10:40–42

Disciples are likened to prophets, the righteous, and little ones, an interesting triad of images that links the disciples to strong prophetic tasks and acts of justice and mercy, even as they are also reminded about their own vulnerability and fragility.

MIHEE KIM-KORT

WHAT IS THE HOLY SPIRIT SAYING TO YOU THIS WEEK?

_____

_____

_____

_____

_____

A SPIRITUAL PRACTICE FOR THIS WEEK

Jesus told his disciples: "Whoever welcomes you welcomes me." How have you felt welcomed by other people this past week? (Has anyone given you a cup of cold water?) What is it like to imagine others welcoming Christ through you? How have you allowed others to welcome you? How have you resisted?

First Reading

Genesis 22:1–14

But the angel of the LORD called to him from heaven, and said, "Abraham, Abraham!" And he said, "Here I am." He said, "Do not lay your hand on the boy or do anything to him; for now I know that you fear God, since you have not withheld your son, your only son, from me." (vv. 11–12)

REFLECTION

The great twentieth-century interpreter of the Hebrew Bible, Gerhard von Rad, describes the test to which God subjects Abraham in this passage as an *Anfechtung*, the German word for a soul-shattering temptation or trial.[1] It is the same word that Martin Luther used to describe the period in his life when he was gripped by the fear that God could never forgive him.[2] The preacher might well approach a sermon on this passage as its own kind of *Anfechtung*, given the odd combination of familiarity and moral quandary the passage presents.

ROBERT A. RATCLIFF

RESPONSE

What is an *Anfechtung* you have faced in your own life? How did you navigate this trial or temptation? How did the experience change or affect your relationship with God? How does your story compare or contrast with Abraham's?

PRAYER

God of Abraham, in this situation I do not understand You. Your behavior violates our covenant; still, I trust You because it is You, because it is You and me, because it is us. Amen.[3]

1. Gerhard von Rad, *Genesis: A Commentary*, rev. ed. (Philadelphia: Westminster, 1961), 244–45.
2. Roland Bainton, *Here I Stand: A Life of Martin Luther* (Nashville: Abingdon, 1978), 31.
3. From a prayer by Eliezer Berkovits; see Weekend Reflections.

Canticle

Psalm 13

But I trusted in your steadfast love;
   my heart shall rejoice in your salvation.
I will sing to the LORD,
   because he has dealt bountifully with me. (vv. 5–6)

REFLECTION

Never are we told what Abraham thought or felt as he and Isaac "walked
on together" (Gen. 22:6). Was it anger, fear, terror, sorrow, incredulity,
regret? . . .
   . . . Perhaps the lectionary's pairing of Psalm 13 with Genesis 22:1–
14 is meant to fill in the blanks. In any case, Psalm 13:1–2 may well
help one imagine Abraham's thoughts and feelings in Genesis 22:1–10:
questioning, apparent abandonment, unsettledness, sorrow. Psalm
13:5–6 may well help one imagine Abraham's thought and feelings in
Genesis 22:11–14, especially the joy of life restored.

J. CLINTON MCCANN JR.

RESPONSE

Read Psalm 13, imagining that it is Abraham who is speaking or singing,
as he climbs Mount Moriah with his son. What do you notice? What
in this psalm could also be you, speaking to God about your journey, at
this time in your life?

PRAYER

How long, O Lord? Will you forget me and my loved ones forever? How
long will you hide your face from me? Consider and answer me, O Lord
my God, that I may know joy in the morning. Amen.

Second Reading

Romans 6:12–23

But thanks be to God that you, having once been slaves of sin, have become obedient from the heart to the form of teaching to which you were entrusted, and that you, having been set free from sin, have become slaves of righteousness. (vv. 17–18)

REFLECTION

Ironically, Paul exhorts his readers to *choose* one form of slavery over another. A modern reader (and perhaps Paul's readers also), accustomed to the juxtaposition of slavery (evil) vs. freedom (good), would find this exhortation jarring. Paul uses a different polarity: slavery to sin (evil, death) vs. slavery to God, a good that leads to life. A feeling, thinking person lives an obedience from the heart that leads to righteousness (v. 17). In this case "slavery" leads to a greater good. . . . Death, the result of slavery to sin, becomes life through submission to God.

RENATA FURST

RESPONSE

"Slavery" is a repulsive word in our society. Could you describe "slavery to God" in such a way that it would have something to teach you about life in Christ? Is there any glimpse of the gospel in such a fraught, painful word? Or is it a bridge too far?

PRAYER

Loving God, I long to follow your way of goodness and love, but I also give thanks for the freedom and integrity of my mind and heart. Teach me the meaning of holy obedience. Amen.

Gospel

Matthew 10:40–42

"Whoever welcomes you welcomes me, and whoever welcomes me welcomes the one who sent me." (v. 40)

REFLECTION

Those of us . . . to whom these prophets come, are asked to consider that a new word is spoken, that a new view of reality is revealed, that a whole new way of life—a way of love and justice and equity—is proclaimed. Those of us who are recipients of this proclamation are asked to listen, not immediately reject . . . [and] to consider whether we will be rejecting the power of Jesus in rejecting the message. Will we miss our chance of gaining our new lives because we will not consider whether the prophet is from God?

NIBS STROUPE

RESPONSE

Consider what prophets are proclaiming a new reality in your life, community, or congregation right now. Notice if you find yourself wanting to listen to or to reject these prophets. What risks exist? How might the power of Jesus be at work? What opportunity for new life is God opening to you?

PRAYER

Jesus Christ, teach me how to welcome prophets into my life and my church, that by welcoming their voices I may also welcome you. Send me, also, as a prophet, to speak with love about what I care about. Amen.

Weekend Reflections

FURTHER CONNECTION

> In this situation I do not understand You. Your behavior violates our covenant; still, I trust You because it is You, because it is You and me, because it is us. . . .
>
> Almighty God! What you are asking of me is terrible. . . . But I have known you, my God. You have loved me and I love You. My God, you are breaking Your word to me. . . . Yet I trust You; I trust You.
>
> ELIEZER BERKOVITS (1908–92), *WITH GOD IN HELL:*
> *JUDAISM IN THE GHETTOS AND DEATHCAMPS*

MAKING THE CONNECTIONS

Choose one or two questions for reflection:

1. What connections have you noticed between this week's texts and other passages in Scripture?

2. What connections have you made between this week's texts and the world beyond Scripture?

3. Does either of this week's two commentary themes speak especially to your life or the life of the world around you right now?

4. What is God saying to your congregation in particular through this week's readings and commentaries?

_____

_____

_____

_____

_____

_____

Sabbath Day

SCRIPTURE OF ASSURANCE

So we do not lose heart. Even though our outer nature is wasting away, our inner nature is being renewed day by day. (2 Corinthians 4:16)

WEEKLY EXAMEN

- Take a quiet moment, seek out God's presence, and pray for the guidance of the Spirit.

- Consider the past week; recall specific moments and feelings that stand out to you.

- Choose one moment or feeling for deeper examination, thanksgiving, or repentance.

- Let go, breathe deeply, and invite Christ's love to surround and fill you in preparation for the week ahead.

- End with the Lord's Prayer.

The Week Leading Up to
Proper 9
(Sunday between July 3 and July 9)

Zechariah 9:9–12

He will cut off the chariot from Ephraim
and the war-horse from Jerusalem;
and the battle bow shall be cut off,
and he shall command peace to the nations. (v. 10a)

Genesis 24:34–38, 42–49, 58–67

And they called Rebekah, and said to her, "Will you go with this man?" She said, "I will." So they sent away their sister Rebekah and her nurse along with Abraham's servant and his men. . . . Then Rebekah and her maids rose up, mounted the camels, and followed the man; thus the servant took Rebekah, and went his way. (vv. 58–59, 61)

Romans 7:15–25a

Wretched man that I am! Who will rescue me from this body of death? Thanks be to God through Jesus Christ our Lord! (vv. 24–25)

Matthew 11:16–19, 25–30

"Take my yoke upon you, and learn from me; for I am gentle and humble in heart, and you will find rest for your souls. For my yoke is easy, and my burden is light." (vv. 29–30)

LECTIO DIVINA

Underline a word or phrase that especially grabs your attention. Pray from that word or phrase and ask God to help you connect to its particular invitation for you this week.

Themes from This Week's Writers

THEME 1: *God Will Command Peace to the Nations*

Zechariah 9:9–12

Whether it be through human royalty, the Messiah, or God's own self, the cessation of hostility and the dawning of peace is a divine gift and a divine calling.

. . . Declaring that none of us can enjoy peace until the last one of us finds justice, God intends to rescue the prisoners from the waterless pit and restore to them double (Zech. 9:11–12).

ROBERT A. RATCLIFF

Psalm 145:8–14

The prophet and the psalmist point in the same direction. God, who is the king in Zechariah 9:9, rules with humility. . . . God the king sets things right by destroying the equipment of warfare in verse 10. . . . In short, God's exercise of power aims for nothing short of world peace.

J. CLINTON MCCANN JR.

Romans 7:15–25a

The God who frees, who is merciful, who brings peace in these texts, is the Jesus who says to those who are weary and bowed down: "Come to me . . . and I will give you rest" (Matt. 11:28). . . .

. . . God is a warrior for peace.

RENATA FURST

THEME 2: *God's Love Redeems Us*

Romans 7:15–25a

Even if we descend into utter darkness, even if we can never quite climb into the light, nothing shall separate us from the love of God (8:39). This is the liberating grace that redeems not only our vices but our virtues too. We are set free to joyfully seek the will of God in the confidence that *God* redeems and is making all things new.

PATRICK W. T. JOHNSON

Matthew 11:16–19, 25–30

Are the children in the parable supposed to symbolize John the Baptist and Jesus? John called for mourning and repentance in the face of judgment, whereas Jesus proclaimed joy because of the presence of the kingdom; in both cases their messages encountered unbelief or indifference.

MIHEE KIM-KORT

Matthew 11:16–19, 25–30

Jesus sees his mission as one of bringing God's love and joy into our lives. . . .

. . . As Fred Rogers emphasized on *Mister Rogers' Neighborhood*, God wants us to hear at our deepest levels that we are loved. What God wants from us, first and foremost, is our passion rather than our perfection.

NIBS STROUPE

WHAT IS THE HOLY SPIRIT SAYING TO YOU THIS WEEK?

_____

_____

_____

_____

_____

A SPIRITUAL PRACTICE FOR THIS WEEK

Draw a person carrying a heavy burden (use stick figures if that helps you draw). Write down on the same page all the things that make up your heavy burden at this time in your life. Then, reread Matthew 11:28–30. What rest is Jesus offering you? How is Jesus inviting you to "learn from me"?

First Reading

Genesis 24:34–38, 42–49, 58–67

"Before I had finished speaking in my heart, there was Rebekah coming out with her water jar on her shoulder; and she went down to the spring, and drew. I said to her, 'Please let me drink.' She quickly let down her jar from her shoulder, and said, 'Drink, and I will also water your camels.' So I drank, and she also watered the camels." (vv. 45–46)

REFLECTION

God involves Rebekah from the outset in one of the most fundamental elements of the entire biblical story: the election of Israel [through her son Jacob] as God's chosen people.

. . . Rebekah employs the means available to her to assert her own agency. When the servant of Abraham shows up to offer a beneficial marriage, she employs the means of the dutiful host and prospective wife. When Isaac is about to give his blessing in chapter 27, she takes on the role of the trickster to make certain that the son *whom God had revealed to her as the heir of promise* will receive it.

ROBERT A. RATCLIFF

RESPONSE

Despite her limited position as a woman, Rebekah acts as a leader and an agent of change. Think of someone in your family or church history who faced a similar challenge. What can Rebekah and that person teach you about leadership in your own life? About how God chooses leaders?

PRAYER

God of tricksters, you choose surprising leaders and work in surprising ways; help me to see power revealed in unexpected people and places, fulfilling your promises. Amen.

Canticle

Song of Solomon 2:8–13

Look, there he stands
  behind our wall,
gazing in at the windows,
  looking through the lattice.
My beloved speaks and says to me:
"Arise, my love, my fair one,
  and come away." (vv. 9b–10)

REFLECTION

Interestingly and importantly, Song of Solomon actually offers a model
of sexuality and marriage that we would do well to emulate. . . . In
short, both partners have voice, and both are free to express what
is clearly their mutual desire. . . . Sexuality is not to be an arena for
domination, but rather it is to be characterized by equality, mutuality
of desire, and the expression of desire. In a culture like ours, where
domination and abuse are rampant, it is a shame that the Song of
Solomon is virtually ignored, even by the church.

J. CLINTON MCCANN JR.

RESPONSE

What connections can you make between your sexuality and your
spirituality? How do you see mutuality of desire in this passage?
Compare this to Rebekah's courtship experience in Genesis 24. Why is it
still so hard to preach or talk about sexuality in church, do you think?

PRAYER

God of desire, just as you created us from your own longing, you invite
us to enjoy longing and desire; teach me to see the connections between
the life of my spirit and the holiness of my sexuality. Amen.

Second Reading

Romans 7:15–25a

For I do not do the good I want, but the evil I do not want is what I do. Now if I do what I do not want, it is no longer I that do it, but sin that dwells within me. (vv. 19–20)

REFLECTION

We live in a culture where sin is easily characterized as mistakes, and a thing like confession sounds too judgmental. A sermon on a text like this can help us understand why we confess, and must confess, in worship. It is not because we have had an especially bad week, but because we are captive to sin. Moreover, we confess not only the personal dimension of sin, but its corporate and universal nature as well. We confess on behalf of communities and societies, and a humanity that is at war with itself.

PATRICK W. T. JOHNSON

RESPONSE

What is the difference between sin as personal "mistakes" and sin as a captivity? What corporate sin—for example, racism, ecological damage, economic inequality—have you been especially aware of in your life or community lately? Write a confession on behalf of your community, society, or all humanity, for this sin.

PRAYER

Gracious God, forgive my personal sins but also the sins done on my behalf, and the sins I benefit from even without choosing them; when we want to do what is good, evil lies close at hand. Amen.

Gospel

Matthew 11:16–19, 25–30

At that time Jesus said, "I thank you, Father, Lord of heaven and earth, because you have hidden these things from the wise and the intelligent and have revealed them to infants; yes, Father, for such was your gracious will." (vv. 25–26)

REFLECTION

Jesus [gives a] prayer of thanks for another relationship, that is, between the Father and the Son, and for "wisdom revealed to infants" (Matt. 11:25). It does not belong to the educated or the leadership; after all, look at how they responded to both John the Baptist and Jesus. In usual fashion, Jesus flips the expectations on where wisdom is located and found, and how it is acquired or cultivated; that is, wisdom belongs to the little ones, to "infants," to children, to the descendants, because it is given and revealed to them, specifically, by and through the Son.

MIHEE KIM-KORT

RESPONSE

What wisdom in Christ have you seen or received from infants or a "little one" recently? What has been an expectation or wisdom of "the intelligent" that may have led you astray? What is a wisdom you had when you were a child, but have lost sight of as an adult?

PRAYER

Christ of the little ones, teach me the wisdom of infants and children and to let go of my stereotypes of intelligence and education, so I may more fully know your love and gracious will. Amen.

Weekend Reflections

FURTHER CONNECTION

"If you love anyone, you cannot help but share his suffering. If we love our Lord, not just admire him or fear him or want things from him, we must recognize his feelings; he must be in anguish over our sins. We must understand this anguish. The Lord suffers with us. He suffers like us. It is a consolation to know this. To know that we are not in fact alone in our suffering."

MIN JIN LEE (1968–), PASTOR SHIN IN *PACHINKO*

MAKING THE CONNECTIONS

Choose one or two questions for reflection:

1. What connections have you noticed between this week's texts and other passages in Scripture?

2. What connections have you made between this week's texts and the world beyond Scripture?

3. Does either of this week's two commentary themes speak especially to your life or the life of the world around you right now?

4. What is God saying to your congregation in particular through this week's readings and commentaries?

_____

_____

_____

_____

_____

_____

Sabbath Day

SCRIPTURE OF ASSURANCE

> How sweet are your words to my taste,
>   sweeter than honey to my mouth! (Psalm 119:103)

WEEKLY EXAMEN

- Take a quiet moment, seek out God's presence, and pray for the guidance of the Spirit.

- Consider the past week; recall specific moments and feelings that stand out to you.

- Choose one moment or feeling for deeper examination, thanksgiving, or repentance.

- Let go, breathe deeply, and invite Christ's love to surround and fill you in preparation for the week ahead.

- End with the Lord's Prayer.

The Week Leading Up to
Proper 10
(Sunday between July 10 and July 16)

Isaiah 55:10–13

The rain and the snow come down from heaven,
 and do not return there until they have watered the earth,
making it bring forth and sprout,
 giving seed to the sower and bread to the eater. (v. 10)

Genesis 25:19–34

Isaac prayed to the LORD for his wife, because she was barren; and the LORD granted his prayer, and his wife Rebekah conceived. The children struggled together within her; and she said, "If it is to be this way, why do I live?" So she went to inquire of the LORD. (vv. 21–22)

Romans 8:1–11

But you are not in the flesh; you are in the Spirit, since the Spirit of God dwells in you. Anyone who does not have the Spirit of Christ does not belong to him. But if Christ is in you, though the body is dead because of sin, the Spirit is life because of righteousness. (vv. 9–10)

Matthew 13:1–9, 18–23

"But as for what was sown on good soil, this is the one who hears the word and understands it, who indeed bears fruit and yields, in one case a hundredfold, in another sixty, and in another thirty." (v. 23)

LECTIO DIVINA

Underline a word or phrase that especially grabs your attention. Pray from that word or phrase and ask God to help you connect to its particular invitation for you this week.

Themes from This Week's Writers

THEME 1: *God's Abundance*

Isaiah 55:10–13

The life of joy and abundance to which God calls them will forever be a sign and remembrance of divine forgiveness.

. . . Just as the prophet insists that God's word does not return empty, Jesus' parable of the Sower (Matt. 13:1–9, 18–23) lets us know that the word planted in the receptive heart yields abundantly.

ROBERT A. RATCLIFF

Psalm 65:(1–8) 9–13

In both texts, it is explicit that the watered earth provides food for people, "bread to the eater" (Isa. 55:10; see vv. 1–2) and "grain" that God has "prepared" (Ps. 65:9). In both instances, God's provision is sufficient, indeed abundant.

J. CLINTON MCCANN JR.

Romans 8:1–11

The mind who hears the word and understands it lives in the Spirit and gives abundant fruit. Deliverance, abundance, and joy are clearly hallmarks of the activity of God in the human person and in the world.

RENATA FURST

THEME 2: *We Are All Sowers*

Romans 8:1–11

Even when one particular form of Christ's community may come to an end—as when a congregation closes its doors—other communities indwelled by Christ generously open theirs. Thus—with reference to Christian community—Paul's promise is confirmed.

D. CAMERON MURCHISON

Matthew 13:1–9, 18–23

This power and this work is given to the readers, whether those of the early church or those in the present-day church, to continue to hold these words, these seeds, wherever we go, so that we may participate in the mission of the kingdom of heaven. We are soil; we are seeds; we are sowers too, laboring alongside the one who calls us to that harvest that is ever in front of us.

MIHEE KIM-KORT

Matthew 13:1–9, 18–23

The sharing of the love of God happens not because of what we do or who we are, but because of who God is and what God is doing. The hearers of this story in every generation are reminded that we are asked to join God in this process of proclaiming the love of God. Most of the time we will never know where or when it will bear fruit, but bear fruit it will.

NIBS STROUPE

WHAT IS THE HOLY SPIRIT SAYING TO YOU THIS WEEK?

_____

_____

_____

_____

_____

A SPIRITUAL PRACTICE FOR THIS WEEK

Reread Romans 8:6. Write "death" and "life" on a piece of paper and make two lists. What is trapping you in feelings of death and sin this week? What is pulling you toward life and peace? Do these lists offer any insights to what "flesh" and "the Spirit" may signify in your life at this time?

First Reading

Esau said to Jacob, "Let me eat some of that red stuff, for I am famished!" (Therefore he was called Edom.) Jacob said, "First sell me your birthright." Esau said, "I am about to die; of what use is a birthright to me?" Jacob said, "Swear to me first." So he swore to him, and sold his birthright to Jacob. (vv. 30–33)

REFLECTION

"Birthright" is a privilege so profound that even to deny it does not dispel it. "Maleness" and "whiteness" might function in comparable ways today.

The simple Esau mistakenly thinks that birthright is a mere idea, a social construct (v. 32), something that he can relinquish on command. . . .

Birthright stood so prominent in the culture that it could not be bartered away. The entitlement was so profound that it became invisible to the holder, who felt free to relinquish what can never go away.

STEPHEN BRECK REID

RESPONSE

What privileges and advantages do you have, but tend to take for granted, in your society? How do you see yourself as Esau, in terms of your social position? How do you see yourself as Jacob? What does God seem to value more than birthright or privilege, in this story?

PRAYER

O God, guide me to self-awareness of my own birthright; I can never give it away—but teach me to use my privilege on behalf of others and, like Jacob, to play the system. Amen.

Canticle

Psalm 65:(1–8) 9–13

O you who answer prayer!
To you all flesh shall come.
When deeds of iniquity overwhelm us,
    you forgive our transgressions. (vv. 2–3)

REFLECTION

Grace is of the essence in both texts. . . . Psalm 65:3 affirms that God's people have been forgiven, and Isaiah 55:10–13 is immediately preceded by an invitation to "return to the LORD, that he may have mercy on them, and to our God, for he will abundantly pardon" (Isa. 55:7). In this context, what makes God's thoughts and ways "higher" than human thoughts and ways is precisely God's ability and willingness to forgive (vv. 8–9). Putting all this together, we conclude that to be God means to exercise sovereignty or power as grace that sustains the life of God's people.

J. CLINTON MCCANN JR.

RESPONSE

What do you make of McCann's countercultural statement that the power and sovereignty of God is rooted in grace and forgiveness? How have you seen God's grace sustain human life? How is God inviting you to be sustained by the power of grace at this time in your life?

PRAYER

God of salvation, by awesome deeds you answer us with deliverance and grace; teach me to receive this grace and be sustained by your power. Amen.

Second Reading

Romans 8:1–11

If the Spirit of him who raised Jesus from the dead dwells in you, he who raised Christ from the dead will give life to your mortal bodies also through his Spirit that dwells in you. (v. 11)

REFLECTION

In these verses Paul describes life . . . as a gift of living "according to the Spirit." . . . It is living that does not make the self with its passions, energies, and ambiguities the center of all values, but instead discovers the center of all values in the gracious embrace of Christ Jesus. Thus, we who are caught in the downward, condemnatory spirals of one addiction or another (drugs, alcohol, money, self) hear in Paul's words a summons to find freedom and release by letting go of efforts at self-determination and accepting the Spirit of Christ's readiness to fill us with "life and peace."

D. CAMERON MURCHISON

RESPONSE

What addictive or compulsive tendencies are you aware of in yourself? What is a way that making yourself the center of your life has made your life worse? What could it look like in your life this week to make "the gracious embrace of Christ" the center?

PRAYER

Spirit of Christ, teach me to make room for you, letting go of burdensome struggles with myself, that you may dwell in me and bring the fullness of my true and whole self to life. Amen.

Gospel

Matthew 13:1–9, 18–23

And he told them many things in parables, saying: "Listen! A sower went out to sow. And as he sowed, some seeds fell on the path, and the birds came and ate them up." (vv. 3–4)

REFLECTION

This parable understands the struggles of the world and of our efforts to live and to proclaim the stupendous love of God. It realistically states that, at best, we will have a 25 percent success rate. . . . Yet it is ultimately a story of hope, a story based in the mysterious and extravagant love of God, a love that is beyond our control and beyond our understanding.

. . . Though there is only a tiny harvest at times (if at all), this parable makes the astonishing claim that God is moving and germinating and producing that which is intended.

NIBS STROUPE

RESPONSE

How have you experienced the 25 percent success rate Jesus describes in this parable? Is this depressing for you? Or a story of hope? How have you felt God's love "moving and germinating" beneath the surface of things lately?

PRAYER

God of hope, most of the seeds of your word do not grow or survive; strengthen me to continue to scatter these seeds of your word and your love, in my life and in your world. Amen.

Weekend Reflections

FURTHER CONNECTION

Every moment and every event of every man's life on earth plants something in his soul. For just as the wind carries thousands of winged seeds, so each moment brings with it germs of spiritual vitality that come to rest imperceptibly in the minds and wills of men. Most of these unnumbered seeds perish and are lost, because men are not prepared to receive them: for such seeds as these cannot spring up anywhere except in the good soil of freedom, spontaneity and love.

THOMAS MERTON (1915–68), *NEW SEEDS OF CONTEMPLATION*

MAKING THE CONNECTIONS

Choose one or two questions for reflection:

1. What connections have you noticed between this week's texts and other passages in Scripture?

2. What connections have you made between this week's texts and the world beyond Scripture?

3. Does either of this week's two commentary themes speak especially to your life or the life of the world around you right now?

4. What is God saying to your congregation in particular through this week's readings and commentaries?

_____

_____

_____

_____

_____

_____

Sabbath Day

SCRIPTURE OF ASSURANCE

> We will not hide them from their children;
> we will tell to the coming generation
> the glorious deeds of the LORD, and his might,
> and the wonders that he has done. (Psalm 78:4)

WEEKLY EXAMEN

- Take a quiet moment, seek out God's presence, and pray for the guidance of the Spirit.

- Consider the past week; recall specific moments and feelings that stand out to you.

- Choose one moment or feeling for deeper examination, thanksgiving, or repentance.

- Let go, breathe deeply, and invite Christ's love to surround and fill you in preparation for the week ahead.

- End with the Lord's Prayer.

The Week Leading Up to
Proper 11

(Sunday between July 17 and July 23)

Isaiah 44:6–8

Do not fear, or be afraid;
    have I not told you from of old and declared it?
    You are my witnesses!
Is there any god besides me?
    There is no other rock; I know not one. (v. 8)

Genesis 28:10–19a

Jacob left Beer-sheba and went toward Haran. He came to a certain place and stayed there for the night, because the sun had set. Taking one of the stones of the place, he put it under his head and lay down in that place. (vv. 10–11)

Romans 8:12–25

It is that very Spirit bearing witness with our spirit that we are children of God, and if children, then heirs, heirs of God and joint heirs with Christ—if, in fact, we suffer with him so that we may also be glorified with him. (vv. 16–17)

Matthew 13:24–30, 36–43

"But he replied, 'No; for in gathering the weeds you would uproot the wheat along with them. Let both of them grow together until the harvest; and at harvest time I will tell the reapers, Collect the weeds first and bind them in bundles to be burned, but gather the wheat into my barn.'" (vv. 29–30)

LECTIO DIVINA

Underline a word or phrase that especially grabs your attention. Pray from that word or phrase and ask God to help you connect to its particular invitation for you this week.

Themes from This Week's Writers

THEME 1: *God Seeks to Adopt the Outsiders*

Genesis 28:10–19a

God has a soft spot for fugitives. Maybe it is the spiritual state that flight causes that God honors. Haste, terror, dread: Jacob experienced them all between Beersheba and Bethel, as refugees do today. . . . In the end it is the fugitive, not the upstanding citizen (or representative of the system), who winds up with the blessing.

JANA CHILDERS

Romans 8:12–25

In Roman culture an adopted son had the full legal standing as an heir. This is a familiar and accepted concept to his readers, even for the adoption of slaves, and Paul . . . develops the metaphor even further.

NICK CARTER

Romans 8:12–25

We may still inwardly await adoption, feeling separated from God and one another, seduced by the lies of our culture. Our deeper truth is that we are already . . . united to the Godhead, "joint heirs with Christ."

WENDY FARLEY

THEME 2: *Let the Weeds and the Wheat Grow Together*

Psalm 86:11–17

It is surprising, perhaps, that the psalmist does not ask God to smite the bullies but, instead, requests a sign of God's favor. When haters see that God helps and comforts the one they have persecuted, then, the psalmist imagines, they will experience shame.

ANGELA DIENHART HANCOCK

Matthew 13:24–30, 36–43

Jesus simply presents the entwinement of good and bad people (seed) in the world as a fact of life. This is nothing over which to lose sleep or into which one need launch a special investigation. It is going to happen, period: let the weeds be.

F. SCOTT SPENCER

Matthew 13:24–30, 36–43

It is not uncommon for Christians to weed out those who, in reality, are good seed sown by God in the world. . . . The parable counsels more than merely being tolerant of others [but] . . . to recognize and rejoice in the goodness of God in others, a goodness freely given without distinctions.

MICHAEL PASQUARELLO III

WHAT IS THE HOLY SPIRIT SAYING TO YOU THIS WEEK?

_____

_____

_____

_____

_____

A SPIRITUAL PRACTICE FOR THIS WEEK

Make a bouquet of the ugliest weeds you can find. Put them in water and reflect on them this week. What do you notice about them? How do they invite you to understand better the weeds or sins that grow inside of yourself, alongside the good?

First Reading

Then Jacob woke from his sleep and said, "Surely the LORD is in this place—and I did not know it!" And he was afraid, and said, "How awesome is this place! This is none other than the house of God, and this is the gate of heaven." (vv. 16–17)

REFLECTION

Jacob thought of himself as a person on the run. He had done x and reaped y and was headed for time in the penalty box—a simple equation. He was, no doubt, thinking his own thoughts as he took off toward Haran. Calculations about ETA, hours of daylight, and the precise location of the next well would have been crowding his mind. . . . It likely never occurred to him that God might see him differently, that there might be deep wells in his personal life, or even that he might be a player in one of God's larger stories.

JANA CHILDERS

RESPONSE

How have you felt like a person on the run, lately? What is taking up your headspace? What deeper wells lie within you? How might you be part of God's larger story, in ways you have not yet realized? How does God see you differently than you see yourself, do you think?

PRAYER

God of presence, you meet me on the roads of life; slow me down that I may encounter you, even if in a struggle, so I may know that everyday life is your house and the gate of heaven. Amen.

Canticle

Psalm 139:1–12, 23–24

Even before a word is on my tongue,
O Lord, you know it completely.
You hem me in, behind and before,
and lay your hand upon me.
Such knowledge is too wonderful for me;
it is so high that I cannot attain it. (vv. 4–6)

REFLECTION

Is there, rather, something menacing about this depiction of God's way
with us? This God haunts our every moment. Stalks us as we go about
our day. Knows everything we are going to do or say before we do. This
is a God we can never surprise, a divine helicopter parent who is not
willing to give us even a little breathing room. Of course, the psalmist
appears to consider this to be a good thing, though there is not much to
go on. Verse 6 displays the psalmist's awe at God's omniscience, but that
is not quite the same thing as welcoming it.

ANGELA DIENHART HANCOCK

RESPONSE

How do you feel about this image of God? What is unsettling? What
is comforting? How could this psalm deepen your sense of the images
of God you carry, and how those images affect your spirituality and
prayer life?

PRAYER

Ever-present God, you know me, inside and out; teach me to live with
this mystery of your omniscience and eternal presence, that I might feel
not suffocation, but intimacy and awe. Amen.

Second Reading

Romans 8:12–25

We know that the whole creation has been groaning in labor pains until now; and not only the creation, but we ourselves, who have the first fruits of the Spirit, groan inwardly while we wait for adoption, the redemption of our bodies. (vv. 22–23)

REFLECTION

Paul uses the contrast between flesh and spirit as shorthand to describe two opposing ways of living in the world. . . . It has not served Christians to despise bodily existence and feel estranged from the earth. We are creatures of flesh: human existence depends on our bodily creation as part of the natural world. Paul could hardly anticipate the ecological meltdown we now face, the weeping of trees and oceans as whole ecosystems succumb not merely to decay but to active destruction. However, he already understands that it is creation itself, including all of humanity, that is "groaning" for the birth of freedom.

WENDY FARLEY

RESPONSE

How do you value your life as a creature of flesh? How do you dismiss it? How do you value or take joy in the life of the created world? How do you dismiss or ignore it? How do you hear creation groaning for redemption and freedom, even in your own backyard?

PRAYER

God of the Incarnation, teach me to honor the holiness of physical life, to hear all creation groaning in pain for healing in these times of constant ecological disaster and speeding climate change. Amen.

Gospel

Matthew 13:24–30, 36–43

"The Son of Man will send his angels, and they will collect out of his kingdom all causes of sin and all evildoers, and they will throw them into the furnace of fire, where there will be weeping and gnashing of teeth." (vv. 41–42)

REFLECTION

While calling for a certain honest acceptance of a mixed good-and-evil world, Jesus is no hopeless fatalist. A judicious "harvest" will ensure the safety (salvation) of the children of God's kingdom and separation (destruction) of evil ones. . . . Jesus offers God's people, and indeed all creation, a firm warrant to wait *in hope* for ultimate liberation from debilitating struggles with evil in the present age, as this week's epistle text from Romans 8:12–25 so poignantly confirms (see esp. vv. 22–25).

F. SCOTT SPENCER

RESPONSE

What are some weeds you see growing in the field of your life, lately? What is the wheat you see? What about in your community? How do you see weeds and wheat intertwined? What does it feel like to be told that it must be God who separates them, and not you?

PRAYER

Lord Jesus, you invite me not to despair at the struggles of the world but to persevere, to love my neighbor, and to wait in hope for you to come and separate the weeds and wheat on the last day. Amen.

Weekend Reflections

FURTHER CONNECTION

I began to find [this] parable absurdly freeing not from responsibility but from the disease of perfectionism. Even the image of fire, which had troubled me so as a child, was transformed into a symbol of hope. . . . I began to see God's fire, like a good parent's righteous anger, as something that can flare up, challenge, and even change us, but that does not destroy the essence of who we are. The thought of all my weeds burning off so that only the wheat remains came to seem like a good thing.

KATHLEEN NORRIS (1947–), *AMAZING GRACE: A VOCABULARY OF FAITH*

MAKING THE CONNECTIONS

Choose one or two questions for reflection:

1. What connections have you noticed between this week's texts and other passages in Scripture?

2. What connections have you made between this week's texts and the world beyond Scripture?

3. Does either of this week's two commentary themes speak especially to your life or the life of the world around you right now?

4. What is God saying to your congregation in particular through this week's readings and commentaries?

_____

_____

_____

_____

_____

_____

Sabbath Day

SCRIPTURE OF ASSURANCE

I pray that, according to the riches of his glory, he may grant that you may be strengthened in your inner being with power through his Spirit, and that Christ may dwell in your hearts through faith, as you are being rooted and grounded in love. (Ephesians 3:16–17)

WEEKLY EXAMEN

- Take a quiet moment, seek out God's presence, and pray for the guidance of the Spirit.

- Consider the past week; recall specific moments and feelings that stand out to you.

- Choose one moment or feeling for deeper examination, thanksgiving, or repentance.

- Let go, breathe deeply, and invite Christ's love to surround and fill you in preparation for the week ahead.

- End with the Lord's Prayer.

The Week Leading Up to
Proper 12

(Sunday between July 24 and July 30)

1 Kings 3:5–12

God said to him, "Because you have asked this, and have not asked for your-self long life or riches, or for the life of your enemies, but have asked for yourself understanding to discern what is right, I now do according to your word. Indeed I give you a wise and discerning mind; no one like you has been before you and no one like you shall arise after you." (vv. 11–12)

Genesis 29:15–28

When morning came, it was Leah! And Jacob said to Laban, "What is this you have done to me? Did I not serve with you for Rachel? Why then have you deceived me?" Laban said, "This is not done in our country—giving the younger before the firstborn." (vv. 25–26)

Romans 8:26–39

For I am convinced that neither death, nor life, nor angels, nor rulers, nor things present, nor things to come, nor powers, nor height, nor depth, nor anything else in all creation, will be able to separate us from the love of God in Christ Jesus our Lord. (vv. 38–39)

Matthew 13:31–33, 44–52

"Again, the kingdom of heaven is like a merchant in search of fine pearls; on finding one pearl of great value, he went and sold all that he had and bought it." (vv. 45–46)

LECTIO DIVINA

Underline a word or phrase that especially grabs your attention. Pray from that word or phrase and ask God to help you connect to its particular invitation for you this week.

Themes from This Week's Writers

THEME 1: *God Works in Unexpected Ways*

1 Kings 3:5–12 and Genesis 29:15–28

What the characters in the story imagine as the most desirable outcomes for themselves, their families, and their future may not always be the most "wise and discerning" choices. God appears to and works among the least expected—doubters, deceivers, ethnically different.

ELIZABETH HINSON-HASTY

Genesis 29:15–28

"I am a scamp," you can almost hear Jacob saying. "It is why you like me."
Indeed, God does seem to like Jacob. Read from this angle, the passage paints a picture of a tolerant God, . . . who loves them in spite of, or perhaps because of, their impish ways.

JANA CHILDERS

Romans 8:26–39

Two thousand years later, we might ask, how are we to live within our religion (Christianity) when religion has come to an end? We are in the position of first-century Jews, who (rightly) love their religion and are not eager to overthrow precious practices for the naked nearness of the divine Spirit. How do we live within a religion, and also beyond it?

WENDY FARLEY

THEME 2: *What Is the Kingdom of God Like?*

Romans 8:26–39

It is useful here to concentrate on Paul's idea of "conformation." The highest good for humanity is to love God, to be conformed to the image of Christ, and to be loved by God. God is (and has always been) at work in us seeking to conform us to, or make us like, Christ.

NICK CARTER

Matthew 13:31–33, 44–52

The parables of the Mustard Seed (13:31–32) and the Yeast (13:33) convey elements of *mystery* and *hospitality* integral to God's economy. The mystery angle relates to the amazing growth of God's kingdom from seemingly trivial beginnings.

F. SCOTT SPENCER

Matthew 13:31–33, 44–52

A common laborer discovers a treasure and a merchant finds a priceless pearl (13:44–46). In both instances, Jesus points to the overwhelming joy and desire out of which the laborer and the merchant act in response to the tangible reality of God's reign.

MICHAEL PASQUARELLO III

WHAT IS THE HOLY SPIRIT SAYING TO YOU THIS WEEK?

_____

_____

_____

_____

_____

A SPIRITUAL PRACTICE FOR THIS WEEK

Read Matthew 13:31–33, 44–52. Choose the miniparable that is particularly speaking to you and write it out on a piece of paper. Then, prayerfully, write two or three of your own miniparables to mirror it. What parable would Jesus use to help you learn this week about the kingdom of God and your own life, right now?

First Reading

"Give your servant therefore an understanding mind to govern your people, able to discern between good and evil; for who can govern this your great people?" (v. 9)

REFLECTION

What does Bathsheba's son ask for God to give him? Solomon does not ask for the defeat of his enemies or for wealth. In contrast to his father David's arrogance, lack of gratitude, and lack of a wise and discerning mind, Solomon acknowledges that his authority comes from God and appeals to God for wisdom to lead a people "so numerous they cannot be numbered or counted" (1 Kgs. 3:8).

. . . Solomon receives that which Wisdom confers on those who seek her, things "far more precious than jewels": prudence, knowledge, discretion, and righteousness in the paths of justice (Prov. 8).

ELIZABETH HINSON-HASTY

RESPONSE

Who is a leader in your life that has disappointed you, or who you have strived to distinguish yourself from in your own leadership or service? What kind of wisdom would you ask God to grant you, in contrast? How would you use it?

PRAYER

Almighty God, you offer wisdom to any who ask for it; grant your wisdom also to me: that I can lead and serve in my own community with understanding and courage. Amen.

Canticle

Psalm 105:1–11, 45b

He is the LORD our God;
  his judgments are in all the earth.
He is mindful of his covenant forever,
  of the word that he commanded, for a thousand generations.
  (vv. 7–8)

REFLECTION

Psalm 105 offers a broader perspective. . . . Jacob falls in love, works for years to win Rachel's hand, and then his uncle pulls a fast one, switching the bride. The ensuing domestic unhappiness is not without its bright spots, but this can hardly be the way Jacob imagined God's promise of abundant offspring would play out. Nonetheless, the psalm reminds us, the twelve tribes were established by means of this particular menagerie: Jacob, Leah, Rachel, Zilpah, Bilhah, and even Laban the dishonest. They are all part of the big story of God's way with God's people, unfurled in Psalm 105.

ANGELA DIENHART HANCOCK

RESPONSE

How has your personal life, love life, or family life been different from what you imagined? How would you describe the "menagerie" of your extended family and friends? How are all of you God's covenant for each other? How are you living into God's "big story" of God's people, do you think?

PRAYER

O God, you are telling a big story about your people; show me how to honor my own story and the difficulties and surprises of this human life as part of that holy story. Amen.

Second Reading

We know that all things work together for good for those who love God, who are called according to his purpose. (v. 28)

REFLECTION

Some have argued that suffering is redemptive; in most cases it is not, and Paul's writing does not support that view. . . . Only suffering that is accepted freely and without coercion (mental or physical)—in love or for the cause of justice—is redemptive. . . .

. . . This is not a Pollyanna passage of blind optimism. Paul is familiar with pain, suffering, and persecution. He is addressing the question of how to live faithfully in the midst of these things. He is suggesting not that God intended these things to happen or that they work for human good but, rather, that God can use them for good.

NICK CARTER

RESPONSE

When was a time when your suffering was purely terrible, where nothing was redeemed by it? When was a time that your suffering has been redemptive, or used by God for good? What was the difference between these experiences? How do Paul's words speak to you about this?

PRAYER

God of all, I know nothing can separate me from your love in Christ Jesus; help me to endure but also to resist and transform the suffering in my life. Amen.

Gospel

Matthew 13:31–33, 44–52

"The kingdom of heaven is like a mustard seed that someone took and sowed in his field; it is the smallest of all the seeds, but when it has grown it is the greatest of shrubs and becomes a tree, so that the birds of the air come and make nests in its branches." (vv. 31b–32)

REFLECTION

Preaching from these parables will call the church to endure faithfully in, with, and for a world that does not acknowledge the kingdom coming in Christ. To say the reign of God is hidden does not mean it is nonexistent. God's revelation both conceals and reveals itself in the world. Its smallness and insignificance according to the world's standards are not challenges to be overcome or obstacles to be removed, since God is sovereign and acts through the freedom by which human beings respond to God's humble self-giving act in Jesus.

MICHAEL PASQUARELLO III

RESPONSE

How has the reality of God's small, hidden, often concealed reign and revelation been a source of delight or challenge in your life? What does it mean to you that smallness and insignificance are "not challenges to be overcome"? How are you watching and waiting for seeds to grow?

PRAYER

Jesus our teacher, you call me to see God's hidden kingdom all around me; show me how what is small and overlooked can be precious and life-giving. Amen.

Weekend Reflections

FURTHER CONNECTION

The striking thing about all of these images is their essential hiddenness—the mustard seed hidden in the ground, the yeast hidden in the dough, the treasure hidden in the field, the pearl hidden among all the other pearls, the net hidden in the depths of the sea. If the kingdom is like these, then it is not something readily apparent to the eye but something that must be searched for, something just below the surface of things waiting there to be discovered and claimed.

BARBARA BROWN TAYLOR (1951–), *THE SEEDS OF HEAVEN: SERMONS ON THE GOSPEL OF MATTHEW*

MAKING THE CONNECTIONS

Choose one or two questions for reflection:

1. What connections have you noticed between this week's texts and other passages in Scripture?

2. What connections have you made between this week's texts and the world beyond Scripture?

3. Does either of this week's two commentary themes speak especially to your life or the life of the world around you right now?

4. What is God saying to your congregation in particular through this week's readings and commentaries?

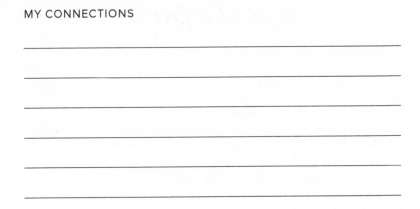

Sabbath Day

SCRIPTURE OF ASSURANCE

> To get wisdom is to love oneself;
>   to keep understanding is to prosper. (Proverbs 19:8)

WEEKLY EXAMEN

- Take a quiet moment, seek out God's presence, and pray for the guidance of the Spirit.

- Consider the past week; recall specific moments and feelings that stand out to you.

- Choose one moment or feeling for deeper examination, thanksgiving, or repentance.

- Let go, breathe deeply, and invite Christ's love to surround and fill you in preparation for the week ahead.

- End with the Lord's Prayer.

The Week Leading Up to
Proper 13

(Sunday between July 31 and August 6)

Isaiah 55:1–5

Ho, everyone who thirsts,
    come to the waters;
and you that have no money,
    come, buy and eat!
Come, buy wine and milk
    without money and without price. (v. 1)

Genesis 32:22–31

Jacob was left alone; and a man wrestled with him until daybreak. When the man saw that he did not prevail against Jacob, he struck him on the hip socket; and Jacob's hip was put out of joint as he wrestled with him. (vv. 24–25)

Romans 9:1–5

I am speaking the truth in Christ—I am not lying; my conscience confirms it by the Holy Spirit—I have great sorrow and unceasing anguish in my heart. (vv. 1–2)

Matthew 14:13–21

Then he ordered the crowds to sit down on the grass. Taking the five loaves and the two fish, he looked up to heaven, and blessed and broke the loaves, and gave them to the disciples, and the disciples gave them to the crowds. (v. 19)

LECTIO DIVINA

Underline a word or phrase that especially grabs your attention. Pray from that word or phrase and ask God to help you connect to its particular invitation for you this week.

Themes from This Week's Writers

THEME 1: *Wrestling with Angels*

Genesis 32:22–31

Scholars suggest that God refuses to disclose God's name because it was not common for God to be seen (32:30) and the power of naming in the Hebrew Bible bears with it the power to control. Jacob ultimately knows the One whom he is dealing with and names the place Peniel, meaning "face of God."

ELIZABETH HINSON-HASTY

Psalm 17:1–7, 15

Like Psalm 17, [the Genesis] story describes a night of struggle, an individual with some gumption, and a dawn that brings fresh perspective. We might say both of these texts are about someone trying to get God to do something, but they both end with the realization that the truest "blessing" is the encounter with God's own self.

ANGELA DIENHART HANCOCK

Romans 9:1–5

That we see the great hero of early Christianity struggling with the limits of his zealous certainties is a powerful witness that frees us to do the same. Paul allows a later insight to displace an earlier one. He allows the Spirit to lead him deeper into awareness of God's goodness and reliability.

WENDY FARLEY

THEME 2: *God Spreads a Feast for All*

Isaiah 55:1–5

You have to love the lavishness of a God who envisions nations coming on the run and ancient Israel shining like a beacon. It is as if Isaiah believes that God's big business with humankind—the thing the heart of God is most after—is to call people to larger and larger versions of life together, to a big tent and a large life fueled and funded by God.

JANA CHILDERS

Matthew 14:13–21

The total number of *seven* loaves and fishes suggests the completeness or fullness of God's creation-week. . . . A simpler mathematical observation may be the most telling: the paltry amount of available food, in contrast to (1) the lavish birthday spread in Herod's palace and (2) the throngs of hungry people in the desert.

F. SCOTT SPENCER

Matthew 14:13–21

Although Jesus initially withdraws—presumably knowing he will face an ending similar to that of John the Baptist—he quickly turns his attention to the great crowd of ordinary people that gathers around him. What follows is a fully public, even political, account by Matthew that shows in concrete, human terms the nature of God's rule and God's way.

MICHAEL PASQUARELLO III

WHAT IS THE HOLY SPIRIT SAYING TO YOU THIS WEEK?

_____

_____

_____

_____

_____

A SPIRITUAL PRACTICE FOR THIS WEEK

Research issues of hunger in your community. See what you can learn about SNAP, public school breakfast and lunch programs, food pantries, and Meals on Wheels. Consider how race plays a role. Pray for the hungry each day. Make a generous donation to a hunger organization.

First Reading

Isaiah 55:1–5

Why do you spend your money for that which is not bread,
   and your labor for that which does not satisfy?
Listen carefully to me, and eat what is good,
   and delight yourselves in rich food. (v. 2)

REFLECTION

You have to love the expansiveness of a God who shouts, "Ho," who flings wide the doors to the banquet house . . . and extends the terms of David's deal so that everyone is included in its embrace (Isa. 55:1–5). . . .

   This is what the people of God celebrate today every time . . . they offer each other the Cup that brims and the Loaf that stretches to feed all. This is what Jesus came for. Died for. This is what his resurrection points us to. This is how the Holy Spirit navigates the twenty-first-century church.

JANA CHILDERS

RESPONSE

What is a way that God has invited you to abundantly feast recently? Did you respond with a yes, or no? When receiving Communion, how do you experience God's generosity and expansiveness? How might the Holy Spirit be encouraging you or your congregation toward a generous future?

PRAYER

God of feasting, why do I spend my money for that which is not bread? Why do I work for that which does not satisfy? Teach me to eat and delight in good foods and abundant life. Amen.

Canticle

Psalm 17:1–7, 15

I call upon you, for you will answer me, O God;
 incline your ear to me, hear my words.
Wondrously show your steadfast love,
 O savior of those who seek refuge
 from their adversaries at your right hand. (vv. 6–7)

REFLECTION

God is named by the psalmist as "savior," specifically of "those who
seek refuge from their adversaries" (v. 7). What is the nature of the
desired rescue? The omitted verse 13 asks God to get up and confront
the predators, overthrowing them. Completely understandable. Yet the
final verse of the psalm imagines the psalmist waking up in the morning
"satisfied," not (necessarily) because all problems have been solved and
enemies subdued, but because "I shall behold your face in righteousness"
(v. 15). God's presence is named as the reason joy comes with the dawn,
even though it is likely that trouble still awaits.

ANGELA DIENHART HANCOCK

RESPONSE

How do you hold in balance the problems and enemies you face with
a sense of joy in God's presence? What is it like to consider that our
problems and enemies will never completely disappear, in this life? What
does "refuge" in God mean for you, this week?

PRAYER

O God, you are my refuge; if I call upon you, you answer me. You
wondrously show your steadfast love to me and all who call on you.
Amen.

Second Reading

Romans 9:1–5

For I could wish that I myself were accursed and cut off from Christ for the sake of my own people, my kindred according to the flesh. They are Israelites, and to them belong the adoption, the glory, the covenants, the giving of the law, the worship, and the promises. (vv. 3–4)

REFLECTION

This passage also provides an opportunity to affirm the place of grief in the midst of our expressions of confidence and hope. Washington Irving supposedly once said: "There is a sacredness in tears. They are not the mark of weakness, but of power. . . . They are the messengers of overwhelming grief, of deep contrition, and of unspeakable love."[1] It is appropriate to recognize that Paul was genuinely distressed over the consequences of his beliefs, particularly the rejection by Jewish Christians, thus leading him to go to great lengths to reconcile those beliefs with them and with Jewish tradition.

NICK CARTER

RESPONSE

Have you ever seen tears as a "mark of power"? What power is there in grief or contrition, in your experience? What was a time when you, like Paul, were led by grief or contrition to attempt change or reconciliation? How did your feelings strengthen your confidence?

PRAYER

Loving Jesus, give me courage to grieve my regrets and the hurt I have caused others; show me the power of tears, so I may find the power to move toward new life and reconciliation. Amen.

1. This quotation is widely attributed to Irving, but it is found without attribution in William C. Brown, ed., *The Mother's Assistant and Young Lady's Friend: July 1843, to July 1844* (Boston: William C. Brown, 1844).

Gospel

Matthew 14:13–21

And all ate and were filled; and they took up what was left over of the broken pieces, twelve baskets full. And those who ate were about five thousand men, besides women and children. (vv. 20–21)

REFLECTION

The largesse of Jesus' feeding well over five thousand people is enhanced by everyone's being "filled," with "twelve baskets full" to spare (14:20). Of course, a dozen matches the number of Jesus' disciples (10:1–4). Strategically, Jesus enlists these Twelve, who had first urged him to dismiss the crowd for dinner, to serve the multitude (14:19). This healing and feeding incident turns out to be a memorable seminar in faith and ministry for Jesus' closest followers.

F. SCOTT SPENCER

RESPONSE

Jesus is grieving and tired. There are only five loaves and two fish. Somehow, he and the disciples have enough to serve a hungry crowd anyway. What is a situation you are facing where you worry you will not have enough? What comfort does God offer you in this Gospel?

PRAYER

O Jesus, through the hands of your disciples you fed a crowd of thousands with almost nothing; teach me to live from the abundance of "enough," and through you, may my hands feed many. Amen.

Weekend Reflections

FURTHER CONNECTION

Miraculous feedings are about something that isn't scarce. At all. They aren't about oil, obviously, or the world's resources or our money or our altruism or our righteousness or our wiliness or our anything. They are about something infinitely abundant, something outside of us that relates to us and to the world in a way that will transform everything. They show us a glimpse of a place where we can believe there is no scarcity, where we can believe in infinite abundance; so of course we're inviting everyone in and handing out plates of cake. And we're not at all afraid someone's going to take our plate or our place or get there first.

DEBBIE BLUE (1965–), *FROM STONE TO LIVING WORD: LETTING THE BIBLE LIVE AGAIN*

MAKING THE CONNECTIONS

Choose one or two questions for reflection:

1. What connections have you noticed between this week's texts and other passages in Scripture?

2. What connections have you made between this week's texts and the world beyond Scripture?

3. Does either of this week's two commentary themes speak especially to your life or the life of the world around you right now?

4. What is God saying to your congregation in particular through this week's readings and commentaries?

_____

_____

_____

_____

_____

_____

Sabbath Day

SCRIPTURE OF ASSURANCE

He said to me: Mortal, all my words that I shall speak to you receive in your heart and hear with your ears; then go to the exiles, to your people, and speak to them. Say to them, "Thus says the Lord GOD"; whether they hear or refuse to hear. (Ezekiel 3:10–11)

WEEKLY EXAMEN

- Take a quiet moment, seek out God's presence, and pray for the guidance of the Spirit.

- Consider the past week; recall specific moments and feelings that stand out to you.

- Choose one moment or feeling for deeper examination, thanksgiving, or repentance.

- Let go, breathe deeply, and invite Christ's love to surround and fill you in preparation for the week ahead.

- End with the Lord's Prayer.

The Week Leading Up to
Proper 14
(Sunday between August 7 and August 13)

1 Kings 19:9–18

And after the earthquake a fire, but the LORD was not in the fire; and after the fire a sound of sheer silence. When Elijah heard it, he wrapped his face in his mantle and went out and stood at the entrance of the cave. Then there came a voice to him that said, "What are you doing here, Elijah?" (vv. 12–13)

Genesis 37:1–4, 12–28

When some Midianite traders passed by, they drew Joseph up, lifting him out of the pit, and sold him to the Ishmaelites for twenty pieces of silver. And they took Joseph to Egypt. (v. 28)

Romans 10:5–15

For there is no distinction between Jew and Greek; the same Lord is Lord of all and is generous to all who call on him. For, "Everyone who calls on the name of the Lord shall be saved." (vv. 12–13)

Matthew 14:22–33

Jesus immediately reached out his hand and caught [Peter], saying to him, "You of little faith, why did you doubt?" When they got into the boat, the wind ceased. And those in the boat worshiped him, saying, "Truly you are the Son of God." (vv. 31–33)

LECTIO DIVINA

> Underline a word or phrase that especially grabs your attention. Pray from that word or phrase and ask God to help you connect to its particular invitation for you this week.

Themes from This Week's Writers

THEME 1: *God Can Turn Evil to Good*

1 Kings 19:9–18 and Genesis 37:1–4, 12–28

According to Irenaeus, [a second-century Christian bishop], tragedies and disasters are present in order for humans to develop a strong character and maturity. He affirms that the created world, with all these challenges and adversities, provides opportunities for humans to grow stronger, and as we overcome these, we will develop a virtuous character.

HUGO MAGALLANES

Romans 10:5–15

This affirmation of God's purposes operating even through human disobedience corresponds with the overarching theme of Romans 9–11: Israel's unbelief ultimately serves God's purpose of saving all (Rom. 11:11–32).

SUSAN GROVE EASTMAN

Matthew 14:22–33

Christian faith is not about the certitude and safety of believing "from the boat," but rather about the productive tension between doubt and trust that leads us ever deeper into a mysterious relationship with the Lord who comes to us in the darkness and the storm, . . . most palpably just when we risk something and begin to sink.

LANCE PAPE

THEME 2: *Everyone Who Calls on the Name of the Lord Will Be Saved*

Psalm 85:8–13

God will respond in the fullness of God's divine nature. By focusing on God's attributes of faithfulness, peace, and righteousness, the psalmist makes it clear that even in lament we must listen for God and expect a response that is a gift of wholeness and well-being, because that is God's nature.

KHALIA J. WILLIAMS

Romans 10:5–15

Our right relationship with God is no longer dependent upon the keeping of the law; rather, it is a gift for all who trust in their hearts and confess with their lips. *Everyone* who trusts in the Lord (those who have come to the realization that God is God and they are not) will be saved.

MINDY DOUGLAS

Matthew 14:22–33

Peter cries out to be saved. . . . His action models for disciples the need to move beyond fear, to faith openly seeking God's saving grace. It is not simply that Peter sank because he took his eyes off Jesus; it is more noteworthy that Jesus the Christ stands ready to save in the midst of both fear and faith.

GENNIFER BENJAMIN BROOKS

WHAT IS THE HOLY SPIRIT SAYING TO YOU THIS WEEK?

_____

_____

_____

_____

_____

A SPIRITUAL PRACTICE FOR THIS WEEK

Find somewhere outside to go by yourself and pray, like Elijah and Jesus. Meditate, read, enjoy the natural world, take a walk, write in your journal, and try in some way to listen for God and what God might want to say to you. (Hint: not in wind, earthquakes, or fire.)

First Reading

At that place he came to a cave, and spent the night there.

Then the word of the LORD came to him, saying, "What are you doing here, Elijah?" (v. 9)

REFLECTION

The passage begins with the statement that "the word of the LORD came to him," a phrase that repeats itself like a refrain throughout the Elijah cycle. This is the fourth of its six occurrences, and its frequent appearance highlights Elijah's reliance on divine guidance and assistance (1 Kgs. 17:2, 8; 18:1; 19:9; 21:17, 28). This time the Deity's message takes the form of a question that suggests the prophet is not where he is supposed to be: "What are you doing here, Elijah?" The question is repeated twice, the second time after he has been told to stand on Mount Horeb.

JOHN KALTNER

RESPONSE

Is there a way that you are waiting for the word of the Lord to "come to you" this week? What do you long for God to say to you? If God asked you, "What are you doing here, my child?" how would you respond?

PRAYER

Lord God, your word came to Elijah out in the wilderness; guide me to the places I need to be to hear your word and receive your presence, to more deeply understand who you are calling me to be. Amen.

Canticle

Psalm 105:1–6, 16–22, 45b

Seek the LORD and his strength;
  seek his presence continually.
Remember the wonderful works he has done,
  his miracles, and the judgments he has uttered. (vv. 4–5)

REFLECTION

The psalmist compels the community to trust God, to seek the presence
and power of God (v. 4), and to trust God based on God's history with
Israel. The psalmist's call to remember and trust is key for this approach
to preaching, because there are times in the life of the church when we
need to be reminded of God's promises to us and our ancestors and
God's faithfulness in fulfilling those promises. The particular use of
Joseph's narrative further solidifies the psalmist's points by showing the
wonderful work of God's restoration in Joseph's life.

KHALIA J. WILLIAMS

RESPONSE

We tend to think of trusting in God as something individuals do. How
have you seen your congregation or faith community trusting in and
seeking the presence of God, together? How does your community
"remember and trust" as it looks toward its future? How could you still
grow in this, together?

PRAYER

God of gathering, you call communities gathered in your name to
seek you and remember your works; help me to seek you alongside my
siblings in Christ, that we may learn to trust you not only as individuals,
but together. Amen.

Second Reading

Romans 10:5–15

Because if you confess with your lips that Jesus is Lord and believe in your heart that God raised him from the dead, you will be saved. For one believes with the heart and so is justified, and one confesses with the mouth and so is saved. (vv. 9–10)

REFLECTION

The focus is not on human belief as an attitude or disposition, in contrast with human "doing of the law," but rather on the effective action of God in Christ, who alone has power to save (3:24). This divine action, which brings Christ so near that "the word" is in our hearts and on our lips (10:8), in turn gifts human beings with faith, so that we may "confess with the mouth, and believe in the heart" (10:9–10). God's saving action does not override human belief; rather, God activates our trust in Jesus Christ.

SUSAN GROVE EASTMAN

RESPONSE

Can you look back on your own life and see ways that your faith in Jesus Christ was activated by God and not your own initiative? What do you notice? What does being saved by Christ, through Christ's power alone, mean to you in particular this week?

PRAYER

Lord of all, everyone who calls on your name will be saved; inspire my heart and activate my belief, that, through faith in Christ alone, I will be saved. Amen.

Gospel

Matthew 14:22–33

He said, "Come." So Peter got out of the boat, started walking on the water, and came toward Jesus. But when he noticed the strong wind, he became frightened, and beginning to sink, he cried out, "Lord, save me!" (vv. 29–30)

REFLECTION

Peter's story suggests that you have to get out of the boat in order to fail in such a spectacular, interesting, and generative way. . . . Even in failure, it does not end in a drowning, but in rescue, and ultimately in grace that swallows up doubt and inspires worship in those who watch from the safety of the boat. On this reading, the scold about "little faith" loses its edge, and we hear in it the good-natured ribbing of one who knows that when it comes to the paradox of faith, a little can go a long way (17:20).

LANCE PAPE

RESPONSE

What is a spectacular way that you have failed because you "got out of the boat," stepping out in faith? How did God rescue you with grace, nonetheless? How hard it is to believe that a "little faith" goes a long way, this week? How is God nudging you to step out of the boat again?

PRAYER

Jesus our friend, you invite me to step out of my boat to take an impossible walk with you; give me courage to take the first step, courage to fail, courage to be changed, and enough faith to call to you for help. Amen.

Weekend Reflections

FURTHER CONNECTION

I can view myself primarily as a person who was terrorized by powerful people against whom I was helpless and whose intentions I could not discern. Or I can see myself primarily as a person who, after some suffering, has been delivered by God and given a new life, somewhat like the ancient Israelites, who in their sacred writings saw themselves not primarily as people who suffered in Egypt but as those who were delivered by Yahweh. I can be angry about suffering. I can be thankful for deliverance. I can be both.

MIROSLAV VOLF (1956–), *THE END OF MEMORY*

MAKING THE CONNECTIONS

Choose one or two questions for reflection:

1. What connections have you noticed between this week's texts and other passages in Scripture?

2. What connections have you made between this week's texts and the world beyond Scripture?

3. Does either of this week's two commentary themes speak especially to your life or the life of the world around you right now?

4. What is God saying to your congregation in particular through this week's readings and commentaries?

_____

_____

_____

_____

_____

Sabbath Day

SCRIPTURE OF ASSURANCE

> O my strength, I will sing praises to you,
>   for you, O God, are my fortress,
>   the God who shows me steadfast love. (Psalm 59:17)

WEEKLY EXAMEN

- Take a quiet moment, seek out God's presence, and pray for the guidance of the Spirit.

- Consider the past week; recall specific moments and feelings that stand out to you.

- Choose one moment or feeling for deeper examination, thanksgiving, or repentance.

- Let go, breathe deeply, and invite Christ's love to surround and fill you in preparation for the week ahead.

- End with the Lord's Prayer.

The Week Leading Up to
Proper 15
(Sunday between August 14 and August 20)

Isaiah 56:1, 6–8

For my house shall be called a house of prayer
    for all peoples.
Thus says the Lord GOD,
    who gathers the outcasts of Israel,
I will gather others to them
    besides those already gathered. (vv. 7b–8)

Genesis 45:1–15

But his brothers could not answer [Joseph], so dismayed were they at his presence.
    Then Joseph said to his brothers, "Come closer to me." And they came closer. He said, "I am your brother, Joseph, whom you sold into Egypt. And now do not be distressed, or angry with yourselves, because you sold me here; for God sent me before you to preserve life." (vv. 3b–5)

Romans 11:1–2a, 29–32

Just as you were once disobedient to God but have now received mercy because of their disobedience, so they have now been disobedient in order that, by the mercy shown to you, they too may now receive mercy. (vv. 30–31)

Matthew 15:(10–20) 21–28

[Jesus] answered, "I was sent only to the lost sheep of the house of Israel." But she came and knelt before him, saying, "Lord, help me." (vv. 24–25)

LECTIO DIVINA

Underline a word or phrase that especially grabs your attention. Pray from that word or phrase and ask God to help you connect to its particular invitation for you this week.

Themes from This Week's Writers

THEME 1: *God Calls Us to Restorative Justice*

Isaiah 56:1, 6–8 and Genesis 45:1–15

Salvation through Christ also . . . seeks to restore the relationship between God and humans—damaged by sin, self-centered desires and practices—by inviting everyone involved to assume responsibilities for their wrongdoings, not to condemn them but as the starting place on the journey to bring healing and restoration.

HUGO MAGALLANES

Romans 11:1–2a, 29–32

We should refrain from judgment, remembering that we have been dealt with mercifully by a gracious and loving God. Recognizing this, we should be the first to dispense such mercy to others.

MINDY DOUGLAS

Matthew 15:(10–20) 21–28

Her faith-impelled action . . . leads her to demand the right of full inclusion in God's redemptive plan. Not only is there the restoration of her daughter's health, but it brings to recognition the reality that a restored life originates from faith in Jesus Christ.

GENNIFER BENJAMIN BROOKS

THEME 2: *God's House Is a House of Prayer for All Peoples*

Isaiah 56:1, 6–8

Groups that had previously been considered outsiders are now on equal footing with the Israelites as part of God's community. Foreigners will observe the Sabbath and be allowed to enter the temple. . . . In addition, those among the Israelites who had previously been shunned, called "the outcasts of Israel," are also invited back into the fold.

JOHN KALTNER

Romans 11:1–2a, 29–32

If even those we consider enemies have their place in God's plan, and if even human disobedience comes within the realm of God's mercy, who are we to judge? . . .

. . . Even when it seems that God has abandoned God's people, Paul finds hope in his very big picture of God.

SUSAN GROVE EASTMAN

Matthew 15:(10–20) 21–28

This all-too-human Jesus cannot magically transcend the limits of the parochial view he inherited, but must learn about God's larger purposes the hard way, by trial and error. Which is the real Jesus? "They both are," Matthew seems to say. "Deal with it."

LANCE PAPE

WHAT IS THE HOLY SPIRIT SAYING TO YOU THIS WEEK?

_____

_____

_____

_____

_____

A SPIRITUAL PRACTICE FOR THIS WEEK

With prayer and holy curiosity, explore the website of a nearby house of worship belonging to a different Christian tradition than yours—whose people you might see as Jesus saw the Canaanite woman. What could you or your congregation learn from their faithfulness and good works? This week, pray for its leaders and people.

First Reading

Genesis 45:1–15

Then [Joseph] fell upon his brother Benjamin's neck and wept, while Benjamin wept upon his neck. And he kissed all his brothers and wept upon them; and after that his brothers talked with him. (vv. 14–15)

REFLECTION

Joseph's reaction is filled with mercy, grace, and forgiveness.

. . . Given his circumstances and all that he endured, many of us would be able to understand and perhaps even justify it if Joseph's reaction was one of seeking some form of retribution for what was done to him (betrayed, attempted murder, sold into slavery). Shockingly there is no sense of revenge or an indication toward retributive justice by Joseph. Rather, his explanation is based on an understanding of salvation as extending God's blessings, grace, and looking for ways to restore everyone involved.

HUGO MAGALLANES

RESPONSE

Joseph may have found it easier to be merciful because of the power and status he now held over his brothers. When was the last time you felt a desire for revenge? What were the power dynamics involved? How has forgiving "down" felt easier than forgiving "up" for you? Has it ever felt harder?

PRAYER

God of grace, you desire mercy, not sacrifice; teach me the compassion and mercy of Joseph, that I may not be overtaken by revenge or anger, but choose redemption and restoration. Amen.

Canticle

Psalm 133

How very good and pleasant it is
when kindred live together in unity! (v. 1)

REFLECTION

Psalm 133 begins with a Wisdom saying about how best to live;
central to the saying is the notion of unity.[1] . . . The psalmist compares
that unity to the anointing of Aaron as high priest, the anointing oil
dripping from his head through his beard and onto his robe. The oil
consecrated his whole being, not just his head. . . . The second simile
is the dew of Hermon falling onto the mountains. . . . Sufficient to
produce a harvest of grapes, [it] falls everywhere. . . . When unity settles
in a community—be it family, church, or even a nation—it brings
blessing and great joy to everyone.

KHALIA J. WILLIAMS

RESPONSE

How would you define "unity"? How do feelings of unity—in your
family, church, or wider community—feed your well-being? How do
feelings of broken unity strain you? Your community? What "dew"
is nurturing you and your community toward greater unity and
fruitfulness right now?

PRAYER

God of blessing, you desire that all may be one; give me and my
community the strength and nurture to seek togetherness in spite of
difference, hurt, and fracture, that we may know your blessings: life
forevermore. Amen.

1. Walter Brueggemann and William H. Bellinger Jr., *Psalms* (New York: Cambridge University Press,
2014), 558.

Second Reading

Romans 11:1–2a, 29–32

I ask, then, has God rejected his people? By no means! . . .

. . . For God has imprisoned all in disobedience so that he may be merciful to all. (vv. 1a, 32)

REFLECTION

Jesus cautioned us not to look upon another with condemnation in our hearts. Instead, we should refrain from judgment, remembering that we have been dealt with mercifully by a gracious and loving God. Recognizing this, we should be the first to dispense such mercy to others. . . .

In the end, those who have knowledge of God's endless mercy, in spite of humanity's undeserving, will seek to embrace such a gift with gratitude and a desire to reflect such mercy in our own lives. This mercy shapes our knowledge of God and our knowledge of ourselves.

MINDY DOUGLAS

RESPONSE

How are you in need of God's mercy and love this week? Make some room in your prayer life to offer your acute hurts, anger, and grief into God's tender care. How can you ease your self-judgment and lean into self-compassion? How might you find yourself reflecting this mercy outward to others in your life?

PRAYER

Loving God, all people are disobedient, and all people are in need of your mercy and help; teach me to be merciful, as you are merciful: to myself, my loved ones, and my neighbors. Amen.

Gospel

Matthew 15:(10–20) 21–28

[Jesus] answered, "It is not fair to take the children's food and throw it to the dogs." She said, "Yes, Lord, yet even the dogs eat the crumbs that fall from their masters' table." (vv. 26–27)

REFLECTION

Like the widow who petitioned for justice in one of the stories Jesus told, this woman will not take no for an answer. She does not naively expect that an inclusive vision will somehow win the day without someone who is willing to take a chance, absorb some blows, and do the hard work of making themselves a nuisance. In this way she sets an example not only for the hard, slow work of justice, but for the mysterious work of prayer. Indeed, her petition sounds very much like the prayer language we learn from the Psalms: "Have mercy on me, Lord!" (v. 22, cf. Ps. 86:3).

LANCE PAPE

RESPONSE

Do you ever make a nuisance of yourself for a good cause? What about in prayer? Why or why not? Is someone nagging or bothering you this week for what they want or need? What would it be like to let your heart be changed or to hear them, as Jesus did?

PRAYER

Lord Jesus, you do not close your ears to nagging or confrontation. You invite me to bother you with my needs; and you invite me, also, to respond to the nagging and needs of my neighbor. Amen.

Weekend Reflections

FURTHER CONNECTION

We commend the woman who quite simply, with all her heart, on behalf of someone she loved, refused to give up. We might think of her act as a "forgiving persistence" towards Christ. We might also wish to ponder a kind of "persistent forgiveness" toward the church.

The woman refuses and persists. And so prevails. And so must we. And so shall we. We must forgive, deepen our love, persist in our conviction that even the church can be redeemed from sin.

DANIEL BERRIGAN (1921–2016), *SORROW BUILT A BRIDGE: FRIENDSHIP AND AIDS*

MAKING THE CONNECTIONS

Choose one or two questions for reflection:

1. What connections have you noticed between this week's texts and other passages in Scripture?

2. What connections have you made between this week's texts and the world beyond Scripture?

3. Does either of this week's two commentary themes speak especially to your life or the life of the world around you right now?

4. What is God saying to your congregation in particular through this week's readings and commentaries?

_____

_____

_____

_____

_____

_____

Sabbath Day

SCRIPTURE OF ASSURANCE

Fight the good fight of the faith; take hold of the eternal life, to which you were called and for which you made the good confession in the presence of many witnesses. (1 Timothy 6:12)

WEEKLY EXAMEN

- Take a quiet moment, seek out God's presence, and pray for the guidance of the Spirit.

- Consider the past week; recall specific moments and feelings that stand out to you.

- Choose one moment or feeling for deeper examination, thanksgiving, or repentance.

- Let go, breathe deeply, and invite Christ's love to surround and fill you in preparation for the week ahead.

- End with the Lord's Prayer.

The Week Leading Up to
Proper 16
(Sunday between August 21 and August 27)

Isaiah 51:1–6

Listen to me, you that pursue righteousness,
   you that seek the LORD.
Look to the rock from which you were hewn,
   and to the quarry from which you were dug. (v. 1)

Exodus 1:8–2:10

She put the child in [the basket] and placed it among the reeds on the bank
of the river. His sister stood at a distance, to see what would happen to him.
(2:3b–4)

Romans 12:1–8

Do not be conformed to this world, but be transformed by the renewing of
your minds, so that you may discern what is the will of God—what is good
and acceptable and perfect. (v. 2)

Matthew 16:13–20

[Jesus] asked his disciples, "Who do people say that the Son of Man is?"
And they said, "Some say John the Baptist, but others Elijah, and still others
Jeremiah or one of the prophets." He said to them, "But who do you say that
I am?" Simon Peter answered, "You are the Messiah, the Son of the living
God." (vv. 13b–16)

LECTIO DIVINA

Underline a word or phrase that especially grabs your attention. Pray
from that word or phrase and ask God to help you connect to its
particular invitation for you this week.

Themes from This Week's Writers

THEME 1: *Assurance of God's Saving Presence*

Isaiah 51:1–6

This part of the book was composed to offer hope and encouragement to a community living far from its homeland, and this passage's reminder that God would save and deliver them from their difficult situation is a theme that is repeated frequently in Second Isaiah.

JOHN KALTNER

Psalm 124

There are hazards and dangers on the road of our Christian journey, but we do not face these hazards alone. God is both present with us and acting for us to deliver us from the dangers, both seen and unseen.

KHALIA J. WILLIAMS

Matthew 16:13–20

Peter is assured that his work as builder of Christ's church will not be defeated. In a sense, Matthew's church is exiled from their Jewish roots and needs assurance for their continued life in Christ. For the church in every time, the assurance of God's saving presence and grace is God's promise to all who confess their faith in God.

GENNIFER BENJAMIN BROOKS

THEME 2: *Not Just Knowing Christ, but Being Transformed In Christ*

Romans 12:1–8

Transformation of both mind and body is a central theme in Paul's letters (see esp. Phil. 3:21). Such transformation is always God's work in us, not something we can manage on our own. It is a participation in the mind of Christ (1 Cor. 2:16), again guiding the shared deliberations of the church.

SUSAN GROVE EASTMAN

Romans 12:1–8

Paul instructs us not to conform to the ways of the world, where people define others by a hierarchical system of worth; rather, to be transformed so that we might "discern the will of God—what is good, acceptable, and perfect" (12:2).

MINDY DOUGLAS

Matthew 16:13–20

In our own time, the church might do well to spend less time insisting that others acknowledge Jesus with the right language, and more time living into his example of spending himself recklessly for the world he loves, and trusting God to vindicate such obedience in God's own time.

LANCE PAPE

WHAT IS THE HOLY SPIRIT SAYING TO YOU THIS WEEK?

_____

_____

_____

_____

_____

A SPIRITUAL PRACTICE FOR THIS WEEK

Read Romans 12:1–2. Then, pray for your body from head to toe, praying a blessing on each part of you, even your inner organs. Bless all members of your body as holy, good, and perfect. How is your body a part of your worship? Your prayer life? Your gifts?

First Reading

Isaiah 51:1–6 and Exodus 1:8–2:10

For the LORD will comfort Zion;
    he will comfort all her waste places,
and will make her wilderness like Eden. (Isaiah 51:3a)

But the midwives feared God; they did not do as the king of Egypt commanded them, but they let the boys live. (Exodus 1:17)

REFLECTION

Is God trying to say here that it is OK to lie and disobey the law?
Why did God not say so in the years when God's people were in exile?
Why does God take a more proactive role in Isaiah and more passive
involvement in the Exodus narrative? Instead of offering concrete
answers to these questions, these passages seem to lead to trust in God
and God's wisdom, but not in a passive way—rather, in a way that
questions and/or challenges the establishment.

HUGO MAGALLANES

RESPONSE

Have you ever broken or bent the law for the sake of God's
commandments, like the midwives? In contrast, have you ever
heard God calling you to rest, like the exiles, to allow God or
others to act instead? How might God be inviting you to resist
the establishment now, actively or passively?

PRAYER

Almighty God, give me wisdom to know when to disobey and subvert,
and when to rest and wait, that all your people may have abundant life.
Amen.

Canticle

Psalm 138

I give you thanks, O LORD, with my whole heart;
   before the gods I sing your praise;
I bow down toward your holy temple. (vv. 1–2a)

REFLECTION

The concluding declaration that God will fulfill God's purpose, and the
petition to not abandon the "work of your hands" further substantiate
the prophet's declaration to Israel. In addition, the embodied nature of
Psalm 138, illustrating bodily acts of worship, connects to the embodied
nature of the Romans 12 passage. Paired together, these texts call for
more than cognitive processing of God's blessings and requirements;
rather, they demand an action of our entire being. In worship, we are
called to offer our whole selves, as seen in the psalm, and in Paul's
address to the Romans, our salvation calls us to do the same.

KHALIA J. WILLIAMS

RESPONSE

How do you worship God with your body in communal worship
with your congregation? In your personal prayer life? In other parts of
your life? What does it mean to you, in particular, that your body is a
pathway to knowing God? To giving thanks to God? To serving God?

PRAYER

Creator God, I am the work of your hands; teach me to worship and
praise you with all my heart, soul, body, and mind. Amen.

Second Reading

Romans 12:1–8

For by the grace given to me I say to everyone among you not to think of yourself more highly than you ought to think, but to think with sober judgment, each according to the measure of faith that God has assigned. For as in one body we have many members, and not all the members have the same function, so we, who are many, are one body in Christ, and individually we are members one of another. (vv. 3–5)

REFLECTION

Humility in this passage is not about lowliness, meekness, or submissiveness (common definitions of humility) as much as it is a call to recognize that all followers of Jesus have a part (a gift, a function) in the body of Christ that is no more and no less important and valued than anyone else's part. Each person brings particular gifts that become a part of the whole. When all parts function together, the body works the way it should. Humility insists that every part honor every other part equally.

MINDY DOUGLAS

RESPONSE

List seven gifts you bring to the body of Christ. Choose someone in your congregation whom you admire and make a list of seven gifts they bring. Then, choose someone you dislike and list their gifts, too. Pray over these lists, honoring that all are part of making the body of Christ whole.

PRAYER

O Christ, in you, we who are many are one body; teach me to value my gifts and the gifts you have given others, that we may grow together into you, more and more. Amen.

Gospel

Matthew 16:13–20

Simon Peter answered, "You are the Messiah, the Son of the living God."
And Jesus answered him, "Blessed are you, Simon son of Jonah! For flesh and
blood has not revealed this to you, but my Father in heaven." (vv. 16–17)

REFLECTION

Jesus, even after embracing the answer Peter gives to the question of
his identity, is not eager to have him (or the other disciples) as his
spokesperson (v. 20). There are situations where even those who have
received the gift of knowing the truth about Jesus are not at all clear
about what to do with that information. In our own time, the church
might do well to spend less time insisting that others acknowledge
Jesus with the right language, and more time living into his example of
spending himself recklessly for the world he loves.

LANCE PAPE

RESPONSE

What was a time you thought you had to act as Jesus' spokesperson
or truth-teller? When was a time you had no idea what to do with
what you know about Jesus? How can you spend less time worrying or
speaking, and more time "spending yourself recklessly" for the world
Jesus loves?

PRAYER

Jesus, son of the living God, you do not need me to say the right words
so much as to love from the heart; help me to know you, not just to talk
about you. Amen.

Weekend Reflections

FURTHER CONNECTION

The liberation of the Israelite people in Egypt begins with Shiphrah and Puah. They are the mothers of a revolution waged by women. They likely enlisted untold numbers of birthing-women and expectant mothers in their resistance movement. It is not clear whether they deliver Moshe (Moses), Aharon (Aaron), and/or Miryam (Miriam). In any case their act of resistance sets the stage for those to follow. Shiphrah and Puah become the first deliverers in the book of deliverance.

WILDA GAFNEY (1966–), *WOMANIST MIDRASH: A REINTRODUCTION TO THE WOMEN OF THE TORAH AND THE THRONE*

MAKING THE CONNECTIONS

Choose one or two questions for reflection:

1. What connections have you noticed between this week's texts and other passages in Scripture?

2. What connections have you made between this week's texts and the world beyond Scripture?

3. Does either of this week's two commentary themes speak especially to your life or the life of the world around you right now?

4. What is God saying to your congregation in particular through this week's readings and commentaries?

_____

_____

_____

_____

_____

Sabbath Day

SCRIPTURE OF ASSURANCE

I thank my God every time I remember you, constantly praying with joy in every one of my prayers for all of you, because of your sharing in the gospel from the first day until now. (Philippians 1:3–5)

WEEKLY EXAMEN

- Take a quiet moment, seek out God's presence, and pray for the guidance of the Spirit.

- Consider the past week; recall specific moments and feelings that stand out to you.

- Choose one moment or feeling for deeper examination, thanksgiving, or repentance.

- Let go, breathe deeply, and invite Christ's love to surround and fill you in preparation for the week ahead.

- End with the Lord's Prayer.

The Week Leading Up to
Proper 17

(Sunday between August 28 and September 3)

Jeremiah 15:15–21

If you turn back, I will take you back,
  and you shall stand before me.
    If you utter what is precious, and not what is worthless,
  you shall serve as my mouth. (v. 19a)

Exodus 3:1–15

When the LORD saw that he had turned aside to see, God called to him out of the bush, "Moses, Moses!" And he said, "Here I am." Then he said, "Come no closer! Remove the sandals from your feet, for the place on which you are standing is holy ground." (vv. 4–5)

Romans 12:9–21

Beloved, never avenge yourselves, but leave room for the wrath of God; for it is written, "Vengeance is mine, I will repay, says the Lord." No, "if your enemies are hungry, feed them; if they are thirsty, give them something to drink; for by doing this you will heap burning coals on their heads." (vv. 19–20)

Matthew 16:21–28

From that time on, Jesus began to show his disciples that he must go to Jerusalem and undergo great suffering at the hands of the elders and chief priests and scribes, and be killed, and on the third day be raised. And Peter took him aside and began to rebuke him, saying, "God forbid it, Lord! This must never happen to you." (vv. 21–22)

LECTIO DIVINA

> Underline a word or phrase that especially grabs your attention. Pray from that word or phrase and ask God to help you connect to its particular invitation for you this week.

Themes from This Week's Writers

THEME 1: *How Does God Call Us?*

Exodus 3:1–15

The call requires Moses to return to the place where he is wanted for murder, to speak for a people who have already rejected him. Moses' vocation, a purpose amid his suffering, comes with only the assurance that God is "with you" (v. 12).

JOHN W. WRIGHT

Exodus 3:1–15

For Moses, this sacred encounter was not just personal and private; it was a time of consecration to serve God in the context of a community, the people of God. Sacred spaces may also be designed to call forth action on behalf of those who live in misery and suffering.

LINCOLN E. GALLOWAY

Matthew 16:21–28

In the setting of Matthew's story line, this account suggests that there is no single "moment of truth" but a series of them, that there are many decision points, instead of one. . . .

Rather, God's call to self-sacrificing service is episodically unfolding, even if unidirectional.

DAVID J. SCHLAFER

THEME 2: *"Take Up Your Cross" Means Love, Not Just Suffering*

Romans 12:9–21

What distinguishes Paul's sketch of the life of the reconciled and reconciling community is not novelty, but the motivating event that animates it: the self-giving love of God expressed in the self-sacrifice of Jesus. . . . The effect of embodying this radically self-giving love—self-giving to the point of practicing gift-giving to the enemy—is to signify the transformation God's Spirit is effecting in the world.

SALLY A. BROWN

Romans 12:9–21

[Paul] cautions the church not to give up when persecuted. In counseling love and kindness toward perceived and real enemies, Paul is preaching Jesus' own message to love all humankind. To feed and give drink to one's enemies here entails sharing material resources with all and sharing Christian spiritual life with all.

KAREN BAKER-FLETCHER

Matthew 16:21–28

Suffering is not a consequence of following Jesus. It should be avoided. However, the cost of avoiding suffering could be the loss of one's soul (vv. 25–26), if avoidance is achieved by forsaking Jesus.

RAQUEL ST. CLAIR LETTSOME

WHAT IS THE HOLY SPIRIT SAYING TO YOU THIS WEEK?

_____

_____

_____

_____

_____

A SPIRITUAL PRACTICE FOR THIS WEEK

Draw an image of Christ carrying the cross (use stick figures if that helps you draw) or find an image created by someone else. Carry it with you this week. Reflect on this question: What is the difference in your life between suffering that leads to new life and resurrection, and suffering that destroys life?

First Reading

Exodus 3:1–15

But Moses said to God, "If I come to the Israelites and say to them, 'The God of your ancestors has sent me to you,' and they ask me, 'What is his name?' what shall I say to them?" God said to Moses, "I AM WHO I AM." He said further, "Thus you shall say to the Israelites, 'I AM has sent me to you.'" (vv. 13–14)

REFLECTION

Moses receives the divine Name through the Word of God as a gift. God reveals God's name as the unchangeable, ongoing act of existence that the divine Word gives as God's Name. God is with Moses because "God *is*." . . . God will not abandon Moses when he returns to Pharaoh. God never has abandoned Moses. God cannot deny God's own Life. God's Life is the One from whom are all things, through whom are all things, and to whom are all things. Moses can move from devastation to call because God's Name, the one who sends Moses, is "I Am-ing."

JOHN W. WRIGHT

RESPONSE

Reflect on God's name "I *am who* I *am*." What does this name say to you about God, at this time in your life? How do you see yourself in Moses? How does this name for God speak to your sense of God's presence and call to you?

PRAYER

Lord God, you are beyond all names; still, teach me to name you in ways that are true, to help me know who it is that has sent me and is always with me. Amen.

Canticle

Psalm 26:1–8

Prove me, O LORD, and try me;
   test my heart and mind.
For your steadfast love is before my eyes,
   and I walk in faithfulness to you. (vv. 2–3)

REFLECTION

While the psalmist trusts "without wavering," Jeremiah wavers.

Yet even in his despair, Jeremiah hears the promise of the Lord, a promise of deliverance and redemption. God's rich history of promise and redemption is what prompts the psalmist to testify to God's wondrous deeds, singing "a song of thanksgiving" while processing around the altar (vv. 6, 7). The company both the prophet and the psalmist choose to keep is the one whose identity transforms theirs in sacramental suggestion, Jeremiah by the eating of the Word and the psalmist by waters of purification.

RON RIENSTRA

RESPONSE

In what ways have you felt despair or wavered in your trust in God, recently? Make a list of God's wondrous deeds in your life or write a song of thanksgiving. Invite God to offer you a "sacramental suggestion," a spiritual practice that could feed you in a surprising, transformative way.

PRAYER

Faithful God, whether I trust you without wavering or waver mightily, your steadfast love is before me; nudge me today with a sign that you are with me. Amen.

Second Reading

Romans 12:9–21

Let love be genuine; hate what is evil, hold fast to what is good; love one another with mutual affection; outdo one another in showing honor. Do not lag in zeal, be ardent in spirit, serve the Lord. (vv. 9–11)

REFLECTION

Instead of rendering verse 11, "Do not lag in zeal, be ardent in spirit, serve the Lord," [Karl] Barth, [Ernst] Käsemann, and others translate, "*. . . serve the time.*" (Barth goes so far as to deem "serve the Lord" an "insipid" translation!) Choosing *kairō* over *kyriō* comports with Paul's concern with the momentous, decisive "time" of God's renewal of all things; the word *kairos* in some form occurs seven times in Romans alone, excluding this occurrence, as well as fourteen times in other Pauline letters, excluding the contested letters.

Such a reading heightens the emphasis and urgency of this entire section of the epistle.

SALLY A. BROWN

RESPONSE

What is your relationship with time? What would it mean to you this week to "be ardent in spirit and serve the time"? What is urgent about what Paul is suggesting? How do you find balance, in your own life, between what is urgent and what is eternal?

PRAYER

Eternal God, we have all the time there is and yet, there is only so much time here on earth; help us to serve the time, holding fast to what is good and loving one another with mutual affection. Amen.

Gospel

Matthew 16:21–28

Then Jesus told his disciples, "If any want to become my followers, let them deny themselves and take up their cross and follow me. For those who want to save their life will lose it, and those who lose their life for my sake will find it." (vv. 24–25)

REFLECTION

Disciples following a Jesus who suffers may become followers who suffer. "Follower" becomes the primary identifying factor, and suffering becomes a consequence that they are willing to endure for continuing the ministry of the one who lived, suffered, died, and was vindicated by resurrection. In other words, the suffering is never the goal or measuring stick of their discipleship. This enables them to see that all sorrow, pain, injustice, oppression, or torment inflicted by life or others is not the will of God for their lives and can be fought against rather than passively accepted.

RAQUEL ST. CLAIR LETTSOME

RESPONSE

When have you felt you must "carry your cross"? When have you suffered as a result of following Jesus? How does Lettsome's perspective speak to or contrast with your own experience? Is there a suffering in your life right now you feel called to fight or refuse?

PRAYER

O Jesus, to follow you, I must not seek to save my life but to take up my cross and walk with you and our friends to Jerusalem. Amen.

Weekend Reflections

The kind of work God usually calls you to is the kind of work (a) that you need most to do and (b) that the world most needs to have done. . . . if your work is being a doctor in a leper colony, you have probably met requirement (b), but if most of the time you're bored and depressed by it, the chances are you have not only bypassed (a) but probably aren't helping your patients much either.

Neither the hair shirt nor the soft berth will do. The place God calls you to is the place where your deep gladness and the world's deep hunger meet.

FREDERICK BUECHNER (1924–),
WISHFUL THINKING: A SEEKER'S ABC

MAKING THE CONNECTIONS

Choose one or two questions for reflection:

1. What connections have you noticed between this week's texts and other passages in Scripture?

2. What connections have you made between this week's texts and the world beyond Scripture?

3. Does either of this week's two commentary themes speak especially to your life or the life of the world around you right now?

4. What is God saying to your congregation in particular through this week's readings and commentaries?

_____

_____

_____

_____

_____

_____

Sabbath Day

SCRIPTURE OF ASSURANCE

"As you have sent me into the world, so I have sent them into the world. And for their sakes I sanctify myself, so that they also may be sanctified in truth." (John 17:18–19)

WEEKLY EXAMEN

- Take a quiet moment, seek out God's presence, and pray for the guidance of the Spirit.

- Consider the past week; recall specific moments and feelings that stand out to you.

- Choose one moment or feeling for deeper examination, thanksgiving, or repentance.

- Let go, breathe deeply, and invite Christ's love to surround and fill you in preparation for the week ahead.

- End with the Lord's Prayer.

The Week Leading Up to
Proper 18

(Sunday between September 4 and September 10)

Ezekiel 33:7–11

Say to them, As I live, says the Lord GOD, I have no pleasure in the death of the wicked, but that the wicked turn from their ways and live; turn back, turn back from your evil ways; for why will you die, O house of Israel? (v. 11)

Exodus 12:1–14

This day shall be a day of remembrance for you. You shall celebrate it as a festival to the LORD; throughout your generations you shall observe it as a perpetual ordinance. (v. 14)

Romans 13:8–14

Owe no one anything, except to love one another; for the one who loves another has fulfilled the law. The commandments, "You shall not commit adultery; You shall not murder; You shall not steal; You shall not covet"; and any other commandment, are summed up in this word, "Love your neighbor as yourself." (vv. 8–9)

Matthew 18:15–20

"If another member of the church sins against you, go and point out the fault when the two of you are alone. If the member listens to you, you have regained that one. But if you are not listened to, take one or two others along with you, so that every word may be confirmed by the evidence of two or three witnesses." (vv. 15–16)

LECTIO DIVINA

Underline a word or phrase that especially grabs your attention. Pray from that word or phrase and ask God to help you connect to its particular invitation for you this week.

Themes from This Week's Writers

THEME 1: *See the Signs, Hear God's Call, Awake from Sleep*

Ezekiel 33:7–11 and Exodus 12:1–14

The blood is a "sign," not for the angel of death, but for the congregation of Israel (12:13). The blood of the slaughtered lamb signs God's preservation of Israel from the plague of death.

. . . The image of the Passover lamb becomes a powerful type for the life, death, and resurrection of Jesus.

JOHN W. WRIGHT

Exodus 12:1–14

The sentinel hears the cry of the people: How then can we live? (v. 10). . . .

Sentinels are set apart for the work because they demonstrate the ability or gifts to hear a word from God's mouth. People of faith are called to be sentinels and to live a life of righteousness.

LINCOLN E. GALLOWAY

Romans 13:8–14

Paul emphasizes the nearness of salvation. He cautions readers to "wake up," because night has gone and the day of salvation is near. Here Paul is communicating a sense of urgency to start living in love immediately, now, today, in the present moment and in each coming moment.

KAREN BAKER-FLETCHER

THEME 2: *How Do We Approach Conflict in a Healthy Community?*

Romans 13:8–14

Keeping alert to this costly, self-giving element is a check against reducing our text's memorable opening line to Hallmark-card simplism, a bland "niceness" that simply goes along and gets along with everyone. The love the apostle has in mind is potentially as costly as Jesus' own.

SALLY A. BROWN

Matthew 18:15–20

It is interesting that the "two or three witnesses" required as a stage in attempted conflict resolution (Matt. 18:16) is the same as the "two or three" who, when gathered in his name, ensure the presence of Jesus among them (v. 20). Individuals alone, be they sinner or accuser, by their very standing apart, dis-integrate the community, the body of Christ.

DAVID J. SCHLAFER

Matthew 18:15–20

Conflict is not new. It is not new to the world at large, and it is not new to the church, individual congregations, or church members. In fact, if there is anything that we can count on, it is the fact that conflict will arise. However, conflict arises in different forms, shaped by the realities of persons and groups involved.

RAQUEL ST. CLAIR LETTSOME

WHAT IS THE HOLY SPIRIT SAYING TO YOU THIS WEEK?

_____

_____

_____

_____

_____

A SPIRITUAL PRACTICE FOR THIS WEEK

Consider someone at church with whom you have a disagreement. What are some ways you might connect with them beyond the disagreement? How might you speak directly with them about the problem? Or how can you call on your community to help you resolve the disagreement? Strive not to grumble about this person to others.

First Reading

Ezekiel 33:7–11

Now you, mortal, say to the house of Israel, Thus you have said: "Our transgressions and our sins weigh upon us, and we waste away because of them; how then can we live?" Say to them, As I live, says the Lord GOD, I have no pleasure in the death of the wicked, but that the wicked turn from their ways and live. (vv. 10–11a)

REFLECTION

[Israel's] inability to remember God's mercy cuts them off from repentance. . . . They cannot see life beyond their own sin. The sentinel, told to warn them of judgment, instead reminds them that God is life and desires their life. The past does not determine the future. God does not desire the death of any. As God lives (v. 11), God desires life. Israel needs to repent from death and turn toward life (God). The house of Israel, as in Exodus 12, does not need to die (v. 11). Israel needs to remember God's mercy and desire for their life.

JOHN W. WRIGHT

RESPONSE

How does self-judgment, perfectionism, or the idea that you are a bad or sinful (or "wicked") person affect your life? How could this lead to death for your spirit or calling? What does it mean to you, this week, to live from God's desire for life and mercy for you?

PRAYER

Loving God, fill my heart with your mercy, that I might not be afraid of shame or unworthiness but turn toward your grace and *live*. Amen.

Canticle

Psalm 119:33–40

Give me understanding, that I may keep your law
and observe it with my whole heart.
Lead me in the path of your commandments,
for I delight in it. (vv. 34–35)

REFLECTION

[This psalm] uses a host of synonyms for the Law (decree, precept,
statute, commandment, ordinance, word, and promise) as a way to
cast a wide net for all that God might speak. Before we can be warning
speakers, we have to be God-seekers. We need to pray continuously
for discernment, for understanding (Ps. 119:34); we need to long to
know what is right and delight in the path of God's commandments (v.
35). This is a constant discipline. We cannot call the church to account
without this relentless listening for the Word of the Lord.

RON RIENSTRA

RESPONSE

Reread the Ten Commandments (Exodus 20:1–17, Deuteronomy
5:1–21), reviewing each one in a spirit of self-examination. What might
God be inviting you to notice?

PRAYER

God of the Torah, teach me to understand and delight in your
commandments, to observe them with my whole heart. Amen.

Second Reading

Romans 13:8–14

Let us live honorably as in the day, not in reveling and drunkenness, not in debauchery and licentiousness, not in quarreling and jealousy. Instead, put on the Lord Jesus Christ, and make no provision for the flesh, to gratify its desires. (vv. 13–14)

REFLECTION

Love entails esteeming one another or, as Paul writes in verse 13, "let us live honorably as in the day." . . .

Paul offers examples of what living honorably does not condone. "Reveling" refers to wild behavior that is destructive of self, neighbors, and property. "Drunkenness" refers specifically to alcohol abuse; it can also include any addictive substances and activities that cause harm to self, neighbors, family, community, and the larger society. "Debauchery" is a referent to wild partying that involves loss of self-containment or self-control, including sexual exploitation and substance abuse.

KAREN BAKER-FLETCHER

RESPONSE

Paul can seem prudish or uptight. What strikes you in Baker-Fletcher's elaborations of Paul's labels? What life habits might God be inviting you to examine or transform, here? How might you more fully "put on the Lord Jesus Christ"? How could you love and honor others more fully, this week?

PRAYER

Lord Jesus Christ, show me how to live honorably, to avoid self-harm, destructive behavior, and damaging thoughts, that I may wear you, alone, as my garment of protection and delight. Amen.

Gospel

Matthew 18:15–20

"If the member refuses to listen to them, tell it to the church; and if the offender refuses to listen even to the church, let such a one be to you as a Gentile and a tax collector." (v. 17)

REFLECTION

While the current social environment tends to make everything public first, this passage emphasizes the relationship between "kinship" and rules that govern communal life (see Lev. 19:15–18). Deviating from the form of accountability outlined in verses 15–17, the court of public opinion is called upon to adjudicate disagreements, oftentimes before the parties involved have a chance to iron things out privately. The preacher can ask, How do we exemplify Christian ideals of reconciliation and community when a fame-shame environment reduces us to silos of like-minded people?

RAQUEL ST. CLAIR LETTSOME

RESPONSE

Most of us no longer live in communities knit together in such a way that we work out conflicts with our neighbors interpersonally. How have you experienced this? How have you experienced accountability and reconciliation at church? Reflect on Lettsome's closing question in your own context.

PRAYER

Loving God, you have gathered us into communities and groups in Christ; help us to better communicate and disagree, that together we may serve you and your people in wholeness and love. Amen.

Weekend Reflections

FURTHER CONNECTION

The Four Elements of Right Speech
1. Tell the truth. Don't lie or turn the truth upside down.
2. Don't exaggerate.
3. Be consistent. This means no double-talk: speaking about something in one way to one person and in an opposite way to another for selfish or manipulative reasons.
4. Use peaceful language. Don't use insulting or violent words, cruel speech, verbal abuse, or condemnation.

THICH NHAT HANH (1926–2022), *THE ART OF COMMUNICATING*

MAKING THE CONNECTIONS

Choose one or two questions for reflection:

1. What connections have you noticed between this week's texts and other passages in Scripture?

2. What connections have you made between this week's texts and the world beyond Scripture?

3. Does either of this week's two commentary themes speak especially to your life or the life of the world around you right now?

4. What is God saying to your congregation in particular through this week's readings and commentaries?

_____

_____

_____

_____

_____

_____

Sabbath Day

SCRIPTURE OF ASSURANCE

So then, putting away falsehood, let all of us speak the truth to our neighbors, for we are members of one another. (Ephesians 4:25)

WEEKLY EXAMEN

- Take a quiet moment, seek out God's presence, and pray for the guidance of the Spirit.

- Consider the past week; recall specific moments and feelings that stand out to you.

- Choose one moment or feeling for deeper examination, thanksgiving, or repentance.

- Let go, breathe deeply, and invite Christ's love to surround and fill you in preparation for the week ahead.

- End with the Lord's Prayer.

The Week Leading Up to
Proper 19
(Sunday between September 11 and September 17)

Genesis 50:15–21

Realizing that their father was dead, Joseph's brothers said, "What if Joseph still bears a grudge against us and pays us back in full for all the wrong that we did to him?" (v. 15)

Exodus 14:19–31

Then Moses stretched out his hand over the sea. The Lord drove the sea back by a strong east wind all night, and turned the sea into dry land; and the waters were divided. The Israelites went into the sea on dry ground, the waters forming a wall for them on their right and on their left. (vv. 21–22)

Romans 14:1–12

Why do you pass judgment on your brother or sister? Or you, why do you despise your brother or sister? For we will all stand before the judgment seat of God. (v. 10)

Matthew 18:21–35

Then Peter came and said to him, "Lord, if another member of the church sins against me, how often should I forgive? As many as seven times?" Jesus said to him, "Not seven times, but, I tell you, seventy-seven times." (vv. 21–22)

LECTIO DIVINA

Underline a word or phrase that especially grabs your attention. Pray from that word or phrase and ask God to help you connect to its particular invitation for you this week.

Themes from This Week's Writers

THEME 1: *Who Are You to Pass Judgment?*

Exodus 14:19–31

Both in our faith communities and also our national conversations, we are invited to reflect on our response when hardship, suffering, adversity, or calamity befalls those who threaten our welfare or seek to do us harm. . . . Do we celebrate their demise, or do we recognize their humanity?

LINCOLN E. GALLOWAY

Romans 14:1–12

Paul suggests the situation requires that the less constrained in matters of food and sacred days need to exercise nonjudgmental self-restraint, protecting the faith of believers more scrupulous in "indifferent" matters such as these, out of love.

SALLY A. BROWN

Romans 14:1–12

For Paul, whether we eat or abstain from certain foods in honor of God, whether we claim a particular day or every day holy in honor of God, we do all these things out of reverence for the Divine.

What is most important is that we make time, space, and ways to honor God from the heart.

KAREN BAKER-FLETCHER

THEME 2: *How Often Should I Forgive?*

Psalm 103:(1–7) 8–13

God is slow to anger and abounding in steadfast love. Then, in the narrative from Genesis 50, Joseph does what God does. . . .

Could this be an invitation to us too? Could this implicit call to forgive others draw us into the grace and compassion and providence of a God who intends that even actions undertaken for evil be turned to the good?

RON RIENSTRA

Matthew 18:21–35

Jesus may well be indirectly referencing . . . Genesis 4:23–24. There a man named Lamech sings a song . . . saying, in effect, "If someone wrongs me, I will repay them, not just in kind, but seventy-seven times over." Forgiveness, as Jesus presents it here, can be understood as the radical, self-sacrificing opposite of—and necessary alternative to—revenge.

DAVID J. SCHLAFER

Matthew 18:21–35

Jesus puts how much we forgive others in relation to how much we have been forgiven. We respond to fouls from a bank that deals in a different currency. We pay back out of the bank of God's mercy, compassion, and forgiveness to us. We refuse to withdraw from the branches of foul behavior we have experienced.

RAQUEL ST. CLAIR LETTSOME

WHAT IS THE HOLY SPIRIT SAYING TO YOU THIS WEEK?

_____

_____

_____

_____

_____

A SPIRITUAL PRACTICE FOR THIS WEEK

Reflect on a way that you have felt forgiven by God lately. Then, reflect on one or two people whom you have had trouble forgiving, yourself. Pray for them and for yourself this week, perhaps using Romans 14:7 as a mantra: "We do not live to ourselves, and we do not die to ourselves."

First Reading

Exodus 14:19–31

The waters returned and covered the chariots and the chariot drivers, the entire army of Pharaoh that had followed them into the sea; not one of them remained. But the Israelites walked on dry ground through the sea, the waters forming a wall for them on their right and on their left. (vv. 28–29)

REFLECTION

In our reading from Exodus, we have the stuff of which movies are made. The visuals in each frame require computer-generated images because the subject matter is supernatural and outside of our everyday experience. . . .

In the Exodus narrative, the divine works supernaturally in cloud, wind, fire, and water to deliver enslaved people from bondage. One of the most enduring and foundational dimensions of theologies of liberation is built on this conviction that God comes to the aid and works on behalf of those who are oppressed, the poor, the outcast, and marginalized.

LINCOLN E. GALLOWAY

RESPONSE

What is it like to think of God as superhero? What new images of God might this bring to mind? How might you imagine yourself as part of the long arc of God's superhero saga? How might God be calling you to help liberate people in your community?

PRAYER

Almighty God, you saved the people of Israel from the Egyptian army and brought them to freedom; teach me radical hope, a sense of fun, and the power of a superhero story to empower and inspire. Amen.

Canticle

Psalm 103:(1–7) 8–13 or Psalm 114 or Exodus 15:1b–11, 20–21

> "Pharaoh's chariots and his army he cast into the sea;
>   his picked officers were sunk in the Red Sea.
> The floods covered them;
>   they went down into the depths like a stone.
> Your right hand, O LORD, glorious in power—
>   your right hand, O LORD, shattered the enemy." (Exodus 15:4–6)

REFLECTION

A word about the use of these texts in an era of politically driven
enmity between Christians and Muslims. . . . It is hard for Christians
who follow the one who said, "Love your enemies," to wholeheartedly
embrace these sentiments, especially when this lection falls close to the
anniversary of 9/11. Yet [we can] boldly speak a word of victory, actual
or aspirational, over God's enemies, without equating those enemies
with those who trace their ancestry to Middle Eastern lands.

RON RIENSTRA

RESPONSE

Have you ever been angry or irritated with Muslims or foreigners?
Acknowledging negative feelings can help us move beyond them, toward
love. When have you wished God would punish your enemies? Or
fantasized about doing so yourself? Does reading these Scriptures relieve
or inflame your feelings?

PRAYER

Lord of all, your enemies are not human beings, but powers and
principalities; help me to read Scripture not in order to judge or blame
others, but to understand who you are and how I should live. Amen.

Second Reading

Romans 14:1–12

Those who observe the day, observe it in honor of the Lord. Also those who eat, eat in honor of the Lord, since they give thanks to God; while those who abstain, abstain in honor of the Lord and give thanks to God. (v. 6)

REFLECTION

Paul advances three reasons, all theological, why the "strong" need to refrain from judgment and defer to the sensitivities of the "weak." First, what the weak do with regard to food choices or observing special days is done in honor of the Lord (Rom. 14:6). Second, we all belong to *one* Lord; and it is this, not agreement on peripheral matters, that establishes our unity (vv. 7–9). Third, God is the only judge; the "weak" are accountable to God, as we all are (vv. 10–12).

SALLY A. BROWN

RESPONSE

What are some ways you look down on the spiritual or religious practices of others in your community? In what ways might you feel that other people judge you? How do Paul's words speak to your situation? What is God inviting you to notice, about yourself or your community?

PRAYER

God, our only judge, all people belong to you and are known by you; strengthen me not to judge or despise the ways of others, but to be curious and generous, and accountable to you for my own life. Amen.

Gospel

Matthew 18:21–35

"'Should you not have had mercy on your fellow slave, as I had mercy on you?' And in anger his lord handed him over to be tortured until he would pay his entire debt. So my heavenly Father will also do to every one of you, if you do not forgive your brother or sister from your heart." (vv. 33–35)

REFLECTION

We tend to bring to the issue of forgiveness some seriously selective perception. This violent story may be an attention getter precisely because, while in the abstract "forgiveness for all without limit" may sound not just reasonable but emotionally engaging, when we find ourselves in situations when we have been deeply wounded or continually inconvenienced by others, we "just do not get it." According to the story, *if* we do not get it—we do not *get* it. Forgiveness does not flow *to* us if it does not flow *through* us.

DAVID J. SCHLAFER

RESPONSE

Think of a petty grievance you have against someone. How does it take up room in your life? What would forgiving this person be like? How could this be a more serious issue than at first it seems, for your spiritual health? How do you long for forgiveness for yourself?

PRAYER

Gracious God, you desire the wholeness and righteousness of all people; show me how to forgive and to receive forgiveness that I may be whole and free in you. Amen.

Weekend Reflections

Simply punishing the broken—walking away from them or hiding them from sight—only ensures that they remain broken and we do, too. There is no wholeness outside of our reciprocal humanity.

I frequently had difficult conversations with clients who were struggling and despairing over their situations—over the things they'd done, or had been done to them, that had led them to painful moments. Whenever things got really bad, and they were questioning the value of their lives, I would remind them that each of us is more than the worst thing we've ever done. I told them that if someone tells a lie, that person is not just a liar. If you take something that doesn't belong to you, you are not just a thief. Even if you kill someone, you're not just a killer.

BRYAN STEVENSON (1959–), *JUST MERCY: A STORY OF JUSTICE AND REDEMPTION*

MAKING THE CONNECTIONS

Choose one or two questions for reflection:

1. What connections have you noticed between this week's texts and other passages in Scripture?

2. What connections have you made between this week's texts and the world beyond Scripture?

3. Does either of this week's two commentary themes speak especially to your life or the life of the world around you right now?

4. What is God saying to your congregation in particular through this week's readings and commentaries?

_____

_____

_____

_____

_____

_____

Sabbath Day

SCRIPTURE OF ASSURANCE

> Help me, O LORD my God!
>> Save me according to your steadfast love.
> Let them know that this is your hand;
>> you, O LORD, have done it. (Psalm 109:26–27)

WEEKLY EXAMEN

- Take a quiet moment, seek out God's presence, and pray for the guidance of the Spirit.

- Consider the past week; recall specific moments and feelings that stand out to you.

- Choose one moment or feeling for deeper examination, thanksgiving, or repentance.

- Let go, breathe deeply, and invite Christ's love to surround and fill you in preparation for the week ahead.

- End with the Lord's Prayer.

The Week Leading Up to
Proper 20

(Sunday between September 18 and September 24)

Jonah 3:10–4:11

But God said to Jonah, "Is it right for you to be angry about the bush?" And he said, "Yes, angry enough to die." (4:9)

Exodus 16:2–15

The whole congregation of the Israelites complained against Moses and Aaron in the wilderness. The Israelites said to them, "If only we had died by the hand of the LORD in the land of Egypt, when we sat by the fleshpots and ate our fill of bread; for you have brought us out into this wilderness to kill this whole assembly with hunger." (vv. 2–3)

Philippians 1:21–30

Only, live your life in a manner worthy of the gospel of Christ, so that, whether I come and see you or am absent and hear about you, I will know that you are standing firm in one spirit, striving side by side with one mind for the faith of the gospel, and are in no way intimidated by your opponents. (vv. 27–28a)

Matthew 20:1–16

"For the kingdom of heaven is like a landowner who went out early in the morning to hire laborers for his vineyard. After agreeing with the laborers for the usual daily wage, he sent them into his vineyard." (vv. 1–2)

LECTIO DIVINA

Underline a word or phrase that especially grabs your attention. Pray from that word or phrase and ask God to help you connect to its particular invitation for you this week.

Themes from This Week's Writers

THEME 1: *God Is Generous Even When We Are Not*

Exodus 16:2–15

The Greek verb translated "grumbled" (*egongyzon*) in Matthew 20:11 echoes the . . . "complained" (*diegongyzen* . . .) in Exodus 16:2. The comparison may help us to hear the grumbling as God hears it in these texts: an invitation to God to continue to reveal Godself to us, confounding our expectations while meeting our deepest needs.

ANATHEA E. PORTIER-YOUNG

Jonah 3:10–4:11

God promises that the nations will turn to the Lord (e.g., Isa. 2:2–4). How will God's people feel when the wicked, tyrannical foreign king actually does this? . . . Jonah is an Israelite Everyman whose responses to God's mercy indicate a too-narrow view of what it means to be the chosen people of God.

PAMELA J. SCALISE

Matthew 20:1–16

Evolution has bred into us the ability to make comparisons and the desire to attain more. God's realm, on the other hand, is a place of plenty and wholeness, where the human hierarchies disappear and every person, regardless of rank or resource, has a place at the table. How does this text speak to us, if envy is human but sharing is divine?

SHAWNTHEA MONROE

THEME 2: *Standing Together in the Struggle*

Philippians 1:21–30

Since the Philippian community is "having the same struggle" that they saw Paul had and now hear he is still having (Phil. 1:30), how are they to live? Paul's advice can be summarized in one word: unity.

CYNTHIA A. JARVIS

Philippians 1:21–30

For Paul, following Christ is grounded in the *koinōnia*, the gathering of disciples, working out new ways of living. This community, he believed . . . is the place where followers are formed and where they support each other. Throughout his letters, Paul lays out aspects of what he calls here "standing firm in one spirit, striving side by side with one mind for the faith of the gospel" (Phil. 1:27).

ELIZABETH M. BOUNDS

Matthew 20:1–16

The first shall be last and the last shall be first, but everyone has to show up.

WHITNEY BODMAN

WHAT IS THE HOLY SPIRIT SAYING TO YOU THIS WEEK?

_____

_____

_____

_____

_____

A SPIRITUAL PRACTICE FOR THIS WEEK

Pay some unearned wages this week. For instance, give a wad of cash to a street musician or panhandler, drop off gift cards at a shelter, pay lunch debts at a school, or research how organizations can purchase and forgive medical debt. Remain anonymous, if possible.

First Reading

The LORD spoke to Moses and said, "I have heard the complaining of the Israelites; say to them, 'At twilight you shall eat meat, and in the morning you shall have your fill of bread; then you shall know that I am the LORD your God.'" (vv. 11–12)

REFLECTION

The memory of "grumbling" or "complaining" is perhaps as central to Israel's testimony as the gift of bread that follows. . . . God's people barely know who this God is or where God has led them (cf. Exod. 16:6). Their hunger is real. When they voice it, God *hears* their complaint, a detail so important it is repeated four times (16:7–9, 12). Instead of responding with rebuke or anger, God responds by meeting the need they have voiced. God also responds by showing up: because God has heard their complaint, the people will see God's glory (vv. 7, 10).

ANATHEA E. PORTIER-YOUNG

RESPONSE

Is "grumbling" a part of your relationship with God? Have you felt God heard you, or ignored you? How has God responded or fed you in a way you did not expect? Do you have a complaint now that you long for God to hear? How does this passage speak to you this week?

PRAYER

Gracious God, you hear my complaining, my need, and my struggle; you respond, you meet my need, and you show up, even if not in the way I first imagined. Amen.

Canticle

Psalm 145:1–8

They shall celebrate the fame of your abundant goodness,
and shall sing aloud of your righteousness.

The LORD is gracious and merciful,
slow to anger and abounding in steadfast love. (vv. 7–8)

REFLECTION

Why do we get so angry when others are blessed by God? Do we expect to earn our blessings by being better than others? Do we think we can take the blessings for ourselves, even out of the hands of others? Do we fear that if others receive blessings, then there will be none left for us?
. . .
This psalm allows us to praise a God who is bigger than our selfishness, bigger than our anger, bigger than any divisions between people, big enough for all that God has made.

DONNA GIVER-JOHNSTON

RESPONSE

What are some blessings you are deeply longing for right now? How do you feel about others who have already received blessings like these? When do you experience envy or feelings of scarcity? Reflect on one or two of Giver-Johnston's questions, above.

PRAYER

O God, you are abundantly good; teach me to sing aloud of your righteousness and love, and to receive your blessings with joy, not envy or fear. Amen.

Second Reading

Philippians 1:21–30

For to me, living is Christ and dying is gain. If I am to live in the flesh, that means fruitful labor for me; and I do not know which I prefer. I am hard pressed between the two: my desire is to depart and be with Christ, for that is far better; but to remain in the flesh is more necessary for you. (vv. 21–24)

REFLECTION

[Paul] could choose death, he explains . . . , pointing to the wonderful eschatological reality of being at home with Christ in the kingdom of God. Yet he instead chooses "to remain in the flesh" (v. 24), in the ongoing realities of this world with all of its pain, suffering, and evil. Like the incarnate Christ, Paul is driven by love and compassion, the desire to be with humans in the midst of suffering. He chooses to "continue with all of you" (v. 25), to be in messy solidarity with others.

ELIZABETH M. BOUNDS

RESPONSE

Does Paul sound melodramatic? What do you hear beneath his words? What do you hear him (writing from jail) saying about the power of community in enduring suffering? Have you been sustained by a beloved community from a distance? This week, what do you need to persevere in the "messy solidarity" of Christian life?

PRAYER

Lord Jesus Christ, you desire to be with us in the midst of our suffering; teach me also to live and endure in messy solidarity with my community of faith. Amen.

Gospel

Matthew 20:1–16

"When those hired about five o'clock came, each of them received the usual daily wage. Now when the first came, they thought they would receive more; but each of them also received the usual daily wage. And when they received it, they grumbled against the landowner, saying, 'These last worked only one hour, and you have made them equal to us who have borne the burden of the day and the scorching heat.'" (vv. 9–12)

REFLECTION

Most Americans came from someplace else; some of us just got here earlier than others. . . .

When a preacher addresses the plight of immigrants, it is important to remember that God does not reward us based on what we deserve. We all fall short of the glory of God, which suggests we are all late-day laborers. Yet God still gives us what we need. This text raises the question, If Jesus means what he says, that "the last will be first, and the first will be last," then what are the ethical implications for the way we think about immigration in the United States?

SHAWNTHEA MONROE

RESPONSE

What was a time you received generosity from God that you did not earn? Think of a person or group that appears unworthy to you of God's generosity. What does it mean if "we are all late-day laborers"? How might you look at what you have and see it as abundance? Or simply enough?

PRAYER

Generous God, teach me to see that you have provided more than enough for all people, including me; show me how to be as generous as you are, that I may live and love as Jesus did. Amen.

Weekend Reflections

For me, and for many of us, our first waking thought of the day is "I didn't get enough sleep." The next one is "I don't have enough time."
. . . We spend most of the hours and the days of our lives hearing, explaining, complaining, or worrying about what we don't have enough of. . . . And by the time we go to bed at night, our minds are racing with the litany of what we didn't get, or didn't get done, that day. We go to sleep burdened by those thoughts and wake up to that reverie of lack. . . .

This internal condition of scarcity, this mind-set of scarcity, lives at the very heart of our jealousies, our greed, our prejudice, and our arguments with life, and it is deeply embedded in our relationship with money.

LYNNE TWIST (1945–), *THE SOUL OF MONEY*

MAKING THE CONNECTIONS

Choose one or two questions for reflection:

1. What connections have you noticed between this week's texts and other passages in Scripture?

2. What connections have you made between this week's texts and the world beyond Scripture?

3. Does either of this week's two commentary themes speak especially to your life or the life of the world around you right now?

4. What is God saying to your congregation in particular through this week's readings and commentaries?

_____

_____

_____

_____

_____

_____

Sabbath Day

SCRIPTURE OF ASSURANCE

So it depends not on human will or exertion, but on God who shows mercy. (Romans 9:16)

WEEKLY EXAMEN

- Take a quiet moment, seek out God's presence, and pray for the guidance of the Spirit.

- Consider the past week; recall specific moments and feelings that stand out to you.

- Choose one moment or feeling for deeper examination, thanksgiving, or repentance.

- Let go, breathe deeply, and invite Christ's love to surround and fill you in preparation for the week ahead.

- End with the Lord's Prayer.

The Week Leading Up to
Proper 21

(Sunday between September 25 and October 1)

Ezekiel 18:1–4, 25–32

Yet the house of Israel says, "The way of the Lord is unfair." O house of Israel, are my ways unfair? Is it not your ways that are unfair?

Therefore I will judge you, O house of Israel, all of you according to your ways, says the Lord GOD. Repent and turn from all your transgressions; otherwise iniquity will be your ruin. (vv. 29–30)

Exodus 17:1–7

"I will be standing there in front of you on the rock at Horeb. Strike the rock, and water will come out of it, so that the people may drink." Moses did so, in the sight of the elders of Israel. He called the place Massah and Meribah, because the Israelites quarreled and tested the LORD, saying, "Is the LORD among us or not?" (vv. 6–7)

Philippians 2:1–13

Do nothing from selfish ambition or conceit, but in humility regard others as better than yourselves. Let each of you look not to your own interests, but to the interests of others. Let the same mind be in you that was in Christ Jesus. (vv. 3–5)

Matthew 21:23–32

When he entered the temple, the chief priests and the elders of the people came to him as he was teaching, and said, "By what authority are you doing these things, and who gave you this authority?" (v. 23)

LECTIO DIVINA

Underline a word or phrase that especially grabs your attention. Pray from that word or phrase and ask God to help you connect to its particular invitation for you this week.

Themes from This Week's Writers

THEME 1: *Is the Lord among Us or Not?*

Exodus 17:1–7

This brief passage contains no fewer than five questions (Exod. 17:2[x2], 3, 4, 7). Physical thirst, fear of death, and confusion regarding the future finally crystallize into one question that displaces the others. . . . It was about a people desperate to know, Where is God in relation to us?

ANATHEA E. PORTIER-YOUNG

Exodus 17:1–7

Several Old Testament passages characterize putting God to the test as rebellion (e.g., Ps. 95:8–9; cf. Luke 4:12), but in our passage the need for water is genuine. God provides it and does not punish them. God supplies the people's need.

PAMELA J. SCALISE

Psalm 78:1–4, 12–16

Throughout the biblical story, God's people can choose to obey God's way or follow the path that leads to destruction.

. . . Despite God's provisions throughout the wilderness and the promise of freedom, still the people doubt: "Is the LORD among us or not?" (Exod. 17:7). Despite Moses' affirmation, the people must answer the question for themselves.

DONNA GIVER-JOHNSTON

THEME 2: *How Do We Understand Humility in Modern Life?*

Philippians 2:1–13

Depending on the community surrounding any congregation, social and economic hierarchies may include education, profession, lineage, political connections, or simply the block a family lives on. Naming some of these hierarchies will help a congregation hear the dissonance Paul is naming between Roman or American society and the Christian life.

CYNTHIA A. JARVIS

Philippians 2:1–13

Christian humility does not require low self-esteem or a rigorous program of self-diminishment. The challenge is not to reduce the self but to reorient it, that is, to "let the same mind be in you that was in Christ Jesus" (v. 5). To have this mind is to walk toward the fullest possible understanding of ourselves and what surrounds us, including God.

ELIZABETH M. BOUNDS

Matthew 21:23–32

In Matthew's parable of the Two Sons, the first son professes obedience but acts in disobedience. The second son rejects obedience but then has a change of heart. He is open to the instruction of God, the counsel of his conscience, which requires the humility to recognize that he has transgressed.

WHITNEY BODMAN

WHAT IS THE HOLY SPIRIT SAYING TO YOU THIS WEEK?

_____

_____

_____

_____

_____

A SPIRITUAL PRACTICE FOR THIS WEEK

Look for an empty jar, box, or container to use as a prayer focus this week. Listen for God's voice to you in Philippians 2:1–13, considering how the Spirit might be inviting you to empty yourself in this season of your life, not as punishment, but to "let the same mind be in you that was in Christ Jesus."

First Reading

Ezekiel 18:1–4, 25–32

Cast away from you all the transgressions that you have committed against me, and get yourselves a new heart and a new spirit! Why will you die, O house of Israel? For I have no pleasure in the death of anyone, says the Lord GOD. Turn, then, and live. (vv. 31–32)

REFLECTION

The command to "get yourselves a new heart and a new spirit" (18:31) balances God's promise to give you "a new heart" and "a new spirit" (36:26), and provides a realistic view of what it takes to turn one's life around. Christians can claim God's help to effect personal transformation, but gaining freedom from hurtful and sinful urges and habits is seldom instantaneous.

. . . [But we] must not flog others or harm ourselves. Such practices linger in our speech, however, when we advise our friends not to "beat themselves up" over a mistake. Christians seek to obey God's command with promise, "Turn . . . and live" (18:32).

PAMELA J. SCALISE

RESPONSE

When was a time you tried to turn your life around? Or away from a hurtful habit? Were you successful? How did you call on God's help? How did you experience guilt or self-punishment? Is there a way, now, that you feel called to get "a new heart and a new spirit"? What advice would Ezekiel give you?

PRAYER

Lord God, show me how to turn away from death, from things that are harming me and hurting you, that I may get a new heart and new spirit. Amen.

Canticle

Psalm 25:1–9

Make me to know your ways, O LORD;
 teach me your paths.
Lead me in your truth, and teach me,
 for you are the God of my salvation;
 for you I wait all day long. (vv. 4–5)

REFLECTION

[We] could focus on exploring the spirit of prayerful petition that is
countercultural. "Instead of living for self, the psalmist offers his or her
life to God; instead of depending on oneself, the psalmist depends on
God in trust; instead of seeking instant gratification, the psalmist is
content to wait for God."[1] Homiletical wisdom can illumine the tension
between seeing prayer as a way to get what we want and seeing it as a
way to seek God's path and be led in the truth. In the end, prayer is less
petition for self and more sacrificial offering of self.

DONNA GIVER-JOHNSTON

RESPONSE

What things you have been longing for, lately? Without self-judgment,
consider how God might be inviting you to wait and depend instead on
God's love and leading, for now. How might you offer yourself and your life
more fully to God, trusting God knows what you want more than you do?

PRAYER

Lord God, you know all the desires of my heart; teach me to walk in
your paths and be led by your truth that, in so doing, I may find more
than I could ever want. Amen.

---

1. J. Clinton McCann Jr., "The Book of Psalms," in *The New Interpreter's Bible* (Nashville: Abingdon, 1996), 7:779.

Second Reading

Philippians 2:1–13

Let the same mind be in you that was in Christ Jesus,
who, though he was in the form of God,
did not regard equality with God
as something to be exploited,
but emptied himself,
taking the form of a slave. (vv. 5–7a)

REFLECTION

There is a subtle distinction to be made here: Christ does not give up
his equality with God but he lets go of it. . . . To have this same mind
means that the Philippian Christian chooses to let go of any status
in Roman society and to humble himself or herself, not as a moral
achievement to be rewarded but by becoming who they are in Christ.
To have the same mind that was in Christ Jesus means they will become,
personally and socially, a community of crucified slaves.

The hymn ends with the one who humbled himself being the same
one who was highly exalted by God.

CYNTHIA A. JARVIS

RESPONSE

What does it mean to you to think of Christ letting go of rather than
giving up divine equality to be human? Are there ways you long to let go
of status markers or societal expectations, to become more fully yourself,
in Christ? How might humility bring you more freedom? More room
for love?

PRAYER

Humble Jesus, you let go of power and status to come close to humankind;
help me to do the same, that I may come closer to you. Amen.

Gospel

Matthew 21:23–32

"What do you think? A man had two sons; he went to the first and said, 'Son, go and work in the vineyard today.' He answered, 'I will not'; but later he changed his mind and went. The father went to the second and said the same; and he answered, 'I go, sir'; but he did not go." (vv. 28–30)

REFLECTION

At a personal level, the parable of the Two Sons fills me with hope. My congregation includes many older adults whose children do not attend church. This "lack of faith" is cause for much concern among a generation raised to believe that church attendance is a requirement for salvation. These children are good people who donate to charities, volunteer at homeless shelters, and work at the food pantry, but rarely attend church. I often use this parable as a way to reassure parents that people who do good work are still doing God's will, even if they will not enter God's house.

SHAWNTHEA MONROE

RESPONSE

How do you relate, or not relate, to Monroe's observations about a generational gap in church attendance? When have you been inspired by good works done outside of a church? When have you been disappointed by people inside the church? Do you ever consider leaving church?

PRAYER

Jesus, you love the people who will not enter your house; whether I am in church or outside of church, teach me to seek you and serve your people with love. Amen.

Weekend Reflections

FURTHER CONNECTION

Humility, Benedict teaches, treads tenderly upon the life around it. When we know our place in the universe, we can afford to value the place of others. We need them, in fact, to make up what is wanting in us. We stand in the face of others without having to take up all the space. We don't have to dominate conversations or consume all the time or call all the attention to ourselves. There is room, humility knows, for all of us in life. We are each an ember of the mind of God and we are each sent to illumine the other through the dark places of life to sanctuaries of truth and peace where God can be God for us because we have relieved ourselves of the ordeal of being god ourselves.

JOAN CHITTISTER, OSB (1936–), *THE RULE OF BENEDICT: A SPIRITUALITY FOR THE 21ST CENTURY*

MAKING THE CONNECTIONS

Choose one or two questions for reflection:

1. What connections have you noticed between this week's texts and other passages in Scripture?

2. What connections have you made between this week's texts and the world beyond Scripture?

3. Does either of this week's two commentary themes speak especially to your life or the life of the world around you right now?

4. What is God saying to your congregation in particular through this week's readings and commentaries?

_____

_____

_____

_____

_____

_____

Sabbath Day

SCRIPTURE OF ASSURANCE

> O give thanks to the LORD, call on his name,
>   make known his deeds among the peoples.
> Sing to him, sing praises to him;
>   tell of all his wonderful works. (Psalm 105:1–2)

WEEKLY EXAMEN

- Take a quiet moment, seek out God's presence, and pray for the guidance of the Spirit.

- Consider the past week; recall specific moments and feelings that stand out to you.

- Choose one moment or feeling for deeper examination, thanksgiving, or repentance.

- Let go, breathe deeply, and invite Christ's love to surround and fill you in preparation for the week ahead.

- End with the Lord's Prayer.

The Week Leading Up to
Proper 22

(Sunday between October 2 and October 8)

Isaiah 5:1–7

For the vineyard of the Lord of hosts
   is the house of Israel,
and the people of Judah
   are his pleasant planting (v. 7a)

Exodus 20:1–4, 7–9, 12–20

You shall not murder.
You shall not commit adultery.
You shall not steal.
You shall not bear false witness against your neighbor. (vv. 13–16)

Philippians 3:4b–14

If anyone else has reason to be confident in the flesh, I have more: circumcised
on the eighth day, a member of the people of Israel, of the tribe of Benjamin,
a Hebrew born of Hebrews; as to the law, a Pharisee; as to zeal, a persecutor
of the church; as to righteousness under the law, blameless. (vv. 4b–6)

Matthew 21:33–46

"Now when the owner of the vineyard comes, what will he do to those tenants?" They said to him, "He will put those wretches to a miserable death, and
lease the vineyard to other tenants who will give him the produce at the
harvest time." (vv. 40–41)

LECTIO DIVINA

> Underline a word or phrase that especially grabs your attention. Pray
> from that word or phrase and ask God to help you connect to its
> particular invitation for you this week.

Themes from This Week's Writers

THEME 1: *Righteousness Is about Relationships*

Exodus 20:1–4, 7–9, 12–20

The Ten Words (the meaning of "Decalogue") . . . are the first of the laws revealed to Israel through Moses at Sinai. . . . With an eye on future, settled life in agrarian villages, these laws aim to shape and guide Israel's life in community with one another and with God.

ANATHEA E. PORTIER-YOUNG

Exodus 20:1–4, 7–9, 12–20

According to Aquinas, the law is about community under God, for which "there are two requirements: the first is that each member should behave rightly towards its head, the second, that he [*sic*] should behave rightly to the rest of his fellows and partners in the community" (*Summa Theologica* 1a2ae, Article 5).

PAMELA J. SCALISE

Philippians 3:4b–14

To be righteous is to orient oneself and one's community to enacting God's justice in the world. Jesus, the embodiment of God's purposes, focused on relationships and community, because those living relationships, which included ensuring basic material well-being for all, were what God's justice looks like in the world.

ELIZABETH M. BOUNDS

THEME 2: *Recognizing and Rejecting Anti-Semitism*

Philippians 3:4b–14

Most congregations may be kept from an anti-Semitic mishearing of the beginning of this chapter if they are reminded that the first Christians were Jews. . . . The so-called "circumcised believers" (Acts 10:45) could have continued as a Christian sect of Jews—except for the fact that God's Spirit inexplicably began falling upon Gentiles (Acts 10:1–11:18).

CYNTHIA A. JARVIS

Matthew 21:33–46

In the first century the two traditions were not yet distinct, that is, it was not Jews vs. Christians, it was Jews vs. Jews. For Matthew, the fight with the Jewish authorities was a family feud; it was personal and it got ugly. Any sermon on this text should be careful not to demonize the Jewish authorities.

SHAWNTHEA MONROE

Matthew 21:33–46

Though this parable, and others in this sequence, have commonly been interpreted as a rejection of Israel, in fact it is a rejection of transgressive authority, equally applicable to the political sphere, then and now, and to the church, then and now. Wherever those given responsibility by God do not return fruits to God, their station is in peril.

WHITNEY BODMAN

WHAT IS THE HOLY SPIRIT SAYING TO YOU THIS WEEK?

_____

_____

_____

_____

_____

A SPIRITUAL PRACTICE FOR THIS WEEK

With prayer and intention, write out the Ten Commandments from this week's passage from Exodus. Then, reflect on them, considering how you may have kept or not kept each one in the past year. Some may catch your attention particularly; consider these with more prayer and some written reflection.

First Reading

Isaiah 5:1–7

And now I will tell you
 what I will do to my vineyard.
I will remove its hedge,
 and it shall be devoured;
I will break down its wall,
 and it shall be trampled down.
I will make it a waste. (vv. 5–6a)

REFLECTION

One expects a love song, like the poetry in the Song of Solomon. Unlike the Song, however, loving care is met by betrayal. . . . The vineyard story is a parable, told to justify God's threat of judgment against Judah and Jerusalem. As Nathan led David to pronounce judgment on himself by means of a touching story (2 Sam. 12:1–14), so this prophet uses a sung parable of betrayal to lead audiences to acknowledge their willful failure to flourish in the place and for the purpose that God had given them.

PAMELA J. SCALISE

RESPONSE

Write a prayer, song, or poem inspired by Isaiah, telling a story of love and betrayal between you and your nation, community, congregation, or family. What was the flourishing God hoped for that failed? What is God's judgment? What new insights do you see? What is God's promise, still?

PRAYER

Lord of hosts, you expected justice in our vineyard but have seen great bloodshed; help me to repent and not to despair, and to believe in your promise of redemption, through us and despite us. Amen.

Canticle

Turn again, O God of hosts;
   look down from heaven, and see;
have regard for this vine,
   the stock that your right hand planted. (vv. 14–15)

REFLECTION

Psalm 80 is sorrowful, but between the lines of despair are signs of faith
and hope. The reading begins, "Restore us, O God of hosts; let your
face shine, that we may be saved" (Ps. 80:7). As the psalmist laments
the current condition of destruction and despair, he also confesses
confidence that God can restore and save, as demonstrated by God's past
faithfulness. . . .

   . . . The psalmist ends with a hopeful chord, plucking the heartstrings
of the Lord, by renaming God's rebellious people as God's own people,
"the stock that your right hand planted" (v. 15).

DONNA GIVER-JOHNSTON

RESPONSE

What conditions of despair and destruction are you most troubled by in
the world or your community this week? What signs of faith and hope
from God do you find "between the lines"? What lines in Psalm 80,
particularly, resonate with you or inspire you to offer them to God in
prayer?

PRAYER

Lord God our gardener, you have planted us to grow and thrive but we,
your people, are ravaged and struggling; nurture us and let your face
shine on us, that we might be saved. Amen.

Second Reading

Philippians 3:4b–14

For his sake I have suffered the loss of all things, and I regard them as rubbish, in order that I may gain Christ and be found in him, not having a righteousness of my own that comes from the law, but one that comes through faith in Christ, the righteousness from God based on faith. (vv. 8b–9)

REFLECTION

A cultural dislike of self-righteousness has developed, perhaps best embodied in fictional characters ranging from the stock Goody Two-shoes to Harry Potter's Dolores Umbridge. With this sense of "righteous," Paul quickly becomes an unattractive guide, apparently calling for renunciation of the joy of living in favor of a life of ascetic self-denial. Such a reading does not honor Paul—or Christianity! . . . The death of Jesus on the cross was a death in service of love and life, enabling the new life signaled by the resurrection.

ELIZABETH M. BOUNDS

RESPONSE

Paul's understanding of "righteousness" can sound snooty; but he did not mean a "privatized ethical purity and piety," as Bounds explains elsewhere. Write a definition for the word "righteous" that has value and meaning for you this week. What does this have to do with "gaining Christ" and being found by him, for you?

PRAYER

Loving Christ, show me how to be found by you, that in gaining you I might live into greater love, new life, and a righteousness that comes from God, through faith. Amen.

Gospel

Matthew 21:33–46

"Therefore I tell you, the kingdom of God will be taken away from you and given to a people that produces the fruits of the kingdom. The one who falls on this stone will be broken to pieces; and it will crush anyone on whom it falls." (vv. 43–44)

REFLECTION

The violence of the response, those "broken to pieces" and "crushed," is discomforting. Is this the recommended way, the way of God or human authorities, to respond to brutality? . . .

Though this parable, and others in this sequence, have commonly been interpreted as a rejection of Israel, in fact it is a rejection of transgressive authority, equally applicable to the political sphere, then and now, and to the church, then and now. Wherever those given responsibility by God do not return fruits to God, their station is in peril.

WHITNEY BODMAN

RESPONSE

How have you seen or experienced abuses of authority at church? Why, from your own experience, would you say Jesus warns against this with such vehemence? How have you seen churches repent for or heal from abuses like this, if at all? What is your hope for your own church?

PRAYER

Lord Jesus Christ, you will take the kingdom of God from any community whose leaders are abusive; show me and my faith community how to serve and love with humility and equanimity, that we may produce the fruits of your kingdom. Amen.

Weekend Reflections

FURTHER CONNECTION

What if [the tenants are] the various nations who conquered Israel:
Babylon, Persia, Greece, Rome?
. . . We do the same thing today. We send battalion after battalion to
the front, and we keep thinking, with "shock and awe," that "they" will
respect us. They do not. Yet we keep expanding our resources even when
we know there is no chance of recuperation. We keep at the quest for
honor and power, even when the cause is lost. . . .
. . . What is the resolution when violence escalates? The landowner
will let the farm out to other tenants. Will the violence be repeated?

AMY-JILL LEVINE (1956–), *SHORT STORIES BY JESUS:*
THE ENIGMATIC PARABLES OF A CONTROVERSIAL RABBI

MAKING THE CONNECTIONS

Choose one or two questions for reflection:

1. What connections have you noticed between this week's texts and
   other passages in Scripture?

2. What connections have you made between this week's texts and the
   world beyond Scripture?

3. Does either of this week's two commentary themes speak especially
   to your life or the life of the world around you right now?

4. What is God saying to your congregation in particular through this
   week's readings and commentaries?

_____

_____

_____

_____

_____

_____

Sabbath Day

SCRIPTURE OF ASSURANCE

"It is the LORD who goes before you. He will be with you; he will not fail you or forsake you. Do not fear or be dismayed." (Deuteronomy 31:8)

WEEKLY EXAMEN

- Take a quiet moment, seek out God's presence, and pray for the guidance of the Spirit.

- Consider the past week; recall specific moments and feelings that stand out to you.

- Choose one moment or feeling for deeper examination, thanksgiving, or repentance.

- Let go, breathe deeply, and invite Christ's love to surround and fill you in preparation for the week ahead.

- End with the Lord's Prayer.

The Week Leading Up to
Proper 23
(Sunday between October 9 and October 15)

Isaiah 25:1–9

Therefore strong peoples will glorify you;
  cities of ruthless nations will fear you.
For you have been a refuge to the poor,
  a refuge to the needy in their distress. (vv. 3–4a)

Exodus 32:1–14

The people gathered around Aaron, and said to him, "Come, make gods for us, who shall go before us; as for this Moses, the man who brought us up out of the land of Egypt, we do not know what has become of him." (v. 1b)

Philippians 4:1–9

Finally, beloved, whatever is true, whatever is honorable, whatever is just, whatever is pure, whatever is pleasing, whatever is commendable, if there is any excellence and if there is anything worthy of praise, think about these things. (v. 8)

Matthew 22:1–14

"But they . . . seized his slaves, mistreated them, and killed them. The king was enraged. He sent his troops, destroyed those murderers, and burned their city. Then he said to his slaves, 'The wedding is ready, but those invited were not worthy.'"(vv. 5–8)

LECTIO DIVINA

Underline a word or phrase that especially grabs your attention. Pray from that word or phrase and ask God to help you connect to its particular invitation for you this week.

Themes from This Week's Writers

THEME 1: *What Are Our False Gods Today?*

Exodus 32:1–14

Those who bow their knees to the golden calf of placing their nation first . . . are the spiritual descendants of the Hebrews who ate, drank, and reveled before the false idol. True worship has less to do with what occurs in a building we declare sacred, and more to do with what we do in secular spaces, demanding justice.

MIGUEL A. DE LA TORRE

Exodus 32:1–14

The image of the golden calf serves as an invitation to explore idolatrous cultural images. . . . What images/metaphors do moderns use for God? . . . Do they subvert the gospel by associating the Lord with a false god rooted in a human ideology or any part of creation itself?

BRIAN D. RUSSELL

Matthew 22:1–14

Come to the banquet table of my realm, says God. Some do. Some do not. Some procrastinate. Some loiter. Some get distracted and wander down the wrong streets and miss the party. Some lose the invitation, or do not have the address, or just never make it. Some say, "I will put on my own party," and set out to do just that.

THEODORE J. WARDLAW

THEME 2: *How Should We Deal with Conflict?*

Philippians 4:1–9

The seemingly disconnected final admonitions . . . when read within the preceding call to unity, come to life as the very "bonds of peace" (Eph. 4:3). . . . When disunity is reigning and a body desperately seeks the unity of the Holy Spirit, these too are the practices for reviving unity.

TROY A. MILLER

Philippians 4:1–9

Paul points to a set of virtues that must be in place in order for justice to be established. These virtues are key to a peaceful communal life. The preacher can reflect on the issue of discrimination involving race, gender, culture, and sexual orientation that often divides a community locally, nationally, and globally.

CAROL J. DEMPSEY, OP

Matthew 22:1–14

The parable of the Wedding Feast . . . cannot be read as an insider's tale that rejects outsiders. No, ultimately this parable connects to broader themes in Matthew about the nature of true discipleship and how any who wish to partake of God's banquet must respond to the invitation with a yes borne out in their lives.

MICHAEL E. LEE

WHAT IS THE HOLY SPIRIT SAYING TO YOU THIS WEEK?

_____

_____

_____

_____

_____

A SPIRITUAL PRACTICE FOR THIS WEEK

"Rejoice in the Lord always; again I will say, Rejoice," Paul writes. This week, make rejoicing your spiritual discipline. Write the word "rejoice" on your to-do list each day; be creative, have fun, and keep it easy. Repeat the words "Rejoice in the Lord always" as part of your prayers.

First Reading

Exodus 32:1–14

The Lord said to Moses, "Go down at once! Your people, whom you brought up out of the land of Egypt, have acted perversely; they have been quick to turn aside from the way that I commanded them; they have cast for themselves an image of a calf, and have worshiped it and sacrificed to it." (vv. 7–8a)

REFLECTION

Here is the question the people of God must answer if they are to claim chosenness: is our church standing with the oppressed, or justifying the actions of the oppressors? "Let your gentleness be known to everyone. The Lord is near," Paul writes to the Philippians (4:5). There is no gentleness in how we have treated the other within our midst, or those from the nations that contribute to our wealth. Our quest for the golden idols of power and privilege has made all who think they are chosen for riches enemies of God.

MIGUEL A. DE LA TORRE

RESPONSE

Is there a golden calf you have found yourself worshiping lately? Something flashy, powerful, or otherwise attractive? What oppressed or outcast people might God be inviting you to pay some attention to, instead? How have you been changed and shaped by what you pay attention to, in recent years?

PRAYER

Almighty God, teach me to turn away from shiny, pretty idols and toward the faces and dreams of my struggling neighbors, where your true worship and riches lie. Amen.

Canticle

Psalm 106:1–6, 19–23

Therefore he said he would destroy them—
    had not Moses, his chosen one,
stood in the breach before him,
    to turn away his wrath from destroying them. (v. 23)

REFLECTION

While the psalm is overwhelmingly a recitation of human sins, it
concludes with a startling portrait of God. Unlike the powerful God
reflected in the opening verses, this God is seemingly held in check
by Moses (Exod. 32:14). Moses' gutsy opposition to God's wrathful
intent to "consume" (v. 10) the "stiff-necked" (v. 9) Israelites is such an
uncommon image of the human-divine relationship that a preacher may
find it fruitful. The psalmist's concise take on Moses as God's "chosen
one [who stands] in the breach" before God to deflect God's anger (Ps.
106:23) will be a provocative, pre-Christian phrase.

LEIGH CAMPBELL-TAYLOR

RESPONSE

Does a wrathful God like this seem unimaginable or old-fashioned
to you? Or is this a familiar image from your childhood, perhaps still
uncomfortably real? How is it to imagine God held in check by Moses, a
human being? What is God inviting you to notice in this story?

PRAYER

Eternal God, you are unchangeable, and yet your heart was moved and
your mind was changed by Moses; help me to live with this mystery and
to know that both your wrath at injustice and your merciful love are
real. Amen.

Second Reading

Therefore, my brothers and sisters, whom I love and long for, my joy and crown, stand firm in the Lord in this way, my beloved.

I urge Euodia and I urge Syntyche to be of the same mind in the Lord. (vv. 1–2)

REFLECTION

Disunity is not a resulting symptom from other problems but the root problem itself. For Paul, unity is not a hoped-for state that occurs when strife, turmoil, and competing interests are not present. It is rather the opposite. Unity is something to be sought after, worked for, and continually practiced in the church when differences are in full view. Unity is also not some content-less state of agreement that masks real issues and problems for the sake of outward harmony. Unity has a content, a practice, and calls for humility and sacrifice within the body of Christ.

TROY A. MILLER

RESPONSE

In what ways does your congregation feel unified? Divided? What strikes you about Miller's descriptions of unity? How could being "of the same mind in the Lord" truly be a practice that gives life, not a faked harmony?

PRAYER

O Jesus Christ, you prayed over your disciples that "all may be one"; teach us how to be one body and of the same mind in you, while honoring our differences and disagreements. Amen.

Gospel

Matthew 22:1–14

"Then the king said to the attendants, 'Bind him hand and foot, and throw him into the outer darkness, where there will be weeping and gnashing of teeth.' For many are called, but few are chosen." (vv. 13–14)

REFLECTION

Most scholars understand the language in verse 7 of invasion, destruction, and burning of the city as a link to the events that occurred in the Roman devastation of Jerusalem in 70 CE. So this is an attempt by the author of Matthew's Gospel to understand those traumatic events and to interpret them for the nascent Jewish Christian community. Though Matthew seems to portray God in a harsh light, it is the situation that is harsh, and the author is trying to interpret it.

. . . After the destruction of the Second Temple in Jerusalem, all Jews had to take stock of their identity and move forward into an unknown future.

MICHAEL E. LEE

RESPONSE

When we are afraid, we want to punish or dehumanize our opponents. Think of a time you have done this. Is there a way you are doing this now? How are you seeing this occur in your community? What more life-giving ways have you found to deal with fear?

PRAYER

Gracious God, be merciful to me and my neighbors when pain and anger move us to be cruel or condemning; teach me to stay awake, to choose Christ and not fear. Amen.

Weekend Reflections

What else does this craving, and this helplessness, proclaim but that there was once in man a true happiness, of which all that now remains is the empty print and trace? This he tries in vain to fill with everything around him, seeking in things that are not there the help he cannot find in those that are, though none can help, since this infinite abyss can be filled only with an infinite and unchangeable object; in other words by God himself.

BLAISE PASCAL (1623–62), *PENSÉES*

MAKING THE CONNECTIONS

Choose one or two questions for reflection:

1. What connections have you noticed between this week's texts and other passages in Scripture?

2. What connections have you made between this week's texts and the world beyond Scripture?

3. Does either of this week's two commentary themes speak especially to your life or the life of the world around you right now?

4. What is God saying to your congregation in particular through this week's readings and commentaries?

_____

_____

_____

_____

_____

_____

Sabbath Day

SCRIPTURE OF ASSURANCE

> The steadfast love of the LORD never ceases,
>   his mercies never come to an end;
> they are new every morning;
>   great is your faithfulness. (Lamentations 3:22–23)

WEEKLY EXAMEN

- Take a quiet moment, seek out God's presence, and pray for the guidance of the Spirit.

- Consider the past week; recall specific moments and feelings that stand out to you.

- Choose one moment or feeling for deeper examination, thanksgiving, or repentance.

- Let go, breathe deeply, and invite Christ's love to surround and fill you in preparation for the week ahead.

- End with the Lord's Prayer.

The Week Leading Up to
Proper 24

(Sunday between October 16 and October 22)

Isaiah 45:1–7

Thus says the LORD to his anointed, to Cyrus,
  whose right hand I have grasped
to subdue nations before him
  and strip kings of their robes,
to open doors before him—
  and the gates shall not be closed. (v. 1)

Exodus 33:12–23

The LORD said to Moses, "I will do the very thing that you have asked; for you have found favor in my sight, and I know you by name." Moses said, "Show me your glory, I pray." (vv. 17–18)

1 Thessalonians 1:1–10

For the people of those regions report about us what kind of welcome we had among you, and how you turned to God from idols, to serve a living and true God. (v. 9)

Matthew 22:15–22

"Tell us, then, what you think. Is it lawful to pay taxes to the emperor, or not?" But Jesus, aware of their malice, said, "Why are you putting me to the test, you hypocrites? Show me the coin used for the tax." And they brought him a denarius. (vv. 17–19)

LECTIO DIVINA

Underline a word or phrase that especially grabs your attention. Pray from that word or phrase and ask God to help you connect to its particular invitation for you this week.

Themes from This Week's Writers

THEME 1: *Do Not Put Your Trust in Human Rulers*

Isaiah 45:1–7

When political leaders like Cyrus, whose lives are antithetical to the gospel message, are defended because they advance the special interests of those who think they are chosen, are we prostituting the gospel for the cheap coins of partisan politics?

MIGUEL A. DE LA TORRE

Isaiah 45:1–7

Cyrus was the Persian king who defeated the Babylonians and permitted Jewish persons in exile to return to their homeland and rebuild the temple. This text is not a blanket blessing of rulers who act wickedly and unjustly. It does not advocate for God's people to silence their prophetic witness for justice and for the blessing of the world through the gospel.

BRIAN D. RUSSELL

Matthew 22:15–22

Rendering unto Caesar does not of necessity mean believing that Caesar is performing the will of God. Paul's First Letter to the Thessalonians and the book of Revelation cast a suspicious eye on the terrible ways that empires treat people.

MICHAEL E. LEE

THEME 2: *Turn Away from Idols to the Living God*

1 Thessalonians 1:1–10

Turning away from idols in the Greco-Roman world was a subversive act, as religion in that culture was not simply one separate facet of life (as in the modern-day Western world) but something infused in every aspect of it. The various gods had authority over one's job, health, home, family, travel, crops, and almost any other area of life one can imagine.

TROY A. MILLER

1 Thessalonians 1:1–10

Paul also commends the Thessalonians for having turned away from idols to serve a living and true God. Paul reminds the Thessalonians that turning away from mainstream Greco-Roman culture calls for new cultural, social, and religious relationships.

CAROL J. DEMPSEY, OP

Matthew 22:15–22

We belong not to our possessions, but to God. We belong not to the partisan political claims we make in election seasons, but to God. We belong not to the demands of our vocations, but to God. We belong not to the charms of our secular world, but to God.

THEODORE J. WARDLAW

WHAT IS THE HOLY SPIRIT SAYING TO YOU THIS WEEK?

_____

_____

_____

_____

_____

A SPIRITUAL PRACTICE FOR THIS WEEK

Paul begins his First Letter to the Thessalonians with beautiful words of thanks and support. Think of some leaders and volunteers in your congregation who might not often hear words like this. Write some thank-you notes, quoting 1 Thessalonians 1:1b, if you like. Finally, write a thank-you note to yourself.

First Reading

Exodus 33:12–23

And the LORD continued, "See, there is a place by me where you shall stand on the rock; and while my glory passes by I will put you in a cleft of the rock, and I will cover you with my hand until I have passed by; then I will take away my hand, and you shall see my back; but my face shall not be seen." (vv. 21–23)

REFLECTION

Spiritual growth is not merely about receiving affirmation and acceptance from God. The Lord responds positively (v. 17) to Moses' requests for God's presence with the people, but Moses is not content at this point to bask in God's approval. Receiving affirmation and blessing moves Moses to want to know God more profoundly. What does it look like for God's people today to desire a deeper relationship beyond one in which God grants our prayers? Moses' response points a way forward. Moses asks to experience God in God's fullness (v. 18).

BRIAN D. RUSSELL

RESPONSE

What does "spiritual growth" mean to you right now? Have you, like Moses, longed to know God more deeply? How would you like your relationship with God to grow? How might you ask God for what you are hoping for? Are there some ways God has already answered this prayer?

PRAYER

Lord God, because he asked to see you, you hid Moses in a cleft of rock and passed by; even if I must hide behind a rock, show me how to know you more and more, that your presence may go with me always. Amen.

Canticle

For all the gods of the peoples are idols,
  but the LORD made the heavens.
Honor and majesty are before him;
  strength and beauty are in his sanctuary. (vv. 5–6)

REFLECTION

No part of creation is exempt from praising YHWH, and no other gods
are to be praised: "all the gods of the peoples are idols" (v. 5). Isaiah
sounds a similar note with "I am the LORD, and there is no other" (Isa.
45:6), which could lead to a sermon on humankind's ageless tendency
toward idolatry. By emphasizing YHWH's initiative, Isaiah warns
against idolizing Cyrus, just one example of earthly powers we must not
worship, because YHWH "is to be revered above all gods" (Ps. 96:4)—
and above all emperors too.

LEIGH CAMPBELL-TAYLOR

RESPONSE

What are some things you deeply love that cannot love you back? What
leaders or celebrities do you idolize? What would it look like to offer
praise and attention to God in a new, even fun, way this week? How do
you know that God pays attention to you, and loves you back?

PRAYER

God of majesty, you created all things; teach me to sing to you a new
song, that I may delight in your strength, your beauty, and your love for
me. Amen.

Second Reading

1 Thessalonians 1:1–10

For we know, brothers and sisters beloved by God, that he has chosen you,
because our message of the gospel came to you not in word only, but also in
power and in the Holy Spirit and with full conviction; just as you know what
kind of persons we proved to be among you for your sake. (vv. 4–5)

REFLECTION

As a leader—in this case, a church leader—[Paul] affirms the church at
Thessalonica and acknowledges the presence of the Holy Spirit among
the believers. By acknowledging the work of the Holy Spirit, Paul
recognizes that the believers are already empowered, and he celebrates
that reality. Paul does not view the believers as people who are less than
himself in stature; instead, he sees them as beloved by God. . . . Such
a leadership style affirms and supports the gifts, talents, and life of a
community and affirms the real strength of a leader whose power is best
when shared.

CAROL J. DEMPSEY, OP

RESPONSE

In your congregation, is power shared? Is it assumed that it is clergy
who will lead and serve the people, or that lay members will also lead
and support clergy in meaningful ways? How might the Holy Spirit be
revealing herself in unexpected places?

PRAYER

Holy Spirit, we are baptized in you for ministry and mission; guide me
to use my gifts and to support others in their gifts that together, we may
serve you with power and full conviction. Amen.

Gospel

Matthew 22:15–22

Then he said to them, "Whose head is this, and whose title?" They answered, "The emperor's." Then he said to them, "Give therefore to the emperor the things that are the emperor's, and to God the things that are God's." (vv. 20–21)

REFLECTION

It takes most of us a lifetime to discern the difference between what we think we own, and who finally owns us. Here we are encouraged in that discernment by the challenge that we not give to the emperor more than the emperor is due. Do not give the emperor your faith, do not give the emperor your ultimate allegiance, do not forge a relationship with the emperor that forces you to figure out how God can rightly fit into the emperor's pocket. . . . For what belongs to God is vastly larger than what belongs to the emperor.

THEODORE J. WARDLAW

RESPONSE

How would you define "the emperor" in your own life or context? What in your life belongs to "the emperor"? What in your life belongs to God? How does it feel to consider that all things, in the end, belong to God? Does this change anything?

PRAYER

Jesus Christ, in you we live and move and have our being; help me to steward what I own, and not to let what I own steward me. Amen.

Weekend Reflections

FURTHER CONNECTION

Throw the powerful off their thrones when they disturb the tranquility of the people. This is the political dimension of our faith. Mary lived it; Jesus lived it. He was truly a patriot of a people who were under foreign domination and that he, doubtless, dreamed of as being free. But, meanwhile, this people had to pay tribute to Caesar! . . .

It is not prestige for the Church to get along well with the powerful. The prestige of the Church is to sense that the poor feel it to be theirs, feel that the Church lives a dimension on earth calling everyone—the wealthy, too—to be converted.

OSCAR ROMERO (1917–80), SERMON GIVEN FEBRUARY 17, 1980

MAKING THE CONNECTIONS

Choose one or two questions for reflection:

1. What connections have you noticed between this week's texts and other passages in Scripture?

2. What connections have you made between this week's texts and the world beyond Scripture?

3. Does either of this week's two commentary themes speak especially to your life or the life of the world around you right now?

4. What is God saying to your congregation in particular through this week's readings and commentaries?

_____

_____

_____

_____

_____

_____

Sabbath Day

SCRIPTURE OF ASSURANCE

For this gospel I was appointed a herald and an apostle and a teacher, and for this reason I suffer as I do. But I am not ashamed, for I know the one in whom I have put my trust, and I am sure that he is able to guard until that day what I have entrusted to him. (2 Timothy 1:11–12)

WEEKLY EXAMEN

- Take a quiet moment, seek out God's presence, and pray for the guidance of the Spirit.

- Consider the past week; recall specific moments and feelings that stand out to you.

- Choose one moment or feeling for deeper examination, thanksgiving, or repentance.

- Let go, breathe deeply, and invite Christ's love to surround and fill you in preparation for the week ahead.

- End with the Lord's Prayer.

The Week Leading Up to
Proper 25

(Sunday between October 23 and October 29)

Leviticus 19:1–2, 15–18

The Lord spoke to Moses, saying:
   Speak to all the congregation of the people of Israel and say to them: You shall be holy, for I the Lord your God am holy. (vv. 1–2)

Deuteronomy 34:1–12

Moses was one hundred twenty years old when he died; his sight was unimpaired and his vigor had not abated. The Israelites wept for Moses in the plains of Moab thirty days; then the period of mourning for Moses was ended. (vv. 7–8)

1 Thessalonians 2:1–8

You yourselves know, brothers and sisters, that our coming to you was not in vain, but though we had already suffered and been shamefully mistreated at Philippi, as you know, we had courage in our God to declare to you the gospel of God in spite of great opposition. (vv. 1–2)

Matthew 22:34–46

When the Pharisees heard that he had silenced the Sadducees, they gathered together, and one of them, a lawyer, asked him a question to test him. "Teacher, which commandment in the law is the greatest?" (vv. 34–36)

LECTIO DIVINA

Underline a word or phrase that especially grabs your attention. Pray from that word or phrase and ask God to help you connect to its particular invitation for you this week.

Themes from This Week's Writers

THEME 1: *You Shall Be Holy*

Leviticus 19:1–2, 15–18

"Holy" has been defined so that one can be holy on a deserted island, but the holiness God calls us to requires a community with whom to be holy. Holy is not a solitary act.

MIGUEL A. DE LA TORRE

Leviticus 19:1–2, 15–18

Biblical holiness is a calling to reflect God's character in deep relationship with God (loving God) and in relationship with the covenantal community, the nations, and all creation (loving neighbor). We love God in some respects by loving our neighbor. Moreover, we love our neighbor by learning to love ourselves as God loves us.

BRIAN D. RUSSELL

Psalm 1

To a sermon on the profound theological claim that, thanks to God's holiness, we too are capable of holiness (Lev. 19:2), today's psalm could add an element utterly lacking in Leviticus: the promise of being "happy" (Ps. 1:1) and experiencing "delight" (v. 2). What a welcome complement to the "shalls" and "shall nots" of Leviticus.

LEIGH CAMPBELL-TAYLOR

THEME 2: *Facing Challenges to Faith and Discipleship*

1 Thessalonians 2:1–8

[Despite] the experience of suffering and mistreatment of Paul and his coworkers in Philippi prior to their coming to Thessalonica, . . . they still came (v. 2). The "great opposition" (v. 2) did not cause them to freeze in fear in Philippi. Rather, they had courage in God to persist.

TROY A. MILLER

1 Thessalonians 2:1–8

Paul's point about suffering and being mistreated has personal implications for believers today. For those who preach the gospel—the liberating word of God's compassionate love for all creation—and for those who choose to live their lives accordingly to the gospel message, suffering will always be a part of their experience, especially for women.

CAROL J. DEMPSEY, OP

Matthew 22:34–46

In the verses immediately ahead of this text, the conflict is with the Sadducees. Now, it is the Pharisees who are closing in on Jesus; and all of this is happening against the emerging backdrop of Jerusalem in the last chapter of Jesus' life. The tension just hangs in the air like a drumbeat that gets louder and louder.

THEODORE J. WARDLAW

WHAT IS THE HOLY SPIRIT SAYING TO YOU THIS WEEK?

_____

_____

_____

_____

_____

A SPIRITUAL PRACTICE FOR THIS WEEK

In the Gospel, Jesus is tested by fierce opponents. Sometimes, our fiercest opponents are in our own minds. Try to picture your inner critic or judge as a character. Perhaps give them a silly name. This week, talk back to them, as Jesus did. Be snarky, if that helps. Remind them of the two greatest commandments, per Matthew 22.

First Reading

Deuteronomy 34:1–12 or Leviticus 19:1–2, 15–18

You shall be holy, for I the LORD your God am holy. (Leviticus 19:2b)

The LORD said to [Moses], "This is the land of which I swore to Abraham, to Isaac, and to Jacob, saying, 'I will give it to your descendants'; I have let you see it with your eyes, but you shall not cross over there." (Deuteronomy 34:4)

REFLECTION

To embrace holiness can be hopeless where the future is not assured, where we may never get to set foot in the promised land that we spent a lifetime walking toward. To be holy can mark us for a life full of suffering and shameful mistreatment. To be holy may very well be the worst transaction in which we can ever engage. Regardless of the love we show our neighbors, our lives may still come to an end on top of a mountain looking toward a reward we will never experience. So again, why bother?

MIGUEL A. DE LA TORRE

RESPONSE

What in God's command "to be holy" appeals to you? (See also Leviticus 19:15–18.) What is most challenging to you? If God cannot guarantee you will reach the promised land or be free from suffering, what in "embracing holiness" is still meaningful?

PRAYER

Lord God, you do not promise me success or protection from all danger, but you call me to be holy, as you are holy; teach me what this means. Amen.

Canticle

Psalm 1

Happy are those
    who do not follow the advice of the wicked,
or take the path that sinners tread,
    or sit in the seat of scoffers;
but their delight is in the law of the LORD. (vv. 1–2a)

REFLECTION

The psalm opens with the formulaic phrasing of a beatitude, "Happy are those . . ." (Ps. 1:1), and then spends its six verses considering the experience of these happy ones as opposed to the experience of "the wicked" (vv. 1, 4–6). The psalmist is unflinchingly dualistic, laying out exactly two paths: the way of those who are "happy" (v. 1) and "righteous" (vv. 5, 6) is contrasted with the way of those who are "wicked" (vv. 4–6). It is worth noting that there is human agency in choosing which path to follow; we are not hapless victims of fate.

LEIGH CAMPBELL-TAYLOR

RESPONSE

Does following God's laws tend to make you a happier person? What factors tend to make you into a more *wicked* person? What is it like to read this psalm as though it were speaking about the interior life of an individual, not two kinds of people?

PRAYER

Loving God, you invite me to be happy, though I will often face wickedness—my own and others'; show me how happiness and righteousness can intersect in my life, that I may delight in your law. Amen.

Second Reading

1 Thessalonians 2:1–8

But we were gentle among you, like a nurse tenderly caring for her own children. So deeply do we care for you that we are determined to share with you not only the gospel of God but also our own selves, because you have become very dear to us. (vv. 7b–8)

REFLECTION

[Paul] writes that he and his two companions were gentle among [the Thessalonians], like a nurse caring for her own children. In a patriarchal, hierarchal Greco-Roman world of Paul's day, this feminine image and metaphor can be refreshing and also challenging to the status quo. . . . For those who tend to read Paul as someone who is prone to autocratic and androcentric language, who is often harsh and offensive to women in his letters, this metaphor comes as a surprise.

CAROL J. DEMPSEY, OP

RESPONSE

What is it like to hear Paul describe himself, Silas, and Timothy in this feminine way? Why would Paul use "nurse" instead of "mother," do you think? How does his tender, loving metaphor of church leadership affirm or challenge your own experience?

PRAYER

Gentle God, all of your children are very dear to you; teach me to serve them as Paul did, so to learn the strength of tenderness and gentleness. Amen.

Gospel

Matthew 22:34–46

"If David thus calls him Lord, how can he be his son?" No one was able to give [Jesus] an answer, nor from that day did anyone dare to ask him any more questions. (vv. 45–46)

REFLECTION

His opponents cannot say a word—Jesus is the authoritative interpreter of Scripture—but what does that interpretation mean?

The invocation of various titles for Jesus is an important part of Matthew's Gospel. . . . In this passage, it is interesting to note that while the crowds called Jesus the "Son of David" (21:9), the Pharisee who asks Jesus about the greatest commandment addresses him simply as teacher. Matthew is clearly indicating that Jesus is a teacher, but more. He is a Son of David, but more. He is the Messiah, but more.

MICHAEL E. LEE

RESPONSE

Jesus was constantly challenged and asked to justify himself during his life on earth. Have you faced this in your own life, or seen someone you love face it? What is most important to you in Lee's point that Jesus is always more than what we think he is?

PRAYER

Jesus the teacher, you were not accepted or trusted by many; even now, you invite me to question you, and yet to know you more and more, even if you will always be more than I can imagine. Amen.

Weekend Reflections

FURTHER CONNECTION

All holiness is God's holiness in us: it is a holiness that is participation and, in a certain way, more than participation, because as we participate in what we can receive from God, we become a revelation of that which transcends us. Being a limited light, we reveal the Light.

ANTHONY BLOOM (1914–2003), *GOD AND MAN*

MAKING THE CONNECTIONS

Choose one or two questions for reflection:

1. What connections have you noticed between this week's texts and other passages in Scripture?

2. What connections have you made between this week's texts and the world beyond Scripture?

3. Does either of this week's two commentary themes speak especially to your life or the life of the world around you right now?

4. What is God saying to your congregation in particular through this week's readings and commentaries?

MY CONNECTIONS

_____

_____

_____

_____

_____

_____

Sabbath Day

SCRIPTURE OF ASSURANCE

> O LORD, you have searched me and known me.
> You know when I sit down and when I rise up;
>   you discern my thoughts from far away. (Psalm 139:1–2)

WEEKLY EXAMEN

- Take a quiet moment, seek out God's presence, and pray for the guidance of the Spirit.

- Consider the past week; recall specific moments and feelings that stand out to you.

- Choose one moment or feeling for deeper examination, thanksgiving, or repentance.

- Let go, breathe deeply, and invite Christ's love to surround and fill you in preparation for the week ahead.

- End with the Lord's Prayer.

The Week Leading Up to
All Saints
(November 1 or the Sunday following)

Revelation 7:9–17

After this I looked, and there was a great multitude that no one could count, from every nation, from all tribes and peoples and languages, standing before the throne and before the Lamb, robed in white, with palm branches in their hands. (v. 9)

Psalm 34:1–10, 22

The LORD redeems the life of his servants;
    none of those who take refuge in him will be condemned.
      (v. 22)

1 John: 3:1–3

See what love the Father has given us, that we should be called children of God; and that is what we are. The reason the world does not know us is that it did not know him. (v. 1)

Matthew 5:1–12

Then [Jesus] began to speak, and taught them, saying:
    "Blessed are the poor in spirit, for theirs is the kingdom of heaven.
    "Blessed are those who mourn, for they will be comforted.
    "Blessed are the meek, for they will inherit the earth." (vv. 2–5)

LECTIO DIVINA

Underline a word or phrase that especially grabs your attention. Pray from that word or phrase and ask God to help you connect to its particular invitation for you this week.

Themes from This Week's Writers

THEME 1: *The Communion of Saints*

Revelation 7:9–17

In the throne room God's radically inclusive plan welcomes people of every racial, ethnic, political, and cultural background (7:9). This . . . encourages the persecuted churches in Revelation to resist oppressive Roman imperial structures and attend to one another's needs and afflictions.

WILLIAM YOO

Revelation 7:9–17

"A great multitude that no one could count," reminds the congregation that the feast of All Saints celebrates *all* the saints. This includes famous saints of the church . . . [as well as] loved ones who have died in the faith *and* disciples who are hard at work in the church today.

ELIZABETH FELICETTI

1 John 3:1–3

All Saints' Day may be a grand time to emphasize the universal scope of God's people—believers from every corner of the globe, from every language and culture, and from all walks of life. . . . The text transcends and overcomes the barriers of time and space connecting believers to all the saints from the distant past as well as the distant future.

ALVIN PADILLA

THEME 2: *We Are All Called to Be Saints*

1 John 3:1–3

First John 3:1 provides a good working definition of "saints": those who are "children of God."

. . . This designation is not our own achievement, but a gift of love from God. It describes our state, who we are; but it also provides us with a future goal, who we are to become.

ARUN W. JONES

Matthew 5:1–12

As we remember all the saints who have lived before us and stand before the Lord, we should be mindful of the life they modeled for us to live through their patience and hope for a better tomorrow. . . . Such is the challenge of the Beatitudes: to live a life worthy of the coming kingdom of God, regardless of any earthly rewards.

SAMMY G. ALFARO

Matthew 5:1–12

It is natural for Christians to want to see themselves among these groups of people Jesus calls blessed, but the Beatitudes are not about trying to "get on the list." . . . These are not tasks that result in rewards. Rather, when we align our aims with God's, we are formed and shaped toward God's purposes.

AIMEE MOISO

WHAT IS THE HOLY SPIRIT SAYING TO YOU THIS WEEK?

_____

_____

_____

_____

_____

A SPIRITUAL PRACTICE FOR THIS WEEK

Set a table or altar in your home with pictures of saints who were spiritual teachers for you, whether traditional saints, family members, or other leaders in your life who have gone before. Speak a prayer of thanksgiving for each of these saints and ask them to pray for you.

First Reading

Then one of the elders addressed me, saying, "Who are these, robed in white, and where have they come from?" I said to him, "Sir, you are the one that knows." (vv. 13–14a)

REFLECTION

Halloween, a cultural celebration just over when All Saints arrives, can contribute to a cultural distancing from death. While Halloween offers an opportunity to focus on macabre costumes of zombies, such depictions are typically anonymous. Skeletons and ghosts on Halloween rarely represent someone specific. Contrast this with the Mexican Day of the Dead, celebrated on All Souls' Day, November 2, and its focus on remembering and communing with loved ones. Celebrations of All Saints should help hearers learn about and better integrate into their worldviews a mature theological understanding of death and the communion of the saints.

ELIZABETH FELICETTI

RESPONSE

How have you noticed this cultural distancing from death in your own life or community? What strikes you in Felicetti's observations about Halloween? Do you celebrate the Day of the Dead? How do you remember and commune with loved ones who have died? Or how do you wish you did?

PRAYER

Lord Christ, you know and love all people, including those who have died; you are with my beloved ones even now, and you will welcome me, too, when I arrive to join them. Amen.

Canticle

Psalm 34:1–10, 22

O taste and see that the LORD is good;
  happy are those who take refuge in him.
O fear the LORD, you his holy ones,
  for those who fear him have no want. (vv. 8–9)

REFLECTION

Help your congregation glimpse the communion of saints and recognize their own place in that faithful throng. Speak of your Communion table as stretching all the way back to Jesus and all the way forward to the eschatological banquet when all will be united "before the throne and before the Lamb" [Rev. 7:9]. Although Psalm 34 is a pre-Christian text, all of our saints and all of us are like the psalmist: each is an individual seeking God.

LEIGH CAMPBELL-TAYLOR

RESPONSE

When you imagine the communion of saints, what do you see? What do you feel invited to see, in particular, in your church's Communion table or altar stretching through time? How do you see your individual journey interwoven with the journeys of others seeking God?

PRAYER

Jesus, you invite us through Communion to a banquet with all our beloved saints, stretching back in time and across the world; let us taste and see your love and goodness together. Amen.

Second Reading

1 John 3:1–3

Beloved, we are God's children now; what we will be has not yet been revealed.
What we do know is this: when he is revealed, we will be like him, for we will
see him as he is. (v. 2)

REFLECTION

Believers of today are to be counted in the same company as those who
have come before, for they too shall gather with them before the throne
of the Lamb and worship! Focusing on the blessing of being a child of
God and our own particular calling . . . might help avoid any tendency
to compare one's worth with that of the saints before them. This is
an excellent opportunity to emphasize the belief that the gathered are
included among the great cloud of witnesses (Heb. 12:1–2) who bring
the good news of the reality of God's kingdom, even in a hostile world.

ALVIN PADILLA

RESPONSE

Make a list of saints, traditional or personal, who have been important
mentors or a spiritual inspiration to you. How do you compare yourself
to them? Or worry you should be more like them? How do you see
yourself as part of the cloud of witnesses? How will we all "be like him"
in the end, do you imagine?

PRAYER

Gracious Jesus, you have made me part of a great cloud of witnesses;
fill me with awe at the love you have given us, that we should be called
children of God. Amen.

Gospel

Matthew 5:1–12

"Blessed are those who hunger and thirst for righteousness, for they will be filled.

"Blessed are the merciful, for they will receive mercy.

"Blessed are the pure in heart, for they will see God." (vv. 6–8)

REFLECTION

What if verse 6 read, "Blessed is the one who has tunnel vision for making things right"? Perhaps this blessing now includes the wrongly convicted death-row inmate, or the lawyer arguing a toxic waste case before the Supreme Court. *Blessed is the Black Lives Matter activist who has lost too many neighbors and friends to gun violence. Blessed is the Syrian refugee trying to gain asylum in a country that did nothing to prevent the war from escalating.* Suddenly the frescoed saints of cathedral ceilings become more multidimensional.

AIMEE MOISO

RESPONSE

Choose a few beatitudes and expand on them in the same way as Moiso. How can these verses be more than nice sayings or a bunch of words? Who are people who are living examples of these blessings in your community? Which blessing draws you as a call or prayer for yourself, this week?

PRAYER

Jesus of upside-down blessings, teach me to see and celebrate my strengths, quirks, and limits as your gifts, all a part of how I am called to serve my neighbor and your kingdom. Amen. Alleluia!

Weekend Reflections

FURTHER CONNECTION

I realized then that one day I am going to be an ancestor. When I have passed on and my spirit is left to lead my children and their children, they will talk about me, about my legacy, about what I left undone or what I did to change things. . . . I remember my ancestors, I remember what they have left for me, and I remember what was left undone. I look at their pictures, searching their eyes for stories they may never have told us when they were alive. Instead, they visit us in dreams, reconnecting us, helping us imagine a new way forward, a way of peace. One day we will become ancestors, but until then, we whisper to our long-gone ones, asking that they remember us.

KAITLIN CURTICE (1990–), *NATIVE: IDENTITY, BELONGING, AND REDISCOVERING GOD*

MAKING THE CONNECTIONS

Choose one or two questions for reflection:

1. What connections have you noticed between this week's texts and other passages in Scripture?

2. What connections have you made between this week's texts and the world beyond Scripture?

3. Does either of this week's two commentary themes speak especially to your life or the life of the world around you right now?

4. What is God saying to your congregation in particular through this week's readings and commentaries?

_____

_____

_____

_____

_____

_____

Sabbath Day

SCRIPTURE OF ASSURANCE

To those who are sanctified in Christ Jesus, called to be saints, together with all those who in every place call on the name of our Lord Jesus Christ, both their Lord and ours:

Grace to you and peace from God our Father and the Lord Jesus Christ. (1 Corinthians 1:2b–3)

WEEKLY EXAMEN

- Take a quiet moment, seek out God's presence, and pray for the guidance of the Spirit.

- Consider the past week; recall specific moments and feelings that stand out to you.

- Choose one moment or feeling for deeper examination, thanksgiving, or repentance.

- Let go, breathe deeply, and invite Christ's love to surround and fill you in preparation for the week ahead.

- End with the Lord's Prayer.

The Week Leading Up to
Proper 26
(Sunday between October 30 and November 5)

Micah 3:5–12

Thus says the LORD concerning the prophets
    who lead my people astray,
who cry "Peace"
    when they have something to eat,
but declare war against those
    who put nothing into their mouths. (v. 5)

Joshua 3:7–17

Now the Jordan overflows all its banks throughout the time of harvest. So when those who bore the ark had come to the Jordan, and the feet of the priests bearing the ark were dipped in the edge of the water, the waters flowing from above stood still. (vv. 15–16a)

1 Thessalonians 2:9–13

As you know, we dealt with each one of you like a father with his children, urging and encouraging you and pleading that you lead a life worthy of God, who calls you into his own kingdom and glory. (vv. 11–12)

Matthew 23:1–12

"Call no one your father on earth, for you have one Father—the one in heaven. Nor are you to be called instructors, for you have one instructor, the Messiah. The greatest among you will be your servant. All who exalt themselves will be humbled, and all who humble themselves will be exalted." (vv. 9–12)

LECTIO DIVINA

Underline a word or phrase that especially grabs your attention. Pray from that word or phrase and ask God to help you connect to its particular invitation for you this week.

Themes from This Week's Writers

THEME 1: *Clergy Are Not More Holy Than Other People*

Micah 3:5–12

God condemns political and religious leaders for ignoring "justice" (*mishpat*) and failing to care for the lowly and the poor. In Micah 3:11, the corrupt leaders are derisively mocked for "lean[ing] upon the LORD" without the faintest hints of remorse, repentance, or reform.

WILLIAM YOO

Joshua 3:7–17

The twelve chosen priests in the reading do not go in front of the people because they are more important but because they carry the holy ark, acknowledging that the mighty God of Israel goes before the people. The waters of the Jordan are parted only by the power of God (3:13); the priests do not have that power on their own.

ELIZABETH FELICETTI

1 Thessalonians 2:9–13

The priesthood of all believers (1 Pet. 2:9) informs us how we are to see the contributions of each person in the advancement of the kingdom of God. Paul's recollection of how he led the flock in Thessalonica . . . [invites] the preacher to exhort and encourage the men and women who lead the church today, be it as church staff or as volunteers.

ALVIN PADILLA

THEME 2: *The Greatest among You Will Be Your Servant*

1 Thessalonians 2:9–13

Paul underscores on the one hand his equality with his congregation— he lived as a manual laborer among manual laborers (4:11)—and urges them to imitate him (1:6). On the other hand, he presents himself in parental terms as a deeply loving provider, guide, and role model.

ARUN W. JONES

Matthew 23:1–12

Jesus expected his followers to model servant leadership. Instead of seeking titles and position (vv. 8–10), leaders in the community of believers needed to serve with humility (vv. 11–12), the hallmark of leadership among Jesus' disciples.

SAMMY G. ALFARO

Matthew 23:1–12

When Jesus points out leaders who do not practice what they preach and who act for the wrong reasons, he contrasts them with a vision of mutual servanthood and humility. Likewise, honorific titles are not appropriate in Jesus' fellowship because all are equal, valued siblings who, together, are the children of God.

AIMEE MOISO

WHAT IS THE HOLY SPIRIT SAYING TO YOU THIS WEEK?

_____

_____

_____

_____

_____

A SPIRITUAL PRACTICE FOR THIS WEEK

Find a synagogue that is in your general neighborhood (in some areas, this may be miles away). Explore their website and learn about their spirituality and mission. What does your congregation have in common with this one? What is strange to you? What inspires you? Pray for their rabbi(s), leaders, and members this week.

First Reading

Joshua 3:7–17

The LORD said to Joshua, "This day I will begin to exalt you in the sight of all Israel, so that they may know that I will be with you as I was with Moses. You are the one who shall command the priests who bear the ark of the covenant, 'When you come to the edge of the waters of the Jordan, you shall stand still in the Jordan.'" (vv. 7–8)

REFLECTION

Writing during the exilic or early postexilic period, the authors looked back to an era of divine favor and human courage to construct stories of military victory, land distribution, and liturgical ceremonies that would remind their contemporaries of God's faithfulness and their ancestors' obedience. Some of the original audience may have felt hope and resolve as they read about Joshua leading the Israelites across the Jordan River with the ark of the covenant (Josh. 3:7–17). Others may have felt a wave of sorrow or a surge of anger as they compared the fragility of their present existence with a glorious past.

WILLIAM YOO

RESPONSE

Think back to an event or time of great change and importance in your life. How do you tell this story to others? In what ways are you emphasizing certain values, memories, or emotions? How does the way you tell the story, even just to yourself, help create your identity?

PRAYER

Gracious God, how will I know you will be with me? Show me how to look back on my life and see how you have been part of my story, and how I have been part of yours. Amen.

Canticle

Psalm 107

O give thanks to the LORD, for he is good;
    for his steadfast love endures forever.
Let the redeemed of the LORD say so,
    those he redeemed from trouble. (vv. 1–2)

REFLECTION

Psalm 107 is clearly a psalm of thanksgiving for all the ways God has
come to the aid of the people of Israel. This too is a psalm written for
liturgical use; a refrain urges the people to "thank the LORD for his
steadfast love, for his wonderful works to humankind" four times during
the course of the psalm (although this refrain does not appear in the
lection as it is assigned). The psalm is both a litany of Israel's troubles
and a listing of the ways God rescued the people.

KIMBERLY BRACKEN LONG

RESPONSE

Are naming your troubles and giving thanks for God's aid both a
part of your prayer life, too? What about the worship life of your
church? Today, write a list or prayer naming your struggles and your
thanksgivings for God's presence and help in the past week.

PRAYER

O God, I give thanks for the ways you have rescued and redeemed me,
and I ask you to hear my pain and struggles now, for I believe your
steadfast love endures forever. Amen.

Second Reading

1 Thessalonians 2:9–13

We also constantly give thanks to God for this, that when you received the word of God that you heard from us, you accepted it not as a human word but as what it really is, God's word, which is also at work in you believers. (v. 13)

REFLECTION

The passage for today may seem a bit odd, even off-putting, in our own context. For here Paul proudly points to himself as a morally upright person—something a contemporary preacher may hesitate to do from the pulpit, lest the congregation think she is inappropriately boastful or perhaps is covering up some serious misdeeds. Paul's milieu was different from ours in this respect. In his day, it was standard practice for philosophers to talk and write this way in order to differentiate themselves from dishonorable figures who presented themselves to the public as moral teachers.

ARUN W. JONES

RESPONSE

Think of a pastor, mentor, or leader whom you deeply admire. Write them a note, "boasting" about them in a way that they might never do for themselves. Give thanks for their gifts and tell them how they have helped you know God better.

PRAYER

O God, I give thanks for holy and encouraging leaders; strengthen these shepherds of your church and all your people, for you are at work in all believers. Amen.

Gospel

Matthew 23:1–12

Do whatever [the scribes and Pharisees] teach you and follow it; but do not do as they do, for they do not practice what they teach. They tie up heavy burdens, hard to bear, and lay them on the shoulders of others; but they themselves are unwilling to lift a finger to move them. (vv. 3–4)

REFLECTION

We are expected humbly to practice true *diakonia* (service) for everyone in the community of believers. In the workplace and community structures we lead, we are challenged to avoid the exercise of authority from a standpoint of power, and instead must have a genuine desire to serve, not those who are "under us," but, rather, those who are next to us. How different might our world be if so-called Christian leaders and politicians actually took Jesus' words to heart and decided to use their position of influence and power to serve with humility the communities they represent?

SAMMY G. ALFARO

RESPONSE

What are ways you are tempted, like the Pharisees, toward a feeling of power over or against other people? What does it mean to you, in this season of your life, that great discipleship is about humility? How does God call you to be a servant, but also to be fully yourself?

PRAYER

Jesus, I know that all who exalt themselves will be humbled, and all who humble themselves will be exalted; teach me the meaning of healthy power and healthy servanthood. Amen.

Weekend Reflections

While we as people of God are certainly called to feed the hungry and clothe the naked, that whole "we're blessed to be a blessing" thing can still be kind of dangerous. It can be dangerous when we self-importantly place ourselves above the world, waiting to descend on those below so we can be the "blessing" they've been waiting for, like it or not. Plus, seeing myself as the blessing can pretty easily obscure the way in which I am actually part of the problem and can hide the ways in which I, too, am poor and needing care.

NADIA BOLZ-WEBER (1969–), *ACCIDENTAL SAINTS: FINDING GOD IN ALL THE WRONG PEOPLE*

MAKING THE CONNECTIONS

Choose one or two questions for reflection:

1. What connections have you noticed between this week's texts and other passages in Scripture?

2. What connections have you made between this week's texts and the world beyond Scripture?

3. Does either of this week's two commentary themes speak especially to your life or the life of the world around you right now?

4. What is God saying to your congregation in particular through this week's readings and commentaries?

_____

_____

_____

_____

_____

_____

Sabbath Day

SCRIPTURE OF ASSURANCE

"Give, and it will be given to you. A good measure, pressed down, shaken together, running over, will be poured into your lap; for the measure you give will be the measure you get back." (Luke 6:38)

WEEKLY EXAMEN

- Take a quiet moment, seek out God's presence, and pray for the guidance of the Spirit.

- Consider the past week; recall specific moments and feelings that stand out to you.

- Choose one moment or feeling for deeper examination, thanksgiving, or repentance.

- Let go, breathe deeply, and invite Christ's love to surround and fill you in preparation for the week ahead.

- End with the Lord's Prayer.

The Week Leading Up to
Proper 27

(Sunday between November 6 and November 12)

Joshua 24:1–3a, 14–25

But Joshua said to the people, "You cannot serve the LORD, for he is a holy God. He is a jealous God; he will not forgive your transgressions or your sins. If you forsake the LORD and serve foreign gods, then he will turn and do you harm, and consume you, after having done you good." (vv. 19–20)

Amos 5:18–24

I hate, I despise your festivals,
    and I take no delight in your solemn assemblies.
Even though you offer me your burnt offerings and grain offerings,
    I will not accept them. (vv. 21–22b)

1 Thessalonians 4:13–18

For the Lord himself, with a cry of command, with the archangel's call and with the sound of God's trumpet, will descend from heaven, and the dead in Christ will rise first. Then we who are alive, who are left, will be caught up in the clouds together with them to meet the Lord in the air; and so we will be with the Lord forever. (vv. 16–17)

Matthew 25:1–13

"Later the other bridesmaids came also, saying, 'Lord, lord, open to us.' But he replied, 'Truly I tell you, I do not know you.' Keep awake therefore, for you know neither the day nor the hour." (vv. 11–13)

LECTIO DIVINA

Underline a word or phrase that especially grabs your attention. Pray from that word or phrase and ask God to help you connect to its particular invitation for you this week.

Themes from This Week's Writers

THEME 1: *God Is Our Righteous Judge*

Amos 5:18–24

One common theme across the prophetic literature is God's delight in those who integrate their passion for steadfast worship with compassion for other people (Isa. 1:10–17; Hos. 6:6; Mic. 6:6–8). In Amos 5:24, justice and righteousness are not presented as alternatives to replace festivals and solemn assemblies. Instead, God is calling for increased and sustained attention to societal inequities.

WILLIAM YOO

Amos 5:18–24

The life and mission of the church extend beyond the Sunday liturgy. Are the people . . . acting as the church after they leave the building on Sunday morning? . . . "Take away from me the noise of your songs" (v. 23) convicts those who come to worship solely as an escape.

ELIZABETH FELICETTI

Psalm 78:1–7 and Psalm 70

We move toward the proclamation that whatever evil the world has conjured, and however we may have taken part in it, Christ is indeed coming to set things right. Justice will come, and with it, God's mercy.

KIMBERLY BRACKEN LONG

THEME 2: *Keep Awake, for We Know Not the Hour*

1 Thessalonians 4:13–18

These readings challenge a far too common contemporary theological assumption: that a focus on getting to heaven diverts our attention from working on salvation in the here and now. In fact, the readings make the opposite claim: that it is the belief in God's coming judgment and salvation that provides the fuel (Matt. 25:13) for our exertions for good in the world.

ARUN W. JONES

Matthew 25:1–13

Believers are cautioned to live with expectancy, cognizant of the imminent second coming of Jesus. This is not a mere pie-in-the-sky existence simply awaiting the coming of Jesus, while doing nothing of earthly good in this world. Rather, this same eschatological hope should guide believers to serve others with their talents, as the next parable in the chapter envisions (Matt. 25:14–30).

SAMMY G. ALFARO

Matthew 25:1–13

In our context, which seems rife with the "delay" of the reign of God, it can be hard to maintain hope. . . .

. . . The bridesmaids who brought flasks of oil also brought hope that though the groom might be delayed, he would still arrive. In the end, they were ready not only for the wedding, but for the wait.

AIMEE MOISO

WHAT IS THE HOLY SPIRIT SAYING TO YOU THIS WEEK?

_____

_____

_____

_____

_____

A SPIRITUAL PRACTICE FOR THIS WEEK

Make a list of beloved people in your life who have died. Read 1 Thessalonians 4:13–18, holding these people in your mind's eye. What words bring you comfort? What is puzzling or off-putting? What hope do you feel for those who have died, with or without Paul's words?

First Reading

Joshua 24:1–3a, 14–25

"Now if you are unwilling to serve the Lord, choose this day whom you will serve, whether the gods your ancestors served in the region beyond the River or the gods of the Amorites in whose land you are living; but as for me and my household, we will serve the Lord." (v. 15)

REFLECTION

"As for me and my household, we will serve the Lord" (Josh. 24:15) can be found on refrigerator magnets, bookmarks, and framed calligraphed plaques in homes. Setting this sound bite in its biblical context enables worshipers to see beyond the snappy verse into the demands being made upon the people of God. . . .

. . . What gets in the way of our relationship with God, with the church, and with each other? We may not carry wooden idols of other gods in our pockets, but we probably have more than one screen to distract us at any given time.

ELIZABETH FELICETTI

RESPONSE

What is your past relationship with this famous verse? Consider Felicetti's questions: What has been getting in the way of your relationship with God, lately? With the church? With other people? What "foreign gods" are in your pockets? What does promising to "serve the Lord," as an individual or household, mean to you at this time in your life?

PRAYER

Lord God, you ask me every day to choose whom I will serve; help me to see—beyond my "foreign gods" and beyond my own household—to your greater purpose of love and justice for the whole world. Amen.

Canticle

Psalm 70

But I am poor and needy;
  hasten to me, O God!
You are my help and my deliverer;
  O LORD, do not delay! (v. 5)

REFLECTION

As a response to the prophet's words, Psalm 70 serves as a kind of confession of sin. Along with Amos, we pray for justice, yet acknowledge that we will be caught up in the upheaval that will come when God rights every wrong. Like bathers in the sea who anticipate with joy the coming waves, then find themselves tumbling in the foam and grit, we both seek and fear the coming of justice, for we know we will be implicated. The psalmist's prayer, then, enables us to acknowledge our own need for salvation, even as we offer our praise.

KIMBERLY BRACKEN LONG

RESPONSE

How do you "both seek and fear the coming of justice" from God? What are some ways you have been working for justice? How would you be implicated still, in injustice? What does it mean to you to "acknowledge your own need for salvation" this week?

PRAYER

O God, make haste to help me and deliver me that I may help and deliver others, so all might rejoice in you. Amen.

Second Reading

1 Thessalonians 4:13–18

But we do not want you to be uninformed, brothers and sisters, about those who have died, so that you may not grieve as others do who have no hope. For since we believe that Jesus died and rose again, even so, through Jesus, God will bring with him those who have died. (vv. 13–14)

REFLECTION

The admonition not to "grieve as others do who have no hope" acknowledges that grieving does take place. How that grieving is processed, however, is culturally bound. One culture may welcome expressive, public modes of grieving, while others may be more subdued to the point of being undetectable. One is not necessarily better than the other. Rather, the text bids us to be aware of the culture in which grieving is taking place and not to impose one cultural style on another, which could very well result in the opposite of the intended consolation. For the believer, this grieving should have in mind the hope of the resurrection.

ALVIN PADILLA

RESPONSE

Have you struggled with the promises of God in grieving the loss of a loved one? What would you say your culture's expectations for grieving are, and how have they affected you? How does the resurrection of Christ offer you hope, for your loved one or yourself?

PRAYER

God of the dead, you meet me in my grief, even when I struggle to hope; give me the joy and hope of your saving help again, that I may not despair, but persevere in love. Amen.

Gospel

Matthew 25:1–13

"The foolish said to the wise, 'Give us some of your oil, for our lamps are going out.' But the wise replied, 'No! there will not be enough for you and for us; you had better go to the dealers and buy some for yourselves.'" (vv. 8–9)

REFLECTION

The parable rubs against Christian inclinations to help one another, foolish or wise. Certainly, there must have been other options, we might want to protest. Light cast by a flame is not a zero-sum resource; if the oil could not be shared, surely the light of the lamps could have been. In any case, an interpretive pitfall is to hear the parable as a call to save ourselves at the expense of others. Acknowledging that the parable is about being ready, not about generosity or distribution of resources, can help mitigate interpretations that are self-serving or congratulatory about our own oil supplies.

AIMEE MOISO

RESPONSE

What does it mean to you to be ready, waiting for Jesus, in this season of your life? What in a spiritual journey or Christian life cannot be shared with others, even if we want to do so? How can you replenish your lamp when your oil feels like it is running low?

PRAYER

Lord Christ, you are coming again to judge and to save the world; show me how to stay awake and keep my oil supplied, that I may meet you whenever you come. Amen.

Weekend Reflections

FURTHER CONNECTION

Our power is first in waiting for the end of darkness, for the defeat of evil; and our power is also in coming upon single sparks and occasional rays, upon moments full of God's grace and radiance.

We are called to bring together the sparks to preserve single moments of radiance and keep them alive in our lives, to defy absurdity and despair, and to wait for God to say again: Let there be light.

And there will be light.

RABBI ABRAHAM JOSHUA HESCHEL (1907–72), *MORAL GRANDEUR AND SPIRITUAL AUDACITY*

MAKING THE CONNECTIONS

Choose one or two questions for reflection:

1. What connections have you noticed between this week's texts and other passages in Scripture?

2. What connections have you made between this week's texts and the world beyond Scripture?

3. Does either of this week's two commentary themes speak especially to your life or the life of the world around you right now?

4. What is God saying to your congregation in particular through this week's readings and commentaries?

_____

_____

_____

_____

_____

Sabbath Day

SCRIPTURE OF ASSURANCE

> But I am like a green olive tree
> in the house of God.
> I trust in the steadfast love of God
> forever and ever. (Psalm 52:8)

WEEKLY EXAMEN

- Take a quiet moment, seek out God's presence, and pray for the guidance of the Spirit.

- Consider the past week; recall specific moments and feelings that stand out to you.

- Choose one moment or feeling for deeper examination, thanksgiving, or repentance.

- Let go, breathe deeply, and invite Christ's love to surround and fill you in preparation for the week ahead.

- End with the Lord's Prayer.

The Week Leading Up to
Proper 28
(Sunday between November 13 and November 19)

Zephaniah 1:7, 12–18

Be silent before the Lord GOD!
    For the day of the LORD is at hand;
the LORD has prepared a sacrifice,
    he has consecrated his guests. (v. 7)

Judges 4:1–7

Then the Israelites cried out to the LORD for help; for [Sisera] had nine hundred chariots of iron, and had oppressed the Israelites cruelly twenty years. (v. 3)

1 Thessalonians 5:1–11

Now concerning the times and the seasons, brothers and sisters, you do not need to have anything written to you. For you yourselves know very well that the day of the Lord will come like a thief in the night. (vv. 1–2)

Matthew 25:14–30

"The one who had received the five talents went off at once and traded with them, and made five more talents. In the same way, the one who had the two talents made two more talents. But the one who had received the one talent went off and dug a hole in the ground and hid his master's money." (vv. 16–18)

LECTIO DIVINA

Underline a word or phrase that especially grabs your attention. Pray from that word or phrase and ask God to help you connect to its particular invitation for you this week.

Themes from This Week's Writers

THEME 1: *The Day of the Lord*

Zephaniah 1:7, 12–18

Concerns about the coming "day of the LORD" find parallels in Isaiah 13 and 22, in Joel 2–3, in Amos 5, and Malachi 3:2. . . . Expectations grow out of the community's yearning for new beginnings and God's desire to create newness where life can flourish. Each generation of the faithful diagnoses the character of that eschatology.

KENNETH N. NGWA

1 Thessalonians 5:1–11

Throughout the Old Testament the end time is understood as a time of destruction for the world. . . . Paul understood it as a time of great pain, like that of a woman in labor (1 Thess. 5:3). These historic Jewish teachings would need to be interpreted to a new people of faith. How do believers live between "the now and the not yet"?

RUTH FAITH SANTANA-GRACE

1 Thessalonians 5:1–11

Particularly for those of us who live comfortably, the end of the world as we know it sounds more terrifying than reassuring. . . .

. . . Could it be that we are living, as Paul suggests, in darkness? What might we do differently now to live in the light and be more hopeful about what is to come?

LEE HULL MOSES

THEME 2: *Trusting in God's Power and Grace*

Judges 4:1–7

We can let the oppression we have experienced and the obstacles in our path convince us that transformation is not possible. Twenty years is a long time to live in fear of Sisera's army, as it were. . . . We are called to trust God's voice despite the obstacles that loom large in front of us.

WM. MARCUS SMALL

Psalm 90:1–8 (9–11), 12

Even the most righteous among us live lives marked by sin, both overt and secret. We deserve God's wrath. Yet the psalmist, in asking God to teach us to count our days so that we might gain wisdom, reassures us that despite all of this, our relationship with God endures.

KIMBERLY BRACKEN LONG

Matthew 25:14–30

If the talents are God's grace, it is given to be multiplied. Paradoxically, sharing grace with those around us yields more. Grace multiplies to the recipient, for others, and with God's abundance. The burying of grace results in a diminution of it; concealing it results in rejection.

KATE OTT

WHAT IS THE HOLY SPIRIT SAYING TO YOU THIS WEEK?

_____

_____

_____

_____

_____

A SPIRITUAL PRACTICE FOR THIS WEEK

On some paper, write down a talent you have been burying—or, reading the parable differently, the name of a corrupt "master" abusing your community. "Bury" it inside a box or container. Pray for Christ's guidance. "Unbury" the paper at the end of the week and reflect on what God is calling you to do about it.

First Reading

Judges 4:1–7

[Deborah] sent and summoned Barak son of Abinoam from Kedesh in Naphtali, and said to him, "The LORD, the God of Israel, commands you, 'Go, take position at Mount Tabor, bringing ten thousand from the tribe of Naphtali and the tribe of Zebulun.'" (v. 6)

REFLECTION

Sometimes we can be dealing with challenges for so long that we can begin to see them as foregone conclusions. . . . The armies we face in our minds have been there for a long time, and we may believe that our adversaries are invincible. . . . [Other people] can tell us about the possibilities with God on our side, but often we are too intimidated to try. . . . The power that would cause Barak to be victorious would not come from the ten thousand soldiers with him; Barak's victory would come from the divine Warrior who fights alongside the covenant people (see vv. 15, 23).

WM. MARCUS SMALL

RESPONSE

What are some of the long-standing challenges or adversaries you face in your mind? Have any of them come to seem invincible? Do you see yourself in Barak? Do you have a Deborah in your life? How may God already be fighting alongside you?

PRAYER

Lord God of hosts, you fought alongside your people of the covenant; show me what could it mean that you are on my side and by my side in my own inner battles. Amen.

Canticle

Psalm 123

So our eyes look to the LORD our God,
   until he has mercy upon us.
Have mercy upon us, O LORD, have mercy upon us,
   for we have had more than enough of contempt. (vv. 2b–3)

REFLECTION

We know that the people of God *do* survive, for even in the worst of
times, God is steadfastly faithful. On this last Sunday before Reign of
Christ/Christ the King, we sing Psalm 123 along with our ancestors,
beseeching God to grant relief to those who have suffered for so long.
Even as we hear the warnings of Matthew's parable as we anticipate
the judgment of God, we do not fear. For, as the writer of the epistle
reminds us, "God has destined us not for wrath but for obtaining
salvation through our Lord Jesus Christ" (1 Thess. 5:9).

KIMBERLY BRACKEN LONG

RESPONSE

What situations in your life or the news are giving you feelings of
hopelessness or doom this week? In what ways are you afraid of God's
scrutiny or judgment? Pray this psalm, perhaps aloud, and see what
words you notice. How might God be inviting you to hope, and not to
be afraid?

PRAYER

Merciful God, my eyes look to you, for I have had enough of contempt;
give me hope and assurance that you have created me not for wrath, but
for salvation in Christ. Amen.

Second Reading

1 Thessalonians 5:1–11

When they say, "There is peace and security," then sudden destruction will come upon them, as labor pains come upon a pregnant woman, and there will be no escape! But you, beloved, are not in darkness, for that day to surprise you like a thief. (vv. 3–4)

REFLECTION

A primary concern for these new believers is the question of the end times. . . . Engaging the metaphor used by Jesus (Matt. 24:43–44; Luke 12:39), Paul reminds them that "the day" will happen when it is not expected. . . .

. . . [Paul] is also aware of the political propaganda of the imperial Roman government, promising "peace and security" to residents of the empire, which could withstand any problem.[1] Countering the claims of such powers, Paul reaffirms that there is no power that can stand against the "breaking in" of God's kingdom, a teaching important across the centuries.

RUTH FAITH SANTANA-GRACE

RESPONSE

What are some ways you try to ensure future "peace and security" for yourself and your household? What are some "powers of empire" that you rely on? What does it mean to you this week that no power can stand against God's kingdom breaking in? Is this reassuring? Or frightening?

PRAYER

Savior Jesus Christ, your kingdom will break into our world and change everything; give me faith and trust that in you we have nothing to secure against, except love and justice, breaking in. Amen.

---

1. N. T. Wright, *Paul for Everyone: Galatians and Thessalonians* (Louisville, KY: Westminster John Knox, 2002), 128.

Gospel

Matthew 25:14–30

"For to all those who have, more will be given, and they will have an abundance; but from those who have nothing, even what they have will be taken away. As for this worthless slave, throw him into the outer darkness, where there will be weeping and gnashing of teeth." (vv. 29–30)

REFLECTION

We might assume the master is Jesus, due to his title, but the harsh behavior of the master toward the third slave makes this association somewhat dubious. Maybe the third slave is Jesus, exposing the reality of the system. If so, [we] could address the question about which character in this story might represent Jesus and why. . . . After all, Jesus was known for addressing economic injustice, overturning tables, and tossing out the money changers in the temple (Matt. 21).

The third slave points out that the slaves were asked to do the master's work for him without the promise of any return.

LAURA MARIKO CHEIFETZ

RESPONSE

What do you notice when you read this story, imagining the third slave as Christ? (Perhaps reread Philippians 2:5–11, to reflect on this further.) What do you admire about this slave? Do you see yourself in him, in any way? Who do the other slaves remind you of?

PRAYER

Lord Jesus Christ, you too were buried in the ground, then rose again to eternal life; help me speak truth to power and bury anything that has become a weapon, even if I must face terrible consequences. Amen.

Weekend Reflections

FURTHER CONNECTION

The hero of the parable is the third servant. By digging a hole and
burying the aristocrat's talent in the ground, he has taken it out of
circulation. . . . When the hero speaks, he utters in the full light of
day what he has learned in the dark, . . . [he] proclaims clearly what
has only been whispered among the elites and their retainers (cf. Matt.
10:26–27). He describes the master for what he is and acknowledges his
fear of his power. The whistle-blower is no fool. He realizes that he will
pay a price, but he has decided to accept the cost rather than continue
to pursue his exploitive path.

WILLIAM R. HERZOG II (1944–2019), *PARABLES AS SUBVERSIVE
SPEECH: JESUS AS PEDAGOGUE OF THE OPPRESSED*

MAKING THE CONNECTIONS

Choose one or two questions for reflection:

1. What connections have you noticed between this week's texts and
   other passages in Scripture?

2. What connections have you made between this week's texts and the
   world beyond Scripture?

3. Does either of this week's two commentary themes speak especially
   to your life or the life of the world around you right now?

4. What is God saying to your congregation in particular through this
   week's readings and commentaries?

_____

_____

_____

_____

_____

_____

Sabbath Day

SCRIPTURE OF ASSURANCE

And let us consider how to provoke one another to love and good deeds, not neglecting to meet together, as is the habit of some, but encouraging one another, and all the more as you see the Day approaching. (Hebrews 10:24–25)

WEEKLY EXAMEN

- Take a quiet moment, seek out God's presence, and pray for the guidance of the Spirit.

- Consider the past week; recall specific moments and feelings that stand out to you.

- Choose one moment or feeling for deeper examination, thanksgiving, or repentance.

- Let go, breathe deeply, and invite Christ's love to surround and fill you in preparation for the week ahead.

- End with the Lord's Prayer.

The Week Leading Up to
Proper 29

(Reign of Christ)

Ezekiel 34:11–16, 20–24

Therefore, thus says the Lord God to them: I myself will judge between the fat sheep and the lean sheep. Because you pushed with flank and shoulder, and butted at all the weak animals with your horns until you scattered them far and wide, I will save my flock, and they shall no longer be ravaged; and I will judge between sheep and sheep. (vv. 20–22)

Psalm 95:1–7a and Psalm 100

For the Lord is good;
  his steadfast love endures forever,
  and his faithfulness to all generations. (100:5)

Ephesians 1:15–23

God put this power to work in Christ when he raised him from the dead and seated him at his right hand in the heavenly places, far above all rule and authority and power and dominion, and above every name that is named, not only in this age but also in the age to come. (vv. 20–21)

Matthew 25:31–46

"'When was it that we saw you a stranger and welcomed you, or naked and gave you clothing? And when was it that we saw you sick or in prison and visited you?' And the king will answer them, 'Truly I tell you, just as you did it to one of the least of these who are members of my family, you did it to me.'" (vv. 38–40)

LECTIO DIVINA

Underline a word or phrase that especially grabs your attention. Pray from that word or phrase and ask God to help you connect to its particular invitation for you this week.

Themes from This Week's Writers

THEME 1: *What Will the Reign of Christ Be Like?*

Ezekiel 34:11–16, 20–24

The divine shepherd is not just restoring the community from the trauma of exile. God is also creating a set of values and principles that will enhance the welfare of the community from within. The focus is on protecting weak sheep from powerful ones.

KENNETH N. NGWA

Ephesians 1:15–23

God's grace has birthed a new humanity (2:16) to which both Jews and Gentiles belong as one family, echoing familiar themes found in Paul's letters to the Galatians (Gal. 3:28–29) and the Corinthians (1 Cor. 12:12–13), in which barriers of race, culture, and social status are removed.

RUTH FAITH SANTANA-GRACE

Matthew 25:31–46

The God incarnate, Jesus, will be gone, but his presence will be experienced in a new way. Whenever we help a fellow human, we are helping Jesus. This changes the popular adage "What would Jesus do?" to "Do I recognize Jesus in you?"

KATE OTT

THEME 2: *What Does God Ask of Us in the Meantime?*

Ezekiel 34:11–16, 20–24

God still speaks up—through you and me—on behalf of those who are pushed to the side. God has a place for those who seem to be left on the margins, forgotten, or just plain ignored. God has a plan for all of God's flock; no one is dispensable to God.

WM. MARCUS SMALL

Ephesians 1:15–23

The lived reality of following Jesus takes on new and dramatic meaning. Yes, we use our hands and feet—the body of Christ—to feed the hungry and house the homeless and clothe the poor. Also, if we are to take Ephesians seriously, we must challenge the very powers that oppose the way of God.

LEE HULL MOSES

Matthew 25:31–46

While in the preceding chapter we learn that we do not know the hour or the day, we face no uncertainty about what we are to do in the meantime.

LAURA MARIKO CHEIFETZ

WHAT IS THE HOLY SPIRIT SAYING TO YOU THIS WEEK?

_____

_____

_____

_____

_____

A SPIRITUAL PRACTICE FOR THIS WEEK

The acts of service in Matthew 25 are sometimes called the Corporal Works of Mercy. This week, plan to offer a work of mercy to someone who is "the least of my family." What is it like to seek to meet Jesus instead of just trying to do a good deed?

First Reading

I myself will be the shepherd of my sheep, and I will make them lie down, says the Lord GOD. I will seek the lost, and I will bring back the strayed, and I will bind up the injured, and I will strengthen the weak, but the fat and the strong I will destroy. I will feed them with justice. (vv. 15–16)

REFLECTION

Deliverance . . . is premised on the divine virtue of justice that rectifies the imbalance between the well-to-do and the poor. Righteous and just shepherding (v. 16) is the virtue around which prophetic proclamation and leadership converge. Justice and righteousness manifest themselves as life in solidarity with the marginalized, rather than *right relationship* within the existing status quo. It requires more than sympathetic patronage to effect spiritual and social transformation.

. . . The divine shepherd is not just restoring the community from the trauma of exile. God is also creating a set of values and principles that will enhance the welfare of the community from within.

KENNETH N. NGWA

RESPONSE

How does this shepherd resemble the shepherd of Psalm 23? How is this shepherd different? What values and principles do you most long to see changed in your community, that would "enhance it from within"? How might God be calling you to join the work of this shepherd?

PRAYER

O Lord, our shepherd, you see how your sheep are treating one another; seek us out, save and heal us, then feed us with justice and teach us to transform the flock. Amen.

Canticle

Psalm 95:1–7a

For the LORD is a great God,
　　and a great King above all gods.
In his hand are the depths of the earth;
　　the heights of the mountains are his also. (vv. 3–4)

REFLECTION

God is lauded as the greatest of all gods and likened to a king (v. 3). . . .
God holds the entire cosmos in divine hands: earth's lowest depths and
its highest heights, both the dry land and the sea (vv. 4–5). God has
made all of creation, including the people of the earth, and this is reason
enough to worship. Yet the people do not worship a God who reigns
from some lofty throne; rather, this God is like a shepherd to them,
giving them shelter and care, and they are like God's sheep.

KIMBERLY BRACKEN LONG

RESPONSE

This week, what are some ways you have noticed the grandeur of God in
the world around you? What are some ways you have noticed God, close
at hand, shepherding you? How do these things offer you a glimpse of
the reality, already and not yet, of the Reign of Christ?

PRAYER

Gracious God, you are majestic like a king and gentle like a shepherd;
we are your people and the sheep of your pasture. O that today we
would listen to your voice! Amen.

Second Reading

Ephesians 1:15–23

I have heard of your faith in the Lord Jesus and your love toward all the saints, and for this reason I do not cease to give thanks for you as I remember you in my prayers. I pray that the God of our Lord Jesus Christ, the Father of glory, may give you a spirit of wisdom and revelation as you come to know him. (vv. 15–17)

REFLECTION

The poetic language . . . brings to mind the language of liturgies and hymns, or the lofty vocabulary of one recently in love. We might even think of Ephesians as a love letter to the body of Christ, flowing from gratitude to adoration to inspiration. Could the preacher take a cue from the lyrical tone of Ephesians and craft her own love letter to her congregation, or to the church at large?

. . . Who are the saints we have loved? For what or whom do we give thanks without ceasing? How does our lived faithfulness express our gratitude for what we have been given?

LEE HULL MOSES

RESPONSE

Write a love letter to the body of Christ: your congregation or the church at large. Copy the style of Ephesians or write in another style of your choosing. Use Moses's questions, above, to help you, or simply write from "gratitude to adoration to inspiration."

PRAYER

Loving Christ, I remember in my prayers and give thanks to you for my faith community; give us a spirit of wisdom and revelation as we come to know you, more and more, together. Amen.

Gospel

Matthew 25:31–46

"Then he will answer them, 'Truly I tell you, just as you did not do it to one of the least of these, you did not do it to me.' And these will go away into eternal punishment, but the righteous into eternal life." (vv. 45–46)

REFLECTION

For a newly forming Christian community awaiting the imminent return of Jesus—the Parousia—the passage is direct and clear. The God incarnate, Jesus, will be gone, but his presence will be experienced in a new way. Whenever we help a fellow human, we are helping Jesus. This changes the popular adage "What would Jesus do?" to "Do I recognize Jesus in you?" . . . There are specific and significant actions one must take in response to specific individuals in order to show one's faithfulness for eternal life (Matt. 25:46).

KATE OTT

RESPONSE

What is the difference, would you say, between asking "What would Jesus do?" and "Do I recognize Jesus in you?" How have you experienced the presence of Jesus in someone you have helped, rather than in someone who has helped you?

PRAYER

O Jesus Christ, the upside-down king, you call me to see and serve you in the stranger, the naked, the sick, and the prisoner; teach me to recognize you, so I do not lose sight or hope of you and your kingdom. Amen.

Weekend Reflections

FURTHER CONNECTION

As the years have gone by, I have accepted that for me to strive to live to the fullest by struggling against injustice is to draw nearer and nearer to the divine. Drawing closer to God and struggling for justice have become for me one and the same thing. . . .

Following the example of grassroots Hispanic women, I do not think in terms of "spirituality." But I know myself as a person with a deep relationship with the divine, a relationship that finds expression . . . in striving to be passionately involved with others more than in being detached.

ADA MARÍA ISASI-DÍAZ (1943–2021), *MUJERISTA THEOLOGY*

MAKING THE CONNECTIONS

Choose one or two questions for reflection:

1. What connections have you noticed between this week's texts and other passages in Scripture?

2. What connections have you made between this week's texts and the world beyond Scripture?

3. Does either of this week's two commentary themes speak especially to your life or the life of the world around you right now?

4. What is God saying to your congregation in particular through this week's readings and commentaries?

_____

_____

_____

_____

_____

_____

Sabbath Day

SCRIPTURE OF ASSURANCE

So you have pain now; but I will see you again, and your hearts will rejoice, and no one will take your joy from you. (John 16:22)

WEEKLY EXAMEN

- Take a quiet moment, seek out God's presence, and pray for the guidance of the Spirit.

- Consider the past week; recall specific moments and feelings that stand out to you.

- Choose one moment or feeling for deeper examination, thanksgiving, or repentance.

- Let go, breathe deeply, and invite Christ's love to surround and fill you in preparation for the week ahead.

- End with the Lord's Prayer.

A Suggested Format
for Small Groups

This book was designed to be used primarily by individuals but can also be the basis for shared study by a Bible study, a sermon group, or any small group. A group session can last one to two hours, depending on the size of the group and which options you choose. Feel free to experiment and tweak the suggestions to make a format that works for your group.

A group meeting on Sundays would easily match the rhythm of the weekly readings, but any day of the week can work. A group might choose to discuss the readings and passages of the past week or the upcoming week.

1. Opening
   Start in one or more of these ways:
   a. A minute of silence
   b. The sound of a singing bowl or bell
   c. An extemporaneous prayer
   d. Any other sign or mark of beginning
2. Introductions
   If introductions need to be made, invite each person to share:
   a. Their name
   b. A personal detail or two
   c. What brought them to join the group or why they keep coming back
3. Discussion Part 1
   Proceed in one or more of these ways:
   a. Discuss Themes from This Week's Writers. What theme resonates most? What commentary quotes stand out? How might the Spirit be speaking to your life or congregation?
   b. Discuss the Spiritual Practice: Who was able to try it? How did the Holy Spirit speak to you through this practice?
   c. Discuss the readings. Choose two or do all four. One person reads aloud the Scripture passage in its entirety from a Bible,

another reads aloud the commentary quote and the response
questions, then all discuss. Close each discussion with that
entry's prayer, said by one person or in unison.

4. Discussion Part 2

   Continue in one of these ways:

   a. Read aloud the Further Connection quote, then discuss
      intersections with the themes and Scripture from the past week,
      and any other outside connections you have noticed.

   b. Choose one or two of the questions from Making the
      Connections and discuss.

5. Closing

   Close in one or more of these ways:

   a. Invite each person to share one word that they are taking away
      from the gathering.

   b. Share briefly in the Weekly Examen (found in each Sabbath
      Day entry).

   c. Read aloud the Scripture quotes from the first page for next
      week.

   d. Ask one person to close the session with a prayer.

Sources of
Further Connections

Berkovits, Eliezer. *With God in Hell: Judaism in the Ghettos and Deathcamps,* 124. New York: Sanhedrin, 1979. *Proper 8*

Berrigan, Daniel. *Sorrow Built a Bridge: Friendship and AIDS,* 230–31. Baltimore: Fortkamp, 1989. *Proper 15*

Bloom, Anthony. *God and Man,* 84–85. New York: Paulist Press, 1971. *Proper 25*

Blue, Debbie. *From Stone to Living Word: Letting the Bible Live Again,* 214. Grand Rapids: Brazos Press, 2008. *Proper 13*

Bolz-Weber, Nadia. *Accidental Saints: Finding God in All the Wrong People,* 47. New York: Convergent Books, 2015. *Proper 26*

Bonhoeffer, Dietrich. *The Cost of Discipleship,* 99. Translated by R. H. Fuller. New York: Macmillan, 1961. First published 1937, in German. *Lent 5*

Boss, Gayle. *All Creation Waits: The Advent Mystery of New Beginnings,* xiii. Brewster, MA: Paraclete Press, 2016. *Advent 2*

Brock, Rita Nakashima, and Rebecca Ann Parker. *Saving Paradise: How Christianity Traded Love of This World for Crucifixion and Empire,* 44. Boston: Beacon Press, 2007. *Lent 3*

Brueggemann, Walter. *Genesis: A Bible Commentary for Preaching and Teaching,* 118. Louisville, KY: John Knox Press, 1982. *Lent 2*

Buechner, Frederick. *Wishful Thinking: A Seeker's ABC,* 118–19. San Francisco: HarperOne, 1993. *Proper 17*

Camara, Dom Helder. *Through the Gospel with Dom Helder Camara.* Quoted in *Dom Helder Camara: Essential Writings,* 152–53. Maryknoll, NY: Orbis, 2009. First published in 1986, translated by Alan Neame. *Easter 4*

Catherine of Siena. *The Dialogue,* translated by Suzanne Noffke. Quoted in *A Little Daily Wisdom: Christian Women Mystics,* edited by Carmen Acevedo Butcher, 284. Brewster, MA: Paraclete Press, 2012. *Christmas Week*

Charleston, Steven. *Ladder to the Light: An Indigenous Elder's Meditations on Hope and Courage,* 1. Minneapolis: Broadleaf Books, 2021. *Lent 1*

Chesterton, G. K. "The Eye of Apollo." In *The Complete Father Brown Stories*, 137. London: Penguin, 2012. *Proper 5*

Chittister, Joan. *The Rule of Benedict: A Spirituality for the 21st Century*, 95. New York: Crossroad Publishing, 2010. First published 1992. *Proper 21*

Claiborne, Shane. *The Irresistible Revolution: Living as an Ordinary Radical*, 113. Grand Rapids: Zondervan, 2006. *Epiphany 8/Proper 3*

Curtice, Kaitlin. *Native: Identity, Belonging, and Rediscovering God*, 88–89. Grand Rapids: Brazos Press, 2020. *All Saints*

Day, Dorothy. *The Long Loneliness: The Autobiography of the Legendary Catholic Social Activist*, 285. San Francisco: HarperCollins, 1997. First published 1952. *Easter 3*

Desert Fathers. Traditional saying, quoted in Thomas Merton, *The Wisdom of the Desert*, 50. New York: New Directions Books, 1960. *Epiphany 7*

Dillard, Annie. "God in the Doorway." In *Teaching a Stone to Talk: Expeditions and Encounters*, 141. New York: Harper & Row, 1982. *Christmas 2*

Douglas, Kelly Brown. *Stand Your Ground: Black Bodies and the Justice of God*, 184. New York: Orbis, 2015. *Easter/Resurrection of the Lord*

Eliot, George. *Middlemarch*, 896. New York: Penguin, 1965. First published 1871. *Epiphany 4*

Francis I. "*Patris Corde* (With a Father's Heart): On the 150th Anniversary of the Proclamation of Saint Joseph as Patron of the Universal Church." The Holy See, December 8, 2020. https://www.vatican.va/content/francesco/en/apost_letters/documents/papa-francesco-lettera-ap_20201208_patris-corde.html. *Advent 4*

Gafney, Wilda. *Womanist Midrash: A Reintroduction to the Women of the Torah and the Throne*, 91. Louisville, KY: Westminster John Knox, 2017. *Proper 16*

Hanh, Thich Nhat. *The Art of Communicating*, 53. New York: HarperOne, 2013. *Proper 18*

Heschel, Rabbi Abraham Joshua. *Moral Grandeur and Spiritual Audacity*, 267. New York: Farrar, Straus & Giroux, 1997. *Proper 27*

Keller, Helen. *The Story of My Life*, 25. New York: Norton, 2003. First published 1903. *Lent 4*

Herzog, William R., II. *Parables as Subversive Speech: Jesus as Pedagogue of the Oppressed*, 167. Louisville, KY: Westminster John Knox, 1994. *Proper 28*

Irenaeus of Lyons. *Against the Heresies*. In *The Early Christian Fathers*, translated by Henry Bettenson, 129. London: Oxford University Press, 1963. *Baptism of the Lord*

Isasi-Díaz, Ada María. *Mujerista Theology,* 33. Maryknoll, NY: Orbis, 1996. *Reign of Christ*

Lee, Jarena. *The Life and Religious Experience of Jarena Lee.* Quoted in Anna Carter Florence, *Preaching as Testimony,* 42. Louisville KY: Westminster John Knox, 2007. *Epiphany 3*

Lee, Min Jin. *Pachinko,* 64. New York: Hachette Book Group, 2017. *Proper 9*

Levine, Amy-Jill. *Short Stories by Jesus: The Enigmatic Parables of a Controversial Rabbi,* 281. New York: HarperOne, 2014. *Proper 22*

Lewis, John. *Across That Bridge: A Vision for Change and the Future of America,* 175. New York: Hachette Books, 2012. *Epiphany 5*

Merton, Thomas. *New Seeds of Contemplation,* 14. New York: New Directions Books, 1961. *Proper 10*

Norris, Kathleen. *Amazing Grace: A Vocabulary of Faith,* 317. New York: Riverhead Books, 1998. *Proper 11*

Ó Tuama, Pádraig. "Stations of the Cross: A Reflection for Good Friday 2020." YouTube video, April 8, 2020. https://youtube/O_o90DCQ6GQ. *Palm/Passion Sunday*

Pascal, Blaise. *Pensées,* 45 (10.148). Translated by A. J. Krailsheimer. London: Penguin, 1995. First published 1966. *Proper 23*

Parker, Rebecca Ann. *See* Brock, Rita Nakashima.

Polkinghorne, John. *Living with Hope: A Scientist Looks at Advent, Christmas, and Epiphany,* 8–9. Louisville, KY: Westminster John Knox, 2003. *Advent 1*

Pope Francis. *See* Francis.

Powery, Luke. *Rise Up, Shepherd! Advent Reflections on the Spirituals,* 51. Louisville, KY: Westminster John Knox, 2017. *Advent 3*

Robinson, Marilynne. *Gilead,* 245. New York: Farrar, Straus & Giroux, 2004. *Transfiguration*

Rohr, Richard. *The Divine Dance: The Trinity and Your Transformation,* 27. With Mike Morrell. New Kensington, PA: Whitaker House, 2016. *Trinity Sunday*

Romero, Oscar. *Through the Year with Oscar Romero: Daily Meditations,* 157. Translated by Irene B. Hodgson. Cincinnati: Franciscan Media, 2005. First published 1999, in Spanish. *Proper 24*

Shillito, Edward. "Jesus of the Scars." In *How Long, O Lord? Reflections on Suffering and Evil,* by D. A. Carson, 191. Grand Rapids: Baker Books, 1990. Poem first published 1917. *Easter 2*

Stevenson, Bryan. *Just Mercy: A Story of Justice and Redemption,* 290. New York: Spiegel & Grau, 2014. *Proper 19*

Taylor, Barbara Brown. *The Seeds of Heaven: Sermons on the Gospel of Matthew*, 42. Louisville, KY: Westminster John Knox, 2004. *Proper 12*

Teresa of Ávila. *The Way of Perfection,* chapter 26, in *The Complete Works of St. Teresa of Avila*, 2:106. Translated by Allison Peers. New York: Burns & Oates, 2002. *Easter 5*

Thérèse of Lisieux. *The Story of a Soul: The Autobiography of St. Thérèse of Lisieux,* 179. Translated by John Clarke. Washington, DC: Institute for Carmelite Studies, 1996. First published 1898. *Epiphany 2*

Thurman, Howard. *Jesus and the Disinherited*, 11. Boston: Beacon Press, 1996. First published 1949, Abingdon Press. *Epiphany 6*

Truth, Sojourner. In "Sojourner Truth, the Libyan Sibyl," by Harriet Beecher Stowe. *Atlantic Monthly*, April 1863, 478. https://www.theatlantic.com/magazine/toc/1863/04/. *Proper 6*

Tutu, Desmond, and the Dalai Lama. *The Book of Joy: Lasting Happiness in a Changing World,* 263–64. New York: Penguin Random House, 2016. *Easter 6*

Twist, Lynne. *The Soul of Money*, 43–45. New York: W. W. Norton, 2017. First published 2003. *Proper 20*

Volf, Miroslav. *The End of Memory,* 26. Grand Rapids: Eerdmans, 2006. *Proper 14*

Waal, Esther de. *Seeking God: The Way of St. Benedict,* 57. Collegeville, MN: Liturgical Press, 1984. *Epiphany 9/Proper 4*

Walker-Barnes, Chanequa. *I Bring the Voices of My People: A Womanist Vision for Racial Reconciliation,* 200. Grand Rapids: Eerdmans, 2019. *Easter 7*

Williams, Delores. *Sisters in the Wilderness: The Challenge of Womanist God-Talk*, 33. Maryknoll, NY: Orbis, 2003. First published 1993. *Proper 7*

Wilson-Hartgrove, Jonathan (@wilsonhartgrove). Twitter, May 22, 2021, 10:10 p.m. https://twitter.com/wilsonhartgrove/status/1396287359600168964. *Pentecost*

Contributors

Numbers in italics are page numbers on which each contributor's reflections can be found.

CHARLES L. AARON JR., Co-Director of the Intern Program, Perkins School of Theology, Dallas, TX; *87, 95, 99, 104*. MARK ABBOTT, Director of Hispanic Distributed Learning, Asbury Theological Seminary-Florida Dunnam Campus, Orlando, FL; *59, 64, 68, 78*. EFRAÍN AGOSTO, Vice President for Academic Affairs and Academic Dean, Professor of New Testament Studies, New York Theological Seminary, New York, NY; *319, 322, 327 337*. SAMMY G. ALFARO, Professor of Theology, Grand Canyon Theological Seminary, Phoenix, AZ; *508, 517, 521, 526*. O. WESLEY ALLEN JR., Lois Craddock Perkins Professor of Homiletics, Perkins School of Theology, Southern Methodist University, Dallas, TX; *197, 198*. RONALD J. ALLEN, Professor of Preaching and New Testament, Christian Theological Seminary, Indianapolis, IN; *198*. WM. LOYD ALLEN, Professor of Church History and Spiritual Formation, McAfee School of Theology, Mercer University, Atlanta, GA; *220*. LINDSAY P. ARMSTRONG, Executive Director, New Church Development, Presbytery of Greater Atlanta, Atlanta, GA; *251, 256, 261, 270*. KIRA AUSTIN-YOUNG, Priest-in-Charge, St. Ann's Episcopal Church, Nashville, TN; *273, 287*. MARGARET P. AYMER, The First Presbyterian Church, Shreveport, Louisiana, D. Thomasen Professor of New Testament Studies, Austin Presbyterian Theological Seminary, Austin, TX; *225, 234, 247*.

KAREN BAKER-FLETCHER, Professor of Systematic Theology, Perkins School of Theology, Southern Methodist University, Dallas, TX; *427, 435, 439, 444*. ERIC D. BARRETO, Weyerhaeuser Associate Professor of New Testament, Princeton Theological Seminary, Princeton, NJ; *149, 152, 156, 161*. RHODORA E. BEATON, Associate Professor of Sacramental and Liturgical Theology, Aquinas Institute of Theology, St. Louis, MO; *227, 233, 236, 242, 245, 251, 254*. WHITNEY BODMAN, Associate Professor of Comparative Religion, Austin Presbyterian Theological Seminary, Austin, TX; *454, 463, 472, 476*. ELIZABETH M. BOUNDS, Associate Professor of Christian Ethics, Candler School of Theology, Emory University, Atlanta, GA; *454, 457, 463, 471, 475*. STEPHEN B. BOYD, J. Allen Easley Professor of Religion, Wake Forest University, Department of Religion, Winston-Salem, NC; *48, 51, 56*. GENNIFER BENJAMIN BROOKS, Ernest and Bernice Styberg Professor of Preaching, Garrett-Evangelical Theological Seminary, Evanston, IL; *400, 408, 417*. SALLY A. BROWN, Elizabeth M. Engle Associate Professor of Preaching and Worship, Princeton Theological Seminary, Princeton, NJ; *426, 430, 435, 444, 448*. JOHN M. BUCHANAN, Pastor Emeritus, Fourth Presbyterian Church, Chicago, and Retired Editor/Publisher, *The Christian Century*, Chicago, IL; *3, 6, 12, 20*.

PATRICIA J. CALAHAN, Pastor, Cornwall Presbyterian Church, Cornwall-on-Hudson, NY; *38, 41.* LEIGH CAMPBELL-TAYLOR, Interim Pastor, Covenant Presbyterian Church, Atlanta, GA; *149, 153, 155, 162, 164, 170, 173, 483, 492, 498, 501, 510.* NICK CARTER, President Emeritus, Andover Newton Theological School at Yale Divinity School, New Haven, CT; *372, 382, 385, 394.* WARREN CARTER, Professor of New Testament, Brite Divinity School at Texas Christian University, Fort Worth, TX; *214.* CHRISTINE CHAKOIAN, Vice President for Seminary Advancement, Pittsburgh Theological Seminary, Pittsburgh, PA; *114, 118, 123, 132, 141, 145.* GARY W. CHARLES, Pastor, Cove Presbyterian Church, Covesville, VA; *113, 115, 123, 131, 133, 140, 142.* LAURA MARIKO CHEIFETZ, Assistant Dean of Admissions, Vocation, and Stewardship, Vanderbilt Divinity School, Nashville, TN; *539, 544.* DIANE G. CHEN, Professor of New Testament, Palmer Theological Seminary of Eastern University, St. Davids, PA; *197, 202, 203.* JANA CHILDERS, Dean of the Seminary; Vice President for Academic Affairs, San Francisco Theological Seminary, San Anselmo, CA; *372, 374, 381, 391, 392.* JIN YOUNG CHOI, Associate Professor of New Testament and Christian Origins, Colgate Rochester Crozer Divinity School, Rochester, NY; *2, 11, 15, 24.* ANDREW FOSTER CONNORS, Pastor and Head of Staff, Brown Memorial Park Avenue Presbyterian Church, Baltimore, MD; *291, 293, 300, 309.* GREG COOTSONA, Professor of Comparative Religion and Humanities, California State University–Chico, Chico, CA; *273, 276, 281.* SHANNON CRAIGO-SNELL, Professor of Theology, Louisville Presbyterian Theological Seminary, Louisville, KY; *113, 117, 122, 131, 135, 140, 144.* JEROME F. D. CREACH, Robert C. Holland Professor of Old Testament, Pittsburgh Theological Seminary, Pittsburgh, PA; *170, 179, 183, 188.*

DAVID A. DAVIS, Pastor, Nassau Presbyterian Church, Princeton, NJ; *2, 4, 11, 20, 22.* MIGUEL A. DE LA TORRE, Professor of Social Ethics and Latinx Studies, Iliff School of Theology, Denver, CO; *480, 482, 489, 498, 500.* CAROL J. DEMPSEY, OP, Professor of Theology: Biblical Studies, Department of Theology, University of Portland, Portland, OR; *481, 490, 493, 499, 502.* JOSEPH A. DONNELLA II, Pastor, St. Mark's Lutheran Church, Baltimore, MD; *50, 56.* MINDY DOUGLAS, Pastor and Head of Staff, First Presbyterian Church, Durham, NC; *400, 408, 412, 418, 421.* SHARYN DOWD, Baptist Pastor, Decatur, GA; *29.* SARAH BIRMINGHAM DRUMMOND, Dean and Professor of Ministerial Leadership, Andover Newton Seminary at Yale Divinity School, New Haven, CT; *152, 161, 165.* JILL DUFFIELD, Editor, *The Presbyterian Outlook*, Richmond, VA; *48, 52.*

SUSAN GROVE EASTMAN, Associate Research Professor of New Testament, Duke Divinity School, Durham, NC; *399, 403, 409, 417.* JAMES H. EVANS JR., Robert K. Davies Professor Emeritus of Systematic Theology and President Emeritus, Colgate Rochester Crozer Divinity School, Rochester, NY; *59, 68, 70, 77, 79.* KEN EVERS-HOOD, Pastor, Tualatin Presbyterian Church, Tualatin, OR; *86, 88, 95, 104.*

WENDY FARLEY, Rice Family Chair of Spirituality, San Francisco Theological Seminary Graduate School of Theology, Redlands University, San Anselmo, CA; *372, 376, 381, 390.* STEPHEN FARRIS, Professor Emeritus of Preaching and Dean Emeritus,

Vancouver School of Theology and St. Andrew's Hall, Vancouver, British Columbia; *60, 63, 68, 77.* ELIZABETH FELICETTI, Rector, St. David's Episcopal Church, Richmond, VA; *507, 509, 516, 525, 527.* JANE ANNE FERGUSON, Associate Minister, Plymouth Congregational Church, Fort Collins, CO; *170, 172, 179, 188.* MARY F. FOSKETT, Wake Forest Kahle Professor of Religious Studies and Albritton Fellow, Department for the Study of Religions, Wake Forest University, Winston-Salem, NC; *292, 301, 305, 310, 314.* JAMES D. FREEMAN, Pastor, Broadmoor Presbyterian Church, Shreveport, LA; *29, 31.* RENATA FURST, Associate Professor of Scripture and Spirituality, Oblate School of Theology, San Antonio, TX; *346, 349, 354, 363.*

LINCOLN E. GALLOWAY, K. Morgan Edwards Associate Professor of Homiletics, Claremont School of Theology, Claremont, CA; *426, 435, 444, 446.* DAVID GAMBRELL, Associate for Worship, Office of Theology and Worship, Presbyterian Church (U.S.A.), Louisville, KY; *207, 210, 213, 216.* DAVID G. GARBER JR., Associate Professor of Old Testament and Hebrew, McAfee School of Theology, Mercer University, Atlanta, GA; *152, 163.* TOMMY GIVENS, Professor of New Testament Studies, Fuller Theological Seminary, Pasadena, CA; *114, 123, 127, 131, 136, 141.* DONNA GIVER-JOHNSTON, Pastor, Community Presbyterian Church of Ben Avon, Pittsburgh, PA; *456, 462, 465, 474.* MARCI AULD GLASS, Pastor, Southminster Presbyterian Church, Boise, ID; *2, 5, 14, 23, 30, 32.* DEIRDRE J. GOOD, Faculty of the Stevenson School for Ministry (Diocese of Central PA), Harrisburg, PA; *42.* BRIDGETT A. GREEN, Vice President of Editorial, Westminster John Knox Press, Louisville, KY; *251, 253, 260, 269.*

W. SCOTT HALDEMAN, Associate Professor of Worship, Chicago Theological Seminary, Chicago, IL; *150, 153, 162, 166, 321, 330, 339.* ANGELA DIENHART HANCOCK, Associate Professor of Homiletics and Worship, Pittsburgh Theological Seminary, Pittsburgh, PA; *373, 375, 384, 390, 393.* HEIDI HAVERKAMP, Author, Episcopal priest, Indianapolis, IN; *272, 285.* CAROLYN BROWNING HELSEL, Assistant Professor of Homiletics, Austin Presbyterian Theological Seminary, Austin, TX; *113, 124, 140.* SARAH S. HENRICH, Professor Emerita, Luther Seminary; Pastor, Atonement Lutheran Church, St. Paul, MN; *292, 295, 300, 310.* MARTHA C. HIGHSMITH, Pastor, McClure Memorial Presbyterian Church, Castle Hayne, NC; *273, 277, 282.* ELIZABETH HINSON-HASTY, Professor of Theology, Bellarmine University, Louisville, KY; *381, 383, 390.* JOHN C. HOLBERT, Lois Craddock Perkins Professor Emeritus of Homiletics, Perkins School of Theology, Southern Methodist University, Dallas, TX; *59, 61, 68, 77, 215.* CHRISTOPHER T. HOLMES, Director of Curriculum Development, Johnson C. Smith Theological Seminary, Atlanta, GA; *87, 96, 105, 109.* SALLY SMITH HOLT, Professor of Religion, Belmont University College of Theology and Christian Ministry, Nashville, TN; *39.* CHRISTINE J. HONG, Assistant Professor of Educational Ministry, Columbia Theological Seminary, Decatur, GA; *39.* PAUL K. HOOKER, Associate Dean for Ministerial Formation and Advanced Studies, Austin Presbyterian Theological Seminary, Austin, TX; *40.* CATHY CALDWELL HOOP, Pastor, Grace Presbyterian Church, Tuscaloosa, AL; *210, 214, 217.* CAMERON B. R. HOWARD, Associate Professor of Old Testament, Luther Seminary, St. Paul, MN; *149, 154, 161.* JAMES C. HOWELL, Senior Pastor, Myers Park United Methodist

Church, Charlotte, NC; *210, 213*. EDITH M. HUMPHREY, William F. Orr Professor of New Testament, Pittsburgh Theological Seminary, Pittsburgh, PA; *213, 218*.

LYNN JAPINGA, Professor of Religion, Hope College, Holland, MI; *291, 300, 302, 309, 311*. CYNTHIA A. JARVIS, Minister and Head of Staff, The Presbyterian Church of Chestnut Hill, Philadelphia, PA; *453, 463, 466, 471*. PATRICK W. T. JOHNSON, Pastor, First Presbyterian Church, Asheville, NC; *355, 358*. ARUN W. JONES, Dan and Lillian Hankey Associate Professor of World Evangelism; Director of the Master of Theology Program, Candler School of Theology, Emory University, Atlanta, GA; *508, 516, 520, 526*. L. SHANNON JUNG, Cole Professor Emeritus of Town and Country Ministry, Saint Paul School of Theology, Overland Park, KS; *281*.

JOHN KALTNER, Virginia Ballou McGehee Professor of Muslim-Christian Relations, Department of Religious Studies, Rhodes College, Memphis, TN; *401, 409, 417*. CRAIG S. KEENER, F. M. and Ada Thompson Professor of Biblical Studies, Asbury Theological Seminary, Wilmore, KY; *282, 286*. ERIN KEYS, Minister, Capitol Hill Presbyterian Church, Washington, DC; *62, 71, 80*. MIHEE KIMKORT, PhD student in Religious Studies, Indiana University, Bloomington, IN; *346, 355, 359, 364*. ERICA KNISELY, Director of Programs for Education Beyond the Walls, Austin Presbyterian Theological Seminary, Austin, TX; *38*.

MICHAEL E. LEE, Associate Professor of Theology, Fordham University Theology Department, Bronx, NY; *481, 485, 489, 503*. JOEL MARCUS LEMON, Associate Professor of Old Testament; Director of the Graduate Division of Religion, Candler School of Theology, Emory University, Atlanta, GA; *291, 294, 303, 309, 312*. RAQUEL ST. CLAIR LETTSOME, Associate Minister, Union African Methodist Episcopal Church, Warwick, NY; *427, 431, 436, 440, 445*. KAROLINE M. LEWIS, Associate Professor of Biblical Preaching and The Marbury E. Anderson Chair in Biblical Preaching, Luther Seminary, St. Paul, MN; *224, 226, 233, 242, 244*. MICHAEL L. LINDVALL, Pastor Emeritus, Brick Presbyterian Church in the City of New York, New York, NY; *171, 184, 189*. MICHAEL LODAHL, Professor of Theology and World Religions, Point Loma Nazarene University, San Diego, CA; *113, 126, 132*. KIMBERLY BRACKEN LONG, Editor, *Call to Worship*, Presbyterian Church (U.S.A.), Louisville, KY; *519, 525, 528, 535, 537, 546*. THOMAS G. LONG, Bandy Professor Emeritus of Preaching, Candler School of Theology, Emory University, Atlanta, GA; *208, 219*. JENNIFER L. LORD, The Dorothy B. Vickery Professor of Homiletics and Liturgical Studies, Austin Presbyterian Theological Seminary, Austin, TX; *272, 274, 281*.

HUGO MAGALLANES, Associate Professor of Christianity and Cultures, Perkins School of Theology, Southern Methodist University, Dallas, TX; *399, 408, 410, 419*. J. CLINTON MCCANN JR., Evangelical Professor of Biblical Interpretation, Eden Theological Seminary, St. Louis, MO; *345, 348, 354, 357, 363, 366*. IAN A. MCFARLAND, Regius Professor of Divinity, University of Cambridge, Cambridge, UK; *224, 233, 235, 242*. SCOT MCKNIGHT, Professor of New Testament, Northern Seminary, Lombard, IL; *87, 90, 95, 105, 108*. TROY A. MILLER, Vice President for Academic

Affairs, Memphis Center for Urban and Theological Studies, Memphis, TN; *480, 484, 490, 498.* AIMEE MOISO, Associate Director, Louisville Institute, Louisville, KY; *508, 512, 517, 526, 530.* SHAWNTHEA MONROE, Senior Pastor, Plymouth Church (UCC) at Shaker Heights, Cleveland, OH; *453, 458, 467, 472.* LEE HULL MOSES, Senior Minister, First Christian Church (Disciples of Christ), Greensboro, NC; *534, 544, 547.* D. CAMERON MURCHISON, Professor Emeritus, Columbia Theological Seminary, Decatur, GA; *364, 367.* ERIC TODD MYERS, Pastor, Frederick Presbyterian Church, Frederick, MD; *86, 89, 95, 98, 104, 107.*

RAJ NADELLA, Assistant Professor of New Testament, Columbia Theological Seminary, Decatur, GA; *3, 12, 16, 21.* ANDREW NAGYBENSON, Pastor, Congregational Church of Middlebury, Middlebury, VT; *175, 180, 189, 193.* KENNETH N. NGWA, Associate Professor of Hebrew Bible, Drew University Theological School, Madison, NJ; *534, 543, 545.* PAUL T. NIMMO, King's Chair of Systematic Theology, University of Aberdeen, Aberdeen, Scotland; *291, 300, 304, 313.*

ANNA OLSON, Rector, St. Mary's Episcopal Church, Los Angeles, CA; *30, 33.* KATE OTT, Associate Professor of Christian Social Ethics, Drew University Theological School, Madison, NJ; *535, 543, 548.*

ALVIN PADILLA, Academic Dean and Vice President of Academic Affairs, Western Theological Seminary, Holland, MI; *507, 511, 516, 529.* LANCE PAPE, Granville and Erline Walker Associate Professor of Homiletics, Brite Divinity School, Texas Christian University, Fort Worth, TX; *399, 404, 409, 413, 418, 422.* SONG-MI SUZIE PARK, Associate Professor of Old Testament, Austin Presbyterian Theological Seminary, Austin, TX; *47, 49, 56, 318, 320, 327, 336, 338.* MIKEAL C. PARSONS, Professor and Macon Chair in Religion, Baylor University, Waco, TX; *153, 157, 162.* MICHAEL PASQUARELLO III, Beeson Professor of Methodist Divinity, Beeson Divinity School, Samford University, Birmingham, AL; *373, 382, 386, 391.* JULIE PEEPLES, Senior Minister, Congregational United Church of Christ, Greensboro, NC; *201, 207.* ZAIDA MALDONADO PÉREZ, Professor Emerita of Church History and Theology, Asbury Theological Seminary, Clermont, FL; *91, 96, 100.* ANATHEA E. PORTIER-YOUNG, Associate Professor of Old Testament, Duke Divinity School, Durham, NC; *453, 455, 462, 471.* BRIAN S. POWERS, Bernard William Vann Fellow in Christianity and the Military, The Michael Ramsey Centre for Anglican Studies, Durham University, Durham, UK; *255, 261.* EMERSON B. POWERY, Professor of Biblical Studies, Messiah College, Department of Biblical and Religious Studies, Mechanicsburg, PA; *26, 30.* SALLY B. PURVIS, Retired Minister, Lakewood United Church of Christ, St. Petersburg, FL; *171, 174, 180, 192.*

MARK RALLS, Senior Pastor, First United Methodist Church, Hendersonville, NC; *47.* MARK RAMSEY, Executive Director, Macedonian Ministry, Atlanta, GA; *318, 327, 329, 336.* GAIL RAMSHAW, Professor Emerita of Religion, La Salle University, Philadelphia, PA; *116, 122, 125, 131, 134, 140, 143, 260, 263, 269.* ROBERT A. RATCLIFF, Editor-in-Chief, Westminster John Knox Press, Louisville, KY; *347, 354,*

356, 363. STEPHEN BRECK REID, Professor of Christian Scriptures, George W. Truett Seminary, Baylor University, Waco, TX; *345, 365.* WYNDY CORBIN REUSCHLING, Professor of Ethics and Theology, Ashland Theological Seminary, Ashland, OH; *318, 328, 331, 336, 340.* RON RIENSTRA, Professor of Preaching and Worship Arts, Western Theological Seminary, Holland, MI; *429, 438, 444, 447.* CYNTHIA L. RIGBY, W. C. Brown Professor of Theology, Austin Presbyterian Theological Seminary, Austin, TX; *225, 237, 242.* RUBÉN ROSARIO RODRÍGUEZ, Associate Professor of Systematic Theology, Saint Louis University, St. Louis, MO; *224, 229, 234, 238, 243.* BRIAN D. RUSSELL, Professor of Biblical Studies and Dean of the School of Urban Ministries, Asbury Theological Seminary, Orlando, FL; *480, 489, 491, 498.*

RUTH FAITH SANTANA-GRACE, Executive Presbyter, Presbytery of Philadelphia, Philadelphia, PA; *534, 538, 543.* STANLEY P. SAUNDERS, Associate Professor of New Testament, Columbia Theological Seminary, Decatur, GA; *60, 69, 73, 78, 82.* PAMELA J. SCALISE, Senior Professor of Old Testament, Fuller Theological Seminary, Pasadena, CA; *453, 462, 464, 471, 473.* KATHRYN SCHIFFERDECKER, Professor and Elva B. Lovell Chair of Old Testament, Luther Seminary, St. Paul, MN; *197.* DAVID J. SCHLAFER, Independent Consultant in Preaching and Assisting Priest, The Episcopal Church of the Redeemer, Bethesda, MD; *251, 260, 262.* BRADLEY E. SCHMELING, Senior Pastor, Gloria Dei Lutheran Church, St. Paul, MN; *272, 281, 283.* MATTHEW L. SKINNER, Professor of New Testament, Luther Seminary, St. Paul, MN; *60, 69, 72, 77, 81.* WM. MARCUS SMALL, Pastor, New Calvary Baptist Church, Norfolk, VA; *535, 536, 543.* DANIEL L. SMITH-CHRISTOPHER, Professor of Old Testament, Loyola Marymount University, Los Angeles, CA; *7, 12, 20, 21, 25.* F. SCOTT SPENCER, former Professor of Religion, Wingate University, Wingate, NC, and former Professor of New Testament and Biblical Interpretation, Baptist Theological Seminary at Richmond, Richmond, VA; *373, 377, 382, 391, 395.* BRENT A. STRAWN, Professor of Old Testament, Duke Divinity School, Durham, NC; *199, 207.* KRISTIN STROBLE, Pastor, Eastminster Presbyterian Church, East Lansing, MI; *38, 43, 47, 57.* NIBS STROUPE, Pastor, Retired, Oakhurst Presbyterian Church, Decatur, GA; *345, 350, 355, 364, 368.* JERRY L. SUMNEY, Professor of Biblical Studies, Lexington Theological Seminary, Lexington, KY; *252, 261, 264, 269.*

DEAN K. THOMPSON, President and Professor of Ministry Emeritus, Louisville Presbyterian Theological Seminary, Pasadena, CA; *346.* DENISE THORPE, Minister of Word and Sacrament, Presbyterian Church (U.S.A.), Raleigh, NC; *319, 323, 328, 337.* PATRICIA K. TULL, A. B. Rhodes Professor Emerita of Old Testament, Louisville Theological Seminary, Louisville, KY; *86, 97, 104, 106.*

LEANNE VAN DYK, President and Professor of Theology, Columbia Theological Seminary, Decatur, GA; *2, 11, 13, 20.*

JONATHAN L. WALTON, Plummer Professor of Christian Morals and Pusey Minister in the Memorial Church, Harvard University, Cambridge, MA; *210, 213.* RICHARD F. WARD, Fred B. Craddock Professor of Homiletics and Worship, Phillips Theological

Seminary, Tulsa, OK; *48*. THEODORE J. WARDLAW, President and Professor of Homiletics, Austin Presbyterian Theological Seminary, Austin, TX; *480, 490, 494, 499*. SONIA E. WATERS, Assistant Professor of Pastoral Theology, Princeton Theological Seminary, Princeton, NJ; *319, 328, 332, 337, 341*. KHALIA J. WILLIAMS, Assistant Dean of Worship and Music; Assistant Professor in the Practice of Worship, Candler School of Theology, Emory University, Atlanta, GA; *400, 402, 411, 417, 420*. PHILIP WINGEIERRAYO, Dean and Professor of Missiology and Methodist Studies, Wesley Theological Seminary, Washington, DC; *252, 265*. LAUREN F. WINNER, Associate Professor of Christian Spirituality, Duke Divinity School, Durham, NC; *29, 34, 39*. REBECCA ABTS WRIGHT, C. K. Benedict Professor of Old Testament and Biblical Hebrew, School of Theology, The University of the South, Sewanee, TN; *170, 179, 181, 188, 190*. JOHN W. WRIGHT, Independent scholar, San Diego, CA; *426, 428, 435, 437*. JOHN W. WURSTER, Pastor and Head of Staff, St. Philip Presbyterian Church, Houston, TX; *179, 182, 188, 191, 197, 200*.

OLIVER LARRY YARBROUGH, Tillinghast Professor of Religion, Middlebury College, Department of Religion, Middlebury, VT; *296, 301, 310*. WILLIAM YOO, Assistant Professor of American Religious and Cultural History, Columbia Theological Seminary, Decatur, GA; *507, 516, 518, 525*.

BEVERLY ZINK-SAWYER, Professor Emerita of Preaching and Worship, Union Presbyterian Seminary, Richmond, VA; *225, 228, 233, 243, 246*.

Scripture Index

About the Editor

HEIDI HAVERKAMP is the editor of *Everyday Connections: Reflections and Practices for Year C* (Westminster John Knox, 2021) and author of *Holy Solitude: Lenten Reflections with Saints, Hermits, Prophets, and Rebels* (Westminster John Knox, 2017) and *Advent in Narnia: Reflections for the Season* (Westminster John Knox, 2015). Having often searched for robust devotional books that could hold her interest, she has tried to write some herself.